AN UNLIKELY HERO

Also by S. J. Taylor

Stalin's Apologist:
Walter Duranty, the New York Times's *Man in Moscow, 1921–1941*
Shock! Horror! The Tabloids in Action
The Great Outsiders: Northcliffe, Rothermere and the Daily Mail
The Reluctant Press Lord: Esmond Rothermere and the Daily Mail

AN UNLIKELY HERO

VERE ROTHERMERE AND HOW THE
DAILY MAIL WAS SAVED

S. J. Taylor

Weidenfeld & Nicolson
LONDON

First published in Great Britain in 2002 by
Weidenfeld & Nicolson

© by S. J. Taylor 2002

A CIP catalogue record for this book is
available from the British Library

ISBN 0 297 64400 9

Typeset in Adobe Garamond by Selwood Systems,
Midsomer Norton

Printed by Butler & Tanner Ltd,
Frome and London

Weidenfeld & Nicolson

The Orion Publishing Group Ltd
Orion House
5 Upper Saint Martin's Lane
London WC2H 9EA

for
the late John Leese,
Editor of *You* Magazine and the
Evening Standard
and his deputy, the
late Genevieve Cooper.

CONTENTS

ILLUSTRATIONS

Sections of photographs appear between pages 146 and 147, 178 and 179.

The author and the publishers are grateful to Associated Newspapers for supplying the illustrations.

The photograph of Lord Rothermere reading the *Daily Mail* is reproduced by permission of Universal Pictorial Press.

ACKNOWLEDGEMENTS

I am grateful to Paul Rossiter who stayed right with me for the twelve years it took to complete three volumes of *Mail* history. In that time he never left a single query unanswered. I must also thank Peter Williams whose patience in explaining 'the dark side' was inexhaustible.

Other people who saw me through were Peter Beal at Sotheby's; Ion Trewin at Weidenfeld & Nicolson; Kathy Campbell at the Daily Mail and General Trust. John Winnington-Ingram read a part of this manuscript and met with me half a dozen times. Charles Sinclair and Roger Gilbert each read a chapter. So did Vyvyan Harmsworth and John Womersley. Nicholas Gold was kind enough to look over the chapter on Reuters. Otherwise, John Hemingway acted as a very valuable resource.

Thomas Grahl in Stockholm took the time to write up detailed accounts of events as he remembered them concerning the launch of London *Metro*. And Steve Torrington who aided me through the last chapters. Sir Bernard Ingham was kind enough to consult with Baroness Thatcher on my behalf. I am very grateful to him, and to the others.

I want to give special thanks to Ruth Liebling, my physical therapist. Without her, there would have been no book. I also want to thank Phill Green for designing the cover as well as Vyvyan Harmsworth and Felicity Swan for their help with the photographs. Liz Gordon and Melanie Bowen were also very kind, and Linda Melvern stayed the course, as always.

Some people never let you down. Jonathan Rothermere, his wife Claudia and his late father Vere are among them. Colin Franey and the late Genevieve Cooper both helped immeasurably. Thank you all very much.

PREFACE

In the twelve years I have spent working on this history of the *Daily Mail* – three volumes encompassing over a hundred years of newspaper history – many of my informants have died. By a strange twist of fate, I have become the last tribunal for the measure of their achievements, and sometimes of their lives. I take this responsibility seriously, and I have done the best I can.

I was an outsider, in every sense of the word. 'How could an American woman possibly understand anything about us?' was the question I encountered time and again. I have no answer to it, except to say, as an Oklahoman I was raised in a wide-open culture that, for all its contrasts to Britain, did offer a host of colourful characters reminiscent of those found in these pages. By the end, I think people pretty much accepted me.

The fact remains that these reminiscences have less to do with me than with the people who shared them with me. I wasn't there. I have tried faithfully to resurrect accurately what happened, but I'm sure I've missed a great deal; that was inevitable. But every word here not assigned to someone else is mine – as is every opinion. My job was to call it as I saw it, and I did that. Let the chips fall where they may.

I quickly became aware that inside Associated Newspapers and the Daily Mail and General Trust, people acted towards me in the same way they had acted towards colleagues and associates throughout their careers. Some were co-operative, candid and unusually generous. Others were obstructive and hostile. I gained tremendous insight into the character of each informant by applying the way they treated me to the way they conducted themselves in the company.

David English was suspicious of me from the start and, simply put, gave me a hard time. In this, he was encouraged by Vere Rothermere, who was a great 'David-baiter'. He pitted us against one another glee-fully. I used to complain to Vere about this and that amused him even more. After about eight years, David warmed to me and then spoke very frankly indeed. Beneath the many layers, he was a perfectly sensible man, marvellous company and terribly funny. In the long run, being subjected to the 'cat's paw' taught me a great deal, although he did make me suffer. I think I understood David, the cruelty *and* the kindness.

I never fully understood Vere and I personally don't believe anyone did. One of his closest associates once said that he was the most complicated individual she had ever known. That was my perception as well. In all the time I knew him, ten years, Vere was never the same person twice. Like the mythological figure Proteus, he changed forms. The media usually portrayed him as a lamb, but I remember him as a lion. Anyone who had ever seen him angry could never forget it and that is the enduring image I carry of him.

That said, he was the kindest of men. One never doubted his humanity. Vere used to divide people into two groups – those with 'heart' and those without. I had never heard the word used in that way, but after a time I got a feel for it.

I guess for all his money and power, Vere had heart. And that was why he succeeded so well.

AN UNLIKELY HERO

The media portrayal of the late Vere Harmsworth, third Viscount Rothermere and proprietor of the *Daily Mail*, owed more to the fictional depiction of Lord Copper than to the real man. In the pages of the popular press, Rothermere appeared at worst as a dimwit, at best an eccentric – and always an enigma. He was the playboy proprietor of the *Daily Mail*, the last native tycoon of the British publishing industry.

This image was perpetuated by Fleet Street's reliance on the cuttings file. Rothermere's file grew fatter by the year with cut-and-paste profiles that had been lifted directly from earlier cut-and-paste profiles, and likewise back through the decades. The sheer weight of the repetitions was enough to convince any reasonable hack that he should not depart from the popular caricature of Rothermere as a kind of idiot savant whose good fortune was nothing short of miraculous. 'Mere Vere' was the favourite catchphrase and Rothermere was presented as right-wing, profligate, philandering and inept into the bargain. He couldn't even tie his own shoelaces, so went the legend.

This was a fairly heavy rap to lay on the only British press baron. And yet, during his lifetime, Rothermere regularly stood up to savage public beatings that few men could have endured. What was it about the proprietor of the *Daily Mail* that invited such ignominy?

Some of it sprang naturally from the competitive nature of Fleet Street. Although there is a reluctance to publish the most embarrassing details of a proprietor's life for fear of reprisal, there is certainly no moratorium on presenting a competitor in an unpleasant light. To this day, the pages of the rival titles are filled with vilifications of the competition, their editors, their columnists and especially their proprietors. 'Open warfare', Rothermere called it. And he was as much as anyone a target of their salvos.

Then again, a part of the contempt for Rothermere stemmed from his lineage. Vere was the great-nephew of Viscount Northcliffe, the progenitor of the modern newspaper, who began as a lowly bicycling correspondent and ended as the greatest press baron in the world. Before his death,

Northcliffe had controlled two-thirds of the titles on Fleet Street, influenced the outcome of two world conflicts and defined the course of the modern media during the twentieth century.

A self-made man in a country that reviles self-made men, Northcliffe counted among his enemies some of the most important figures of the time. He held no position in English society that he had not plundered from the ranks of his betters and, after his death, they repaid him in kind by reminding posterity that he died mad and probably of syphilis.*

If possible, Vere's grandfather had been even more controversial than his great-uncle. Harold Harmsworth, the first Viscount Rothermere, accumulated sufficient capital to rank as Britain's fourth richest man and, in addition, controlled the *Daily Mail* with an iron hand. To the astonishment of his readers and the dismay of his staff, he was an early supporter of Oswald Mosley. This explains how the famous headline HURRAH FOR THE BLACKSHIRTS made its way so often into the cuttings file of his grandson Vere.

As to Vere's father Esmond, he rocked fashionable London with his marital scandals twice during his lifetime, once by perpetuating the longest divorce proceeding in history, against Vere's mother, and again by divorcing his second wife Ann after her shocking affair with the journalist Ian Fleming, later of James Bond fame.

The Harmsworths were too controversial to occupy a place in English society. They were outsiders who could never fit in. Nor could they hope to wedge in as a consequence of power and money – since English society was too frequently the quarry of their newspapers. Sooner or later, the powerful sword of the free press would cut too close to one society figure or another and the family would be ostracised once again. If, in the early days before he took over the publishing dynasty, Vere believed he could have friends in high places, or friends at all, he was quickly disabused of the notion. The sword cut two ways.

Then, too, there was the problem of Vere himself. As a young man he had been viewed as a frivolous playboy. Women adored him and he had access to almost unimaginable wealth. He married a film starlet, Patricia Matthews, who gave parties that were attended by first-rank celebrities. The lifestyle was enough to excite envy and hostility, and the couple came in for enormous criticism.

If all this weren't enough to create an enduring sense of enmity among the journalists who wrote about him, there was also the fact that Vere had

---

*Northcliffe actually died from malignant endocarditis. But Fleet Street is not known for letting the truth interfere with a good story.

inherited everything – the money, the power, the newspapers. Among the press corps, indeed the country, there was hardly a man who didn't believe he better deserved the inheritance than Rothermere, or that, if he had been the one to get it, he couldn't have done a better job.

All these factors militated against Vere and his image. Still, even all this – the family, the power, the fortune, the lifestyle – might have been forgiven if it hadn't been for the fruits of one terrible moment, a single evening that for ever blackened Vere's reputation and that of the *Daily Mail*.

It was 12 March 1971, popularly known as 'The Night of the Long White Envelopes', when a group of the most talented men and women on Fleet Street were dismissed in a particularly brutal mass sacking.

The industry was set reeling, and the number of enemies who despised the *Mail* and its playboy owner proliferated. Those who had been fired, their friends and families, their fellow hacks, began baying for blood. Few outside the portals of Northcliffe House wished the new *Daily Mail* any luck in its quest for survival. A great many eagerly awaited its demise.

As to Vere Rothermere, so thoroughgoing was the sustained attack on his reputation that, decades later, the prevailing assessment of the man and his achievements remained unchanged. The journalists believed the publicity they themselves had generated and Vere's rating remained low.

So how could it have happened that the *Daily Mail* not only survived but flourished, that Associated Newspapers expanded phenomenally, that the Daily Mail and General Trust became one of the most highly respected companies in the City?

The general assessment was that, however it came about, it couldn't have been Vere Rothermere.

Or *could* it?

ONE

THE NIGHT OF THE LONG
WHITE ENVELOPES

The original plan had been to post the envelopes on 15 March. If the men in charge had stayed with the plan, perhaps the bitterness of the night would never have occurred, and the sackings would have remained a personal matter, shared among friends and family, and dealt with in solitude.

But that possibility was lost for ever when Donald Young, Father of the Chapel* of the *Daily Mail*, and Peter Burden, who held the same title on the *Daily Sketch*, issued a joint statement. In it they said they shared the 'firm belief that the 277 journalists who were to be made redundant should be notified as soon as possible'.

Howard French, former editor of the *Daily Sketch* and a director on the board of Associated Newspapers,† took them at their word. If the union wanted the notices to go out early, then so be it. Besides, he agreed with the notion. The sackings were inevitable and he wanted to get the whole thing over with as quickly as possible. Otherwise, word of who was in and who was out might leak, with disastrous results.

So short-term was the decision to deliver the form letter early that it was actually dated three days later than the night it went out. Its language was, as these things go, par for the course. 'A very careful examination has been made … I am extremely sorry to have to tell you … I am aware you will be facing a period of personal stress … With many thanks for your past services …' It was signed by Mick Shields, the new managing director of Associated Newspapers, who had been appointed by the new chairman, Vere Harmsworth.

The *Daily Mail* and the *Daily Sketch* were being merged, and a group of journalists had been targeted from each of the titles to be made redundant. This was a first in Fleet Street. If a paper folded, its staff was summarily sacked. People expected that. It was regrettable, tough, even

---

* The newspaper's chairman of the National Union of Journalists.
† Associated Newspapers controlled the *Daily Mail* and Daily Mail and General Trust was the name of the holding company. Although Vere Harmsworth was chairman of Associated, his father retained the chairmanship of the holding company.

heart-wrenching, but there was nothing personal. This time it seemed as if there *was* something personal. The *Daily Mail* was surviving, but many of its best people weren't.

David English, who had been editing the *Sketch*, had been named the editor of the surviving *Mail* and, although only a handful of men at the top knew it for sure, the ailing broadsheet was to be scuttled in favour of a tabloid format. Later there would be bitterness as those who were sacked came to realise that many from the *Mail* were being ousted in favour of journalists from the *Sketch*. English and his team would be dubbed 'The *Sketch* Mafia', and the entire operation would be condemned wholesale by the industry.

Only a few months before, in a highly controversial move, Esmond Rothermere, then proprietor of the *Daily Mail*, and Max Aitken, proprietor of the *Daily Express*, had tried to work out a merger between their two rival newspapers. What they envisaged was a kind of joint operating agreement, styled after the American prototype, that would allow at least one of their newspapers to survive in the prevailing atmosphere of union demands, rising costs and falling circulations. But that effort failed after Vere Harmsworth made it clear he wanted to take over the family publishing dynasty and try to save the *Daily Mail*.

There followed a series of dramatic events in which Esmond resigned as chairman in favour of his son. Esmond absented himself from the scene by taking a long sojourn in South Africa and the die was cast. These events had taken place in late December of 1970 and early January of 1971. Since then, the management had been working feverishly with David English and his hand-picked team of journalists to produce a plan that would modernise the *Daily Mail* and make it a going concern in what looked to be the dying middle market of the newspaper industry. Now that plan was ready.

There was a persistent rumour that Howard French had made the list of those who were to go. A second rumour pegged Arthur Brittenden, the outgoing editor of the *Daily Mail*, whose pay-off was rumoured to be very high.* Still another had David English as the list maker. In the event, all three rumours proved correct. French made the initial list from the staffs of both newspapers, Brittenden made his own list of those who should be retained from the *Daily Mail* and English had the final say. In making his decisions, English relied heavily upon Alwyn Robinson, tagged to be the managing editor of the new *Daily Mail*, because he felt that Brittenden might have a number of axes to grind.

* Brittenden's pay-off was £36,000.

French believed it wasn't a matter of picking superior journalists over inferior ones. In redundancy, he would say later, it was a matter of choosing 'horses for courses'.

> You want some educated people, some who came up in the provinces, those good at crime, politics, investigation, so it was less to do with good or bad than what you need.

That was the stated objective. But others at the management level believed in a hidden agenda. They deplored the so-called 'culture of infallibility', that is, a culture of people who resisted change. They were, so went the theory, a group of writers and sub-editors who believed their way was the only way of doing things.

Viewed as highly uncooperative and likely to block the transition from broadsheet to tabloid, these men and women were thought to adhere to a deeply held ethos. The only way to change that ethos was to get rid of the adherents, right down the line. And that was the only way David English would get a straight shot at saving the *Daily Mail*. That was the theory.

The 'culture of infallibility' didn't include everyone sacked that night, but the suspects were on the list, slotted in purposefully. But although they might not have known about the hidden agenda, many on the list harboured suspicions about how they got there. The feature writer Julian Holland believed for many years afterwards that Arthur Brittenden told David English to get rid of him and Barry Norman 'at all costs'. It was a highly dramatic scenario.

But for English the matter was more casual:

> I went out with Arthur and I think the way it actually worked was he gave me a list of people we should keep at all costs. And then he gave me a list of people that we didn't need. And I think French also produced a list.
>
> But in the event, I didn't pay close attention to either of these lists because I was going to edit the paper myself. I made my own enquiries, and the names overlapped with a lot of their names. I was quite keen to keep Barry Norman, I think, but then I thought, 'Oh, he's been around a long time.' Anyway, I think he wanted to go.

The letters were ready at 4 p.m. on 12 March. By then, downstairs in the newsroom, a sense of imminent disaster had taken hold. Hacks telephoned hacks and a steady stream of journalists began to trickle in either to Northcliffe House, where the *Mail* was published, or to Old Carmelite House, home of the *Daily Sketch*. Some of the journalists drove up from their homes in the country to be there for the débâcle. Nine o'clock was the time fixed for handing out the bad news.

David English was not involved in the night's events. He and his hand-picked team of journalists were away from the scene of the disaster. Louis Kirby, who would be David's deputy editor on the new *Mail*, had taken charge of the outgoing *Sketch*. But all David's people were very much aware of the drama playing itself out only a few offices away.

The day before, David had called in the top *Mail* people earmarked for the sack, giving each of them the bad news face to face. 'As you know,' he began in his brief speech of dismissal, 'the paper's being merged.'

I want——to take over your job. I think it's best if you leave straight away. You'll be getting——amount of money. I hope you find another job and I'm sure you will…Would you now please go…and pick up your cheque?

It was later said that David faced such anger and hatred in these terminal interviews that he was glad he had a bottle of whisky in his bottom drawer.

In the case of Ken Donlan, however, the scenario played out a little differently. Donlan was called in *with* his successor, John Womersley, and the two of them sat there uncomfortably while English delivered the news to Ken that he was 'the unlucky one'. In the meantime, would he take the time to help John sort out the newsroom so that the changeover could take place in an orderly fashion?

For Womersley, it was an 'extremely traumatic moment'. He didn't know Donlan personally, but he knew him by reputation and was well aware how highly regarded he was by all his subordinates. Ironically, Ken had been secure in his job of many years as news editor of the Manchester *Mail*, but he had been persuaded only five months before to come down to London and take over the same job on the national title.

Now, Donlan and Womersley ploughed out of David's office and into the cold, windy March morning side by side. Neither of the two men had his overcoat and as they made their way up Whitefriars Street to Fleet Street they were both feeling the chill, so to speak. If the pubs had been open, they would have fallen into a sentimental reverie over a glass of beer. But it was too early. So they stopped at a café near El Vino for a coffee and Ken proceeded calmly to outline the problems John would face in Ken's old job as news editor on the *Daily Mail*.

Impressed by Donlan's conduct, Womersley couldn't help asking himself if he would have shown the same high level of professionalism if he had been the one facing the sack.

Alwyn Robinson likened the sackings to an accident that takes place during mountain climbing. Sometimes the danger of all the climbers falling to their deaths becomes so great that it is necessary to cut the rope, sacrificing those at the bottom so that those at the top can live.

It was Robinson who carried the envelopes, boxed and alphabetised, on to the editorial floor that night. 'Robbie', as he was called, had been in all the meetings to finalise and double-check the lists that morning. In his own words, 'It got easier as it went on, not because the choices became less difficult, but because you got used to the idea somebody should go.'

But nothing could prepare him for the actual night. When he finally walked out to face the lions, Robinson found that all the emotion had gone out of him. 'I felt numb, detached,' he said later. Otherwise he couldn't have done it. Then people swamped him, coming up in bitterness or sadness or anger. And as he carried the envelopes past them into the office, they were all clamouring, 'Where's mine where's mine where's mine?'

Later, he stayed on the floor, 'viewing the process as if through an opaque glass'. He didn't feel guilty. And in the days to come, he wouldn't lose any sleep over the events of that evening. Instead, he felt as if he had been through a bereavement.

In the long run, he said later, 'You have to remember that although half the staff were losing their jobs, half the staff were saving theirs.'

The *Mail*'s well-known political correspondent, Walter Terry, helped Robinson carry in the envelopes, commandeering the office that had been selected for giving out the bad news. Terry had never fired anybody in his life, but he had been assigned the onerous task of delivering the blow to those on the *Mail* who were being made redundant that night. Brittenden had already left and it was thought that Terry, who was popular with almost everyone on the newspaper, would be the right man for the job. Terry himself agreed to do it because he believed that a *Mail* man was the only person to sack another *Mail* man.

Terry looked at the first name on the envelope and called in the assistant editor, Geoffrey Bayliss, who was in charge of that night's printing.

'How's the edition?' 'Oh, it'll be all right.' 'Good. Well, better get on with this business. Sorry, Geoff. You're the first. Here it is.' So it went on, senior men being summoned to Terry's room to pick up their own white envelopes and those of their staff who were to be axed.

Iain Smith, features editor in charge of 'Femail' and 'Money Mail', remembered seeing the light go on and hearing the buzzer go.

We all looked at each other and said, 'This is like the roll of the tumbrels. People are being summoned to the guillotine. We're not stupid. We know what is happening.' Then, when the first person came out... he was looking a bit shaken.

So we shot along into Walter's office and I said, 'Walter, I think we know what you're doing and I don't think it's going very well. Can we just pause and think this through a bit?' And Walter said, 'Oh, God, am I doing it all wrong?'

I was then handed about fifty envelopes to give out. I gave out the envelopes in the Features Office.

And the bottom one was mine.

David English had been right about Barry Norman. He wanted to go.

At least, that was what he and his friend Julian Holland had each decided after dickering about it all morning on 12 March. The two of them were just about to take the long walk down the hall to inform the management they wanted to be put on the list for voluntary redundancy when the announcement came that the whole thing had been brought forward. The notices were going to be handed out early, that night in fact.

But the truth was, Norman didn't really expect that the *Mail* would sack him because he was one of the newspaper's main feature writers. Well known for his light and chatty style, he had built up a following and he was accustomed to getting a huge byline with a thumbnail photograph. Although he hadn't been particularly happy at the newspaper for the last three years, in his own words, 'I simply didn't have the courage to leave.'

Then I remember Iain Smith came up to me and said, looking very sorrowful, 'Would you go in and see Walter.' So I went and there was Walter Terry, I mean, looking very unhappy, because he was one of the writing journalists. He wasn't one of the executives. And he gave me this envelope and said, 'I'm sorry about this.' And I said, 'Well, what *do* you say? It's all right, Walter.' And he said, 'No, it's not all right, it's bloody awful, you know it is.'

Barry said nothing to this because there wasn't anything else to be said.

So you came out waving your envelope! You know, pretending that... I don't know, putting on as brave a face as possible. People would then come up to you and say, 'Christ, they haven't let you go, surely!'

Outside Barry was bold and brash. But inside he had suddenly become painfully aware he had 'a wife, a mortgage, two daughters, two cats, two dogs and two guinea pigs to support. I needed to work!' And all around him were people in the same boat.

They just couldn't stay seated at their desks. They were wandering from person to person asking, 'Are you in? Are you out?' There was an atmosphere 'of euphoria and of hysteria', Barry remembered. 'People were frightened, let's face it.'

Just about then, a TV unit arrived and began questioning the journalists about how they were reacting to the dramatic events of the evening. To let them know exactly how they felt, one *Mail* journalist pulled down his pants and mooned the camera.

In the midst of this madness, to Barry's absolute disbelief, a guide appeared leading a tour of *Daily Mail* visitors right through the editorial floor. Barry found himself imagining what the tour guide must be telling his entourage, 'And here are all the *Daily Mail* writers and over here in the corner at the moment is one of the famed journalists hanging himself.'

To Barry Norman the atmosphere took on a surreal quality. Later, as he struggled for an image to describe the events of the night, Barry, who was to make his name as a film critic for the BBC, realised the whole thing was exactly like *Night of the Living Dead*.

Possibly the brightest star among those from the *Daily Mail* who were to go was Rhona Churchill. She had made her name as a war correspondent and had since become a kind of roving commentator in hot spots all over the world. When the crowd discovered her name was on the list a cry of anger went up across the newsroom, adding to the accumulating fury of the night.

What they didn't know was that Rhona had requested redundancy several weeks before and it had been quietly arranged. Her husband had been ill and she had wanted to retire for a long time in order to be with him. This gave her the opportunity to go out with a pay-off.

Then again, Peter Black, who had created for himself the position of television critic on the *Daily Mail*, was furious he was being retained. If his friends were going, why couldn't he? He barged into David English's office, demanding to be made redundant. English good-naturedly promised him he would duly be sacked in three years, if Peter still wished. Then he 'could buy that villa in the south of France' he was hankering after. In the event, Black never did manage to get the sack – or to get his villa. Instead, David gave him lunch at the Savoy and that was that.

Peter Burden, who had laboured long and hard as the Father of the Chapel to get a good pay-off for those who were going, naturally assumed he would be among them. He was the chief crime correspondent on the *Daily Sketch* and, because he had been apprised early of the newspaper's closure, had already had an interview in London for a job in Australia. A newspaper in Canberra wanted to take him on and train him as a sub-editor, and Burden had agreed. He had sold his house in England, and his wife, the daughter of a Fleet Street journalist, was enrolled in a degree course in Australia when, to his surprise, English told him he wanted him to stay.

'So I bought a new house and my wife enrolled in a programme here,' he said later. Many years after the event, Burden and his wife finally managed to take a holiday in Australia and, ironically, they 'just fell in love with the place'.

Brian James was at home in Essex when one of his fellow reporters on the sports pages gave him a call, ostensibly to talk about golf. But after only a few minutes the reporter suggested Brian drive in from the country. Something important seemed to be going on and he thought Brian should be there. It was late at night and the drive took forty-five minutes, but Brian went in, wondering all the while whether his colleague knew something he wasn't telling him. But when he walked into the newsroom, Brian was totally unprepared for the scene that greeted him.

> The entire staff was there, people who normally wouldn't have been at that time of the evening. But the city editor, sports editor, heads of departments were absent. They were all at a meeting.
>
> Then the door opened and they came in, looking a bit grey-faced. And they all had these bundles of letters in their hands.
>
> And they all kind of said, 'OK, lads, will you gather round here,' gesturing in their shirtsleeves. We were expecting an announcement. But they started reading names out. 'John Smith, sorry, John.' Next person, next person. This was the way people found out they were being fired.
>
> One or two of the executives called in people one by one, into their offices, everyone had his own way of doing it. People were standing around crying. Then someone said, 'Oh, Brian, sorry.' And immediately Charlie Wilson, the sports editor, handed me an envelope, saying, 'Right, Brian, you got what you wanted.'

Not quite comprehending Charlie's words, Brian opened the letter and, for just a minute, looking over the language of the form letter, he thought it was a cut in expenses. He couldn't actually grasp what it said. Then he had a wayward thought, 'Christ, I've been sacked! It was totally out of the blue.'

Brian James was in shock because he was 'fairly hot' on the sports circuit. Only a short time before he had been offered a major job as a sports announcer at the BBC. At that time the *Mail* had made a successful effort to keep him on the newspaper. So now Brian was in a state of utter confusion.

He also remembered that a short time before, when there had been a series of nationwide power cuts at short notice that played havoc with the production of the *Daily Mail*, he and the other reporters rallied. They had gone in to work in the early hours of the morning to write their stories, so they could be set in hot type immediately just in case there was a power cut that day. Other times, when the cut came, Brian had written his story with a candle stuck to the top of his typewriter. 'So this is how they thank us!' he thought savagely, as he stood there, reading over his letter.

Then something dawned on him. 'Why did he say I got what I *wanted*? Hey, wait. *Wind this back!* Why would Charlie imagine this was what I wanted? I have a mortgage and three kids!'

So Brian went down to the Mucky Duck and it was the wildest night in his memory. He didn't even remember where he finished up, but he slept on somebody's floor. And the police actually had to come to break up the party at about four in the morning. Hung-over and miserable, Brian vowed, 'I'll never work for that bunch of bastards again!'*

He vaguely remembered, some time during the night, saying, 'This is just like the Night of the Long Knives, only it's the Night of the Long White Envelopes.'

He mentioned it to somebody else and somehow the name stuck.

When Arthur Brittenden offered Charlie Wilson the job of sports editor in 1969, Charles was a bit nonplussed. 'Me?' he asked Brittenden. 'I was never a sports editor in my life.' Over a lavish lunch, however, he allowed himself to be persuaded, even though he didn't feel he brought anything special to sports reporting over and above enthusiasm.

But he attacked the job in the same way he always attacked everything, doing a lot of extra reading and research, and pretty soon, 'Not only could I name the Arsenal team but I could name the Blackburn team and any other team as well. And I spent a lot of time, particularly at weekends, watching sport, and it did not do my first marriage any good at all.'

---

* As of 1999, Brian James was still working for the *Daily Mail*.

In fact, Charlie believed his marriage foundered during the year or so he edited the sports pages at the *Daily Mail*. The night he gave the envelope to Brian James, Charlie noticed that 'he looked at me in huge astonishment because there was no question he was one of the most talented soccer writers in the country at the time and here was I telling him he wasn't wanted'.

But Charlie sincerely believed that Brian had told him, if it came to the crunch, he wanted to be given redundancy.

Brian and I had lunch together in a little dark corner of a restaurant. And during that lunch he said to me, 'I would like to go if there is a possibility of redundancy.' That's how I remember it. And I said, 'OK.' And off I went.

A few weeks later I sat down to discuss who should go and who should stay, because we were merging two sports staffs. And I was asked, 'Who was the Number One soccer writer, the *Sketch* guy or the *Mail* guy?' I said, 'I can solve that problem. Brian wants to go.'

Everybody said, 'Wonderful.' A very painful problem solved.

'I arranged it because I thought he wanted it,' Wilson said later.

But Brian James was deeply offended and the misunderstanding became the basis for a kind of feud between the two men. They didn't get back together for years, until they thrashed the matter out properly. So, all in all, even though Charles Wilson was not one of the journalists singled out for sacking that night, it still went down in his memory as one of the worst nights of his life.

Because, after he had sacked James and the others on his list, he went home, 'sat down with my then wife, Anne Robinson, and carved up the furniture between us. The splitting of the goods because the marriage was ending...'You have the cutlery, I'll have the china.' So item by item, we split the house up.

'It was the perfect end of a perfect day.'

The journalists from the *Sketch* who were going were able practitioners, known for their talent and competence. But those from the *Mail*, a respected broadsheet with an intellectual following, included some of the top names in the field. Especially to their own way of thinking, it was inconceivable that such eminent journalists as they were could be given the sack.

True, the redundancy payment was generous – four weeks' pay for every year of service, plus a deferred pension. Union leaders had hammered out the agreement during the turbulent weeks preceding the Night of the Long White Envelopes. But to get these favourable terms they had been forced to wage a sustained fight with management.

They pointed to the group's successful diversifications that included television holdings and exhibition sites. And although Blackfriars Oil hadn't begun producing a profit, it was widely believed that when and if it did, it would turn out to be a bonanza. Already extremely profitable was the provincial newspaper chain, Northcliffe Newspapers, which Harold Rothermere had ruthlessly acquired during the 1930s, fighting it out with the Berry brothers who, until then, had enjoyed clear sailing in the market. Northcliffe Newspapers had long been recognised inside the company as one of Harold's most astute, if hard-won, investments.

But the profits from the provincials, as well as those from the company's other ventures, were constantly being seconded to support the languishing national titles. Now their losses had grown too big for that and Associated Newspapers could no longer underpin this kind of loss.

At a certain point even the union leaders realised that trying to do so 'would begin to conflict with the directors' legal responsibilities to share-holders not to run the company on a course that endangered collapse'. To show the company was negotiating in good faith, Vere Harmsworth 'invited [union leaders] ... to send their own accountants to look at the books'. Vere's openness helped to quell all but the most militant negotiators.

But the employees, and especially those who had lost their jobs, couldn't bring themselves to believe the crisis was real. They suspected the company was playing them for fools. According to this scenario the cutbacks were a new kind of sinister money-saving device and Associated was ridding itself of workers to bolster profits.

Suspicions like these arose from the absolute secrecy with which Vere's father Esmond had always operated the family business. Even the emergency talks that had taken place in December between Esmond and Max Aitken, attempting to merge the two rival newspapers, had been kept so quiet that no one, except for the top brass inside Associated, knew anything about them. So the gravity of the situation remained unknown outside an élite circle of company negotiators.

The continuing blackout on bona fide information created an atmosphere of distrust and a rumour mill arose to feed the employees' worst suspicions. In the last days before the sackings near panic prevailed and when the long overdue disclosure telling the depth of the fiscal crisis finally did take place it came as a shock. Seemingly out of the blue, workers were told that the future of the national newspapers was hanging in the balance, and only the most draconian of measures could prevent the closure of all three titles – the *Daily Sketch*, the *Daily Mail* and the *Evening News*.

All this did very little to assuage the anger on the floor of the newsroom at Northcliffe House on the night of the sackings. The journalists were enraged and searching for a scapegoat. Their first instinct was to blame Arthur Brittenden, who wasn't present that night. He was their editor and there was a strong feeling that he should have been there.

Others held the union leaders responsible. Never mind the terms of the redundancy. No amount of money could compensate them for their loss of dignity.

Eventually people came to realise that Arthur Brittenden had also lost his job. And realistically, the union leaders had done the best they could in difficult circumstances. Even David English had only been putting together a team of men and women he knew from personal experience he could depend upon.

No, if they wanted the real villain of the piece, they need look no further than the new chairman of the company, Vere Harmsworth.

It was not difficult to cast Vere Harmsworth in the role of a sinister manipulator whose greed was responsible for the blood on the newsroom floor. Until the moment he took over the firm he was an invisible man. His father had instructed his top people 'not to pay any attention to him' and none of them did. Corporate politics ebbed and flowed around him, but didn't involve him.

Common sense should have dictated that Vere would eventually take over the firm, but even in the last few days before he did so no one could imagine it. Esmond had controlled the firm for over three decades. Nobody could remember a time when he wasn't in charge.

As to his son, Vere was eccentric and hard to know. He was given to long silences and that alarmed people. When he did speak, it was in strangely coded language that was almost oracular. Any meaning to be derived was extremely subtle. It was far too subtle for men of action to stop and consider what he intended to convey. Everyone was far too important and far too busy.

Now, here he was, the boss of them all, and nobody knew him.* One thing they did know. Vere Harmsworth was directly to blame – not for the fiscal crisis itself perhaps – but for the draconian measures devised to stop the rot. In fact, the 277 journalists who were sacked on the Night of

* Howard French knew him. But there were sides to Vere nobody knew.

the Long White Envelopes were the tip of the iceberg. In all, 1733 jobs were lost that spring.

Nearly half of the redundancies came from closure of the *Sketch*, and the *Evening News* lost 355, mainly in production. Otherwise firemen, timekeepers, hall porters, cleaners, office workers, switchboard operators, everybody took a cut.

Harmsworth, who took an active hand in the negotiations, hoped to stem the crisis, make the *Daily Mail* fiscally independent and perhaps save not only that newspaper but the *Evening News* as well. To this end he had set in motion the series of events that culminated in the sackings on the Night of the Long White Envelopes.

Earlier, he had found the proposed merger between the *Daily Express* and the *Daily Mail* unacceptable and had been quick to seize the opportunity to end those negotiations. From the start he had opposed the talks and, the very moment his father forfeited the chairmanship of the company to him, he set about trying to find another way out of the fiscal conundrum the company faced. He took advice from his senior management and editorial staff, of whom David English was fast becoming the most pre-eminent member, having been lured from the *Daily Express* eighteen months before to edit the *Daily Sketch*. But it was Vere who made the decisions. There was no one else who could.

His first was to close the *Sketch*. That in itself was regrettable – but perhaps understandable. His second decision, to make the *Mail* into a tabloid, was less so to the outside world. Inside Associated it seemed an important part of changing the ethos of the paper, of giving it a completely new revamp that left the past behind.

But it was a high-risk solution and there was no guarantee it would work. The great danger lay in the fact that, heretofore, the tabloid format had been associated with downmarket newspapers. The *Mail* was traditionally middle market and it was feared its readers would depart in droves from a format generally associated with newspapers like the *Sun* and the *Mirror*.

So Harmsworth and his managerial team came up with the term 'compact', an in-house euphemism for the tabloid format. The term became a comfort word that minimised the extent of the risk they were taking and gave them respectability.

But changing over remained a highly controversial move and so was bringing David English over from the *Sketch* to edit the *Mail*. English knew the tabloid format inside out and he brought an energy to his editing that suited the smaller newspaper.

Anyone who knew the *Mail* was going to go tabloid would see a kind of logic to the list of those dismissed from the newspaper. But because they didn't want to tip off their competitors, the management kept that information under wraps. Indeed, David English went to great lengths to hide what he was doing, code-naming the plan 'Fox and Fury' and exporting trial print runs to Amsterdam.

Few of those sacked would have wanted to work on a tabloid, most especially a *Daily Mail* tabloid. But until the Night of the Long White Envelopes, most people believed it would only be the *Sketch* that closed and only *Sketch* journalists would go. The attitude was very much: 'It was really very sad and no doubt the *Mail* would have to make room for some of the *Sketch* people.'

So the final shock that the two papers were going to be merged, with the *Sketch* editor at the helm, took people unawares. It was 'a bit like Harrods buying a corner shop in Milton Keynes and bringing its management in to run Harrods'. This was the way one *Mail* journalist put it.

If the journalists were sceptical, the media critics were even more so. In an uncharacteristically harsh leader the *Spectator* condemned the entire exercise out of hand:

> When journalists looked at the list of *Mail–Sketch* redundancies ... the consensus was that on the whole the principle behind the sackings, if principle there was and not a blindfolded man with a pin, had been to fire the best. There was a story of a journalist weeping because he had not been fired: 'they must have thought I wasn't any good.' 'Let's say we'll kill the *Sketch*,' some bright management fellow among the Harmsworths and their ghosts must have said, 'it will sound far better than saying we're killing the *Mail*.' And so they've killed the *Mail*, labelled the corpse the *Daily Sketch*, and renamed the *Sketch* the *Daily Mail* ... the *Daily Mail* was twice the paper the *Daily Sketch* ever was.
>
> It would be very rash to predict either a long or a healthy life for the new tabloid ... While wishing it well, its probable death need cause little concern outside Fleet Street.

Vere Harmsworth protested immediately to the *Spectator*, calling the leader a 'tendentious, unworthy and misleading attack by one important press medium on another. Faced with the kind of losses we have been making,' he continued,

> I can think of many other publishers who would have closed all their titles and not just one. Had we done so over 7500 of our staff – instead of 1733 – would have become redundant. But it was because of our firm belief in the

future of the *Daily Mail* and the *Evening News* that we decided to make essential economies in our total operation … There is no basis whatever for your assertion that it is the *Mail* and not the *Sketch* which has been killed …

But too many were too angry to listen to Harmsworth's rationale. In the mass sackings that took place on the Night of the Long White Envelopes there were too many friends of friends in the media, too many colleagues, too much anger.

In a *Times* article entitled PROFIT AND DISHONOUR IN FLEET STREET, Bernard Levin, the former star columnist for the *Daily Mail*, launched an attack so vigorous that the only answer Harmsworth could make was a libel action. True to form, Levin's highly emotional article was written on behalf of 'hundreds of men and women, some of whom are my dear friends, and all of whom were lately my colleagues'.

Levin said that 'the great majority of the serious journalists' had been let go as well as 'every expert … almost every specialist, almost every foreign correspondent, almost every *Mail* journalist noted for thinking before taking the cover off his typewriter'.

The merger, he continued, would be 'hugely profitable', especially after the redevelopment of the office space left empty by the *Sketch*. As for the new chairman, 'Mere Vere', he

had not yet found the manhood to meet the members of his staff or even the courtesy to write to them.

Do I seem angry? Well, I *am* angry. …

I am angry … because … in the city of the Rothermeres loyalty is a one-way street. … I am angry because men who have personal fortunes counted in tens of millions of pounds are haggling over pennies with men who have not even tens of hundreds.

Not only Levin was angry. Fleet Street was angry.

There would be no impartial evaluations of the new *Daily Mail* or of its new chairman. Nor would its editor go unscathed. This was how it was going to be – and pretty much for the duration. Thus began Vere Harmsworth's trial by fire in the media.

The honeymoon had ended before it began.

TWO

POISON

No matter how strong Vere's character – and he was an unusually strong-minded child – the bitter forces prevailing during his early years were destined to haunt him for the rest of his life.

Vere was born on 27 August 1925, the youngest and last of the three children of Margaret and Esmond Harmsworth. His two elder sisters, Lorna, born in 1920, and Esmé, in 1922, basked in the halcyon days of their parents' early married life. But by the time Vere was born the marriage was foundering. The effect of this upon the boy's sense of well-being was devastating.

Esmond was the youngest son of Harold, first Viscount Rothermere and the only one of Harold's three sons to survive World War One. That fact in itself carried serious repercussions. Esmond, though privileged on an almost unimaginable scale, suffered greatly from survivor's guilt. It was clear that Harold believed him inferior to the two elder brothers who died valorously in battle, both of them heroes in a war that cost England two-thirds of its finest young men.

And Harold complicated matters by expecting Esmond to compensate for 'all the sacrifices of those great personages your two elder brothers'. So, by the time he married, Esmond was completely subservient to his father and, to a large degree, beaten down.

Esmond must also have been intimidated by his father's achievements. He was the brother of the great Northcliffe, and together the two of them founded a vast newspaper and magazine empire.

Northcliffe was the progenitor of the modern newspaper, a publishing genius. He founded the *Daily Mail* in 1896 and with it the publishing principles that a hundred years later would still dominate the industry. Rothermere was reckoned to be the financial brains behind the business. From a childhood of gruelling poverty, he fought his way up to become the fourth richest man in England.

More controversially, Harold had during the 1930s supported Oswald Mosley's Blackshirts. The support lasted six months, long enough to tarnish his name in perpetuity. It also provided enemies of the

Harmsworths with the opportunity to undermine the family. Esmond never could outrun his father's controversial reputation. Even Vere had to contend with the legacy of Harold's opinions.

Thus, on his father's side, Vere Harmsworth would have to find his way through a veritable labyrinth of complicated personal and political realities. It was as bad on his mother's side.

Vere's mother Margaret, called 'Peggy' by her friends, was a sultry brunette of striking beauty. A slender reed of a woman with a flair for dressing well, Peggy had high cheekbones and wavy hair, a captivating manner and a lively sense of humour. By the time she was twenty she had already had a number of shocking affairs, one of them serious. But when that young man went away to war, she blithely took up with young Vyvyan Harmsworth, heir to the Harmsworth publishing dynasty.

Harold Rothermere was generous by nature and, especially where women were concerned, a soft touch. He had met Peggy's mother sailing home from a business trip to Canada and was struck with sympathy for her plight. She had been married and widowed three times, with four daughters and a son. Pregnant with a sixth child when her last husband was killed, she was penniless and vulnerable. It was typical of Harold to try to help her. He offered her and her children a house to live in on his Benenden estate. Thus he coincidentally brought her daughters into daily contact with his sons.

It was later said that Harold was appalled at the manner in which Peggy had insinuated herself into a relationship with his son Vyvyan. The truth was that Harold had foisted her off on the boy, taking Peggy under his wing and putting her forward. A relentless meddler, Harold often invited her to stay at his house, and the night before Vyvyan left for the front Harold invited Peggy and her sister to stay at the Ritz where he was giving his son a farewell party. Peggy thus became a fixture in Vyvyan's life and they eventually reached a tentative attachment. Afterwards, when Vyvyan died, Peggy became attached to Esmond.

Within the Harmsworth family, there were two views on Peggy. The first was that she was aristocratic and colourful, a charming woman who had been blessed with numerous graces. The second that she was poison. In fact, the two views were not mutually exclusive.

Certainly, Peggy knew what she wanted and set out to get it. It would be easy to dismiss her actions as unbecoming, even predatory, but Esmond was cultured and handsome and powerful, not an unworthy object of affection.

The war was on. Young people were acting recklessly and Peggy had never learnt to moderate her feelings; throughout her life she remained emotionally extravagant. She overpowered the surviving Harmsworth with her sophistication and beauty, and Esmond determined to marry her. He did so in a private ceremony in St John's Church in Bromley on 12 January 1920. He was only twenty-one. Neither his father nor his mother attended the wedding, a fact seized upon by disapproving elders in the Harmsworth clan, who blamed her for acting unbecomingly.

Whatever the truth, by 1925 when Vere Harmsworth was born, the relationship between his parents was showing strain. It was strange to consider how the couple grew apart. So many lives had been lost or broken in the war, and there were so few men left to go round that it seemed unconscionable for a couple lucky enough to be healthy and whole not to treasure one another and their children. Nevertheless, in the midst of opulence most people could only dream about, the disenchantment began.

Their life was a movable feast, with Esmond and Peggy constantly travelling from one of their houses to another, along with the children and the nannies and an entourage of servants. Esmond found and decorated a holiday home on the Isle of Wight – Malta Cottage. The children were carried by paddle steamer across the Solent from Lymington to Yarmouth, a thirty-minute journey. When they arrived, an old grey Rolls took them the remaining mile to their summer home.

There, while Vere lay tucked up in his pram, his elder sisters played in the garden that surrounded the cottage. These were later called 'the sunshine years' by Vere's sister Esmé.

Esmond liked art deco and decorated the interior of the house after that style, in orange and black. There were balconies across the top, where one could sit and enjoy the good weather. Below were the garden and the tennis court, and Vere's sisters could remember their father in his long white flannels, usually carrying a tennis racket and crying out for someone to give him a game.

Peggy's mother, 'Granny Janet', her sisters and a great many friends were frequently about, and strains of the Charleston could be heard wafting from the gramophone late at night. An army of servants, including a footman, two housemaids, a kitchen maid and a cook, were there to look after the guests. Nanny Radcliffe took care of the children, and an under-nurse took care of Nanny Radcliffe, seeing that her laundry was done, her shoes cleaned and her bed made every morning.

When the children misbehaved, Nanny Radcliffe would don her hat and coat, threatening to leave and sometimes actually walking out of the door, until they ran after her, begging her to stay and promising never to commit the offending act again. Nanny was plump and comfortable, more of a mother than Peggy, and the children loved her.

Back and forth they travelled, from their grandfather's villa in the South of France, to Warwick House in St James's in London and later to

Villa Allegria, on the outskirts of Cannes, where their father had a second summer home. It was a twenty-four-hour rail journey from London to the villa, and the girls remembered arriving and watching the maid put pink silk sheets on the bed for Peggy. Waiting in the garage was Esmond's green Hispano Suiza and a blue Bugatti with scarlet leather seats for Peggy. Esmond had engaged the London designer 'Rufus' to decorate the villa. He hung the stone walls with ornate tapestries and furnished the interior with Spanish tables and lamps with parchment shades.

For the children there was an elkhound named Naga, and their Shetland pony Violet. They owned a brown bear cub and their father took moving pictures of them playing with their pets.

Peggy had her own flat in Paris as well, on the rue de la Tour Faubourg, where she stayed when she visited the Paris couturiers. Speaking fluent French, she took the girls along to the designer Coco Chanel, where she was a regular client. For the Deauville races she dressed them in designs like hers, in little cloche hats and linen suits of pink and pale-blue. When beige was considered chic, they all had beige suits.

During her first summer in Deauville, Peggy suddenly found herself pursued by an admirer some fourteen years younger than herself – Prince Aly Khan. Aly easily made friends with the little girls, letting them steer his Alfa Romeo on the road along the shore. Half Indian and half Italian, Aly was lively and gregarious, and the children adored him, considering him their special friend. It never dawned on them that he was attracted to their mother.

Aly Khan was a far cry from Esmond, a strict disciplinarian who closely scrutinised their activities. It was a carefree existence with their mother in France, unlike the one the family led in London when they were with their father.

There the family lived a regimented life in Warwick House. The children were whisked past the butler and footman, up the thickly carpeted stairs to the nursery on the third floor, where they lived amid Spartan furnishings, plain wooden furniture and a linoleum floor. Nanny Radcliffe took them for long walks in Green Park and they could hear Big Ben chiming as they strolled.

They saw their mother for ten minutes in the morning and during children's hour, between five and six in the evenings. Otherwise, Nanny Radcliffe was their mother. She snored loudly at night and talked to herself, but she was a figure of stability in their lives.

Esmond at first pursued a career in politics, the field he truly loved, and he would have chosen it for his life's work had he been free from family obligations. As the Conservative Member of Parliament for the

Isle of Thanet from 1920, he was at twenty-two the youngest member of the House of Commons, serving in Westminster for nine years.

His wife didn't share his enthusiasm. Peggy sat on the platform during elections, 'and looked bored', her daughter Esmé later wrote. Although Peggy did charity work and oversaw celebrations and fêtes, she harboured deep resentment. Some of it stemmed from the narrow existence she was leading. She had always been wild and now she was conformist. It didn't suit her.

Then there was her jealousy. Peggy accused Esmond of having an affair with her youngest sister, Baba, and named other women as well. Esmond didn't deny it. But Peggy was too spirited to take Esmond's peccadilloes in her stride.

She struck back with the young Prince Aly Khan, causing gossip even among the jaded sophisticates of the French Riviera, not because the couple obviously shared more than an interest in racing – but because of his colour. Aly was stigmatised for being half Indian, a 'non-white' in the upper-class parlance of the day, and the affair became a scandal, infuriating Esmond and bringing about the final rupture of the marriage.

Peggy retreated to her sitting room, Esmond to the library and for weeks they barely spoke. The break finally came when the children were aged ten, eight and five. Lorna heard her father say to her mother, 'You can get out.' After that, the children fled with their mother to Claridge's where they took a suite. When Esmond sent a bouquet to try to make it up, Peggy flung the flowers out of the window.

In the midst of this family crisis, Peggy turned on everyone and, in an angry moment, sacked Nanny Radcliffe, a terrible mistake considering how frightened the children already were. Nanny put on her hat and coat, as she had so many times, but this time she carried her luggage with her. As always, the children begged her to stay, 'weeping and hanging on to her clothes and promising to be good'. They followed her down the corridor, crying after her. But this time Nanny didn't stop.

As the eldest of the children, Lorna fared best in the face of this adversity. A self-directed child, she had developed a sense of independence that guided her through. But Esmé and Vere both believed they were somehow to blame for Nanny's leaving. They felt guilty over the break-up of the marriage. Esmé started compulsively performing her tasks twice, in a subconscious attempt to get them right and bring back her nanny. The little girl began to think herself backward and suddenly found it difficult to learn.

All of us were bad at school, all three kids. I don't know why we were stupid, or whether a child psychologist would say it was the divorce when we were young. I think a child psychologist would say that was the root reason. We were not interested at all in learning anything. We had a built-in resentment against all teachers…

The effect of the divorce upon Vere was even more severe. He underwent a complete personality change.

Until now, he had been a rambunctious boy, 'full of life and mischief and into everything'. After Nanny Radcliffe left he withdrew, becoming a sad, solitary figure, prone to long periods of silence. In photographs taken at the time he had the haunted look of a changeling.

He was always pictured standing alone, some few feet away from the others. Sometimes he stared intently into off-camera space, making himself even more a figure of isolation. If he faced the camera, his eyes had a look of distrust, even bitterness. He gave off a tremendous sense of understanding everything that was happening, with the hopeless acceptance of someone who is powerless to effect the outcome of events.

Vere's grief manifested itself in his health. He became ill with unde-fined illnesses. He developed painful boils and for a long time was forced to wear bandages on his legs. Peggy hired a hospital nurse to look after him. But Vere hated the nurse and began throwing tantrums. Nurse Grade responded by locking him in a cupboard for hours at a time, warning, 'Mind the rats don't bite.' At five years old he became traumatised, withdrawing completely into himself and saying nothing.

To Esmond, Vere was a problem child. If he couldn't keep up with the others, whose fault was it? Esmond, who had suffered so much from his father's overbearing manner, visited his father's methods of child rearing upon his son. A twentieth-century gentleman, he remained Victorian through and through. He never thought his conduct might have an effect upon Vere. He blamed the boy, saying he was a weak link.

Then, when Vere was nine years old, there was a traumatic incident. The children had gone skiing at Kitzbühel with their father. Esmond was in the habit of going up a smaller mountain, having lunch at an inn at the top and skiing down. Vere couldn't keep up. He was left to find his own way back down, even though it was dark. Esmond believed this would imbue him with character and teach him a lesson.

But on one occasion when Vere reached the top of the mountain the inn was closed. He was thirsty and ate the snow, not realising it had absorbed the bacteria from the fields ploughed below. He contracted hepatitis and nearly died.

But despite this Esmond never made a connection between his treat-ment of his son and its effect upon the boy. He took on an unfortunate sardonic tone of voice when he spoke to Vere. More cruelly, he spoke about him to others, in front of Vere, as if he couldn't hear or understand what was being said. It appalled visitors and confused the servants. One of Esmond's closest friends, Aidan Crawley, the former MP who later became editor-in-chief of ITN, frequented Esmond's house in London, disliked the way Esmond treated his son and made friends with the boy. 'In later years,' Crawley remembered, 'Vere remembered me for being kind to him. I didn't lose by it, I assure you.'

The break-up of the marriage of Esmond and Peggy took on all the characteristics of a military engagement. They both dug in with a stubbornness and selfishness that was irrational, cruel, vindictive. They were destroyers bent on revenge, locked in a war with one another that seemed absurd to outsiders.

And the first casualty of the private war between Esmond and Peggy Harmsworth was their son Vere.

For many years Peggy nurtured the belief that she and Esmond would get back together.

Instead, Esmond instigated the longest divorce proceedings in the history of English jurisprudence, beginning in 1930 and lasting for eight years. There were amusing sidelights, as when Peggy cited twenty-six co-respondents. Less amusing was Esmond's side paying informants to report on Peggy.

It was a nasty piece of work, a lawyer's field day, the children caught in the crossfire. The divorce proceedings were omnipresent in the background, poisoning the children's pleasure in living and their peace of mind. At the same time, they were highly privileged and felt loved by each of their parents, an emotionally confusing state of affairs. As to the effect of the divorce upon Vere, the boy was mummified – buried alive, eyes wide open, watching everything.

Ironically, much of the rancour between Peggy and Esmond stemmed from their continuing attraction, their mutual fury providing a frisson of the passion they had once shared. Neither of them could let go and, if the truth were known, neither wanted to. Peggy's hope that they could rebuild the marriage was not altogether fantasy. And although Esmond went through women at a startling rate, he might eventually have renewed his marriage vows to Peggy had he not met Ann O'Neill, whom he later married. His obsessive fixation on the small dark Ann at last obliterated his obsessive fixation on the small dark Peggy.

But Peggy still loved Esmond, although she was very angry and increasingly embittered. She had over the years entwined her own identity with his. Now, caught in the toils of her desire for revenge, she was slow to catch on that her own position in society eroded in direct relation to her estrangement from her husband. And of course, Peggy had no money.

Deprived of Warwick House, the summer homes and finally her flat in Paris, her lifestyle scaled down gradually without her actually noticing. In August 1931 she rented a house in Cornwall where she continued to entertain Aly, who provided a distraction with his charm. Once he filled her shoes with freshly gathered violets.

It was Harold who came to Peggy's rescue. A penthouse flat was purchased, overlooking Park Lane with views of Hyde Park. And in Dorset Harold bought Peggy a stately home, suitable for the children and their station in life. Athelhampton Hall had a river running through the estate and thirteen Tudor gardens. There was a crown garden, a sunken garden, a river garden and, to the delight of the children, a nut walk.

The house had six grand reception rooms, all lit by candlelight since there was no electricity until 1936. When Aly visited he delighted the children by playing hide-and-seek or taking them for rides in his chauffeured car. He was constantly showering them with little gifts.

A stable was built, and Aly and Peggy indulged their mutual passion for horseracing. At the dinner table they talked incessantly about horses and Peggy began raising thoroughbreds.

The servants were aware of the relationship but remained discreet. Aly and Peggy were popular with the staff. In Peggy's territory, Esmond was considered a cold and distant figure who had broken the heart of their lovely mistress. Peggy's behaviour was beyond reproach.

Into the house came the sixteen-year-old Florence Oakley, engaged for the summer to take charge of Vere, by now eleven years old and considered a troubled child. Florence's father had been a linguist, stationed in India, and during his lifetime her family had enjoyed genteel status. But when he suddenly died the family was plunged into crisis and Florence was forced to go into service. She chose childcare as her area because she loved children and she adopted the ethical values of the teaching profession.

Athelhampton Hall was a happy house, she remembered later, with an unpretentious staff who were genuinely friendly. At the railway station Florence was impressed when the chauffeur met her in a Bentley. But she hadn't guessed what a fabulous old house it was.

> In the entrance hall hung old guns and pistols, two huge arches, a stone floor. When I saw the Great Hall, with suits of armour, candelabra placed on each side of the massive fireplace, I looked up what a height, at least eighty feet, flags hung so high one could not discern what they were. A huge oak table was set in the centre on huge flagstones. I was absolutely fascinated.

Florence was employed as an assistant to Nanny Radcliffe who had, since her sacking, been re-engaged. But the beloved nanny was now so ancient she stayed in her room most of the time and Florence had complete responsibility for young Vere.

The day Florence arrived, Lorna and Esme were away with their mother, and the new nanny found the boy in the charge of the servants. Vere seemed depressed, unhappy, difficult to reach, they told Florence with concern. He was a 'mopey' child who spent all his time alone, his only companion his dog PeeWee. Vere slept late, went to bed early and, although he was no bother, the staff didn't know how to deal with him. 'He is an odd boy,' the cook told Florence in confidence.

Vere was always alone, Florence discovered, hiding himself under grapevines, or in unused rooms throughout the house, or beneath his covers – wherever he could find. When Florence Oakley discovered he took all his meals alone, she was appalled. But the butler said, 'Master Vere *likes* eating alone.'

Vere told Florence stoically he was always 'told off' for everything; it was his lot in life. Florence didn't believe him. 'Just wait,' he told her. Later on the day they first met, Florence and Vere went into the kitchen for tea and cherry cakes, when Vere happened to say he was hungry. 'That's what comes of not eating your lunch, Master Vere,' the butler said automatically. Vere lifted his eyebrows at Florence, winking. 'See what I mean?' he asked.

Florence set about changing all this. Only five years older than her charge, she was an unconventional nanny who thought what was missing from the boy's life was a bit of fun. With this in mind she organised games and outings into town and down to the river.

Under this regime Vere flourished and he soon began calling Florence 'a good sport'. It seemed a high compliment from the inhibited boy. But although he did have a better time that summer, it quickly became apparent that he was a deeply unhappy child.

'What an effect his parents' divorce was having on poor Vere!' Florence said later. 'Unfortunately, we servants were not in a position to point this out to them. But we could at least give him a bit of happiness here. He was such a dear lad.'

It was true. Vere was charming. That August, on the morning of his birthday, when she went up to ask him what he wanted for breakfast, she found the boy still in bed, the covers pulled over his head. 'What do you want for breakfast, Master Vere?' she asked. 'Sausages or nothing!' he answered, pulling down the covers. But wouldn't he like to have something else as well, she ventured. 'Sausages or nothing!' he yelled again in a loud voice.

'If ever I have a little boy, I will love him and I will call him Jonathan,' he said, jumping out of bed.

'Why Jonathan, Master Vere? Why?' she asked.

'Cos I will, that's all.'

Vere wasn't giving up on life, despite the isolation of his early years. He had plans that he shared with no one. Indeed, there was plenty of time to make them. Alone and bored, he turned to the comics, devouring *Tiger Tim*, *Rainbow* and the Bruin Boys, a family of bears. A short time later he switched to books, quickly turning to history, something his teachers never knew.

At Eton, Vere continued to live in a world apart, doing poorly at his school work and making a bad adjustment. He resisted the regimentation of the classroom, withdrawing into silence. But he was a surprisingly good-natured child. With the other boys he embraced the myth of his own imbecility with enthusiasm and he was well liked despite his slowness. When he won the heavyweight boxing championship for the school, he took everyone by surprise, demonstrating a competitive spirit that none of his classmates suspected.

But for the most part Vere preferred to remain a secret person. He amused himself by observing the behaviour of his classmates and he never lost the habit of living reclusively, within himself, even when surrounded by others. He was shy to the extent of backwardness, his social skills stunted by the isolation of his early years. Vere was nothing like his father, whose astounding good looks, social graces and ready wit made him one of the most sought-after gentlemen in the realm. No, Vere was more like his grandfather Rothermere, whose shyness was such that he was tongue-tied and garrulous by turns. And somewhere, buried deeply within the boy, was a streak of the wild brilliance of his great-uncle Northcliffe.

But for now his wayward and undisciplined intellect was a law unto itself.

Florence continued to work for Mrs Harmsworth that winter, returning to London to continue her training while Vere was away at Eton. Some time later a number of significant changes took place, one of them being that Prince Aly ceased coming to visit and another that the divorce became final.

Then, after one of Vere's trips home, Florence thought she detected a change in the boy. He had slumped back into his old ways, seemed very depressed and unhappier than ever. The next summer revealed the reason. Mrs Harmsworth returned to Athelhampton Hall with someone new. Not long afterwards Commander Hussey and his two children came to visit. The Commander had custody of his children and it was soon revealed that he and Vere's mother were to be married.

Peggy had been round to each of the three children, asking whether they thought she should marry Commander Hussey. Hussey was proud and distant, and the two girls answered with a resounding, 'No!' But when Peggy asked Vere, he said, 'You must do whatever will make you happy.' It was an odd answer. But the boy seemed to understand intuitively his mother's need to be loved and the inevitability that her needs were not going to be met. But he said nothing.

Nor did the servants have any faith in the Commander. Overnight, the atmosphere at Athelhampton Hall changed – from pleasant to 'no guests, no fun'. Peggy gave all the servants a photograph of herself and the Commander at their wedding at the Register Office, but young Florence thought she looked terribly unhappy. The Commander was 'obnoxious' and Florence made plans to leave.

Unsurprisingly, one of Commander Hussey's first acts as master of the house was to tell Florence she must make her own way.

> I was asked to go to the Drawing Room, and Commander Hussey said that I must not expect me or my luggage to be transported, etc., etc., in quite an offensive manner. I replied I expected nothing from him. I was quite capable of making my own arrangements...

Peggy's family thought the Commander had married her believing she would receive a handsome divorce settlement. When she didn't, he became angry and even violent. For the second time in her life Peggy found herself with a husband who wasn't faithful, increasing her tendency to be bitter about the opposite sex. Later, one of the children discovered that Commander Hussey himself had been one of the paid informants in the divorce proceeding their father had pursued against their mother.

All this folly fell heavily upon the children and particularly on Vere. For all his wealth and privilege, he was miserable. In his later years he once said to his sister Esme, 'I spent the first forty-five years of my life getting over our childhood.'

'So did I,' she answered vehemently. 'So did I.'

After he took over Associated Newspapers, Vere Harmsworth sometimes surprised his subordinates by exhibiting a high degree of suspicion towards people and their motives. It came out of nowhere and seemed almost paranoiac. When one of his employees asked him about it, Vere replied cryptically, 'If you had had my upbringing, you would be suspicious too.'

THREE

TERMS OF ENDEARMENT

Vere's escape from domestic strife came with the start of World War Two. In June 1940 his father decided that he and Esme would join the thousands of children being evacuated to America.

Esme, who was seventeen, wanted to stay in England with her friends, no matter what the risk. Vere, not quite fourteen, was more amenable to his father's wishes. But the children's grandfather was firmly against the crossing. He feared for the safety of the two teenagers as they crossed the submarine-infested North Atlantic. Nevertheless they made the journey in a steamship, with 600 other children, all of them bored and seasick and heartbroken to be leaving home.

For Esme the move was disastrous. She was sent to stay in the house of one of Esmond's business associates, Frank Humphrey, in Ridgewood, New Jersey. She felt lonely and isolated, and managed to make her way home again only six months later.

For Vere the brief sojourn in America had its advantages. First, he was away from his parents and their problems, giving him a fresh perspective on his own identity. Then, too, he attended Kent School in Connecticut, where he at last began to enjoy his studies. His work improved and he made friends with the gregarious American students in his classes, and altogether he began to love learning in ways he had never before considered. In America he wasn't cosseted and protected by a large staff of well-meaning servants. He had a sense of freedom and discovery. The world was a big place, he was finding out.

His host, Frank Humphrey, was critical of the boy, matching almost perfectly Esmond's own sardonic tone when he wrote to the press lord reporting on his son's adjustment. Vere was no trouble at all, he said. Whenever he visited Humphrey's home in New Jersey, all he did was eat and sleep. Nevertheless, Humphrey admitted, Vere was doing well at school, even excelling in certain subjects, so there was no cause for alarm on that front.

But if Humphrey found Vere wanting, the feeling was not mutual. Vere was riveted by Frank Humphrey. Despite his sleepiness, he was very much aware that Humphrey kept, not one, but three mistresses in New York, each of a different race. The propensity of wealthy Americans to live conformist lives while quietly pursuing private pleasures fascinated the boy and his fascination was entirely non-judgemental.

Vere was to make other observations on his way home when, the following year, he became one of the first to cross the Atlantic aboard the Boeing Flying Clipper. Like his sister Esme he had to go by way of Lisbon and, also like her, had to spend time in Estoril queuing for passage. Following in her footsteps, he went to the Grand Hotel to wait it out.

Portugal was a neutral nation and Estoril became a kind of way station for refugees from both sides during the war. The place was a hotbed of spies and intrigue, and the casino attracted underworld characters as well. Free to go wherever he liked, Vere roamed the halls of the hotel during the day and visited the casino at night, more interested in the people than the gambling. The circumstances of his childhood had forced him into the role of observer and here in Estoril he became a full-fledged student of human nature. Ironically, no one in his family even realised he was in Estoril, his father's involvement with Ann O'Neill having reached a crescendo and his sisters frantically seeing friends off to war. When at last Vere did manage to get passage home, he was amazed at the airport to see the British aeroplanes lined up side by side with the German planes and their swastikas.

Vere Harmsworth was passive by nature; it appeared to be one of his early defences against the powerful personalities of his parents. But beneath his benign exterior he had inherited the strong character of both his parents. His mother, though she had her faults, had tremendous courage and, especially in the face of adversity, she could keep her head, making her way despite any difficulty. Vere was very much like her. He could stay the course. He also had inherited the devastating Harmsworth charm and he was capable of disarming people with it, frequently to their surprise. His father was witty and Vere had a good sense of humour too, but his jokes tended to be dry and ironic. Like everything else with Vere, the humour came across as a coded message, a secret from those who didn't understand irony. If the listener wasn't attuned to his wry tone, Vere's witticisms sailed right over his head.

He remained a recessive character all his life, becoming garrulous and outgoing only with the selected few with whom he felt comfortable. Strangely, and although it was a source of shame, one of the best things that ever happened to him was being passed over for a commission in the army. He joined the ranks in 1943 and found himself completely at ease among the ordinary soldiers.

Later on he would rely upon these men and their skills, first to help him shore up the fading fortunes of the family publishing empire, then to bring it back to its former glory. The class system that had prevented so many talented men from achieving all they could would work to the advantage of Vere Harmsworth, who liked them much better than the people he had known since birth.

But for now, Vere was stationed in Alexandria and, practically on the eve his company was shipped out, became violently ill. Misdiagnosed, he languished, near death, in an ear, eye, nose and throat hospital, until a surgeon happened to diagnose his illness as glandular fever, transferring him immediately to an intensive care unit. He was injected with the new wonder drug penicillin every two hours and his life was saved.

His convalescence remains something of a mystery. He later spoke of it only cryptically and confidentially. For in Alexandria he was enlisted by a British espionage agent to make the rounds, reporting back on whatever he was instructed to observe. Nothing could have been more natural to Vere, who somehow always managed not to be noticed, a habit he picked up in his youth. With plenty of money in his pocket and a reputation for being a playboy, he seemed particularly gullible to any fast-talking racketeer or master of intrigue. His natural eccentricity provided a cover and no one would ever have suspected he was systematically reporting back what he learnt. He discovered great advantages then to being underestimated. He also discovered, to his continuing amusement, that he felt at home in the company of pickpockets, women of dubious reputation and knaves of all sorts.

Vere had an encyclopaedic curiosity and along with it a lifelong fascination with corruption, whether it stemmed from questionable business practices or moral turpitude. He always wanted to know why people did what they did. But he also had an interest in corruption for its own sake, occasionally shocking a friend or colleague with his prurient interest. They made up excuses to account for his straightforward questions about things they found embarrassing, most usually based on his being some sort of holy innocent. But Vere made no excuses for himself. He was interested in what people did, that's all.

One of his favourite stories about Northcliffe was about the press magnate's aquarium with two fighting fish separated by a panel of glass. From time to time, Northcliffe lifted the glass to study the results. Vere Harmsworth found this story utterly riveting. He was interested in the mayhem committed by nature's predators, yes. But he was also interested in Northcliffe's fixation upon brutality, one he shared. The power and prestige Vere wielded meant he rarely found it necessary to participate in life on this level. But he was fascinated by it, if not amused. Throughout his life he enlisted others to carry out the uglier necessities of business for him, preferring to keep the high ground for himself. But if and when someone confronted Vere face to face with his own culpability, if he had any, he would own up to it.

Few knew this side of him because he chose to reveal it very seldom. Until the very end of his life he never grew tired of playing the fool, or being amused by the various explanations of his personality others would advance. His double or even triple identity was his little joke on the world, providing amusement for all and a means of participation for a very shy man.

Ann O'Neill's husband was killed in the war in 1944 and she was free at last to marry her long-time lover Esmond. It was typical of Ann that at the very moment of realising her goal to marry Rothermere she was entering into her affair with Ian Fleming. As one of Ann's greatest friends, Evelyn Waugh, put it, 'It makes perfect sense. She's marrying Rothermere and Ian's round the corner in a flat.' Thus did Ann manage to continue her exciting life of intrigue and subterfuge, merely changing one man for the next. In 1946 Ann reopened Warwick House and Vere Harmsworth, now twenty-one, returned to St James's, taking up residence in one of the upper bedrooms.

Ann turned her attentions to entertaining and quickly made a reputation for herself as one of the pre-eminent social hostesses of London. But she had very little time for Esmond's son Vere, seldom including him in her entertainments. For a time he studied on his own, ignored by the household, as he struggled to win a place at Oxford. But when he failed his exams, in a state of disgrace he understood only too well, he had no choice but to go to work for his father's firm.

For two years he worked for the Anglo-Canadian Paper Mills that his grandfather Harold had founded in Quebec. This was at least better than the paper mill Northcliffe had founded in Grand Falls, Newfoundland. Vere believed its remote location would be unbearable and fought successfully against being assigned there.

While he was in Quebec, Vere renewed his interest in North Americans. They were more open than his fellow countrymen, less likely to categorise him according to position or class, less judgemental. He always prospered whenever he lived or travelled there, and he grew to trust Canadians and Americans probably more than his own countrymen. Among his new acquaintances was Bob Morrow, a colleague of his father's. Bob was a shrewd young attorney from Montreal who had been a pilot during World War Two. His business acumen would result in a remarkable contribution to the fortunes of Associated Newspapers. He would also become one of Vere's few lifelong friends. But for now they were simply two young men, each trying to find his footing in the business world.

When Vere returned to London he set up in an apartment of his own and started working his way through each of the departments at Associated Newspapers, learning as much about the business as he was able. To all intents and purposes he now became a playboy in post-war London, driving a sports car, taking out beautiful girls and going to nightclubs like the Milroy on Park Lane. Women were crazy about him and they sought him out as an escort.

Vere was tall like his father, six feet four inches, but instead of sharing Esmond's blond colouring, Vere was dark like his mother, with high cheekbones and steamy good looks. In fact, during this period he believed he looked like an Italian gigolo. But if he was attractive to women, he seemed not to know it.

It was easy for them to mistake Vere's basic shyness for indifference. When this happened they could misread his character, imputing to him a higher level of sophistication than he possessed. Thus he was considered a challenge among the young ladies of his set.

But Vere was a far cry from the worldly playboy many believed him to be. True, he did have all the trappings – the car, the money, the looks. Women fell for him in the same way they had fallen for his father, but with very different results. Vere was nothing like a polished philanderer and he resisted the role as successfully as he could. Nevertheless he gained the reputation for being a dilettante when in fact no one could have been more diligent or well-meaning.

In the summer of 1953, just after the Coronation, Helen Fitzgerald gave a dinner party. She was the sister-in-law of Lord Beaverbrook, the Rothermeres' great competitor, who owned the *Daily Express*. Beaverbrook's granddaughter, Lady Jeanne Campbell, attended the party and Vere was there as well. Jeanne Campbell knew Vere from their child-hood days because her grandfather's house, Stornaway in St James's, adjoined Warwick House. But she hadn't seen Vere for several years. Although Jeanne remembered very little of the actual dinner party, Vere's presence registered with her and, subconsciously at least, she began to think about him.

Jeanne's parents were divorced and she had been more or less 'given' to Beaverbrook when she was only one and a half weeks old. Beaverbrook grew increasingly attached to her and she became, in her own words, 'the child of his heart'. Hers was an extraordinary childhood, living alone with her grandfather at Cherkley, along with the forty servants who cared for the place. She had a loving Scottish nanny to look after her, but in large part she had been included among Beaverbrook's friends and colleagues since she was very small. The effect upon her was to make her highly precocious. But she was very lonely as well.

It may have been because of this remarkable set of circumstances that now, at twenty-four, she had fallen 'into the toils of an adventurer'. Prince Radziwill, whom Jeanne called 'Stash', was a complicated character in his late thirties who acted as a kind of Svengali to the young girl. He was married, but that hadn't stopped him from more or less taking over Jeanne's life. He was like a mother and a father to her, filling 'all the holes of her childhood', and she adored him.

Beaverbrook deplored the relationship. He knew about disreputable activities the Prince had been involved in during the war, including gold smuggling, and he told Jeanne he wanted to get her away from this man at all costs. The press baron threatened and cajoled her by turns to leave Radziwill, once even going down on his knees and begging her to give him up in an extravagant gesture that had no effect whatsoever upon the young girl. Another time he threatened Jeanne, saying, 'If you don't give him up, I'll destroy him.' At the very least, he told her, he had 'called in the lawyers to make sure that damn black prince doesn't get hold of my newspapers'. Jeanne thought all this hilarious, but when she later told Radziwill about the incident he actually turned white. In later years she reluctantly concluded that at least part of his attraction to her had been the desire to make use of her grandfather's position.

Now Beaverbrook, who had never taken much interest in Jeanne's social life, came up with the idea of giving a number of little dinner parties for her. He hoped she would meet someone nearer her age, a suitable young man who would take her mind off the Prince.

Against this background Jeanne happened one afternoon to be in Piccadilly, just round the corner from Stornaway House, and ran into Vere in front of the Ritz. She remembered he was standing on the kerb in a very bad suit and 'he looked adorable'. On a whim, she invited him to a dinner party and he accepted. Her friends Alex Romanov and Mary Millington Drake were there, and by the end of the evening Jeanne was a fair way towards being smitten. Vere offered to drive both women home and, since he took Mary first, it gave Jeanne the opportunity to invite him to her flat for a private dinner the next night.

Vere accepted. The two of them had a marvellous time, eating their meal on Jeanne's balcony. She thought Vere intriguing, mysterious and, above all, subtle. At twenty-seven he was young and vital, and she was intoxicated by being with someone in her own age group. As they talked, she discovered what very few people knew, that Vere was widely read and an intellectual, and she saw this as common ground that could lead to a long relationship. At the end of the evening he invited her to go to Sark aboard his yacht. She brought Julian Plowden and his girlfriend Denise, Lady Kilmarnock. It was a great excursion and Jeanne ended up driving Vere's car back to London. When she got to her flat she asked him up for a nightcap.

The men Jeanne had dated invariably 'pounced' whenever they saw the opportunity, but Vere did not. In Jeanne's eyes this made him even more attractive. When they reached the top of the stairs she said to him, 'Vere, I want you to marry me. I've fallen in love with you.' There was a slight pause, then he replied, 'You wouldn't want to marry me if you knew what I was really like.'

This took Jeanne aback. She decided this was a playboy's subterfuge, thus transforming Vere into a mysterious and appealing character when he was probably just trying to give her his own impartial and honest view of himself. But she believed more than ever that she and Vere were soul-mates and belonged together. When, the next day, Prince Radziwill returned from Ceylon, she met him to break off the relationship, telling him she had fallen in love with someone else. His response was 'cold fury' since he had already asked his wife for a divorce and actually had with him the emerald he had intended to give Jeanne. Later, in 1958, when he married Lee Bouvier, Jacqueline Kennedy's sister, Jeanne was amused to discover that the emerald had found its way 'into her coffers'.

In Jeanne's mind she and Vere were practically engaged. 'It never occurred to me', she said later, 'that he wouldn't marry me.' Meanwhile Jeanne confessed to Beaverbrook whom she had fallen in love with.

Nothing could have pleased the press magnate more than the joining of the rival newspaper dynasties through marriage. Wily and observant, Beaverbrook had always seen in Vere the potential to become a capable newspaper proprietor, and he made immediate plans to give Jeanne and Vere the *Evening Standard* as their wedding gift, so enthusiastic was he about their impending nuptials.

But Beaverbrook was actually right about young Harmsworth's news-paper instincts, to the extent that Vere realised the relationship between himself and Jeanne Campbell was impossible. He knew enough about human nature to understand that Beaverbrook would be incapable of letting Vere find his own way in the business and he also knew, without a shadow of doubt, that Beaverbrook's meddling would create an untenable situation, both in the marriage and in the business. The two rivals could never join forces. Beaverbrook's domineering nature made that impossible.

Vere resisted. Typically, he didn't actually believe Jeanne's affection for him was real; instead he suspected she was acting cynically at Beaverbrook's behest. But he never told this to Jeanne. Later, when Jeanne invited him to join her and her grandfather at his villa in the South of France, he accepted but never showed up. Although the couple enjoyed a long friendship, Vere never evinced any romantic interest in her, which distressed her.

'In a way, we were like two kids playing,' she would later say. She called him 'Ty', short for 'Tycoon', although at the time he was the furthest thing from a tycoon she could think of. But they did decide to start a magazine together called 'Fumati'. Although both of them treated the idea as a serious one, it never got off the ground.

Thus it went, the two of them locked in a kind of ill-defined on-again, off-again relationship until something happened to change Jeanne's mind. In the summer of 1955 they decided to drive down to the South of France together. On the way they stopped at an inn where, as Jeanne was preparing for bed, she took out the five unlabelled bottles she always carried with her. Each of them contained a different potion, among them a sleeping draught, Lysol and complexion milk. 'I've got to sleep,' she thought, but she accidentally took the Lysol instead of the sleeping draught. Her reaction was complete hysteria. She called Vere and he had her drink milk before taking her to the hospital where she had her stomach pumped. Jeanne had believed he would be full of concern for her. Instead, on the way to the hospital, he said in an outraged voice, 'You would do this *to me!*'

For Jeanne it was the ultimate eye opener. She had always thought he would eventually come round, but now she realised it would never happen. For whatever reasons, Vere would never marry her and indeed, she no longer wanted to marry Vere.

And so the affair ended.

The woman Vere did marry was Patricia Matthews, a young Rank starlet whose stage name was Beverley Brooks. Patricia was married to Christopher Brooks, whom she had met at Brands Hatch where he was driving a racing car for one of his friends. Patricia had a baby daughter by him, Sarah. But by the time Sarah was born, the marriage had already begun to founder.

Brooks was an old Etonian who had made a bad business investment, finding himself much the worse off in a deal with a partner. It was also possible he had strayed during Patricia's difficult pregnancy. Patricia sometimes said so. But whether or not this was true, she remained friends with him and her family always enjoyed seeing him come to visit, even after it became clear that the marriage wasn't going to work.

As for Patricia, she was a wild card in every sense. Born into the middle class, she quickly discovered another world. She was lively, ambitious, bold. She was also stunningly beautiful. It would be possible for her to escape the limitations of the British class system.

In a way she was aided by her mother, Doris Matthews, who was something akin to all the stage mothers in the world. She urged Patricia on to higher and higher achievements. She poured everything into her daughter that she herself had wanted to be, and she lived her life vicariously through her daughter.

Like so many of her generation, Patricia's mother had long wanted a child, but it was nine years before she felt secure enough in her marriage both financially and emotionally, to have her first baby. Thus, when Patricia finally was born, she became her mother's primary reason for living.

Patricia was reminded, almost every day of her life, that physical appearance was the most important aspect of a young girl's life. Indeed, both parents constantly referred to the way people looked and how their appearance would inevitably determine what would become of them. Patricia *was* a very pretty girl and she came to believe her appearance was the best means she had of achieving a better way of life.

But there was something far more attractive about Patricia than the way she looked. She was bursting with life, full of enthusiasm and exuberance. It was exciting just to be around her and whenever she talked about her plans for the future she seemed sure to succeed. Hers was a volatile personality, extremely appealing and highly explosive. With Pat, one had the feeling anything could happen.

Her sister Jenny, seven years younger than Patricia, remembered waiting for her at the bus stop when she was a child, eager to find out what had happened to her that day. She hero-worshipped her elder sister, taking pride in everything she did.

To please her parents Patricia had started secretarial school when she was seventeen. But she soon dropped out, fashioning herself into a model. Her method of getting work was to show up at a fashion salon or a department store and inform the management that they needed her to sell their clothes. Such was the nature of her enthusiasm and appeal that they would often agree with her, and she made her way without difficulty.

Patricia had no stop mechanisms. She would brook no failure. Whatever it took, that's what she would do. 'To achieve the possible,' she would often say, 'you must attempt the impossible.' Another of her sayings was, 'Keep your eye on the doughnut, not on the hole.'

She was very good at school, achieving two credits and a distinction for her school certificate. In later life she would amaze people by her ability to remember all kinds of minutiae, reeling off with ease telephone numbers of people she had called only once. Yet in large part she left the intellectual side of herself undeveloped, probably because young women of her generation weren't customarily encouraged to develop their minds. Patricia nevertheless believed intensely in self-improvement and Norman Vincent Peale's *How to Win Friends and Influence People* became her bible, as it was her mother's before her.

More troubling, Patricia early on showed a lack of imagination that seemed undesirable, even self-destructive. During the last air raids of the war, when the family were scuttling below ground as fast as they could go, Patricia would refuse to get out of bed. On one level this made her seem fearless. But on another it appeared she didn't seem to realise she could actually be harmed.

Then, too, from childhood, she had been difficult to control and in school, despite her high marks, she showed an unwillingness to accept discipline from her teachers. Her mother always sided with her daughter, backing her totally. But Doris did realise that controlling Patricia was a complicated matter.

Her mother nevertheless did not seem to disapprove of this mindset and the two of them often drew into their own world of fantasy of how it would be when Patricia achieved the high goals her mother had instilled – a distinguished and well-off husband, a glittering social life, a brilliant career.

Patricia missed very little when it came to putting herself forward. She had genuine stage presence. After appearing at the Edinburgh Festival, she enrolled in the Royal Academy of Dramatic Art and was quickly picked up by the Rank Film Organisation, Britain's major film producer of the time.

The film industry was just emerging from its wartime function of producing propaganda films to keep up the morale of the public. Rank Studios, under the auspices of Production Facilities Films, had initiated a stunt that ended up becoming a highly successful public relations venture, dubbed the 'Rank Charm School'. It was a slightly derisory term that indicated a system of contracting beautiful young people as actors and actresses in the movie industry. But it sounded terrific, resulting in thousands of column inches of free publicity in the popular press.

In England almost everyone in the acting world had come up through the theatre, but theatre actors didn't always translate well on to film because they tended to exaggerate their movements for the stage. Hence, the 'Charm School' was a method of attracting and tying up potential film stars for the industry. These fledgling actors and actresses were paid £10 a week, and for that they entered into a public relations scheme that included a great deal of press attention and a lot of photographs, most often taken by the well-known Russell Sedgewick.

For the girls it was an opportunity to be escorted by fabulously handsome actors to a lot of first nights, wearing glamorous furs and diamonds that were collected at the end of the evening. After the performance, more often than not, the aspiring actress had to take the tube home since England was still reeling from the privations of war.

In this milieu Patricia quickly won her first film role in *Reach for the Sky*. She played Douglas Bader's feckless girlfriend who deserts the war hero after he loses his legs in action. It was a small part, but a prominent one and it gave Patricia a start. The photographer Baron then named her as one of the top ten beauties in England and the studio suggested that Darryl Zanuck wanted to give her a screen test in Hollywood.

Patricia had been taught immaculate clipped English by the studio, which she performed to perfection, always managing to sound slightly imperious. She also showed a certain verve and flair. Then, too, the camera liked her, picking up a vulnerability that made her special on screen.

At the time Patricia met Vere Harmsworth it was apparent that she was destined to have at least a degree of success and perhaps more. And, at twenty-four, she was at the absolute peak of her beauty.

A friend of Patricia's, Duggy Gordon, introduced her to Vere and Patricia never forgot, remaining a lifelong friend to Gordon. The young couple were immediately drawn to one another. Patricia recalled later that Vere was very patrician and very handsome, if scruffily dressed.

For his part Vere quickly realised that, for all her affectation of being a member of the upper classes, her impressive command of perfectly enunciated English wasn't entirely real. But it wasn't how she spoke or looked that was the true basis of his attraction to the young actress. What drew him in was her liveliness, her playful charm, the childlike enthusiasm she displayed for living, that vulnerability that distinguished her from other girls. He had for so long been sequestered from life, living in a kind of emotional vacuum resulting from his position and money, that it was a pleasure to be around someone whose *joie de vivre* was so open and easy.

The mutual attraction developed into love and in 1957 they married, neither of them suspecting how difficult it would be to bridge the differences in their backgrounds. Complicating matters further, each was carrying the baggage of the older generation. Much later, most people who knew her well would say that Vere was 'the love of Patricia's life'. And until the end of his life, Vere never stopped saying how much he loved his wife.

In many ways, however, and by a later standard of evaluation, it was a shame for Patricia that she married Vere before she had fully tested the level of success she might have achieved, because she actually did have something and might very well have made a name for herself if she had not stopped there.

But she did stop there. She gave herself over to Vere's life and value system, without developing her talent or her intellect, and she spent her time trying to please the very people whom she could never please, because of her humble background. For Patricia and Vere, the attraction they felt for one another would lead to a roller-coaster relationship without the stability necessary to bring lasting satisfaction. In later years people around the couple would come to realise that the relationship had been doomed from the beginning.

What was less obvious was the harm it would do Patricia Matthews. Seduced by the illusion of power and happiness that great wealth often gives, she sought her sense of self-worth from her looks and social standing. It was an attitude typical of the age she lived in. The idea of a Prince Charming who solves all a young girl's problems and introduces her to an opulent lifestyle was a dream shared by many young women of her generation.

It was Patricia's great sadness that she didn't push on, to see what she could have accomplished on her own mettle, and in that sense the tragedy of the age contributed strongly to her later lack of self-worth and eventual unhappiness.

FOUR

EVERY WOMAN NEEDS HER *DAILY MAIL*

Much like his private life, Vere's career was complicated by contingencies few understood. Although he had been given charge of Associated Newspapers in 1971 when he was forty-six, and this included the *Daily Mail*, still Vere remained under the control of his father. It was the result of a structural anomaly that gave ultimate control of Associated Newspapers to its holding company, Daily Mail and General Trust. Although Vere became chairman of Associated, his father kept the title chairman of DMGT. So it remained possible for Vere's father to challenge his authority.

By now Esmond was suffering from Alzheimer's, and on bad days he could be remote and domineering; in short, undependable. Adding to this muddled state of affairs was the fact that Vere's father had left behind a number of people on the board of Associated 'to save me from myself', as Vere would later put it.

Yes, Vere had taken over, and yes, he was the man in charge – up to a point: the point at which his father raised objections to any of his plans. This Byzantine arrangement was typically deceptive and typically Harmsworthian. If nobody else understood the full implications of the set-up, Vere did. It was a classic case of Catch-22.

On 2 April 1971 the board of Associated Newspapers held a meeting crucial to the survival of the *Daily Mail*. The directors were to consider the unanimous recommendation from Vere and others who were directly involved that the relaunch scheduled for 3 May go forward.

As we have seen, much had happened since Vere took over. He had made the decision to merge the *Daily Mail* with the weaker Associated title, the *Daily Sketch*. Controversially, he had appointed the *Sketch*'s editor David English as editor of the merged paper, and he had made a further bold and far-reaching decision about the new paper's format. It would go tabloid, or 'compact', as it was called. English had already selected his staff for the new paper, singling out 277 of the two newspapers' journalists for redundancies. But in fact that was only the tip of the iceberg. In total, Vere dismissed 1733 employees, a move that hardly endeared him to Fleet Street.

English had prepared secret dummies for the new *Daily Mail* and had them printed in Amsterdam. He had organised the news, features, entertainment and sports teams. A relaunch date was set and an advertising agency had been engaged.

Now, barely a month before the relaunch, Vere's brother-in-law Neill Cooper-Key, who was a director on the board of Associated Newspapers, led a mutiny against Vere's leadership. Cooper-Key enlisted the support of another board member, Eric Graham, who set forth a proposition that the board should re-instigate the discussions between the *Daily Mail* and the *Daily Express* for a possible merger. Speaking in support of the proposition, Cooper-Key reminded the other members of the board of the recommendations made by a group of management consultants in a document called the McKinsey Report. It had predicted the ultimate failure of any attempt to resuscitate the *Daily Mail*.

Neill Cooper-Key's action was tantamount to a vote of no confidence, and it extended not only to Vere Harmsworth but also to David English, Mick Shields, John Winnington-Ingram and the entire relaunch team.

The figures that alarmed Cooper-Key had been prepared by Allan Wilkie, the financial controller of a subsidiary of DMGT. He was also present at that important meeting on 2 April 1971.

On the basis of sales and advertising projections, Wilkie estimated that if the new *Daily Mail* achieved a circulation of 1,800,000, the paper would move into a £243,000 profit. At the top figure forecast, a 2,250,000 circulation, the newspaper would produce an £842,000 profit. However, if the new *Daily Mail* achieved a circulation of only 1,600,000, it would deliver a first-year *loss* of £192,000.

Calculated against the one-time cost of the relaunch, even if the newspaper achieved the highest projected circulation – a highly unlikely outcome– the newspaper's profit would sink to only £67,000. And that was if it fulfilled the wildest dreams of the team.

The odds against that level of success seemed so remote to Cooper-Key that he introduced a course of action that would essentially nullify the entire venture. Rather than invest in a new compact *Daily Mail*, it was much safer, Cooper-Key reasoned, to join forces with Beaverbrook's *Daily Express* and spread the risk between two faltering companies. What Cooper-Key was suggesting was to go back to an earlier deal that had already been discredited. But he was determined to try one more time to bring a halt to the plans he believed were doomed to failure.

Vere was ready for him. He remembered that Cooper-Key had been one of those who helped to persuade his father Esmond to withdraw from the fledgling commercial television company Associated-Rediffusion in 1956, a disastrous move costing the company untold millions in future profits as well as a stronghold in the television industry. As the profits of Associated Rediffusion soared within a month of DMGT's exit from the venture, the City quickly labelled Esmond's tactics as 'Doing a Rother'.

As a precaution against Cooper-Key's achieving a similar result now, Vere had spoken to his father by telephone in South Africa the week before. He now stood to read out a telegram he had received from his father in response:

> warmest congratulations on the way you have faced the most difficult times ever known in Fleet Street you have done splendid work organising merger which is only solution to our problems if we are to carry on the daily mail, which all wish for in our hearts we believe your plans for new mail are excellent and have a touch of the northcliffe spirit you have my complete and unqualified support with good wishes to you and all who are working with you much love rothermere

Vere then urged the board to accept the recommendations to relaunch the *Daily Mail*. He pointed out that any delay would be fatal to the relaunch plans.

Without further discussion, Vere's resolution passed. Not unanimously... but it passed.

Cooper-Key wasn't the only one expecting disaster on 3 May. Most of the media pundits in London had published predictions that put the new compact newspaper's chances of survival at slim to zero. And, of course, the *Mail*'s competitors were letting it be known that they didn't expect much from Vere Harmsworth *or* David English.

What they couldn't know was that inside Associated Newspapers, an unbelievable *esprit de corps* had taken over. Said John Winnington-Ingram,

> For the first six to nine months, we were fighting for survival, and Vere was unsure of himself. And to his aid came this terrific spirit about the place. Everybody was supportive of Vere, and dozens of us formed great affection for him.
>
> And he returned it.
>
> It was almost as if his lack of confidence was driving all of us forward.

That was inside. Outside, the critics held sway. But what was really alarming was the advertisers' growing fear that the critics might be right.

Everyone on the relaunch team understood the importance of retaining their old advertisers and attracting new ones. Morale was then struck a stinging blow when the trade weekly *Campaign* reported that Masius Wynne-Williams and Ogilvy and Mather, both leading advertising agencies at the time, believed the new *Mail* was too much of a hybrid to survive. This, six weeks before the newspaper had even appeared on the market.

But despite all this negativity, Harmsworth remained confident. He believed in the marketing strategy he had devised of targeting women as the readers of the new *Daily Mail*. Each of the newspapers on Fleet Street had carved out a market niche for itself, he reasoned. The *Daily Express* had captured the lower-middle-class market and the *Daily Mirror* the working-class market. 'Then Rupert Murdoch floated to the surface by using the sexual revolution,' he said later.

Vere saw women as 'the last big market' and they were exactly the readers he intended the *Mail* to pursue. The way to tailor a newspaper to the woman reader was not by putting in women's pages and adding a few features for the women's readership. 'You appealed to women by orientating all the news stories, all the persona of the newspaper into something that was attractive to women,' Vere said.

David English and Vere had discussed the basis for the appeal many times, and the pair of them even hammered out a special strategy to capture the young mothers' market, agreeing to a special morning edition for them. By catering to this group, Vere reasoned, the new *Daily Mail* would attract young readers who would stay with the newspaper for life.

Crucially for the survival of the newspaper, this was the readership that advertisers would find most attractive. Since women controlled the purse strings in most households, their buying power made them extremely attractive targets for most advertisers and eventually the advertisers themselves would come to realise this. This was Vere's logic and it went a long way to explaining his high level of confidence.

Yet it appeared at first as though David English didn't fully understand what Vere intended. Either that, or he might have wished to scupper the strategy without actually saying so. When he prepared the briefing guide for Foote, Cone and Belding, the advertising agency that was handling the relaunch account, David neglected to emphasise the vital importance of the female readership.

English wrote that this was 'the age of the transistor. The age of planned, efficient packaging. The age which demands the maximum information in the most convenient form.' His new *Daily Mail* would have 'vitality', 'authority'; it would be 'easy to handle'. There would be 'planned sections for news, sport, City, entertainment and women's interest features'. It would cover 'industry', 'education', 'fashion'. There would be a hot news team, background information, pace-setting foreign news, great pictures, the list went on. In this context the women's pages would take on 'the many real issues facing women in their day-to-day lives.'.

But nowhere did English give a clue that the major thrust of the marketing strategy he and Vere had agreed was to concentrate on cultivating a female readership.

* * *

VIDEO: Tiny World in distance. Rotating very fast. It comes towards camera, but slows down...

AUDIO: 'This is the world you're living in today. Moving fast. Bursting with news. There's never been a more exciting time to be alive. Starting tomorrow we'll be capturing all that excitement in the New Compact *Daily Mail*... Tomorrow. Every page makes sense of this exciting world.'

Known among the staff at Associated Newspapers as 'the spinning globe' advertisement the television campaign planned by Foote, Cone and Belding for the relaunch of the *Daily Mail* reflected perfectly the advertising brief prepared for them by David English, and everyone within the company appeared satisfied at first.

But somehow the advert left Vere Harmsworth feeling vaguely disappointed. What did a spinning world have to do with his original marketing strategy for the *Daily Mail*? He didn't know.

In the interests of preserving morale, however, he muffled his objections, saying very little. Besides, at this point, Vere didn't have the confidence to rebut the reactions of his own professional staff simply on the basis of what he called 'a personal hunch'.

The first issue of the new compact *Daily Mail* appeared on the morning of 3 May 1971, right on schedule. But in his attempt to distance his newspaper from the downmarket *Sun* and *Mirror* tabloids, David English went overboard, producing a first issue so conservative that many regarded it as dull. It was mainly the front page that created that impression. The use of rounded rules to encircle both the masthead and the body of the newspaper was intended to give the paper an elegant look. Instead, it looked overly fancy, like an invitation to a party. And the overall appearance was vertical, more appropriate to a broadsheet than to a tabloid format. The traditional three-deck head over the lead story increased the height of the page, so it literally had a stilted look.

Asked for a defining comment about the new *Daily Mail*, the highly successful editor of Rupert Murdoch's *Sun*, Larry Lamb, said on a radio broadcast that the first issue of the *Sun* hadn't been a very professional product, but the character of the newspaper was obvious from the start. Although David English's *Daily Mail* was much more professional, the character of the paper had yet to be established. It was obvious from Lamb's comments that he admired the product and his newspaper's official response was right in character: 'a smashing new beefcake series for lively girls everywhere – The Daily Male', a series of pin-ups.

Even the *Daily Express*'s response was less antagonistic than it might have been. That newspaper's proprietor, Max Aitken (son of Lord Beaverbrook who had died seven years before), called the paper 'a strange new hybrid' and welcomed the *Daily Mail*'s old readers to the *Express*, saying he was sure they would feel more comfortable there. But he refrained from criticising the new newspaper outright, perhaps because he secretly admired it or possibly because he was still hoping for a merger if this attempt to revive the *Mail* failed.

Campaign was more forthcoming. It reported 'an air of puzzlement or disappointment about the paper's first looks'. David Phillips, media director at Bensons, said its first impact was 'a little feeble; but put alongside the *Evening Standard*, the *Mail* does grab you'. Basil Spice, Press and Media manager of J. Walter Thompson, said that clients for whom they were buying space in the new *Mail* would have used the old paper had it continued to exist. He had seen the dummy for the new paper, and 'when it finally appeared I felt a bit disappointed... the front page does make it look a bit like a religious weekly'.

In the face of this comment and criticism, David English did what he could do best. He quickly remade his newspaper's front page, dropping the rounded rules and changing the column widths. The latter innovation, instigated as a desperate measure, was actually a stroke of genius. For the widened six-column make-up led naturally in a horizontal flow to the next page in the newspaper, and the next, and the next.

Form and function were at one stroke merged, and his new compact or tabloid newspaper suddenly cohered.

Another of David's bright ideas, one he dubbed 'a perfect solution', failed utterly. This was a two-page wraparound of the *Sketch* over the *Daily Mail* to show *Sketch* readers a copy of the *Mail* and thus attract them as readers. He decided that the *Sketch* would begin publishing a slam-bam serialisation the day before it closed. It would be continued first in the wraparound and then in the *Daily Mail*, thus keeping on readers who had been hooked by it. Eventually the wraparound did appear, minus the serialisation, an idea that was dropped as being too complicated. But the wraparound didn't work as David had planned. One circulation representative reported back that some newsagents were throwing the wraparound away, saying, 'What's the point of selling a paper that's already dead?'

Another *Sketch* anomaly occurred. The sales of the *Daily Mail* before the relaunch had been 1,720,000 and during the exciting first two months of its existence, sales of the new *Daily Mail* increased to 2 million. But all too quickly management came to realise that the increase was entirely down to *Sketch* readers. The newsagents substituted the new *Daily Mail* for the *Daily Sketch*, and it was three weeks before the subscription ran out and *Sketch* readers could cancel. They then defected to their natural home, the *Daily Mirror*. This was not a total defeat, for *Sketch* readers were not exactly the type of readership the new compact newspaper needed to attract. But it was still a blow to morale.

Then the summer doldrums began, a price increase of three pence was tacked on and the paper began to haemorrhage readers. In total, counting the lost *Sketch* readers and others, some quarter of a million ceased to buy the new paper.

True the *Mail* was losing the 'right' readers. That is, part of the new *Daily Mail* strategy was to dispense with the older and less affluent reader, and since the losses in circulation were mainly off the *Sketch* and in the north, this aim was being accomplished. However, the newspaper was not attracting the younger and more affluent readers that it needed in order to survive.

Under the pressure of defecting advertisers, John Winnington-Ingram fell back on a contingency plan devised earlier for just such a case. That was to publish a number of twenty-four-page newspapers during August, thus cutting editorial to fit the exigencies of the shrinking number of adverts. In truth the *Mail*'s major competitor, the *Daily Express*, obviously encountering something of the same problem that summer, had already gone down to the equivalent twelve-page issues a number of times. Indeed, as Winnington-Ingram pointed out to a disappointed editorial, the advertisements in the *Daily Mail* no longer justified even a twenty-four-page paper. Under the circumstances, what Winnington-Ingram was seeking was hardly draconian. David English, as a member of the board of directors of Associated Newspapers, had himself agreed to such an exigency.

But English nevertheless decided to make a stand on the issue. In the highly theatrical manner that would come to characterise his personal style, English argued passionately to Vere Harmsworth against what he thought was a false economy. The paper was too young, too fragile to sustain so severe a pruning. It might threaten the important development of the newspaper's character, losing more readers as a result. In the meantime, Winnington-Ingram was pursuing his own more fiscally prudent arguments with Harmsworth.

Vere was out of the country on his annual holiday when the two men butted heads and said he would give his decision upon his return at the end of August. It was to become the hallmark of Vere Harmsworth's own personal style – that he took his time in making any decision. Another distinct advantage his delay gave was to consolidate his own power as the overlord whose word meant life or death to his underlings. Harmsworth would develop this tactic into an art form.

In this case he came down in favour of David English. It was a victory for editorial over management and those at the *Mail* read much into Vere's decision. But barely three weeks later, after a short but worrying printers' strike, the paper again faced being shrunk to twenty-four pages. Again Vere sided with English.

Now David pulled out all the stops, reinforcing his side dramatically in a personal letter of gratitude to Harmsworth:

My Dear Vere,

I write this letter to thank you from the bottom of my heart for your decision to make today's paper 32 pages.

I can honestly say, Vere, that we on the Editorial were in total despair yesterday at the news that the *Daily Mail* was going back into the battle with only 24 pages...

All yesterday afternoon, I pleaded, fought, cajoled and argued for a larger paper. I was told categorically 'It is out of the question. It is physically impossible to produce a larger paper. 24 is our maximum.'

And then, last night, I got the news that you had stopped it. The word came down that the Chairman had rejected a 24-page paper and insisted on a 32-page paper. And now there is a 32-page paper. It will be rough and tough and we will have to work like hell to get it out. But it can be done. And we must do it. Are we the only people to see this?

Without your will and determination, Vere, we wouldn't have had a competitive paper today. I have to thank you. The reason I am writing this rather emotional letter (and I can write these things better

49

than I can say them) is to tell you of the profound conviction on the Editorial floor that, without you, we don't stand a chance...

But despite Vere's unwavering support, the newspaper continued to hover at the 1.7 million mark, even declining to 1.6 million by September. If not languishing, the fledgling *Mail* was still worrying its editor and owner. Although English had put on 130,000 women readers to replace those who had defected, many of those readers were not in the desirable ABC1 category the paper had to attract. Instead, they were C1s. In itself, the new readership constituted a concealed threat to maintaining the 'quality' readership that directly affected advertising prices.

During these dark days, when it seemed that the circulation would drift further down, even to the 1.5 million mark, Vere invited David to his office. 'Have a drink and keep your nerve,' he told the worried editor.

You are producing a very good paper and it is going to work. You should change nothing about it. Just go on improving it; but keep to the same style and plan. The old *Daily Mail* kept tacking and changing course... There was no consistency; that's why it didn't work. You are producing a good paper. Believe in it, and in what you and the other journalists are doing.

This was Vere Harmsworth at his best. He had become a figure of stability who was able to provide the rock-solid foundation his more volatile and creative editor needed.

David English was all fire and flash, almost neurotically driven. Vere Harmsworth was cool, reflective and stable. He had the courage and will to stay the course. Between the two of them they would find a way.

With the *Daily Express* at over 3.3 million circulation and the *Daily Mail*'s circulation plummeting, the new compact newspaper was rapidly becoming the Number One underdog on Fleet Street. As such, it was secretly popular with a number of powerful advertisers, who believed the *Mail* was worth keeping an eye on. At any rate, this is what a number of executives at Associated believed.

However, the advertisers weren't putting their money where their hearts were. Advertising was not piling in at the rate the *Mail* required and drastic steps were needed if they were to find a way to change the advertisers' minds.

Vere Harmsworth had heard that a small new agency, known for its 'in-your-face' adverts, might be able to help. He had met Maurice Saatchi and Tim Bell, and he was frankly impressed by the agency's maverick style, a style he believed matched the fledgling *Mail*. Said Bill Muirhead, then a young man in charge of the campaign,

> We in Saatchi's then were very very small and very very anti-establishment … I think what happened with us was that we came along and we were seen as a bunch of young people who broke the mold and were prepared to question the rules. We had a small office in Soho, the ground floor and the basement, Number 6 Golden Square.
>
> We were launched in 1971 and we were controversial and to do what we were trying to do you had to be unique. And for Vere Harmsworth to appoint us was itself a controversial thing to do. So we were employed to boost the advertising revenue into the *Mail*.

Saatchi's decided to shock the industry into sitting up and taking notice. They invented a fictitious advertising agency of the most conventional type that they called Conwell, Smarm and Drone. In this agency was an 'old-style media director' who dropped in to work at about eleven in the morning, went through the newspapers and put on a few bets. He then had a couple of gin and tonics and went off to lunch, from which he returned at about 5 p.m.

While Reg droned away, a bright young assistant named Eric did all the work. Eric used the most advanced statistical tools to determine who should be on the advertising schedule for the firm. This naturally led him to place the *Daily Mail* on it.

When Reg returned from his late lunch he was presented with this schedule that he needed to take to a meeting with his chairman and a big client. Although he gave Eric a drubbing for including the *Daily Mail*, it was too late to change it and, lo and behold, the client was delighted to see that the schedule included the new *Daily Mail* as was the chairman. So Reg, quick off the mark, took all the credit for Eric's hard graft.

That was the basic set-up: Eric, in a number of clever ways, kept determining the statistical value of putting the *Daily Mail* on the schedule; Reg kept scoffing and then taking all the credit. It was chancy material and Vere Harmsworth loved it.

In order to get attention for this unconventional swipe at the industry, Saatchi's bought twenty small white portable television sets and sent them as a gift to the media directors of the top twenty agencies. Over the screen was an acetate overlay that said, 'Turn this on at 10.50 on Sunday morning and see something that will improve your business.'

Advertising was inexpensive on television on Sunday mornings and

Saatchi's featured a three-minute comic commercial starring Reg and Eric. 'So all the agencies were then talking about this Reg and Eric, the Erics were laughing and the Regs were feeling guilty and it just raised the profile of the *Mail*', said Bill Muirhead later. 'And it created a much more dynamic image for their display ads department.'

Not surprisingly, Saatchi's was attacked over 'Reg and Eric' by one of the more conventional agencies. But Harmsworth, who had taken a passionate interest in everything Saatchi's was doing, held firm. 'And it was very brave of him because this could have backfired on us,' said Muirhead. 'That was to Vere's eternal credit.'

But David English ultimately didn't take to the controversial young agency. They were far too original for his taste – and perhaps too independent. At least, that's what a few of the executives at Associated Newspapers came to believe.

Vere was a patient man, a reticent man, a diffident man. But it *was* possible to push him too far, as an incident that took place in the autumn of 1972 revealed to a staff wide-eyed with surprise.

The circulation of the new *Daily Mail* continued to decline to the extent that it was approaching the danger mark. Those on the staff had begun to wonder whether it actually was going to survive. Yes, the paper was attracting a more desirable readership, but not to the extent that had been hoped for. So a crisis meeting was called for a weekend retreat in a hotel near Hove. Here, management and editorial would thrash out a viable way forward. Importantly, the advertising agency Foote, Cone and Belding was chosen to give a presentation outlining its new approach to the advertising campaign planned for the spring of 1973.

The night before, FCB gave a taster of their campaign plans. The media director of the agency, Alec Joyce, stood before an interested editorial staff of the *Daily Mail*. Vere was also present, along with managerial and circulation personnel from Associated.

Joyce was aware of the downward-drifting circulation and knew that Vere Harmsworth intended women to be the focus of the reading audience. But up until this point, FCB claimed, the agency had not been aware of the importance Vere placed upon the direct appeal to women.

Indeed, Joyce's research showed this was not a practicable course of action and he now explained to the gathering 'that newspapers are read by men and women, people of all ages, and therefore one had to say the prime target must continue to be men'. Joyce had several suggestions, among them that the *Mail* should look into sponsoring a number of sporting events in order to attract the right kind of male reader—

But Joyce was cut short. For, in the words of one observer, Vere Harmsworth 'rose up like Neptune from the sea, in all his wrath'. Harmsworth verbally attacked the surprised man, chiding him for paying no attention to the thrust of the *Daily Mail*'s appeal to women. Then he physically removed all the agency presentation cards and dumped them on the promenade outside, where a small delegation from the agency formed, worriedly talking over this unexpected turn of events.

Inside, there was a certain amount of shock, for it was a Vere Harmsworth nobody had seen before. Certainly, men from Foote, Cone and Belding didn't know this man, but frankly, neither did anyone from the *Daily Mail*. One thing was certain: this was the defining moment in the future of the new *Daily Mail*. It was certainly the moment when staff members became aware themselves of how serious Vere was in his marketing strategy and when perhaps they realised their jobs depended upon a quick grasp of that strategy.

The change in attitude was instantaneous and not only for those from the advertising agency.

John Standen, vice-chairman of FCB and an account director who had recently been put in charge of the *Daily Mail* campaign, was one of those present at the meeting, along with Mervyn Francis, the managing director of the agency. Standen had recently been assigned the *Daily Mail* account, in his words, at the perfect moment, 'with everything going downhill and the client getting increasingly concerned'. Now they stood on the sea front, discussing the ominous possibility that they could lose the account and, indeed, before they left the meeting they were told that Saatchi & Saatchi was going to be invited to submit to the *Daily Mail* in competition with them for the commercial side of the market. This was not music to John Standen's ears. He returned to London facing the stark realisation that if the account went down, he would be responsible, because, technically, although he had only been handed it recently, it was his baby. Standen knew he had no time to lose if he were to save the day.

It was the age of transatlantic headhunting in the advertising business and the agency had just hired two new senior creative men, one of them American, the other British. John Standen asked that the American, Bill Jenkins, be immediately assigned to him.

By 4 p.m. on the afternoon of Standen's return from Hove, the two men had already begun talking over how they could save the account. Jenkins was a thin man of medium height, rather slight in appearance but wiry and tough-looking. He was in his late thirties or early forties, a New Yorker, who had somehow picked up a slight Southern accent along the way. He wore his hair longish, as was the style, with a *Viva Zapata*-type moustache, like Robert Redford in the 1969 film *Butch Cassidy and the Sundance Kid*.

John Standen had every issue of the *Daily Mail* for the last two months on his desk and the two men, total strangers to one another, went through them one by one. For his part, Jenkins understood only too well he was coming in at the 'Jesus Christ Stage'; that is, he would either save the account and become 'Jesus Christ', or he would take on an altogether less attractive rubric.

What the two men established was that the appeal Vere Harmsworth talked about so avidly was a fixed theme in David English's *Daily Mail*.

> We went through every issue of the paper, day by day, page by page, and we analysed the female appeal that had been built into the writing, the news items. All this had an appeal to women in it. Not just fashion and cosmetics, but we went right into the depth and the heart of the paper ... trying to figure out if this appeal was really there.
>
> And we didn't find a single issue in which there was not a continuous thread of journalism that appealed to women. It was the reverse of a feminist newspaper, but it acknowledged the woman's point of view.

At 9.15 that night the two men ended the meeting and Bill Jenkins told John Standen he would report back to him when he had something.

At 10.30 the next morning Bill Jenkins was standing outside John Standen's office. He came in and spread half a dozen rough layouts across John's desk saying, 'This is what I think we ought to do, John.' It was essentially a woman's magazine campaign and it was built on the theme 'Every Woman Needs Her *Daily Mail*'.

'That was within twenty-four hours,' Standen said later and he couldn't have waited much longer. He had three weeks to get the entire campaign ready, because they had to have it by the beginning of November if it were to be finished in time for a spring launch.

'I bought Bill's campaign 100 per cent,' said Standen, 'and drummed up £15,000 for a series of finished advertisements. We took the pictures for the posters, we shot on 16mm, we did a thirty-second television commercial. If we're going to go down, we decided, let's go down fighting.'

By 1 November they were ready. They invited a deputation of executives from the *Daily Mail* to a full presentation. Vere Harmsworth was present, David English, Mick Shields, John Winnington-Ingram, Alwyn Robinson and a number of men from the Circulation Department. But they didn't look too hopeful as they arrived at the FCB headquarters.

For John Standen the stakes were high. Certainly, if the agency didn't keep the account, heads would roll, perhaps even his own. He could feel the pressure bearing down on him. He rose from his seat and began by saying what the team had learnt at Hove. Then he quickly handed over to Bill Jenkins.

I sat back down. From where I was I could see the perspiration running down Bill's face as he got up. But when he spoke, his husky voice began calmly, showing no signs of nervousness.

This Zapata-type figure unveiled the pieces of creative work one by one, done like a woman's magazine, a double-page spread in full colour and two posters, in all eight pieces of creative work.

He unveiled the pictures and they looked stunning, ahead of their time, on posh layouts, and Bill read his copy. 'Every woman needs her *Daily Mail*,' he said.

'And why?' Bill read his text. 'So that you are not just a good listener at parties. So that you can interrupt your hairdresser once in a while. So that in the evening you can tell *him* a few things *he* might have been too busy to learn during the day. So that you can keep an eye on how your taxes are being spent. So that you know every day what the famous and infamous are doing and saying. So you always have a picture of the changing scene. So you can increase the children's awareness of the world around them ... So that you are not just another pretty face, Every Woman Needs Her *Daily Mail*.'

The silence was palpable as the *Mail* delegation took it all in. Then David English said he was delighted and the dam broke. Standen could tell they'd made it.

The attention turned back to Bill Jenkins and he added his *coup de grâce*:

Every Woman Needs Her *Daily Mail* ... And *Every Man Knows Why*.

It was a two-tiered approach that would reach out to women and then begin to draw in men as well. Yes, they were focusing on the female reader. But they would go for the men readers as their secondary goal. It was exactly what the *Mail* needed to put it on the map and everyone at the presentation agreed it was a fabulous success. In particular, Vere Harmsworth was pleased to see his own plan at last put into operation so effectively.

Bill Jenkins's advertising campaign put on about 85,000 readers in three months, so estimated the *Mail* managing editor, Alwyn Robinson, and it pushed the *Daily Mail* over into the kind of 'circulation solvency' it needed in order to make it. But more than that, it gave English and those on his editorial staff the coherent rationale they needed to understand how they could attract first the women readers the paper needed, and second the men readers, who had to follow in their wake if the paper were to survive.

It also served to attract the right *kind* of readers into the fold, the high-income, ABC1 readers whom advertisers wanted to reach. In that sense Bill Jenkins was a hero both to the management and to the editorial at the newspaper.

The apparent ease with which Bill Jenkins created the dual slogans for the *Daily Mail* belied the immense pressure under which he and other men in the highly competitive field of advertising laboured. As the 'Jesus Christ' figure who saved the *Daily Mail* account for Foote, Cone and Belding, Jenkins enjoyed a remarkable first year of success at the agency. He basked in the praise of the upper management and, in fact, was invited by John Standen to work with him on the British Airways campaign, a prestigious account that also produced another success for Jenkins.

But the story didn't end there. It was difficult for Jenkins to measure up to the success he had achieved so quickly. A little bit at a time, Bill began slipping at the agency. The pressure was coming on harder and harder, and it seemed to his colleagues that it was getting to him. He became more emotional than he had been at the beginning, and irrational. He started to lose his temper over little things and he lost control of himself in front of his staff. These were the early signs that he wasn't going to make it.

As sometimes happens in cases like these, Jenkins began to hit the bottle. He showed up at work with alcohol on his breath and his work started to suffer. In the end, John Standen said later, 'he'd blown it at FCB, blown it in himself, really, and went back to the United States'. Standen was truly saddened by this. He understood the pressures of the industry only too well and he still respected Bill Jenkins for his rapid save of the *Mail* account.

Some time later Standen discovered that Bill didn't fare any better in America. He was burnt out and he knew it. But it still came as a terrible shock when he learnt that Bill Jenkins had taken his own life.

The pressure on an ad agency director, John Standen philosophised later, is more intense than outsiders can readily imagine. Some men can't stand up to it and Bill Jenkins, for all his creativity and ability, was one of them.

FIVE

SHELL GAMES

On 15 November 1974 two emissaries from the Abitibi Paper Co., a North American corporation based in Toronto, stood on the Embankment in London. One of them, Ross LeMesurier, had arrived on a transatlantic flight from Toronto that morning and he held open the door of a red telephone box while his London colleague, Trevor Spurgen, dug into his pocket for 10p coins. The two men were keeping a line open to Spurgen's London office by feeding in coins whenever the disconnection blip began to sound.

The transatlantic line had been opened an hour before in order to send an important message from Abitibi in Toronto via this crude relay system to the two men camped on the Embankment. There was nothing simple about the means of communication the men were using that afternoon and there was nothing simple about the message they were waiting to receive. Miraculously, the relay worked, and a few minutes before 3 p.m. Spurgen got what he was waiting for and hung up the telephone.

The two men walked the hundred yards to Carmelite House, took the elevator to the executive floor and asked to see Vere Harmsworth, the chairman of Associated Newspapers.

For the past fourteen years Associated Newspapers had enjoyed a primary position in the Canadian paper milling industry by virtue of its controlling interest in Price Brothers & Co., a profitable Quebec-based paper company. In fact, the Price Brothers' 'reverse merger', as it was called in 1960, had been largely a peaceable affair. Price Brothers and the Associated-owned Anglo-Newfoundland Company merged in order for the two companies to fill their order books by availing themselves of a good sales organisation based in Manhattan.

This reverse merger had been the brainchild of Robert Morrow, an earlier acquaintance of Vere who was now an enterprising director on the board of Anglo-Newfoundland, vice-chairman of Price Brothers on behalf of Associated Newspapers.* Bob was a character such as only

* For an account of the reverse takeover of Price by Anglo-Newfoundland Company, see *The Reluctant Press Lord*, pp. 130–3.

North America can produce. He was a shrewd country boy of tremendous sophistication, a living oxymoron, who knew where his bread was buttered, as the saying goes, and that was with the Harmsworths in London, whom he represented.

Beyond that, Bob Morrow was like a hero out of a 1940s war film. Indeed, in real life Bob actually *was* a war hero who had flown many flights over Europe during World War Two. Bob resembled the Hollywood film star Dana Andrews and in 1974 he still wore his hair in the wavy style of the old-time movie stars of the 1940s. Bob was, like the characters they played, straight as a die, honest, forthright and bristling with integrity.

But the relationship with Price Brothers – along with Associated Newspapers' high-profile placement in the Canadian paper milling industry – was about to be brought to an abrupt halt. For LeMesurier and Spurgen were making a courtesy call on behalf of Abitibi to inform Vere Harmsworth that the Toronto-based company was staging a takeover. The net result was that the 'Brits', as the Abitibi management called Associated Newspapers, were about to suffer a disastrous loss of control and prestige at Price Brothers.

When Vere Harmsworth returned from lunch at 3.10 p.m. that day he invited the two men into his office, despite the fact that they had no appointment. They all took seats round his conference table, making the customary pleasantries. But just as they began to explain their mission Vere's telephone rang, interrupting them. What they didn't know was that it was the *Mail*'s City Editor, Patrick Sergeant, on the line, informing Harmsworth of the takeover bid, which he had picked up on the wires. Vere took in the information blandly and, in behaviour highly typical of the chairman, returned to the table with a slight smile on his face, patiently waiting for the men to state the business he was now fully apprised of.

LeMesurier explained that Abitibi wished to buy 49 per cent of the stock held by Associated for $18 a share, the offer was firm and there was no minimum to the number of shares Abitibi would buy. Trading had been halted and wouldn't resume until 9.45 a.m. on Tuesday.

A crucial decision by Abitibi in making the takeover bid had been to proceed by what the executives there nicknamed 'the quickie route'. That is, the Ontario Securities Commission required twenty-one days for a company to complete the necessary requirements for a takeover bid. During that time the takeover company, in this case Abitibi, sent out a circular to all Price's shareholders, informing them of the offer and giving them time to consider the bid. But a recent innovation on the exchange allowed a 'lightning' raid capacity to take over companies, with a time lapse of only a few days in which to complete the bid. Abitibi believed that by going the 'quickie route' they would shut out any competitors who might see this as an opportunity to cut into the action with a counter-offer.

Then, too, Abitibi had taken the decision to buy only 49 per cent of the stock because of a technical hitch in Canadian tax law. At 49 per cent any dividends paid to Abitibi would not be taxable, but above 51 per cent they would.

Now Ross LeMesurier and Trevor Spurgen sat in Vere Harmsworth's office, sanguine in their belief that he would accept their offer, even though, as Vere now calmly pointed out, the share price was worth at least $10 more than they were offering. But even beyond that, there were compelling reasons why the deal Abitibi was offering was completely unacceptable to Vere.

What the representatives could not have known was that the two well-reasoned decisions taken by Abitibi – to go the short route and to offer for only 49 per cent of the stock – would be the very petards by which their own company would be hoisted.

By the time Vere Harmsworth landed in Montreal on a hastily scheduled flight two days later, Bob Morrow had already arranged for the pair of them to fly on to Toronto via a Price Company DH125. There, he had scheduled a meeting with the two architects of the takeover, Harry Rosier, the president of Abitibi, and Tom Bell, the company's chairman.

Seated in Abitibi's posh suites on the twenty-second floor of the Toronto-Dominion Centre, the British contingent explained why they weren't able to accept the offer extended by Abitibi. Bob Morrow said,

> We've got tax problems in England, the problem of repatriating the money and the problem of capital gains tax if we don't roll it over. We would like to sell our whole interest. This is our major objective.

What Morrow was referring to was the complex British tax law affecting Associated Newspapers' investment in Price Brothers. In this regard the 49 per cent cut-off was crucial, for if Vere Harmsworth accepted that offer, he would then be left with less than 10 per cent of its shares in Price, thus losing double-taxation relief in Britain on dividends from the remaining holdings in the company.

Moreover, if Vere took the proceeds from the sale home, he would not automatically be allowed to invest again outside the UK, but would have to go through cumbersome and costly procedures that were aimed at discouraging corporations from taking British sterling outside their homeland. That meant Harmsworth could not even take the profits from their sale to Abitibi and buy sufficient stock to put himself over the 10 per cent tax relief mark, because of the general prohibition against buying new stocks abroad. So the offer Abitibi was making placed Associated Newspapers in an untenable position both in regard to taxation and to reinvestment.

But there was something more. With less than 10 per cent of the stock, Associated wouldn't even be entitled to a seat on the board of the company they had once dominated. The company would suffer a loss of prestige and, from Vere Harmsworth's personal point of view, a loss greater than that. For him, it would bring an anticlimactic ending to his family's history in the papermaking industry in North America.

At the beginning of the century his great-uncle Northcliffe and his grandfather Rothermere had set up the Anglo-Newfoundland Company in Grand Falls, Newfoundland. Northcliffe had become obsessed with the small poverty-stricken interior community of Grand Falls, building it into a model city for its inhabitants with housing, medical care and education for each and every employee. In fact, Northcliffe had overseen in the most minute detail the improvements to Grand Falls, practically bankrupting himself in his zeal to extend to his employees the standards of modern living in the twentieth century.*

Despite this nostalgic background, Vere Harmsworth was stuck. He was faced with the implacable Abitibi management team, who refused to budge an inch on their offer. There was nothing Morrow and Harmsworth could do except capitulate.

Or was there?

As Bob Morrow summed up the situation, 'it couldn't have been a worse deal'. On the one hand, if Associated accepted the 49 per cent offer, 'this would have split the Associated holding, and part of it would have gone for Abitibi shares, and part of it for Price shares. Associated would be left with Price – a divided and substantially weakened holding. It also entailed a hefty tax penalty.' On the other hand, not to have accepted the offer and just stayed with Price meant that 'we would have been left in a company that Associated had controlled and was now going to be controlled by Abitibi. A complete loss of control of the company.' This was why Bob Morrow, upon hitting the turf in Montreal after flying home from Toronto, went straight to his house and began making a series of desperate telephone calls.

* For a full account of Northcliffe's papermaking activities in Newfoundland, see *The Great Outsiders*, chapter 6.

In the meantime it was up to Vere to telephone his father in Palm Beach, Florida, where he and his wife Mary had a winter home away from their main residence in Newport, Rhode Island. He had to explain the situation Associated Newspapers now found themselves in. It was at such a time as this that Vere became very much more aware of his father's position of control as chairman of Associated Newspapers. And, true to form, Esmond was in his most dithering mood, ready to blame Vere for not taking the Abitibi offer, and to blame him if he did. Esmond and Mary also had personal shareholdings of about 1 per cent in Price Brothers, and they were worried about the best way to invest those in what appeared to be a growing crisis.

With the advent of family pressure, the situation in Montreal had quickly descended into the kind of nightmare power play that only families who love one another can perpetrate.

Just when Harmsworth and Morrow thought it couldn't get any worse, a letter arrived from the Bank of England to the effect that the kind of investment represented by owning shares in Price was classified as a 'direct investment'. This meant essentially that after liquidation, the proceeds from any sale to Abitibi would have to be repatriated to England at a low-rated currency exchange rate. Associated would therefore suffer an actual loss from the transaction, be liable for capital gains taxation and lose its tax relief on the remaining investment. All this, and the proceeds of the sale could not be reinvested abroad without the permission of the Bank of England. If that permission *was* granted, it would be at a high currency exchange rate.

Against this background, a blizzard descended upon the city of Montreal, blackening the skies and adding to the general desperation of the moment.

Bob Morrow reached for the telephone again, calling colleagues to seek a way out of the dilemma, although the odds were stacked against him. Morrow was well connected in the élite financial community of Montreal and among his close acquaintances was the prominent financier Paul Desmarais. The two had met on a trip to Russia and immediately struck up a friendship. Now the word went out that Morrow was seeking a solution to his crisis. Desmarais was involved in heavy business meetings in Winnipeg, but as soon as he got out he gave Morrow a call.

Paul Desmarais was the chairman of Power Corporation, a $500 million investment and management company with holdings in major transportation, paper and financial concerns. He was also mentor to the talented Bill Turner, president of Consolidated Bathurst, the Power

Corporation paper subsidiary. Desmarais was something of a cult figure in Montreal finance, with a reputation for innovative deal-making. Now, the three men turned their full attention to Associated Newspapers' crisis, to see if they could work out a way to save the day.

Vere Harmsworth was experiencing pressure not only from his father. Travelling with him were Mick Shields, the managing director of Associated, and Peter Saunders, the company secretary. Their reason for being there was practical; together, the three of them formed a quorum and could vote instantly on any important decision Associated needed to make. Mick Shields was also present to act as Vere's adviser.

But Mick now began to experience doubts about the deal that Bob Morrow was cooking up with Desmarais and Turner. 'Mick was like a hen on a hot rock,' was how one neutral observer privately put it. Now Mick began to advise Vere that any solution to their problems offered by Desmarais might bring about more trouble than it solved.

Vere Harmsworth realised Mick had taken an irrational dislike to Desmarais that perhaps went beyond business. Vere said later,

> Mick was certainly a bit ambivalent, but Mick was always ambivalent. You never quite knew where he was going because he didn't get on with Bob Morrow. He was jealous of Bob and he didn't like the deal Abitibi was offering either. It wasn't the ideal deal at all. So Mick was growing more and more ambivalent by the minute.

Added to this was the continuing pressure from Vere's father, who was bearing down heavily upon his son; but because of the fact of Esmond's advancing Alzheimer's disease, Vere knew 'the real person I was dealing with was Mary'.

Mary was Esmond's third wife and the mother of Esmond's second and only other son, 'Little Esmond', who at this time was seven years old. Since the elder Esmond had become more and more incapacitated, Mary had made herself knowledgeable about the Rothermere financial holdings and was a power centre in her own right. Bob Morrow reluctantly admitted that he believed Mick was 'too close to Mary', considering he worked for Vere. But Mick would have seen himself as loyal to both power centres since he was managing director of both DMGT, which Esmond chaired, and Associated Newspapers, which Vere chaired.*

* Since the names of the companies involved in these business dealings have changed several times over the years, I have taken the final names assigned for consistency and for the convenience of the reader.

No doubt Mick was speaking to Mary privately during these delicate negotiations in Montreal, so the internal politics were at best complicated, and at worst Machiavellian. The resultant pressure on Vere was immense, to put it mildly.

> I was frightened. Yes I was. I was inexperienced. I was a new boy. It was my first time in this kind of thing. I was a late developer, I suppose. I went through these things rather late. It was very, very scary. There was a lot of money at stake, and we had to do the deal right. I had a very able ally in Bob, but he wasn't used to this kind of thing either. And Mick wasn't very good at that kind of thing, not really.

All the while, too, Vere's father kept reiterating that he was 'very suspicious about this deal and he didn't like Desmarais' reputation'. Vere knew this could be coming indirectly from Mick, or it might be Mary's opinion, or it might actually be his father's opinion if he was having a clear day. But Vere also knew that since he had taken over the company his father had become 'a bit jealous of me, I suppose', and 'so perhaps he was just giving me a hard time'.

So in the middle of this wrangling, Bob Morrow and Paul Desmarais worked out a deal, eventually arranging an agreement that would entail the exchange of the shares owned by Associated Newspapers in Price Brothers with shares in Consolidated Bathurst, and the two companies formed a consortium.

A shares swap of course, in one fell swoop, neatly sidestepped the threat of double taxation, capital gains on profits and the repatriation of British sterling that would have been entailed in the UK by a forced sale. Moreover, it offered Associated Newspapers a stronghold in Consolidated Bathurst and a seat on the board, so the prestige of Associated was also assured. More personally, the Harmsworth family's involvement in the Canadian paper-milling industry would continue.

Bill Turner, the president of Consolidated Bathurst, had been instrumental in working out the swap with Paul Desmarais and Bob Morrow. In Turner's mind it was a very good deal for Associated Newspapers *and* for Consolidated Bathurst. He was present when the deal was done and he remembered what happened next.

> After we finally made the agreements, Vere called his father again. And his father gave him a dressing down on the telephone, said he was naïve and he'd ruined a good investment... And Vere turned to Paul Desmarais and said, with tears in his eyes, 'Paul, I've made a mistake and I shouldn't have

done it.' Paul said, 'Vere, if I'd thought you'd made a mistake, I wouldn't hold you to this thing. But you haven't made a mistake.'

There were bad feelings all round, with Vere completely discouraged by his father's embarrassing drubbing of him in front of his business colleagues. But in a few minutes Esmond called back, for although he was still very angry with his son, his concerns had shifted. Perhaps inspired by Mary, he was now worried whether their personal shareholding of 1 per cent in Price Brothers could be included in the swap-over to Consolidated Bathurst.

So Bob Morrow telephoned Esmond, with Mary on an extension, and Bob assured them that it could.

At the same time these squabbles and high-powered manoeuvres were taking place in the Power Corporation–Consolidated Bathurst–Associated Newspaper camp, Abitibi were on the move.

In order to complete their takeover bid of Price Brothers at $18 per share, Abitibi had asked for and received a one-day extension from the Ontario Securities Commission. The Abitibi chairman Tom Bell, and his president Harry Rosier, were optimistic all would be well by the new closing time, that is, until they received a call from Vere Harmsworth.

In view of the one-day extension, Harmsworth now explained to Bell blandly, Power Corporation and Associated Newspapers had sufficient time to form a consortium and as a result were planning to make a counter-bid to the $18 per share bid tendered by Abitibi. This left Bell and Rosier stunned.

In *Takeover*, a book that explained the Abitibi manoeuvrings during the fateful days of what would go down as the biggest takeover in Canadian history, Peter Mathias explained what happened next.

> Harmsworth elaborated on the consortium's plans only so far as to tell Bell the bid would be $20 per share, and it would be for all the holders' shares, not just a percentage. The consortium's bid looked far superior to Abitibi's...

Upon hanging up, Bell turned to Harry Rosier and a number of advisers to try to think of a way out of what was fast becoming a quagmire. But they could come up with nothing. They then rang Harmsworth back. 'We're finding it very difficult to manoeuvre,' he explained. Fine, Harmsworth told him. He would just have to wait to find out what Abitibi were planning in response. But in future Bell was to 'conduct any further conversations with our Mr Saunders'. He gave Bell Saunders's telephone number and rang off.

Now it was panic stations all round for the Abitibi camp.

All Bell's attention was now absorbed in a great fear: that Power Corp. would buy control of Price through the back door... and leave Abitibi with a bid hanging out on the exchange – which could only bring in perhaps 30 per cent or 40 per cent of Price's stock ...

Bell reminded everybody tartly that the Abitibi board hadn't authorised him to spend $30 million to $40 million on a simple investment in Price, with no representation on Price's board and no option to go forward to merger, and with somebody else in control.

Jack Haire summed up Abitibi's plight eloquently: 'If the Price share-holders tendered only 25 per cent of the stock to our bid, we'd have to eat it.' And if that happened, the consequences for Bell's and perhaps others' employment might well be terminal.

With their minds thus concentrated wonderfully, the Abitibi camp hurriedly revised their earlier 'take-it-or-leave-it' offer to Associated Newspapers.

Understanding fully, perhaps for the first time, the awkward situation Associated had been placed in by their original offer, they came up with a new, more acceptable exchange that they described as 'elegant' in its fairness to all parties. Abitibi would take up 65 per cent of Associated Newspapers' holdings in Price Brothers by issuing two million Abitibi treasury shares, giving the Brits just over 10 per cent of Abitibi. They would thus get the Brits off the hook in terms of their tax liability and repatriation problems. With high optimism, an Abitibi representative now rang Peter Saunders with the offer.

Saunders agreed to put the offer to Harmsworth and said he would call them back 'shortly'. The Abitibi team was jubilant, believing they had successfully passed through the Valley of the Shadow of Death.

But as time passed, it became amply clear to the team that Harmsworth wasn't going to ring back. Abitibi, they realised, was about to 'either lose $30 million or be totally discredited'. By now they were completely exhausted and fresh out of ideas as to how to save themselves. At a little after 1 a.m. the Abitibi team dispersed, totally dispirited.

Back in Montreal, Bob Morrow and Bill Turner had just completed the swap of shares. Later, Morrow described the situation as it stood at that moment.

Connie Bathurst was now holding a substantial number of shares in the Price Company that they had just exchanged for with Associated. So Paul Desmarais and I and Vere sat down in Bill Turner's office, and we called a number of Price Company stockholders and whereas Abitibi had been offering for 49 per cent of the company at $18 a share, we were making the offer of $20 a share to close the next morning at nine o'clock.

Come nine o'clock in the morning, we had made enough deals that Connie Bathurst would have wound up with control of Price Company.

But by the next morning at eight, Abitibi was bouncing back. One of the team had come up with a welcome thought. Abitibi didn't have to withdraw its bid because trading would be suspended when the Power Corporation–Associated bid hit the floor in an hour, the expiration time for trading Abitibi's offer at 9.45 would come and go and 'Abitibi would be released without obligation'.

Now, with the sweat drying on their brows, the Abitibi team came up with a new idea. They would make a counter-bid to the offer that Desmarais, Turner and Harmsworth had been pitching throughout the night. After considerable wrangling and revenue raising, they decided to counter-offer $25 per share for Price Brothers stock. But this time they let the tax incentive hang, bidding for 51 per cent of the company. Suspicious of what might happen next, they needed 51 per cent just to be sure they had full control.

All said and done, in a hastily called meeting the Board of Directors at Abitibi Corporation approved a $125 million expenditure for a new bid for Price Brothers.

Bill Turner, president of Consolidated Bathurst, was now holding 17.5 per cent of Price Brothers, and had taken in as well the 1 per cent that had been personally owned by Esmond and Mary Rothermere.

Upon receiving word that his consortium's share offer for Price Brothers' stock had been bettered by Abitibi to the tune of $25 per share, Turner withdrew his consortium's offer of $20. Instead, he tendered his entire holding of Price Brothers to Abitibi.

According to the reckonings of several prominent Canadian financial writers, Consolidated Bathurst, and by implication Power Corporation who had control of Consolidated Bathurst, made a killing of $10 million on the stock market in 1974 money. This in exchange for two hectic days of wheeling and dealing by the two companies' president and chairman.

When he discovered the amount of the profit made by Bill Turner and

Paul Desmarais, Esmond Rothermere immediately rang his son and berated him for not having made that money himself for Associated Newspapers. Never mind that the offer had never been there for Vere to make, it was quite clear to Esmond that Vere was to blame. It took a little time for Esmond and Mary to realise that they shared in any profit realised by Turner and Desmarais on the Price Brothers' deal, since they and Associated owned a great deal of stock in Consolidated Bathurst.

As soon as the deal hit the Canadian press, Bill Turner felt compelled to call a news conference. There, he publicly chided the irresponsible financial journalists who had mistakenly concluded that Consolidated Bathurst had realised a $10 million profit on the Abitibi–Price Brothers takeover.

The way Turner and Consolidated Bathurst calculated the transaction, they made no profit at all on the deal, meaning, of course, they would pay no taxes. In fact, the way Consolidated Bathurst calculated the deal, it generated a tax *loss*.

Bill Turner then had a notion and he went to his Board of Directors to explain it to them.

> The moment we tendered the shares that last time, we all knew the price was going to drop dramatically in Price shares. So I explained to the Board of Directors of Consolidated Bathurst and said, 'We're going to tender our shares, and I proposed at that time to buy back a whole lot of shares when the price dropped, because I know that eventually Abitibi will want to merge with Price Brothers.'
>
> According to the Canadian merger laws, anyone with 10 per cent of the stock can block a merger. So I said, 'I propose to go back and buy 10 per cent of the stock at a low price and get another premium from them when they wanted to merge,' which is what we did.
>
> We tendered our stock at $25 a share. And we bought back 10 per cent at $11 a share.
>
> Time went by, a couple of years, they wanted to merge. They paid $25 a share for our holding.
>
> Then we took the money from that and bought 10 per cent of Abitibi. Then we eventually sold that for a profit.

Safely back in England, Mick Shields invited David English to lunch, where he showed English an account he had written of the events that had taken place in Montreal and Toronto only a short time before.

David English told how Mick explained himself:

'I have written my own account of these negotiations. And I'm not going to be caught by this deal, when it comes out or if anyone writes anything about this,' he said.

He gave his account to me over lunch, and it was self-serving naturally, that he, Shields, had done everything to organise the deal properly, and Vere had got everything wrong or lost his nerve and he had completely screwed up Mick Shields.

He was very bitter with Vere, and he was often bitter with Vere, yes…So of course I thought this was an incredibly dynamite piece of paper. I didn't really want to have anything much to do with it.

So I said, 'Well, is that your account, Mick? You know, I'm not even going to make any comment on it. And if you publish it, I don't see how you can continue to work here.'

Mick answered, 'Well, you know, I'm not publishing it. I'm keeping it in my safe.' And he obviously went round showing it to more than one person on the board to explain why the deal had gone wrong.

Mick Shields's account of the largest takeover in Canadian history presumably did go into his safe, from whence it never emerged.

So then it was 'Ball game over', Bob Morrow recalled years after the event. '*But not quite.*'

In January of 1989, Stone Container Company of Chicago made an offer to buy Associated Newspapers' shares in Consolidated Bathurst, offering approximately $378 million. History would show that the offer came at a propitious time for Associated, since the papermaking industry in Canada was just beginning to show signs of what many believed would be a terminal decline.

The offer from Stone Containers was accepted by Bouverie Investments, a holding company for the Consolidated Bathurst shares and a subsidiary wholly owned by Associated Newspapers that had been incorporated in Canada. Bouverie Investments in turn invested £180 million in its UK subsidiary, which in turn lent £180 million to Associated Newspapers in London. In this way tax efficiency could be maximised. Later, Bouverie Investments was moved from Canada to the Yukon in a further drive towards tax harmonisation.

This, then, was the end of the Harmsworth family's venture into papermaking in Canada, started so many years before by Northcliffe and Rothermere.

SIX

THE GLOVES COME OFF

The same kind of pressure that drove advertising executive Bill Jenkins to suicide was also bearing down on David English. Like Jenkins, English was highly creative and as a result was subject to pressures that more prosaic talents did not have to confront. But unlike Jenkins, English knew where to unload the pressure – on his staff.

English exhibited an unusual mixture of journalistic know-how and *joie de vivre* that caused a sense of euphoria among those who worked for him. He was the dream editor of every young and talented journalist. He was wildly charismatic, and according to his then Number Two man, Stewart Steven, he made the *Daily Mail* 'a place of fun. One looked forward to going to work.'

An oft-repeated maxim on the *Daily Mail* editorial floor was that whatever job you were doing, David English could do it better. Because of this, he incurred the respect of the staff while challenging them to do the best work of their lives.

But English not only understood the need of his staff to be inspired; he also understood their need to be rewarded and it was his policy to be the sole distributor of rewards. Salary, expenses, travel, prestige: these were his and his alone to parcel out and his reporters vied for them with undisguised zeal. And the punishment? That was David's special province as well. Nobody could inflict pain like David.

Beyond all that, there was also the 'special relationship' phenomenon. David managed to give each of his chosen favourites the feeling that he or she had a special relationship with him like no other. Pleasing David brought out the sunshine. Displeasing David? Well, it was better not to think about displeasing David.

The list of journalists English recruited for the *Daily Mail* would later read like a journalism hall of fame. People like Brian Freemantle, John Edwards, Ann Leslie, Jack Tinker, Anthea Disney and Lynda Lee-Potter were the young talent. David English provided them with the security they needed to become the stars of tomorrow. He was the impresario, the demanding Diaghilev who orchestrated their talent. In some cases he actually invented them.

Lynda Lee-Potter, for example, was a sparkling feature writer and columnist whose gift for interviewing was well known among the *Daily Mail* staff. The story of how David plucked her from the chorus line and thrust her into this leading role typified his ruthless methods. Nevertheless, Lynda was the eventual beneficiary of what amounted, on David's part, to an act of revenge.

Jean Rook had been his star columnist, an outrageous character who dominated the newsroom with her salty language and imperious manner. But Rook accepted a lucrative job offer from the *Daily Mail*'s arch opponent, the *Daily Express*, thereby incurring English's undying wrath. To get even, English held Rook to the last day of her contract, a peevish act that demonstrated how angry he was. But he also had something else up his sleeve. He wanted to prove to Rook that she wasn't irreplaceable. So he filled her post with Lynda Lee-Potter. Peter Black, who watched the process with growing alarm, was among those who observed darkly as English

processed her column into a likeness of the strident Rook's as ruthlessly as Colonel Sapt processed Rassendyll into a likeness of the Prisoner of Zenda. The satirical magazine *Private Eye* published extracts from the columns of the two women, and from its own invention Glenda Slag, and invited readers to detect the parody.

Some staff members disliked what English was doing, believing he was subverting the very real talent of Lee-Potter to a model vastly inferior, but once David English made up his mind, trying to stop him was like trying to halt an oncoming train. Lynda Lee-Potter, under David's tutelage, was destined to become 'the voice of the *Daily Mail*', embodying David's vision of the ideal woman reader he was seeking for the newspaper. In some guises she was the conscience of middle-class womanhood; in others a carping fishwife; in still others a highly sophisticated social commentator. It was a tribute to the flexibility of Lee-Potter's talent that she could carry out David's scenario without compromising her own creativity. Indeed, in only a short time, Lee-Potter outpaced her original brief, becoming the best-known star on the *Daily Mail*, perhaps on Fleet Street itself.

But all too often, if David English created you, you became his creature and then you belonged to him. That was the long and short of it.

His managing editor, Alwyn Robinson, couldn't help commenting that the forceful new editor of the *Daily Mail* wasn't always good with people. Later on, Robinson said David got better, learning to lighten his touch. But in the early days he could be tough – too tough. This apparently was understatement. For David's difficult temperament was to become the stuff of legend in Fleet Street and when the pressure of a declining circulation threatened to create too much pressure on the man, David English responded by cooking up the heat under his staff. As his news editor, John Womersley, put it, 'after the first halcyon days, when it became obvious it was going to be a fight to the finish, the gloves did come off.'

One of English's brightest stars, Anthea Disney, who went on to edit America's *TV Guide* and head the American publishing giant HarperCollins, remembered David as being 'autocratic at the best of times' and certainly, during the uphill battle when the circulation was falling, David moved into the realm of the dictator. 'He issued orders,' Disney recalled.

> He always had the best idea, in his opinion.
>
> He liked to think that he listened to other people but he didn't. He certainly didn't when he was up against it. All of us who worked for David felt that we had special relationships with him and now there wasn't time for any relationships. It was just fight, get your nose down and fight and be yelled at and come back and do it again and again and again and get yelled at a lot.
>
> He was very abusive to people, but it was a very hard time, and I think all of us understood that there was something that was going on here that was crucial and I think all of us desperately wanted the paper to survive.
>
> I don't think David ever had a foul mouth, but he would yell across the newsroom, and he would also do it for effect.

It was, according to Disney, a complicated matter, because he also possessed the ability to make you extremely fond of him and to make himself seem vulnerable to the extent that many of his staff wanted only to protect him.

The flip side of this vulnerable man, however, was a martinet who enjoyed playing the puppet master. A common phrase to describe David when he was like this was that he was the most 'feline' of men and if you ever got on his bad side, he would 'cat's-paw' you to death.

But for the young Anthea Disney, who liked and admired David English, it was disappointing to encounter this side of him.

> I certainly learnt that he could be evil and dreadful and he would play with people and toy with people and I would watch him and I would just curl up inside knowing he had the power to do this to me.

Somehow, Disney understood intuitively that if David English knew she feared him it would be fatal, so she exercised extreme care around him, avoiding him when he slipped into his more terrible rages and moving out of the range of his cruelty when he was overtaken by his own fury. She described herself at these times as having the ability to become wallpaper.

Her mentor Gordon MacKenzie was not as adept at keeping out of harm's way. MacKenzie had a complicated relationship with the editor. David was extremely fond of him, but at the same time he sensed that MacKenzie was frightened of him. To English, this was a red flag. He tended to enjoy torturing people who feared him, even if basically he liked them and they were his creatures.

MacKenzie shared an office with Anthea Disney, Room Eight, a corner office 'out of which used to come this incredible quantity of features every day'. Generally, when things went wrong, MacKenzie didn't lay the blame on Anthea. Instead, he took over a mentor role, encouraging her to do better. When things went right, MacKenzie not only praised her, but he was quick to give her the credit with the editor. But English's treatment of MacKenzie was not as open-handed as MacKenzie's treatment of Anthea.

David used to taunt him mercilessly and I remember one night David was sitting on the backbench, jacket off, shirtsleeves rolled back rather cleanly, and he was sitting there holding court. There was Ted Jeffery, Peter Grover and Stewart Steven with David in the middle. So there was this table of people, all very important, all sitting back and watching, knowing you were about to be eviscerated.

One night David was in a dreadful mood. He had had this idea for a piece for page six, and it had not been written to his satisfaction. I was in charge of rewrite and Gordon was in charge of trying to soothe things over.

Gordon read what I had written and said, 'I think you've got it, I think it's great.' He took it over to David, who said, 'What do you call this? This isn't the story I was talking about in conference, this is nothing like the story I was talking about in conference!' And there was Gordon, standing there miserably, crumbling these pieces of paper in his hands.

I walked over and said, 'If you've got any complaints about that feature, you can discuss them with me because I'm the poor hack who rewrote it twice to try and get it the way you wanted it.'

And David looked at me and he had this really kind of mean look on his face. And then, suddenly, he relaxed and let out this big laugh, and he said, 'Well, I suppose we're going to have to live with it then, aren't we?' And everyone laughed and had a drink together. But it could have gone the other way.

That was life on the *Daily Mail* those days, pretty much. You never knew which way it would go.

Anthea never believed she was actually frightened of David but she was wary of him. So when, for several years, she enjoyed David's patronage from the comfortable distance of being the New York correspondent for the *Daily Mail*, it was the ideal situation. She derived full benefit from his knowledge and ability, with 4000 miles between him and his temperament. But even then he exercised enormous power over her. Once, when the *Daily Express* had a story on a Lady Godiva stunt at Studio 54 that Anthea had not chosen to send him, he snapped at her, 'Well, Madame, I hope you are satisfied, you've ruined my newspaper.'

Many years later, when Anthea reminded David of this, he burst out laughing and said, 'Did I really say that?' It was this kind of charm that endeared him to people. Nevertheless, after Anthea returned to London to the *Daily Mail* to become the first and only woman features editor on Fleet Street, she knew she could never relax her guard.

Another story that showed how David could react to resistance involved Jack Tinker. David had just had the entire editorial floor redecorated and was rather proud of his matching colour scheme. Tinker, who began as an assistant on the gossip column but quickly advanced to become the colourful and witty drama correspondent of the *Daily Mail*, didn't want to leave his office. But David said, 'You have to come into the main office with the rest of us.' Jack came, but he brought with him his terrible, battered, filthy old chair, which he loved and which was comfortable. David said, 'Jack, you are not going to have that in this room. I've just spent all this money getting this right.' Two days later David noticed that Tinker still had his old chair. David said, 'Jack, you've got to get rid of that chair.' Jack said, 'David, I can't.' So English picked up the chair, carried it down in the lift, walked down Carmelite Street and threw it in the Thames.

This was a delightful story, the kind David English was happy to perpetuate himself. He told it frequently on occasions when he had to speak, because he rather liked the image it portrayed of him. But the truth was that the new *Daily Mail* was created entirely to fit David's preconceptions. It was a dramatic scenario that was very exciting for the staff. Entirely by chance, they found themselves at the centre of the world, David's world, the hottest place to be in the newspaper industry, and the benefits just kept coming.

One of the great frustrations in any journalist's life is the familiar situation wherein he finds his material being ignored and unpublished for reasons never explained. It is a blow to the ego from which many are unable to recover. But David English was putting out the *Mail* with the smallest staff on Fleet Street. There was no time for staff members to stand grousing in pubs as to the unfairness of having their stories spiked. Their stories were not being spiked. They were being published and read. They were being stretched to the limit and it was the most exhilarating time of most of their professional lives.

It was also the most difficult. One of his diarists described the worst of David's personal tantrums as very much like what he imagined Caligula's might have been. Others spoke in terms of David's continuing 'psychodrama'. Everyone participated in David's psychodramas, that is if they intended to stay at the *Mail*.

One of David's more diabolical techniques to prod staff into a high level of performance came to be known as 'creative tension'. It was said he discovered the technique in the United States, when he was the *Daily Express* foreign correspondent there. Others believed it was a carry-over from David's days on the *Express* itself, where Beaverbrook had pioneered the technique. It involved sending two or more reporters out on the same assignment, thus goading them into direct competition with one another.

One reporter who was 'the victor' in a creative tension exercise gave short shrift to David's system. He explained off the record that he didn't in the least believe the technique produced a better product. In his estimation it simply set staff members against one another, fomenting unrest in the newsroom. He was assigned, along with another news reporter, the same story based in Australia. The two of them set to work, each getting in touch with his own sources, and this reporter had the good fortune of catching his source on the telephone in the middle of the night.

The other reporter had a source every bit as good, but didn't manage to raise him until two hours later. So 'the victor' received lavish praise in the public arena of the editorial floor and the reporter who failed was publicly humiliated in front of his colleagues. At the end he was 'mentally devastated'. The great irony was that 'the victor' found the whole thing distasteful. To his way of thinking it was a costly procedure that was largely futile and based mainly on luck. But he never wanted David English to know his true opinion because, inevitably, that would have meant he would not have received regular and prestigious assignments, his career would have been stunted and he would have become an outcast. So he played the game.

Creative tension was the bane of the diarists' desk when two very able and competitive men were drawn into a fight to the finish. The whole situation began with what David English later would call his biggest mistake – the importation of Suzy Knickerbocker from the *New York Post* for the launch of the new *Daily Mail*.

David thought she would create a high profile for the fledgling newspaper by bringing a bit of glamour from Manhattan to London. In this he was backed up by Vere Harmsworth's wife Patricia who adored her. 'Suzy', as she was known, was featured heavily in a few of the *Daily Mail*'s television advertisements, one of which had been largely produced and directed by Patricia herself. Patricia believed, as did David, that Suzy embodied the womanly spirit they were trying to instil in the new *Daily Mail*. She was very attractive and outgoing, terribly witty on the page, with a lot of bite. But Suzy turned out to be too American, showing little understanding of British institutions, and the readers rejected her.

She was dispatched back to New York in short order. But her absence created a vacuum. English knew the position on the paper was a key one, and he was on the lookout for someone as colourful and flamboyant as the New York columnist, someone who would become one of the *Daily Mail*'s top celebrity writers.

Enter Paul Callan, editor of the 'Londoner's Diary' on the *Evening Standard*. Callan caught the attention of designer Harold Keeble, who was working hand-in-glove with David English and Peter Grover to put the layout of the *Daily Mail* in good order. Callan had noted in the diary that potential advertisers in the *Mail* were being given a special viewing party at the Ritz, as fate would have it in the Marie Antoinette Room. It struck Callan's fancy that after having sacked some 277 journalists, the lavish party given at the Ritz was perhaps inappropriate, so he wrote up a short item on the affair entitling it, 'Let Them Eat Cake'. When Keeble spotted the piece, he advised English to go and get him. 'He's just the kind of man we want on the diary,' Keeble told English.

Callan was duly enlisted as the new *Mail* diarist at a wage double what he was making at the *Standard*. Callan admitted that he was warned not to go, most notably by Malcolm Muggeridge, who said, 'Oh, my dear boy, what a ghastly idea, going to that ghastly paper full of vulgarians.'

'So naturally I went,' Callan said. And in turn, Callan invited a junior on the diary by the name of Nigel Dempster to join him in his new job. Thus began a famous or infamous relationship that would become known as the signal example of creative tension on the *Daily Mail*.

Callan was a character. Told there was no office space available for him close to the newsroom, he took over a tiny top office on the fourth floor of Northcliffe House that had a small balcony. There he swiftly installed a table and chairs, and during the 'beautiful summer of '71', with its many strikes, he and Dempster sat on the balcony drinking Pimm's and basking in the sunshine. They installed a dart board and if one or another of those whom Callan referred to as 'the awful little lick-spittle creeps' who worked at the *Mail* happened to come into their office, he made it a practice to ignore them. He and Dempster would start a game of darts, saying nothing to 'the poor wretches'. As an added insult Callan posted his wage statement on the door so everyone on staff could see how much he was making ('more than Vincent Mulchrone!').

One day David English, having heard of the entertainment on offer in the diarists' office, showed up for a Pimm's, took stock of the situation and the next day Callan, Dempster and their assistant were installed in an office downstairs, quickly becoming part of the news apparatus at the *Mail*. Perhaps to annoy the others or possibly just because the two of them had a theatrical bent, they fell into loud arguments, much of it posturing. 'I might add', said Callan, describing these innocent days, 'that drink had no small part in all these proceedings.'

But despite all the joviality, Dempster and Callan were actually beginning to get on one another's nerves and, according to Paul Callan's version of events, it was largely caused by creative tension. 'We really fell out badly, Nigel and I, and English encouraged this friction, this mutual aggravation. I don't work like that.' English believed that creative tension brought out the best in people. Callan disagreed. Callan complained to English and, soon afterwards, Dempster was sent to the United States, where he made a big hit. Callan always claimed, 'I breathed life into Dempster's journalistically inert body... but sometimes I wondered if it was Frankenstein creating the monster!'

Callan was soon thereafter offered a programme on radio with LBC. He had just got married and he welcomed the change. So he left the *Mail*, with a retainer to write features for the newspaper.

Nigel Dempster was drafted into returning from New York, largely against his will, because life in New York had become very pleasant and because he had been on a winning streak there. His first major victory came on 3 July, when word filtered out that Richard Burton had left Elizabeth Taylor.

The bureau chief at the *Mail*'s New York office on 42nd Street, Dermot Purgavie, got word that Burton was hiding out in Quogue, near the Hamptons, and Dempster drove out there, spending the night in Southampton with a friend. As he was working to London time, with a five-hour difference, it was imperative he get to Burton early.

And first thing in the morning about 6 a.m. I drove to the back of the guest house where the actor was staying and parked beside a hedge. On the other side of the hedge was Richard Burton asleep in the guest house.

I waited and waited until about 11 a.m. when I heard a consumptive cough. It was getting close to deadline in London. I gave it five minutes, then I went round and knocked on the door, and there's Burton.

I said, 'Good morning, I write for the *Daily Mail*,' and he said, 'Great paper, I write for the *Mail* as well. Come in.' And I said, 'Is it true that you and Elizabeth Taylor are getting a divorce?' And he said, 'Mrs Burton to you. Would you like a drink?' He had a bottle of vodka and a carton of orange juice which he started drinking, and I took a beer. So we went through it all. He gave an interview while drinking this bottle of vodka. After about an hour he'd drunk most of the vodka and he's reciting *Hamlet* for me, not saying very much about Elizabeth Taylor but it's an interview. Burton now says, 'I've had enough, I've got to go to sleep.' He had to because by now he was pissed out of his mind.

And when he finished the vodka I leave, and at the front gates of the house now are fifty or sixty press people, cameras, radio people, television people, journalists, a lot of them. So I go back to my car and drive out front, and I say, 'I've just interviewed Richard Burton and he won't be giving any more interviews.' 'Why not? they ask.

'Well, I'm afraid he's hopelessly drunk.'

This was Nigel Dempster's first big break, and his story was bylined and picked up across the world. He followed that up by reporting on Watergate and by going to South America to cover the Allende assassination in Chile.

But since no one could get into Chile, he was reporting the entire putsch from Argentina. In the middle of all this chaos David English rang him and said, 'Callan has left.' 'And', said Dempster later, 'I'm to return to London and take over, and I say that I don't really want to.' And why should he? At this point his reputation was made and he could get work elsewhere. But he was persuaded by Purgavie at least to go to London to hear the offer.

Nigel duly returned and David English gave him lunch at the White Tower, where he outlined his offer, including the added inducement of a Mini-Cooper. So 'I then go back to New York, wind up my affairs, say goodbye to all my girlfriends and come back and start work on 7 October 1973. The first column is published on 8 October, and it is the longest-running personal column in Fleet Street and here I still am.'

Thus ends the longest-running feud caused by creative tension on the *Daily Mail*.

But if creative tension brought David English's methods under critical scrutiny by those in the journalism trade, his penchant for stunt journalism made him a controversial editor by anybody's standards. It was typical of English never to be satisfied with simply reporting the news. He intended to affect the *outcome* of the news. It was speculated that this was a function of his personality – a peculiar form of control-freaking specific to David. Equally, it was said that this was a function of his great genius.

Whatever the case, it was this characteristic that was destined to become his calling card. He went far beyond the realm of the traditional newspaper editor; he became the primary proponent of what has been called euphemistically 'news management'. At the beginning it was David English slanting his news stories towards the women readers he coveted. By the end he was instrumental in putting a woman into the Prime Minister's office. And he loved it, he loved every minute of it.

A typical instance of David reworking reality: he rings up a sports reporter, telling him how to write his dispatches on an up-and-coming tennis player. This girl is, in David English's peculiar argot, not just a talented newcomer; this is 'a wonder player'. In fact, she is 'the greatest player of all time'. This hyped-up overstatement was David's way of creating a swell of interest that would increase circulation. He also intended to create a sense of excitement at the birth of a star. More than that, it reflected David's intention to control the celebrity factor, himself creating or destroying the stars of today and tomorrow. It would become a pattern in the world of sports, in politics and in West End drama.

If David liked something he would push for it to become the big thing of the moment and everybody around him, from his sub-editors to his reporters, was expected to share the enthusiasm. It was impossible for him to grasp the concept that he could be wrong. And if he did turn out to be wrong, it didn't matter. The public had a short memory. He moved to the next thing. But if a sports writer disagreed with him, as he did in this case, it was possible David would view that disagreement as a lack of loyalty. Or he might not. It was purely a matter of English's whim.

Many of his staff, watching David manipulate the news, felt uneasy when he was in this mode. It was often said that when David's better judgement was overcome by his enthusiasm, only one man could influence him: his associate editor Peter Grover. Grover was well grounded and centred, and English would sometimes listen to him. But not always.

Surely the most controversial news management event ever undertaken by David English had to do with the rescue of ninety-six orphans from Vietnam on the eve of the fall of Saigon. The original idea did not come from English, but from his news editor Brian Freemantle, who later became well known for his thrillers.

Freemantle and English went back – way, way back, in fact, to the time when they were youthful competitors at their first jobs. English was reporting for the *Christchurch Times* and Freemantle was on the *New Milton Advertiser*. Although Freemantle had no very good memory of the young English, David did remember him, and when the two men ended up on the *Express* together they became friends. Later, when David became editor of the *Daily Sketch*, he brought Freemantle over to be the 'travelling' foreign editor. Then, when English was named editor of the new *Daily Mail* he took Brian with him. In this position Brian covered the Israeli Six-Days' War and was three times sent to cover Vietnam.

So Freemantle knew the score regarding the impending fate of the young orphans who had been fathered, in many cases, by American military men. He also had good contacts in Vietnam and when he proposed to David that they 'rescue' as many orphans as they could, David replied, 'Terrific if it works.' David would go along, and so would a number of the editorial and reportage staff.

It was left to Brian to charter the airliner 'if I could get it insured through Lloyd's of London', because the existing insurance of the other charters didn't cover them going into a war zone.

We offered this plane to Project Vietnam Orphan, a British adoption organisation. I just said, 'I have this aircraft. Do you want to get these kids out?' And they said yes.

We evacuated the entire orphanage. There were also some children that another adoption agency wanted us to carry. And the Save the Children Fund gave us some nurses. And there was a condition imposed by the South Vietnam government. The children had to be brought out in advance of the overnight to 9 a.m. curfew, because it was feared there would be a panic if they saw a coach going out. People would run after the coach and perhaps engulf our aircraft...

There was the inevitable delay. The kids were sitting in the hot coach for a long time. The eldest was thirteen and the youngest was a baby in arms. Many had operational scars. All were malnourished. All looked very ill. I was very frightened when I saw them. I thought we would get off with ninety-six little coffins.

What I didn't know was they had been sedated for the trip, and by the time we reached Bombay they were running up and down the aisles from the excitement of being on an aircraft.

The baby I was holding lost control of her bowels. I didn't find out until later that she had been aboard the American Galaxy Aircraft that thirty-six hours before had crashed and she was one of two kids who had survived that. So when our plane took off, she simply lost control from fear.

We went out and we got the children and off we flew.

What followed was 'seventeen hours of non-stop concentrated nursing for the health and the comfort of sick and traumatically disturbed children'.

For Freemantle, who had masterminded the project, there was still the news to get out. When the plane landed in Bombay, Brian dropped off a photographer and reporter with the story. But he wasn't completely confident that the stories had got to the *Daily Mail* in London. So 'as extra insurance', he repeated the entire procedure in Dubai. A reporter, David Pryke, was sent off the plane to phone in the story again.

Then a comedy of errors began that has gone down in the annals of Fleet Street history as legend. It was said that David Pryke tried to take his jacket, but David English stopped him saying, 'We won't leave without you, David.' Others said that Pryke knew the first priority of Freemantle was to get the children safely home and so he realised he could be left behind. Whatever the case, the plane was being refuelled and when this was completed it took off, leaving Pryke in Dubai without any money, without his passport, completely stranded. He did have with him a dirty handkerchief and a Polo mint.

'Pryke was incandescent with rage,' Freemantle said, and as soon as he persuaded the British ambassador to come out to the airport and get him, he called the office and 'resigned on the spot'. Brian Freemantle arranged for Pryke's air passage home and called the Foreign Office in London, arranging for him to walk straight through customs and be met by a chauffeured car from the *Daily Mail*. Said Freemantle later,

Well, the plane was delayed and the customs officials at Heathrow told to expect him changed shifts. So when Pryke tried to walk straight through as he had been told he could, he was detained and had to explain. The car I sent, the guy got fed up waiting, so he pushed off. So David Pryke resigned again.

Pryke was eventually persuaded to stay, but the story that David English and Brian Freemantle abandoned him stuck in the telling, and that's the way it is remembered.

In the aftermath of the event controversy raged, with readers writing letters to the editor that vociferously condemned the airlift as an inappropriate stunt. At the same time readers were writing in that it was a wonderful humanitarian effort.

The *Evening News* took up the subject in an editorial that sided, predictably, with the *Daily Mail* and its controversial decision to transport the children to Britain.

> The bickering that has developed over the Vietnam 'Baby Lift' is unfortunate. It is also spurious.
>
> There are suggestions that the suffering children of Saigon would have been 'better off' in their own country.
>
> There are claims that some of the babies may not be orphans at all.
>
> Does it matter? ...
>
> The fact is that a hundred helpless infants have been plucked from a situation that promised death for some, danger for others and an uncertain future for the rest.

But the leader had little effect. So hot was the topic that the question whether the rescue was ethical continued to rage. Even years later, the *Spectator* published a piece in which it was suggested that the *Mail*'s airlift of babies from Vietnam to England was 'a squalid operation'. The article went on to say 'that the *Daily Mail* wrongly represented the children to be orphans or in need of special medical attention, that they were taken away from their parents and home backgrounds purely as a "promotional stunt" ...'

The *Mail* brought a successful libel action against the *Spectator*, and eventually the magazine withdrew its allegations and apologised for the embarrassment these had caused. The *Mail* received undisclosed damages and was awarded legal costs.

As to David English, he took an uncharacteristic back seat to all these proceedings. Brian Freemantle said,

> He gave me my head completely.
>
> On the face of it, the idea of chartering an aircraft and going into a war zone is pretty unusual. What David said to me was, 'See if you can make it work.'
>
> The perimeter of the airport was in control of the Vietcong. We all knew that the Galaxy had gone down.
>
> But David English was on that flight as well. If it went down, David went down. The same went for me. So if we were willing to go down with the plane it wasn't only a publicity stunt.

Soon after the rescue of the orphans from Saigon, an incident occurred that would have been more appropriate to the pages of a John le Carré novel than to the editorial floor of the *Daily Mail*. No one had any expectation of such an event and the evening before it occurred was as convivial as any that was ever celebrated by the senior journalists on the *Mail* staff.

It was 28 February 1976 and David English was holding one of his informal dinners, this time at the Waldorf Hotel. The celebration had been organised to mark the retirement of Bob Findlay, the *Mail*'s sports editor. As the evening drew to a close and the men spilled out into the Strand in London, a light rain was falling. John Golding, the managing editor of the newspaper, carried with him an open bottle of good cognac, no doubt an ad hoc reward for his work in organising the dinner. He said goodnight pleasantly to his colleagues and climbed into a taxi that would take him to his home in Norwood in south London.

It was the last time English or any of the staff was ever to see the newspaper's managing editor.

The following Monday morning a perplexed John Womersley found himself writing an entry into his desk diary: 'A human drama unfolds in the office as David tells me that John Golding is missing. He left home on Saturday and has not been seen since.' Soon thereafter Womersley was put in charge of an investigation to find out what had happened to the missing editor.

The day after the dinner had been a Saturday and Golding had the day off work. Usually, he and his wife would go shopping together on Streatham High Road. But this particular Saturday his wife went alone while Golding extracted some tiles from the fireplace that he wanted to replace. There was the suggestion that John and his wife had had a minor argument before she left, perhaps over his decision to remain at home. There was the possibility that he had also argued with his son who no longer lived with his parents. But there was no sign of a serious altercation, certainly nothing on a scale to initiate what took place next.

Later John Womersley recalled the details of the disappearance.

Mrs Golding had not yet returned from her shopping when her husband, wearing his usual Saturday casual clothes, decided to leave the house. It was some time after 2 p.m. when he got into his car and drove away, never to return. The last person known to see him was an *Evening Standard* photographer of his acquaintance. They met by chance at a road junction not too far from Golding's house. The photographer was on his way to cover a Saturday afternoon football match. Golding hailed him and said, 'I'm glad I don't have to work Saturdays any more.' The photographer later said that he appeared to be his normal self.

Later that weekend Mrs Golding telephoned David English, saying that her husband hadn't returned from his trip, she hadn't heard from him at all and it was completely out of character. The following Monday his colleagues at work were similarly baffled because it was equally out of character for Golding not to turn up for work.

John Womersley went out to visit Mrs Golding at the family home in Norwood and she allowed him to go through John's personal possessions. There he found 'nothing to suggest a premeditated or organised departure'.

No suitcase or clothes were missing. No cash had been withdrawn from the joint bank account. Even his reading glasses were still on the table.

The single clue that Womersley uncovered had to do with Golding's briefcase. Journalists on the staff were required to carry a briefcase with their contacts book, a clean shirt and a passport in case it became necessary to leave the office at short notice on a foreign assignment. When Womersley searched Golding's briefcase, which he found in Golding's car, the passport was missing. Other than that, Golding's bank accounts showed no sudden withdrawals, no unusual amounts of cash had been withdrawn, even on a regular basis.

What Womersley did manage to establish was that instead of driving to find replacements for the tiles he was repairing, the logical errand, John Golding got into his car, drove to Liverpool Street Station, parked in a legal parking spot, then 'vanished off the face of the earth'.

By all accounts Golding was a popular member of staff, well-liked and respected by his colleagues, and extremely good at his job. Golding had begun on the *Mail* as a staff photographer, working his way up through the editorial ranks to picture desk executive, then art editor. It did come as something of a surprise to several of them when David English decided to make Golding the managing editor of the *Mail*, given that background. In the new position, Golding would have to take on administrative assignments that many journalists considered political and dull, including dealing with militant trade unionists. They doubted Golding would have a tolerance for that. But Golding showed a penchant for the work, to the extent that David rewarded him with a plum assignment.

Not long before he disappeared Golding had flown to California to secure the publishing rights to the autobiography of Doris Day for serial-isation in the *Mail*. During his sojourn the managing editor was fêted as any high-level media executive could have expected to be. He attended 'champagne receptions and villa poolside lunches, meeting wealthy pub-lishers and agents, and being entertained at dinner parties', Womersley said later.

It was all that was needed for David English to put one of his characteristic spins on what might have happened with Golding. Said Womersley later,

> David speculated that on this trip Golding had met and fallen for a wealthy Californian widow who had persuaded him to forsake the stress of London's Fleet Street and to succumb to her charms and lead a sybaritic life in the sunshine of southern California. 'So why didn't he stay out there?' we asked David. 'Ah,' David replied, 'he wouldn't let the paper down. He'd bring back the story first!'
>
> It was as good a theory as any. American stringers scoured Hollywood and its affluent suburbs for any sign of Golding with a doting widow. Their expenses arrived, but no sign of their elusive quarry. Scotland Yard also favoured the 'another woman' theory. But no woman or love nest was ever discovered.

The *Mail* published several accounts of John Golding's disappearance with the result that all across England there were dozens of 'sightings' of the missing managing editor. He was seen sitting on a bench on Plymouth Hoe, on Brighton Pier, on the ramparts of Edinburgh Castle. John Womersley said later, 'He was even seen walking along the central reservation of the Oxford bypass.'

None of these leads panned out.

From dealing with similar stories, every journalist on the *Mail* was familiar with the usual reasons for a mysterious disappearance, but in no way did Golding fit the pattern. 'John Golding', stated Womersley, 'was not a womaniser, not a gambler, not a big spender, not in ill health, not a criminal and not living a secret life.'

So the matter was left to rest, with no clues as to the reasons for Golding's mysterious disappearance until later that summer. In July the *Daily Mail* received a tip from 'an underworld informant' saying that 'John Golding was alive and well, and living in Tangier'. According to Womersley,

> He was said to be working for Billy Hill, a notorious member of the

London criminal fraternity at that time. I immediately flew out to Tangier armed with a portfolio of enlarged photographs of John Golding.

I checked into the El Minzah Hotel, got a large-scale map of the town, quartered it and for five days checked out almost every bar, hotel, bank, taxi office and travel firm where an Englishman could have visited. In the 1970s Tangier had a largish British expatriate population, many leading escapist lives in a city where morals were not particularly guarded. There was a strong homosexual community and Tangier was not known for nothing for its reputation of free trade and free love.

John was soon making the rounds of some of the seedier nightspots, armed with his photographs. At one club he encountered 'a swarthy bartender' who seemed friendly. When Womersley held up his picture saying, 'Excuse me, I'm looking for this man. Have you seen him?' the bartender promptly jumped ever the bar, pulled down the blinds and said, 'Never mind your friend, you have found me instead.' Said Womersley, 'I had to fight my way out.'

Womersley finally located the opulent residence of Billy Hill, 'a lavish high-security apartment on the fifth floor on the Avenue Hassan II'. There he was allowed to enter past 'two burly minders' by Billy's stylishly decked-out wife, who told him that neither she nor her husband had ever heard of John Golding. 'What use would he be?' she asked the journalist. 'My husband tries to keep out of the newspapers, not get involved with them.' But she did agree to talk to her husband in London about the matter.

Within hours Billy Hill had called David English direct, telling him he had never heard of his managing editor and would English please call off his dogs in Tangier. Womersley again:

> My last contact with the story came over seven years later when Mrs Golding successfully applied to have her husband legally declared 'presumed dead' so all his estate could be properly dealt with. I provided an affidavit saying that despite the most strenuous enquiries I could find no evidence that he was alive.

But Womersley could find no evidence that Golding was dead either. Nor did anyone on the staff ever discover the outcome.

It was destined to remain one of the mysteries of the *Daily Mail*, talked about for years to come but never solved.

SEVEN

ON THE ROAD

Nobody could help your career more than David English, especially if you were crazy enough to want to go *into* Saigon when everybody else was trying to come *out*.

Foreign correspondent John Edwards had been in Cambodia and Vietnam so many times during the late 1960s and early 1970s that he found it more economical to take a share in an apartment in Thailand than stay in a hotel. When it became obvious Saigon would fall, Edwards said to English, 'I've just got to get back there.' David raised the obvious objection: it was dangerous. But Edwards protested that he had been in comparable situations: the Indo-Pakistani War, Northern Ireland, Beirut, the list went on.

So David said, 'Well, I won't stop you.' It was late April 1975 and the Vietcong were no more than forty miles outside Saigon when John managed to get on to an Air France flight. There was only one other passenger, a Norwegian radio reporter.

> As we were landing, I looked out of the left-hand side window and it was a sight I'll never forget. The whole of the airport terminal was like an anthill that had been disturbed, thousands of people waiting to get on any plane, any flight to anywhere. My Air France Boeing 707 stopped at the end of the runway. They just opened the back passenger door and let the chute down.
>
> We didn't have bags, just carry-ons. We jumped down and the stewardesses let bottles of wine and cigarettes slide down after us. Then they waved and flew off empty. The Norwegian and I were on the grass beside the runway and we just walked through the holes in the fence.

The Saigon Edwards found was in a desperate panic, with stories going round that the Vietcong were already in the suburbs. He took a room in the Caravelle Hotel on an inside well in the building. All around him were people evacuating as fast as they could, in a state of high panic.

He was given an evacuation procedure that explained what part of the city the American helicopters would come from. They were coming from a battle fleet in the Gulf of Tonkin and they would take the journalists back there. Edwards said later,

> You were given a station, letters 'a' or 'b' or 'c', and you had to listen continuously to American Forces Network, AFN-VN, for Vietnam. Bing Crosby would sing 'White Christmas' and when the record finished, a man would say, 'and the temperature is rising in downtown Saigon' and then 'White Christmas' would come on again. Then the jolly green giants [the helicopters] would come and get you.
>
> I had never intended to evacuate. But I went down to the US embassy and saw oceans of people hanging on to niches in the wall to get on to the roof, where the helicopters were taking off from. The machine-gun bullets were chipping everywhere plus artillery from the North Vietnamese army, and the Americans firing back in mad panic.

After watching the last helicopter take off, John left the scene. Tens of thousands of people had been at the embassy and now John watched them, walking hopelessly with their suitcases through the streets. He went into a hotel and nobody was there. He walked back into the restaurant, searching for something to eat. Later, he said,

> There was nobody in this hotel. And I thought, 'Christ, they've all gone. I'm left. I'm on my own.' I went into the kitchen and there was a big vat of soup, gently simmering. I ladled some into a bowl, stood beside one of the windows. I put this into my mouth and I couldn't swallow it. I didn't have the ability physically to swallow the soup. I guess it was fear or anxiety.

Edwards left the hotel and went to the Reuters office, along with a few other reporters who were still left in the country. In a short time the Vietcong and North Vietnamese army started coming by, and John stood watching the now-famous sight of the tanks rolling in. John wrote about 800 words on the subject and commandeered the only telex line still available. It went out to Hong Kong. He said,

> I gave the operator all the money I had, $300, equivalent to a year's salary, and he got 471 words out on that. And that was the last bit out from Reuters for a month. One or two got some stuff out from AP and others from UPI. But all the lines went down at the same time.

A group of reporters left the Reuters office, following the tanks into the presidential palace. A few of them jumped on the backs of the North Vietnamese army tanks for a lift. But John just walked along behind. Suddenly, they all found themselves in the middle of the 'biggest bloody firefight ever, mortar and machine-guns blasting, bloody stuff was flying everywhere'. Elements of the South Vietnamese army had decided, suicidally, to hold out against the Cong.

Edwards and the others went down on their stomachs, crawling along, fifty or sixty yards, when at last they got back into the Reuters office and holed up there. After a while they went back to the hotel, where there was a roll-call. Peter Arnette, then with the Associated Press, and Sandy Gall of ITV were there, and Gall agreed to be the leader since he spoke fluent French.

John Edwards asked, 'Have you heard the song "White Christmas" yet?' He was shocked to find out that the message was a different song altogether, 'Mother Wants to See You'. In some kind of internal panic, somehow Edwards had got the message wrong in his mind and to this day he still can't explain that. He thought he knew the message as well as his own address. In fact, if he had been intending to evacuate he couldn't have, because he simply got it wrong.

Still, the story he was covering was the 'biggest for decades', of such importance historically that Edwards couldn't allow himself not to be there. He had got out 471 words, about 200 more than anybody else.

'*Been there, done that*,' he said later and mentally marked it off his list.

Ann Leslie had met David English when she was at the *Daily Express*. Simply put, she thought he was the greatest editor of the age. So when David left she decided to resign. She was summoned to Max Aitken's office where he asked her why she was leaving.

> So I answered, 'Well it's not money, Sir Max. I'm very tired of doing the things I do, like interviewing cricket players' wives, and I've been sent to Cliff Richard three times and if we ever had anything to say to one another we've run out by now.'
>
> And I said, 'I also quite frankly want to work with David English as editor.' Aitken just looked out of the window. That was one of the many reasons the Beaverbrook family lost control of the *Daily Express*, because they simply didn't know how to do it after Beaverbrook went.

Eventually, she took a contract with the *Daily Mail* as a freelance feature writer specialising in foreign affairs.

In due course she became one of the *Mail*'s brightest stars. But none of her adventures compared with the fall of the Berlin Wall.

In November 1989 David English called Ann into his office, saying, 'I'd like to talk to you about East Germany. What do you think is going to happen?' Ann replied that it would be a bloodbath... *or* they would open the wall. When David asked her which, she plumped for the wall.

'Well,' said English, 'I think so too. So that's why I want you to go in.' Ann pointed out she couldn't get a visa into East Germany since she was on a list of reporters prohibited from going there. David told her to do a tourist day-trip entry and just get in.

Ann thought that if they caught her they would simply expel her. So why not go?

The second day I was there the politburo resigned. The third day the government resigned. We knew something was going to happen, but we didn't expect it that week.

I was there illegally, but realised the thing was crumbling so fast that I went round to the Foreign Ministry and said, 'I'm here illegally, but I want Press Accreditation.' The woman in charge just looked at me and said, 'Well, why not? It's all going, isn't it?'

And I said, 'Yes, it's all going.' I was so tired. I had been writing yards of stuff. I went to this amazing press conference that evening and everybody in East Germany was exhausted who had been covering this, and there was this official who was droning on about the make-up of the next Communist Party. Everybody was asleep and I was gently dozing off.

Then he said casually, 'Oh, by the way, this might interest you. As of now, the borders will go down.' I just felt as though I'd had a cattle prod up my bum! Cameras were switched on. Everybody came awake.

We were trying to get clarification of this amazing statement but he didn't have any, he'd just been handed this bit of paper. He then fled into the Gents. I said to Tom Brokaw of NBC, 'Get into the Gents with him, strangle him with the lavatory chain and find out what he's talking about.' Then everybody started to move and there was pandemonium.

It suddenly occurred to Ann that this press conference was being broadcast live on West German Cable TV, so this ambiguous statement had gone out. She thought that everybody watching must have thought he meant you could go now, if you wanted, across the border. On the phone to the office she said, 'Everybody has been watching this, and they will interpret this as the border's open.'

Leslie went down to Checkpoint Charlie, then rushed to the other crossing point. She saw groups of people gathering and they were all arguing, saying, 'Can we go or can't we?' Then, of course, the thousands began to turn up. The whole place became pandemonium. People just started hacking down the wall. The cry of every journalist was, 'Where's the phone?' There were very few lines anyway, you could wait for hours to get a phone out. Said Leslie later,

It was the most amazing night of my life. People just started hacking down the wall. I would rush to a hole in the wall and I'd get through the hole, then get a phone, file some stuff, rush back and find that the hole in the wall I'd just come through was now full of people.

So I couldn't get back into Berlin that way so I'd shout, 'Where's the next hole?' I don't think I slept for about forty-eight hours or more. I was crying and all these West Berliners were crying.

I rang David and said, 'Look I'm just going to write off the top of my head.'

I wrote this thing out of sheer exhaustion, wildly over the top, and I said to David, 'I'm just going to keep writing' because by then even the West German phones were jammed because the world and his wife were turning up. I said, 'Just tone it down a bit.'

David English let the story stand just as Ann Leslie wrote it and the piece won her the Feature Writer of the Year Award for 1989. It was called 'What a Momentous Night to Remember'. Leslie wrote,

I cannot believe this is happening.

Here I am in a massive queue of East German cars approaching Checkpoint Charlie and tears are streaming down my exhausted face.

At this exultant moment, I feel convinced that I will never feel such an intensity of emotion again in my life...

...sitting beside me in the car and sobbing like me is teacher Wiebke Reed, who today has become free for the first time in her grey and fear-filled 48 years.

We are hugging each other and she's screaming, 'I love you, Ann!' and I'm screaming back, 'I love you, Wiebke!' We're screaming the same at the huge crowd of West Berliners who are cheering our battered little red Wartburg as it inches and coughs its way slowly across the no man's land where so many have died...

We crank open the Wartburg's sunroof. I jump on to the car seat and, emerging bodily out of the roof into the freezing sunshine, I wave my arms in victorious salute...

For Ann Leslie, who was later to receive the coveted Edgar Wallace trophy, it remained the most momentous event in a career of momentous events. And David English had put her there.

Ian Wooldridge, prizewinning sports reporter and columnist, was at Munich in September 1972, staying in the Olympic Press Village. He knew that the Dachau Concentration Camp was only about twelve miles from the outskirts of Munich. Wooldridge went there with photographer Monty Fresco to write a story about the concentration camp two days before the games were to start.

They photographed a few things. Then, just as they were coming out, they saw the entire Israeli Olympic team in front of a great monument that had been erected there as a tribute to the Jewish nation. Monty Fresco quickly took a series of pictures and neither he nor Ian thought anything about it. It would turn out that those photographs were the last pictures ever taken of the Israeli Olympic team.

On the day of the assassination, Wooldridge was due to interview an American writer, and when he arrived at the meeting he found the man wringing his hands in grief and saying, 'Oh, God there's no point in going on.'

> And I didn't know what had happened. He told me the terrorist group Black September had captured nine of the Israeli team and I said, 'We have to get down there.'
>
> So we went down and everyone was trying to get into the Athletes' Village. We went in through the laundry lift. We were lying on the ground with hundreds of other reporters waiting for the sounds of gunfire to stop, and we stayed there for something like seventeen hours.

But eventually the hostages were bussed out with their captors, then taken by helicopter to a military airfield twenty-eight miles from Munich. There a last-stand battle took place and all the captives and four of their captors were killed.

> Later, the memorial service was held around the quarters where the team had been shot. I was in charge of taking the wives of the first two men who were killed. There must have been a thousand guards. If there had been a single guard there on the day, it wouldn't have happened.

Wooldridge couldn't come to terms with the fact that the games went ahead and the column he wrote on the occasion, 'We Just Wanted to Weep Alone', has become a classic:

The XXth Olympic Games broke stride in Munich yesterday just long enough to pay tribute to the massacred Israelis. By teatime, they'd carried out the dead and the show was on the road again...

In fierce midmorning heat, [the spectators] witnessed a memorial service so precisely staged for world television that it was more like a Hollywood Bowl spectacular. You found yourself looking for the drum majorettes.

What started as a solemn act of remembrance turned into a political rally and ended as a symphony concert.

To Wooldridge's mind this was the sorriest moment he ever had to report.

On 2 May 1984 Brian Vine was summoned to the editor's office where David English was waiting for him. 'There's a brilliant idea around,' said David, 'and it's more brilliant than usual because it's mine.'

It seemed that Ian Wooldridge had just written a column about a seventeen-year-old Afrikaner who had recently broken the world record for the women's 5000 metres at 15.01, at a little-known location called Stellenbosch in South Africa. The record bettered that of Mary Decker, America's leading contender in the event, by 6.45 seconds. The runner was an amateur contender who ran barefoot and her record-breaking run was unofficial. But after reading about her in Wooldridge's column, David English had developed one of his 'enthusiasms'. The name of the young runner was Zola Budd.

He told Brian to fly to South Africa, along with the *Mail*'s athletics correspondent, John Bryant, and assess her running abilities, her power, her ease, her talent. 'Your job', English told Vine, 'is to make contact with the people around her, those interested in her career, and ask them if they would like to see her career promoted internationally. Would she be able to come and live in Britain as a British citizen?'

By noon, Brian Vine was at the embassy getting a visa and by 6 p.m. he was on an overnight plane, flying directly to Johannesburg because Zola Budd was running at nearby Port Elizabeth. As Vine recalled, 'We were in such a hurry, we had to take the tube to Heathrow.'

Vine and Bryant had made contact with Budd's father by four o'clock that afternoon.

David had been intrigued by the fact that her parents had British heritage and his mind had just clicked like a Rolls-Royce into place. He said, 'Here is this great story of a young girl shut out of international competition by

apartheid. The athletic spirit is something that shouldn't be bottled up.'
He wanted her to come to Britain and run in the Olympics for this
country. She was entitled to a British passport because her grandfather was
a British citizen.

And this was the proposition I put before Zola Budd's father.

But the *Mail* was competing against the IMG Agency, one of the top
athletic agencies in the world. In fact, the agency man had been Ian
Wooldridge's source for the original story, an ironic touch that made
Wooldridge nervous about the whole deal. For that reason and a number
of others, he opposed David's 'brilliant idea'.

My first reason was that my friend gave me that tip-off. They had hired
her, we stole her off that agency. Of course I wish I'd never written it. I
had literally let down my contact who had given it to me totally gratu-
itously, and he came in when it was all going on and said to David, 'You
can't do this. You can't just come here and steal this woman runner.' And
David said, 'I'll tell you why you can't do it, you can't get her the passport.
I can pick up this telephone now and get her this passport.'

That became the clincher in the deal with Zola Budd's father: David
could get her a British passport to compete *that year* in the Olympics.
The *Mail* was willing to pay all her expenses, the expenses of her coach
and bring her family to England to allow her to train for the British
Olympic team.

The story became a blockbuster with many ramifications, not least
whether a runner blocked because she came from a country that had officially adopted apartheid should then be allowed to run for another
country.

As a second string there was the question of whether a contender
should be imported into Britain at all in order to compete in the
Olympics. One of Wooldridge's main objections was simply whether
Zola Budd was ready to run in the Olympics. She didn't have the experience she needed, Wooldridge told English. Speed was one thing; experience another. But David chose not to listen and Vine brought Budd to
Britain. The resulting chorus of disapproval could be heard from one end
of the country to the other.

In the middle of this furore was David English who, having secured
the contract, made a statement about his attitude in the *Daily Mail*:

The *Daily Mail* firmly believes that Zola Budd will become a great British athlete. That is why we have helped her and her family to come to this country so that she can run for Britain – the country she wants to represent in world athletics. As a British citizen she will be able to run against international competition and we felt it would be a tragedy if she had to run for any other country when her heart lies here.

But did Zola Budd really *want* to represent England? Later, in her autobiography, she gave her own rather sad account of the story from the point of view of an unsophisticated seventeen-year-old girl who couldn't even speak English at the time she came to England to compete. She said she felt 'harshly exploited by the *Mail*, which paid £100,000 for exclusivity of my "story"'. And she lambasted the newspaper for bringing her before she was actually ready to compete.

More pathetically, she told of being under her father's dominance. He ended up keeping £45,000 of the money for himself, splitting the rest among family members and leaving Zola only £20,000 in her British Trust Fund. She believed that David English was interested only in circulation and controversy, and that she was left in an untenable position.

Because of her age, the question of 'human bondage' was bound to arise and the *Mail* never adequately answered the charge. It coined the expression, 'She's blonde, beautiful and British', and pressed forward, helping Zola jump the long queue waiting for a British passport. She would later say that, to her, the passport became a symbol of her abuse.

But Brian Vine pointed out that the contract was exclusive of commercial endorsements, and Budd and her father were free to benefit from making their own deals independent of the *Mail*. And they did make deals, although it remained unclear whether Zola Budd herself got any of the money.

From the *Mail*, she was given the use of a house in a village in Hampshire, her coach was brought over from South Africa and her family were supported. They were paid, and that was the deal. But Brian Vine knew she was in over her head:

> She was a fairly uptight little girl with a lot of running talent, very naïve, with little experience. It was not a brilliant relationship with her father, who as far as we were concerned was the dominant factor because he had to sign the contract. She was in a foreign country. It was wet. Everything was alien, from the food to the climate, and she had broken off from her athletic training at home. Then there was the anxiety whether she would be granted a passport, which she didn't know, and in what time-frame. Would it be in time to get her into the Olympics?

Then all the time there were photographers asking her to pose and me dragging her biography out of her. Her coach, Pieter Labuschagne, was brought to England. He was her history teacher and I think she had a crush on this guy. She wasn't happy until he had been flown over, but that was part of the agreement. He was here in time for her first race. And that caused arguments.

There were a lot of family rows. This internecine warfare was going on behind these lace curtains in Guildford where they had bought a house.

I was pressing her for information all the time and she said in her auto-biography that I was putting the *Mail* before human relations. But, even with all this, I had to say she was talented, TALENTED! And what we were doing seemed right.

Zola Budd arrived in Britain in March, received her passport in early April and contended in the Los Angeles Olympics in August.

And there, as history showed, she wasn't ready for international com-petition. During the race, Zola became entangled with Mary Decker and the two of them went down in one of the greatest upsets ever in the Olympic Games. Maricica Puica, a relative unknown, was the eventual winner.

This was the barefoot girl who had run with the ostriches. It was left to Ian Wooldridge to say the unspeakable:

David's concept, I think, was wrong. He was going on for a 'Gold Medal for Britain', but to his advisers, of whom I happened to be one, it wasn't right.

Brian Vine disagrees. It was, he believed, a unique story in the annals of British journalism, 'plucking a person from one country and into another, harbouring her, then launching her on a world stage. But we received more brickbats for that than for anything we ever did.'

EIGHT

IN LOVE WITH THE PIG

In 1968, when the youth of America were preoccupied with burning bras and American flags, a newly graduated alumnus from the University of Tennessee, Phillip Moffitt, had already determined to swim against the tide. He and two friends were starting up a small computer business at a time when such an effort was easily dismissed as crass commercialism.

The former president of the student body, Moffitt was a campus mover and shaker who had accepted a job as assistant dean of students while he considered whether to pursue his lifelong dream, a law degree. He was put in charge of programmes for new students and came up with the idea of giving freshmen a magazine listing activities on offer in the surrounding city. 'Sounds like an interesting idea,' his immediate superior said, 'but you'd better take it upstairs to get an OK.' Once upstairs, Moffitt was sent even further upstairs. Eventually, he was told he would have to wait a year or more to get the idea approved.

Out of frustration, Moffitt went to his two partners in his computer business and asked them how they would like to go into the field of publishing. Thus, in the autumn of 1969, the first magazine edited by Phillip Moffitt, *Knoxville in a Nutshell*, appeared on sale at the University of Tennessee. 'It made a couple of thousand dollars, it seemed very easy to do, make money in publishing, right?'

Right. The following year, Moffitt expanded his magazine to twenty issues, renamed his company 13–30 for the age group he wished to reach and lost $100,000. In the autumn of 1971 the group covered forty different campuses and lost $200,000. By the time Phillip Moffitt was twenty-five years old, he and his company owed a million dollars 'with no way to pay it'.

There was a memorable trip to the printers wherein Moffitt explained that he understood he owed them $100,000, but unless they extended another $100,000 credit, they could never hope to get their money. Said Moffitt,

One guy, I'll never forget it, he peeled every inch of my skin off, he told me what a completely horrible human being I was.

This one banker had loaned us everything he could loan us at one bank up to their limit, and then he started working at another bank, and to the dismay of the board of that bank, he started loaning us money again. His name was Lawrence Frierson and they asked him, 'Why are you doing this?' And he answered, 'Well, I like the look in their eye.'

In 1974, the year 13–30 changed over from the calendar year to the fiscal year to do their books, the company went into profit for the first time, chalking up $30,000. The following year they made $300,000 and every year thereafter they grew at a rate of 30 per cent a year. The change in their fortunes came from concentrating on single-advertiser periodicals for companies that wanted to reach the youth market.

It had started when the then Datsun automobile manufacturer in Japan, now Nissan, had asked 13–30 to develop a new approach for their company's advertisements. Moffitt responded by publishing a magazine called *America* that featured travel tips and articles written by students about trips they had taken. From that moment on, the company was in profit.

To us it was the world and in early 1976 I started questioning what I was doing. I'd never intended to be a business person. The thing I liked was that it was hard, quantitative measurement versus the soft measurement of the academic world, where nothing is right or wrong, and that had got on my nerves. I liked the fact that you either made money, or you didn't make money. You either got to stay in business or you didn't.

By now, Phillip's original partners were long gone, one to work for the National Security Council and the other to help in his family business. So Moffitt had tied up with Chris Whittle. It was Whittle who had masterminded Moffitt's election campaign for student body president when they were both undergraduates. Another former student, Wilma Jordan, who graduated from the University of Tennessee, was also a founding shareholder in 13–30.

Whittle had sold the adverts for the original publication *Knoxville in a Nutshell* and, as the company expanded, he had taken over the management side of the business while Moffitt concentrated on editorial. Jordan began as a kind of financial controller, and her hard head for figures and her emotional balance quickly brought her to the forefront of 13–30.

Within three years of making their first profit, the company had thirteen speciality magazines, sales of $12 million and pre-tax earnings of about $1.8 million. The turnaround had happened so quickly that the business attracted potential buyers, and the three partners were tempted to sell out and make an incredible profit for each of them. But at the last minute Lucas Bonnier from the Bonnier Newspaper Company in Sweden called Moffitt and said, 'I'll buy half your company, no more no less.'

> We said no, we were selling it all, and then at the last minute I had second thoughts and got on a plane and flew to Stockholm. Lucas met me at the airport, and we basically agreed on the spot. So he bought half the company.
>
> What I told myself was that it's OK for us to stay in because we will get into paid circulation magazines and this will give me more pleasure and *Esquire* is available. And we'll get *Esquire* with their backing.

This was the circuitous routing by which Phillip Moffitt, Chris Whittle and Wilma Jordan found themselves sitting across from Mick Shields and Charles Sinclair of Associated Newspapers at the Pierre Hotel in New York City in the autumn of 1978.

Two years before the meeting at the Pierre, Vere Harmsworth's determination to get into the American market had culminated in the purchase of *Esquire* magazine by Associated Newspapers in a combined publishing takeover with Clay Felker, former editor of *New York Magazine*.

Felker was old-time New York, knowledgeable in the ways of the world, and at the time he joined forces with Vere Harmsworth he was very angry. He had recently been ousted by the company he and his partner had founded when shareholders in the New York Magazine Company sold out to Rupert Murdoch over Felker's objections. Still smarting from the defeat, Felker and his partner Milton Glaser plunged right back in, starting discussions with *Esquire*, which was up for sale and which Felker had edited in the fifties.

When Felker and Harmsworth began their joint venture, *Esquire* was losing money and Felker's first brief was to stem the haemorrhage of cash that endangered the survival of the fifty-year-old men's magazine. But the magazine was plagued with disastrous circulation problems that, along with its sagging reputation, Felker inherited as well.

The magazine had been subjected to the then popular practice of 'field selling', a door-to-door operation that involved the simultaneous selling of dozens of magazines on one card in an effort to get circulation up and thus attract more advertisers. But the effort had backfired badly in the case of *Esquire*. The magazine had until then enjoyed a trendy image, but now, with over a million subscribers, advertisers discovered that the readership had been corrupted in terms of market desirability. As a result, advertising dropped to only 496 pages a year.

'If somebody bought a five-year subscription,' Felker said later, 'and these were very cheap, that meant they were due sixty copies in five years.' So not only did he have an undesirable readership, but he was also going to have that readership with him for a very long time.

His solution was to upgrade the content of the magazine while at the same time upping the number of issues per year. In this way he planned to rid himself of his undesirable readership more quickly while attracting the right readers. 'It was more expensive than the monthly magazine in terms of the overall costs, but I wasn't paying more than the previous people had paid,' Felker said. But his approach was viewed suspiciously by the management at Associated who thought the plan illogical and extravagant. And as the magazine's losses began piling up, alarm bells started to ring.

The managing director of Associated Newspapers, Mick Shields, drafted into action a thirty-year-old executive who, until now, had been in charge of Associated Newspapers' tax affairs. Charles Sinclair was to fly over and cast a long look at the *Esquire* operation. Although he was young, Sinclair was unusually level-headed and even in these early days he already had the distinctive pallor of the serious financier. Educated at Winchester and Magdalen College, Oxford, he was showing signs of the business acumen that would eventually carry Associated Newspapers into a golden age of investment.

For now, he objected to being sent because, as he said later, 'I didn't have any publishing experience.' But Mick Shields simply said, 'Don't worry about that. Just get on with it.' Sinclair continued,

I was to go and look at the numbers and see where the money was going and what the chances were of the business ever being rescued from the ashes of what Clay had done with it.

Mick Shields didn't believe in spending money if it could be avoided and there was no income stream in America to offset the expenses. He naturally encouraged a certain amount of tight-fistedness. So I was flying stand-by to New York and back to London on a regular basis.

Charles was unimpressed by Felker's multiple-issue strategy to get rid of undesirable readers. He took the hard-headed view that it cost more to put out twenty-six issues annually than twelve, especially if you had no extra pages of advertising to support the policy.

At the same time rumours were filtering down about Felker's high pay-outs to big-name writers. Another bone of contention was his high personal salary. For this and other reasons, Sinclair did not believe Felker was the man to steer the magazine into profitability. It was a tough stance for a relatively inexperienced man to take against one of the high flyers of Manhattan, but Sinclair stuck to his guns. He believed his first and last duties were to Associated Newspapers. He didn't care what Felker thought.

Among other things, he had compared the content of the magazine with a list of writers and contributors and found a poor match. There seemed to be many non-producers. But Felker was less than pleased with this approach.

Insofar as his new proprietor was concerned, even a society hound like Felker was a little stunned at the company Vere kept. He recounted a story when Vere offered to get him invited to Monaco for the weekend. 'If you want to go,' Harmsworth said to him, 'I have to know right away because Patricia has to tell Grace.'

Clay enjoyed impressive social prominence, both in New York and in the enclaves of the rich and powerful across the United States. But this worked against him in terms of his credibility as a careful manager. A story that made the rounds had the *Esquire* editor offering to fly Vere and Patricia Harmsworth from London to New York on Concorde, then on a chartered plane to Palm Springs for a Christmas party of bigwigs, all expenses to be paid for by *Esquire*.

This Felker denied categorically. The only possible grounds for the claim of extravagance against him was the multiple-issue question, he said, but he compensated for that by taking up a cheaper binding for the magazine.

After examining the books, Sinclair still remained unconvinced that Felker was the man to save *Esquire* and that was the message he carried back home. Felker disliked Sinclair, saying he was a control freak who wouldn't have minded getting his hands on editorial. The two men were totally at odds and there could only be one winner in what was developing into a head-on confrontation.

There was no denying that in the first eighteen months of running *Esquire*, Felker had used up the $5 million Associated Newspapers had invested in the magazine and that money had been intended, at least in Mick Shields's mind, for use over the next four years. In fact, behind the scenes, Shields was going 'absolutely bonkers about Clay Felker', his son later said. He believed that Clay was a drain on Associated funds, with 'his huge salary and unreal demands'. The honeymoon had clearly come to a crashing halt.

Just as the skirmishes were threatening to break out into actual war, the Tennessee contingent came on the scene.

With the backing of the Swedish group Bonnier, to whom they had sold half of 13–30, Phillip Moffitt and Chris Whittle were now offering to buy *Esquire* from Associated Newspapers for just over $3 million. They knew the magazine was in trouble, but in a way they didn't care. Moffitt was enamoured of the publication and wanted to see if he could save it. With this in mind he travelled to Stockholm to see his partner Lucas Bonnier, telling him of this great new opportunity. Bonnier told him, 'Phillip, it's a dead magazine now.' But he agreed Moffitt should have his try.

So Moffitt took his idea to Vere Harmsworth and eventually, after many negotiations, Moffitt said, 'we reached a handshake deal to buy the magazine'.

> We were in his apartment on the Ile St Louis. We shook hands and raised champagne glasses. It was all very storybookish, these young guys on their way to the great adventure.

So far as Mick Shields and Charles Sinclair were concerned, they had favoured selling *Esquire*, recouping what they could of their original investment. But something about Phillip Moffitt and Chris Whittle impressed them, and Sinclair said about them,

> We got along with the Tennessee people very well. We told them we didn't think it was sensible for them to buy *Esquire* outright. They offered us what they could.
>
> We said, 'Well, that wasn't really enough,' so we only sold them 80 per cent of *Esquire* and kept 20 per cent. We came to the figure of 80 per cent because that was the cut-off for them to be able to offset the inevitable losses of *Esquire* against the growing profits of 13–30 for tax purposes.*
>
> And we put the assets of the company into a new company so Felker's old company died on the vine. We were of course pleased to sell *Esquire* because there was nothing else we could do with it.
>
> We got some money for it and we stayed in for the ride.

And what was about to happen *was* a ride, one of the most exciting that Associated Newspapers would take in the next decade as they became more and more deeply invested in first 13–30, then Whittle Communications.

* Sinclair immediately saw the advantages of the 80 per cent figure in terms of maximising 13–30's tax efficiency and acted accordingly.

What made the management at Associated believe that Moffitt and Whittle could turn *Esquire* around when an old hand like Clay Felker had failed? Although they were young, there was something about the pair that reeked of integrity and grit. To Mick Shields and Charles Sinclair, they seemed committed and idealistic, and willing to put in the incredible effort it was going to take to turn the tide.

In other words, they liked the look in their eye.

Associated Newspapers and 13–30 signed their deal on a Saturday in the autumn of 1978. On the following Monday Phillip Moffitt had a meeting at the Waldorf Astoria with all the employees at *Esquire*. There, he spoke to them for the first time about his plans for the future.

At the time Moffitt was thirty-three years old, but he looked a lot younger. He had long curly hair and a round cherubic face. The speech he gave, stressing the platonic ideal he was seeking for the magazine, was naturally delivered in a soft Tennessee dialect. He was surprised to look out and see the shock registering on everybody's faces. 'I was speaking conceptually,' he said later, 'and people in New York do not speak conceptually, and so this dismayed them more than the way I looked or sounded.'

In the wake of this encounter Phillip Moffitt was taken aside by one of the former editors, who said, 'You know, Phillip, there's not any inventory.' And I said, 'That can't be true.' He said, 'It is true. Clay just ran the company out of his briefcase. We never knew what was there until it showed up, because that was just his style.'

So the nightmare began. For the next four years, he and Wilma Jordan would commute back and forth every week, 'working four days in Tennessee, three in New York, four in New York, three in Tennessee, we never stopped'.

Chris Whittle also did that for about a year, but then he returned to handle all the marketing in Tennessee. So Phillip Moffitt took over the advertising sales for *Esquire* as well as running the editorial. 'I did this, I did everything. I basically traded my life for the business.'

Starting in 1974, Wilma Jordan had assumed an increasingly important role in 13–30, finally becoming the chief financial officer in the company and second in command at the magazine.

My first year at Number 2 Park Avenue on the twenty-fourth floor in this corner office, I cannot tell you what happened day to day the first six months, I was in such a daze. We were working so hard that there was nothing to tell. I never had a date between 1979 and 1982!

It was a project of total, single focus because everything was riding on it and everything was wrong and we were so naïve about the business climate and so naïve about what it took to really reposition a consumer magazine.

We started losing money! That was the first crisis. We had a three-year business plan, and it turned out we lost all the money we had planned to lose in three years in one year!

One saving grace, Jordan said later, was the frequent presence of Charles Sinclair. Far from viewing his visits as adversarial, as it had eventually developed with Clay Felker, Wilma Jordan saw him as a resource:

Charles Sinclair was a very hands-on financial type, and he made suggestions and helped us refine things. How often do you have a consultant more sophisticated than you are?

And Mick Shields flew to New York every month. I always thought Charles was the financial brain and I thought Mick was really the person with the insight because he understood the business and the research. He had his finger on that pulse.

The first thing Phillip Moffitt decided to do was junk Clay Felker's plan to run twenty-six issues and cut the magazine down to twelve issues a year. At the time, they were down to about 450 pages of advertising and it just made sense to reduce the publication expense. 'The circulation had died,' he said, and news-stand sales had dropped down to 30,000, with a renewal rate on subscriptions at just under 30 per cent.

We did a mailing when we walked in the door that the magazine already had prepared. It cost us a quarter of a million dollars and we got something like 50 subscriptions.

We had to our name $3.5 million in cash and a $1.5 million credit line. We went through that $5 million in five months.

Phillip had a vision for the magazine and he already had inside his head a picture of the person to whom it would speak, a kind of sophisticated male reader between the ages of twenty-five and forty-five. And the advertising sales people 'would not go out and sell my vision', he said.

At the original employees' meeting at the Waldorf Astoria, there had been 115 employees. Within eighteen months there were only seven left of the original staff. 'It was unbelievable,' said Moffitt later. 'We fired more than bailed. And at last we got a staff of sixty who were with us.'

The next thing that happened was that the Swedish investors felt they wanted to withdraw. In fact, when he made the original deal with Bonnier, Moffitt wasn't certain how the relationship would develop. So he wrote a clause into the contract giving 13–30 an option to buy back their shares at what they had paid, plus a money market return on the investment. Now, in a shrewd move, Charles Sinclair suggested that 13–30 transfer this option to Associated Newspapers and allow them to buy the Swedes out in exchange for extra funding. In this way Associated Newspapers bettered the quality of their assets for a low price and *Esquire* received more investment capital.

In the original deal with Associated, 13–30 had bought 80 per cent of *Esquire*, with Associated staying in to the tune of 20 per cent. With this deal Associated swapped their ownership in *Esquire* for an ownership position in 13–30, which included *Esquire*. So in this reconfiguration of the ownership, Associated Newspapers then bought 42 per cent of the shares in 13–30 and eventually Associated took full ownership of the business. Indeed, Associated was getting in deeper and deeper, as it had with Clay Felker, but with one difference: the continuing profitability of 13–30. The Knoxville-based company seemed to be benefiting from its high-profile relationship with *Esquire*, in spite of the fact that *Esquire* itself was on the ropes.

But even though Associated's faith in the parent company investment was gratifying, it wasn't solving the continuing fiscal crisis Phillip Moffitt, Chris Whittle and Wilma Jordan were facing in 1981. They needed more money and at that point they knew they couldn't attract another investor. Yet they all believed that by cutting back on the staff, building up the editorial and pruning the number of issues, it was only a matter of a year before *Esquire* would turn around.

In a panic the trio flew to London and spent the entire weekend in meetings with Mick Shields, Charles Sinclair and Vere Harmsworth, 'literally meetings all day Saturday and all day Sunday', Moffitt said later.

The going was rough in light of the earlier history when Clay Felker was running the magazine. But by the end of the weekend Phillip and Chris thought they might have persuaded Associated to provide the funds they needed. The only hitch was that the Board of Directors of Associated had yet to be convinced.

But we believed there was nothing to be gained by our being in front of the board, because something could go wrong. So the solution was for us to just literally leave town and leave poor Wilma there to face the board and disarm them. There would be nobody to shoot at, in a sense, and

Wilma is very glued together and nailed down. She was a detail person who could tell the story better than we could.

When they said they were going to leave her to persuade the board, Wilma Jordan didn't realise at first that the presentation was probably crucial to the survival of the magazine.

I was so naïve at the time. I really didn't understand the impact of my being left there. I was in this boardroom filled with, shall I say, older gentlemen?

So I did about a two-hour presentation of what we had done and where we were going and why it was going to work and they asked me to leave the room and I stayed out in another room for about an hour.

Then I came back in and they said, 'We've decided to keep supporting you guys and give you additional money to get you through next year.'

In all the blood, sweat and tears the young entrepreneurs were shedding, Vere Harmsworth and Mick Shields were perhaps getting a glimpse of themselves in 1971 when they were trying to save the *Daily Mail*.

But Charles Sinclair viewed what was happening as 'a bigger business opportunity'. He believed the three were 'the kind of team you very rarely come across in business'. To his way of thinking, they had a proven track record with what they had achieved with 13–30.

So we provided debt finance for 13–30. Of course, we drove a hard bargain. We required more equity. But we liked the way they handled themselves in adversity, because they inherited nothing from Clay but adversity.

Not long after this Mick Shields came over to New York. He looked at what was happening on the magazine, took Phillip Moffitt aside and said, 'Phillip, you can't fall in love with the pig.' Phillip Moffitt answered, 'Mick, the reason I'm here is because I'm in love with the pig.'

In the days that followed Phillip Moffitt restored many of the original features of *Esquire* and discarded Clay Felker's stapling for the expensive square-backed binding that had originally covered the magazine. On a more nostalgic note he brought back some of the best-known writers as contributors to the new *Esquire*, including Gay Talese, Tom Wolfe and Truman Capote. New writers like Nora Ephron began to appear regularly and bi-annual special issues called 'publishing events' came into being. They became so popular that a New York book publisher rang Moffitt saying they wanted to publish it and it eventually came out in hardback form.

Just as the team had promised the board of Associated, sales began to improve. The meagre 30,000 news-stand sales figure had, by 1983, advanced to 130,000 and overall readership soared by 51 per cent.

The same year, when the magazine celebrated its fiftieth anniversary with a 616-page special issue, the number of ad pages had jumped to 1312. There was a party at the Lincoln Center in New York City to celebrate the magazine's survival and also, in 1984, Whittle and Moffitt received the *Adweek* award as magazine entrepreneurs of the year.

At about this time Phillip Moffitt instituted focus groups of readers to talk about their impressions of the new *Esquire* and from time to time a managerial team from the magazine would sit behind a one-way mirror in order to see for themselves how the readers were reacting to the new product. At one of these, Moffitt was amazed to hear the focus groups using the very phrases he had used at his first fateful meeting with his new employees at the Waldorf Astoria. 'It was eerie how right-on we were,' he said later.

Associated Newspapers' capital investment in *Esquire* had been between $5 and $6 million, and when they sold their share to Hearst the profit came to $25 million. In 1988 Associated sold half their share in 13–30 to Time-Warner, an investment of some $40 million, reaping a profit of $125 million.

These profits were not the end of Associated's investments abroad, nor were all their holdings in the United States so profitable.* But they did signal a change in focus, as the investment arm of the company started to become as successful as the newspaper arm, if not more so.

* See chapter 19 for a discussion of less profitable investments in the United States.

NINE

THE MONTAGUES AND THE CAPULETS

If only the circumstances of his birth had been different, so said the journalists on the *Daily Mail*, Vere would have made a first-rate sub-editor. They steadfastly believed Vere was a frustrated newspaperman.

At the same time, Vere gave the managerial team the impression that he was a manager at heart. His managing director of operations, John Winnington-Ingram, said they all believed Vere was one of *them*, thus bolstering morale immensely. Again, on the investment side of Associated Newspapers, Mick Shields and his protégé Charles Sinclair believed their efforts were the most important for the firm and it certainly appeared as if Vere agreed.

In America the same principle was at work. To those for whom social prominence was an important aspect of the media business Vere appeared as a substantial society figure. To those who were entrepreneurial he appeared to be an entrepreneur. In the élite investment communities of Montreal and Toronto he fitted easily into the mould of a high-flying financier.

In fact, Vere was a chameleon who shared the values of each and every arm of his business. He rewarded loyalty and gave credit wherever it was due. Yet he constantly encountered hostility, most of it based on envy of his position as head of Associated Newspapers. 'It was very hard at the beginning,' Vere would later say. 'A lot of people were suspicious of me. But once I became a father figure, it was suddenly all right.'

Vere was everywhere, putting in a working day that began around 10 or 10.30 in the morning and ended whenever it ended. He had enormous stamina. He wore out his employees with hard work and, as often as not, with long nights of revelry at restaurants and nightclubs in London or abroad. To a surprising degree he managed to become all things to all men, engendering profound loyalty. But contrary to the popular belief of the journalists that Vere was a journalist at heart, or of the managers that he was a manager at heart, Vere was first, last and always a businessman, forever on the lookout for his next profitable acquisition.

He would have loved to be a reincarnation of his great-uncle

Northcliffe and he certainly had a streak of the press baron's newspaper savvy. But he was actually more like his grandfather Harold, the first Viscount Rothermere, who started with nothing and went on to become the fourth wealthiest man in England. Vere had an innate understanding of the newspaper business that came to him naturally, perhaps even genetically. But what he really understood best was money and competition.

During the 1960s, when it looked very much as if the national newspaper market would dwindle away to nothing because of unrealistic union demands, Associated Newspapers diversified and, long before he took over the dynasty, Vere endorsed the move.

Another of Harmsworth's innovations was the dividing of the company into independent entities, loosely held together under the auspices of a single holding company. Vere wanted to make sure any action by the national unions could not affect the financial health of other arms of the business, especially the provincial newspaper chain Northcliffe Newspapers, where union relations continued to be excellent.

Vere's father Esmond had continued to develop the highly profitable chain acquired by his father Harold and Vere often said he would have been unable to fund the nationals if it had not been for Northcliffe Newspapers. Along with Blackfriars Oil and other of the company's diverse holdings, Northcliffe Newspapers had by 1977 transformed Associated Newspapers into a growing concern, with its latest half-year pre-tax earnings coming in at £6.1 million.

So far as the national titles were concerned, Harmsworth was satisfied that the *Daily Mail*, under David English's leadership, had turned a corner and was on its way to becoming the pace-setter for the middle market. That uphill battle was all but won. But even before the *Mail*'s future was certain, Vere was casting about for his next big challenge. He would have liked to have a Sunday title as successful as the *Mail* and this led him to try to acquire the *Observer*. But he was defeated, to the extent that his competitors believed the matter was finished, when in fact the idea of a successful Sunday newspaper was only beginning to become a continuing preoccupation with him.

In the meantime Vere turned his attentions to the evening market. In 1977 the *Evening News* was a constant drain on Associated's resources. It was a newspaper that had never found its niche, a loss maker that showed no signs of ever really paying its own way, much less making it into profitability. The demands of the unions, of course, were making it almost impossible for the *Evening News* to survive, but that wasn't all. Television and the broadcasting media were eating into the evening market as well.

Then there was the problem of the *Evening News* itself. Casually identified as 'a cockney newspaper', the *News* was distinctly working-class and therefore less appealing to advertisers than its upmarket competitor, the *Evening Standard*, which was owned by Beaverbrook Newspapers. It was said that newsagents could identify which of the two evening newspapers an approaching customer would buy simply by the way he was dressed.

Yet Vere was attached to the *News*, aware of its nostalgic place in the annals of Harmsworth newspaper history. It had been Alfred Harmsworth's first newspaper, an ailing Conservative news sheet that was three days away from closure when, in 1894, Alfred and his brother Harold took it over. They paid £25,000, a waste of money according to the journalistic pundits of the time, who predicted the two inexperienced brothers would soon come a cropper. But Alfred and Harold, with the help of their entrepreneurial partner Kennedy Jones, transformed the *Evening News* into a paying proposition and, more important, gained an understanding of the rudiments of production and distribution that would eventually lead to their dominance in Fleet Street.

But even though Vere Harmsworth loved the *News*, he knew that in the fiercely competitive market of 1977 two evening newspapers could not survive. Either the *News* or the *Evening Standard* would have to fold. The outcome Vere envisaged was to merge the two titles, creating a single profitable newspaper that united the best characteristics of each. He saw the chance for both Associated and Beaverbrook Newspapers to derive long-term benefits from the deal. That was the stated agenda.

Privately Vere remembered only too well that Beaverbrook Newspapers was Associated's main competitor. He was still sore that, in 1971, his inheritance had very nearly been bartered away by his father and his managers, by merging the *Mail* with the *Express*. If the deal had gone ahead, the *Daily Express* would essentially have gobbled up the *Mail*, Vere would have lost his stronghold in the newspaper industry and the Harmsworths would have gone down in history as having suffered defeat at the hands of the Aitkens. It was a close call and Vere still viewed Beaverbrook Newspapers with suspicion. In the long term, he believed the only way to insure the stability and security of the *Mail* was either to kill Beaverbrook Newspapers or to buy it.

He would have liked to kill it. Failing that, joining forces with them, with Associated in the ascendant position, was the next best thing. So he, Mick Shields and John Winnington-Ingram devised a plan that would give Associated the upper hand.

Secret negotiations began in January 1977 and by 3 February, with Lord Goodman acting as mediator between the two rival firms, an agreement was hammered out. Associated would pay £5 million 'for the goodwill of the *Evening Standard* title', plus an amount equivalent to the net book value of the newspaper at completion. Associated then would gain editorial control of the surviving evening newspaper. They would pay half the redundancy costs for closing the *News*, estimated at £4.3 million, and later buy 50 per cent of a jointly owned printing plant, which would be called Fleet Street Printers, now owned solely by Beaverbrook Newspapers. The plant would then take over the printing of the *Daily Express*, the *Daily Mail*, the *Sunday Express* and the surviving evening newspaper.

It was an offer Beaverbrook Newspapers, which had recently bought new presses, could not afford to refuse. In the seven months before January 1977 it had sustained a £1.5 million loss, but with annual losses expected to soar to between £4 and £5 million. And because Beaverbrook himself had made no effort to diversify before his death in 1964, 99 per cent of the revenue of Beaverbrook Newspapers came exclusively from the newspapers themselves. But both the *Daily Express* and the *Evening Standard* were losing money; only the *Sunday Express* could be said to be generating a healthy revenue. As Jocelyn Stevens, managing director for Beaverbrook at the time, explained the situation,

> Beaverbrook Newspapers was sinking. The banks were not prepared to bankroll us unless we made all the shares voting, and if all the A and B shares had got votes, then the Aitkens would have lost control.
>
> Sir Max Aitken had had several heart attacks, which were concealed, and he was gradually becoming less and less able. And there was no question about it, if the Beaverbrook Foundation in Canada were not prepared to help with money, then the company was in dire trouble.
>
> But the trustees explained they were prevented from helping by the terms of the trust deed. It was as if Beaverbrook didn't want the newspaper company to go on after his death. And we suddenly found ourselves no longer negotiating a deal with Associated Newspapers as equals, but fighting for our lives.

Stevens himself realised, however, that any truce between Beaverbrook and Associated would by necessity be an uneasy one since neither side could forget the decades of deadly competition between the two firms. Privately he referred to the Harmsworths and the Aitkens as the Montagues and the Capulets, even naming the file where he kept details of the deal by that name. At Associated, John Winnington-Ingram reported a similar situation, with Vere 'growing increasingly nervous about agreement with Beaverbrook. He kept saying over and over, "Am I being done? Am I being done?"'

Perhaps these circumstances were not the most propitious under which two companies sought to join operations for the mutual benefit of both.

During March and April, David English was spending 60 per cent of his time on the merger with Beaverbrook Newspapers and only 40 per cent on his editorial duties at the *Daily Mail*. But there was a very good reason for David's participation: David's man, Louis Kirby, was at the time editing the *Evening News*. Between the two of them, English and Kirby knew more about the evening market than anybody at Associated and it was widely assumed that Kirby would take over the merged paper, if negotiations between Associated and Beaverbrook succeeded.

Kirby had earned his spurs in 1971 by taking over from David on the *Daily Sketch* when David assumed the editorship of the *Daily Mail*. In 1974 Kirby had become editor of the *Evening News*, overseeing its changeover into a tabloid. But despite Kirby's high level of professionalism he hadn't been able to overcome the paper's problems. By 1977 the *Evening News* had a circulation of 536,000, well above the *Evening Standard*. But it had been the *Standard* that developed the highly lucrative classified ads section that was sustaining the newspaper. That and the fact that its 418,000 circulation was made up largely of ABC1 readers.

Most important, the *Standard* had been edited for seventeen years by the legendary Charles Wintour. Somewhat unusually for a Fleet Street editor, Wintour was a highly intellectual man who had earned first-class honours in English and History at Cambridge. He had put his personal imprint on the newspaper, having achieved a title with both style and substance. In the process he had become known in the industry as 'an editor's editor', attracting a highly desirable readership to the newspaper's pages. Among his protégés were Max Hastings, Trevor Grove, Magnus Linklater and Roy Wright, all of whom eventually went on to edit newspapers themselves. In terms of sheer talent and colour, Wintour had also made his mark. He had helped to develop, among others, the skills of Fay Maschler, Nicholas Coleridge, Sue Arnold, Jak, Valerie Grove, Nicolas Tomalin – the list went on ...

But Wintour was possessive of the *Evening Standard*, and in its defence he could be fiery and obdurate. In the early 1960s, when he was casting about for a successor, he decided upon Tom Pocock and for a time Pocock had difficulty convincing Wintour that he wasn't the man for the job. Pocock felt more comfortable as a writer and reporter, planning eventually to write books, and he refused Wintour's offer to become deputy editor of the *Standard*.

By the time the merger idea had become a serious consideration, Wintour had handed over to thirty-three-year-old Simon Jenkins, and Wintour himself had taken a less active position in Beaverbrook Newspapers, overseeing publication of the *Daily Express*. Nevertheless, once he perceived that the *Evening Standard* was in play, he suddenly became a force to be reckoned with.

In a way, Associated Newspapers never knew what hit them. Upon discovering the bare bones of the deal, Wintour did not mince words. He wrote to Lord Goodman on 18 March, 'The point which concerns me is the identity of the surviving evening newspaper.' He continued,

> If it is to be the *Evening Standard*, then there are no problems. The present editor and editorial staff can perfectly well maintain the character and quality and integrity of the paper under different ownership and management.
>
> If, however, the survivor under the scheme were to be the *Evening News*, then a great injustice is contemplated and an act which is clearly contrary to the public interest...
>
> If therefore the deal involved closure of the *Evening Standard*, I would clearly have to oppose it...

Wintour had been greatly disturbed by 'The Night of the Long White Envelopes' and he determined the fate that befell the old *Daily Mail* was not going to be shared by the *Evening Standard*.

But Vere Harmsworth was eager to placate Wintour, and there followed a series of dinners, luncheons and conversations between Jenkins and Kirby, Wintour and Harmsworth, English and Kirby and Wintour and Jenkins and Harmsworth that culminated in a five-page memorandum sent by Wintour to Harmsworth. It was clear from the tone that Wintour was personally taking up the negotiations on behalf of Beaverbrook Newspapers, although he had no brief to do so. But such was the power of his personality that Associated opted to deal with his demands.

Essentially, Wintour wanted to keep the staff of the *Evening Standard* intact and, after discussion, Harmsworth agreed in theory to an 80/20 per cent staffing ratio in favour of the *Standard*. Wintour was unable to take on board the fact that this was a great concession on the part of the *Daily Mail* proprietor who had himself envisioned something like a 50/50 cut between the *News* and *Standard* staffs. But Wintour kept on insisting the staff of the merged newspaper had to be 100 per cent from the *Standard*.

What Harmsworth refused to agree was Wintour's demand that the new editor be Simon Jenkins. At a luncheon that included both Jenkins and Kirby, the two sides lined up.

Harmsworth's courteous manner was no help to him in convincing Wintour that Jenkins was not his man. His soft-spoken objection was subtle, belying his stubborn intentions. In the first place Harmsworth would never agree to having his choice of editor dictated to him by anyone else, and most especially by someone in the Beaverbrook camp. Throughout his career Vere would consider and often appoint someone else's candidate, and he certainly welcomed input. But for Wintour or anyone else to dictate an appointment, that was a categorical impossibility, given Harmsworth's character.

But Vere's quiet objections didn't stop Wintour from presenting Jenkins as the best candidate, even in front of Louis Kirby. Lewis Chester and Jonathan Fenby recorded Wintour's astonishing attack in their book *The Fall of the House of Beaverbrook*:

> Wintour proceeded to list Jenkins's great qualities against what he suggested were the more modest accomplishments of Lou Kirby. [Jenkins] was younger, abler, a better writer and better in appearance, a fact deemed relevant as editors frequently had to appear on television...
>
> 'It was', according to one of those present, 'like the assassination of Marat by the occupants of the asylum at Charenton, with Kirby as Marat.'
>
> Harmsworth frequently said: 'Oh, dear.'

Adding injury to insult, Wintour later that afternoon rang David English and said he would agree to an 85/15 per cent split between the two papers. But Jenkins must edit the paper.

Years after the fact, Vere Harmsworth admitted he had never for a moment entertained the idea of retaining Simon Jenkins as editor of a merged evening newspaper. Of Wintour's insistent outburst, he said,

> It was a bit embarrassing actually, so I had to rather diplomatically tell him that there was no way in which Jenkins – no way I would accept Simon –...
>
> So that must have been why Wintour was so vitriolic. Privately, I didn't think Jenkins would be the right editor, and David and I were quite in agreement, and no, I wasn't having him.

But Wintour was like a dog with a bone. David and Vere admitted to one another that in a way they admired his spirit, David even suggesting to Wintour that he might himself be the very man to edit the merged evening paper. But Wintour was made to understand there was no way he was going to name the editor for a newspaper owned by Associated Newspapers, even if the deal came unglued as a result.

In any case, Wintour's dream ticket would have been impossible to implement, because the unions at Associated would never have accepted a deal that substituted the entire staff of the opposing title for their own. Just to prove their mettle, the *Evening News* journalists speedily went out on strike, demonstrating in the process that Kirby and his deputy, John Leese, were seasoned newspaper professionals. They got out the paper almost single-handedly, using a few stringers and wire copy.

In the meantime, Associated and Beaverbrook Newspapers scheduled a secret meeting at the end of April, in the basement of the Bonnington Hotel on Southampton Row, a suitably unpretentious environment in which to reach the final terms of the deal. But in the meantime, and unbeknownst to the Associated team, Charles Wintour had been in touch with James Goldsmith, who said he was willing to put his considerable resources into an alternative bid for the *Evening Standard*.

The night before the fateful meeting Jocelyn Stevens arranged to meet Goldsmith for dinner. At the same time, across town, Vere Harmsworth and Simon Jenkins were meeting at Vere's flat in Eaton Square. So at about the same time that Jocelyn was agreeing to put Goldsmith's offer before the board, in effect scuppering Beaverbrook Newspaper's deal with Associated, Vere was explaining to Jenkins that Kirby was going to be the editor of the newly merged newspaper.

After leaving Eaton Square, Jenkins wandered around for about an hour before calling Wintour to report what Harmsworth had confided, somewhat of two minds about whether it was proper to do so. But Jenkins wasn't the only one feeling ambivalent that night.

Vere Harmswotth was getting cold feet about actually consummating the deal with the *Daily Mail*'s decades-old rivals. For one thing he didn't believe Jocelyn Stevens wanted to bring the agreement to fruition and he continued to expect the worst.

I wasn't so keen any more on doing a deal with the *Express* because the Aitkens were being so bloody difficult. Max and Jocelyn were not the sort of people I wanted to be in business with.

I don't know what the hell got into me. Pat was away and instead of going to bed I decided to go out. I went to Raffles nightclub in the King's Road. There was Emma Soames. And I sat and I talked. Drinking and drinking and I got very drunk, and I told her about this secret meeting [the next day at the Bonnington] where the deal would be done.

And she must have told Wintour... [that night]. The next day, when we all met in the Bonnington, Jocelyn was late and there were all these vans parading up and down. And they did that overnight, and it had all started when I had got drunk and made that remark to Emma Soames.

Subconsciously, I didn't want to do the deal. And years later, I said to Emma, 'I owe you one. If it hadn't been for you, I would have never got that bloody *Evening Standard* without the Aitkens.'

All his life, Vere Harmsworth believed Charles Wintour and Jocelyn Stevens had arranged to have a fleet of vans blocking Southampton Row on 28 April, the day of the meeting that would finalise the deal between Associated and Beaverbrook Newspapers. The havoc those vehicles wreaked that fateful afternoon went a long way towards dismantling the carefully constructed agreement that had been in the making since the beginning of the year.

So was it Emma Soames who, as Vere believed, rushed to tell Wintour the deal was about to be signed and thereby subverted the agreement?

Or was it Vere Harmsworth himself, who inadvertently scuppered his own deal by getting drunk and spilling the beans to Emma Soames?

Or was it Charles Wintour, whose stalwart opposition to any editorial change at the *Evening Standard* caused him to prevent the merger of the two companies?

Or was it the machinations of the wily and flamboyant Jocelyn Stevens as he positioned for his firm's best advantage?

Or was it James Goldsmith who, by making an offer, tore the deal irrevocably apart?

Or was there some other secret reason why the *Daily Mail* and the *Daily Express* and all their sister publications are not joined in perpetuity at the hip, thus changing the history of Fleet Street for ever?

TEN

THE OLD DAVID WAS NO MORE

It turned out that Charles Wintour had nothing to do with the assembling of the vans outside the Bonnington Hotel on the morning of 28 April 1977. 'I am not the man who did it,' Wintour said years later.

Jocelyn Stevens also denied involvement and, indeed, that morning he received a call from Goldsmith who was ready to make an offer. So Stevens called on him on his way to the Bonnington and Goldsmith handed over a written bid of £5 million pounds for the *Standard* saying, 'You're bound to report this to your board because it is material.'

After this encounter, Jocelyn carried on to the Bonnington and struggled to get into the meeting.

> I got kicked. It was one of the two times I was actually kicked on to the ground by members of the trade unions. And it was the *Evening Standard* staff who felt very badly about the deal.

The near riot taking place outside the Bonnington came as a surprise both to Stevens and to Wintour. But throughout the years Vere persisted in his belief that these two had engineered it.

Lord Goodman also believed Jocelyn was the perpetrator. He remembered having to have his way cleared by police who rushed him through the angry crowd of union members. In his mind, only one man could have organised such a disruption overnight and that was Jocelyn. John Winnington-Ingram, too, believed it was Stevens and Wintour.

Whoever had done it, Jocelyn's arrival and his announcement of a formal offer from Goldsmith finished off the meeting and the Associated team straggled out of the hotel. But Vere, who had been close friends with Goldsmith for years, knew he didn't actually have the stomach for the newspaper business. For years he had viewed with tolerance 'Jimmy's' need for publicity and he suspected that, in the long run, that was the true motive behind his friend's offer. Vere decided to double and redouble his efforts to secure the *Standard*. After the insults and double-dealing he had endured, if anything, he was more determined than ever.

It fell to David English to renew relations with Max Aitken and, after a cordial lunch a short time later, English was able to report back to Harmsworth that Aitken had been personally aggrieved by the events taking place outside the Bonnington. He hadn't given up on a merger with Associated, he told English, and it looked very much as if it were possible to revive their deal. In the meantime, just as Vere had predicted, James Goldsmith's offer was looking softer and softer.

This was the backdown Vere had been expecting. But now other events had been put into motion. Tiny Rowlands had expressed an interest in buying into Beaverbrook Newspapers, Rupert Murdoch was stepping up to the plate and Victor Matthews had quietly indicated that Trafalgar House might make an offer. The stakes had risen considerably. Now it looked as if Aitken might be persuaded to offload the entire enterprise. Sir Max himself initiated a meeting with Harmsworth to try to persuade him to jump back into the bidding.

It was against this background that the *Daily Mail*, after weeks of investigation, broke a story destined to have a far-reaching and unanticipated effect upon any designs Vere Harmsworth had upon the *Evening Standard* or Beaverbrook Newspapers – the British Leyland slush fund story, published on 19 May 1977.

In the story, one of the most notorious of the age, the *Daily Mail* accused Britain's state-owned car makers of imposing a 'worldwide bribery web' in an effort to win overseas orders. The newspaper spoke of 'damning evidence of large-scale corporate corruption'.

In addition, in a box labelled 'Men … and letters', Lord Ryder, chairman of the National Enterprise Board, and Mr Alex Park, the chief executive of British Leyland, were pictured, along with a quote from a letter attributed to Lord Ryder. It purported to implicate the Secretary of State in setting up 'Special Account Arrangements'.

The byline above the story was that of Stewart Steven.

This was not Steven's first run-in with controversy. Five years earlier, in 1972, when he was foreign editor for the *Daily Express*, he had written an extraordinary story headlined MARTIN BORMANN ALIVE.

The British Leyland exposé bore all the hallmarks of Steven's exposé of Martin Bormann's whereabouts. But, like the Bormann story, it would turn out to be false. In this case it would cost Associated Newspapers immense pay-offs in libel damages. It very nearly cost David English the editorship of the *Daily Mail*.

It also probably prevented Vere Harmsworth from getting the *Evening Standard* for many years.

On Friday, 20 May the *Daily Mail* continued its exposé of British Leyland, leading with the headline SLUSH MONEY: THE SECRET BANK DEALS. But a companion piece on the front page admitted that Lord Ryder had denied writing the letter published by the *Mail* the day before. Despite Ryder's denial, the *Mail* was sticking to its guns. At least publicly.

Inside Northcliffe House, however, doubts were beginning to surface. At about ten o'clock on Thursday morning, only hours after the publication of the initial story, David English walked into Room Six, the office of his assistant editor John Womersley, holding a small piece of yellow tape-machine paper. It was the Press Association 'rush' denying the story was true and David wanted to know 'what it was all about'.

He was pulling John Womersley off his regular duties and putting him in charge of an internal investigation to be certain the essentials of the Leyland story were correct and, if they weren't, to ascertain who was at fault. At the time, Womersley had the impression that David wasn't particularly perturbed and still retained full confidence in the story. This would change.

For his part, Womersley was surprised to find himself in charge of the investigation, considering he had not been consulted about the story before its publication, an oddity, since he was assistant editor in charge of News. In fact, practically no one besides the original investigative team knew anything about the publication of the exposé, not Gordon Greig, who was the political correspondent, nor Ted Jeffery, the night editor.

Jeffery had found out about it in a circuitous manner. His son David had been recently hired by British Leyland and worked in the same department as the man who was Stewart Steven's informant. By strange coincidence, the day before the *Daily Mail* printed the story, Jeffery had gone to the headquarters to take his son out to lunch. When he went in to fetch him, Jeffery had to leave his name with Reception. Later, when British Leyland began to investigate their own staff, suspicion immediately fell on David Jeffery, who was called in by the management to account for himself. He was quickly exonerated because the facts pointed elsewhere, but it was slightly unnerving to begin a job under such circumstances.

Meanwhile, Ted Jeffery returned from his lunch, and soon afterwards was taken aside by Stewart Steven and told they were doing a big story on British Leyland the next morning. 'And it did seem ironic to me at the time', Jeffery said later, 'that I had virtually just come from British Leyland Headquarters when he told me that.'

The reason for all the secrecy, of course, was to prevent leaks, either to British Leyland, which might have tried to put an injunction on the articles, or to the *Mail*'s competitors, who would have tried to put together a spoiler. In stories of this type, keeping the lid on was standard operating procedure. But this time the secrecy deprived the investigating team of the expertise of their colleagues.

One man who did know about the *Mail*'s exposé was Jonathan Holborow. Holborow was news editor on the *Mail* and had originally brought in the 'Leyland Dossier'. He had received a call from an informant and set up the original meeting to look into the matter. Afterwards, Holborow took the dossier to deputy editor Peter Grover and Grover read it. He said, 'This is very interesting' and Holborow said, 'I'm a bit worried about the signature of a Lord who would sign himself "Don Ryder".'

Three days later David called Jonathan in saying, 'I want to give this story to Stewart Steven to run and you're off it.' Later on, quite coincidentally, when the campaign started, Jonathan had taken the day off. When he came back into the office on the Friday, there sat Stewart and David, looking glum. 'David was all pale and haggard,' Jonathan said later, 'and he flashed that brilliant "David" smile. "Ah," he said, "the man who got off the jumbo jet just before it crashed."'

Later, when people asked Holborow what his input into the story had been, he invariably answered, 'It was my day off.' The phrase became a catch phrase around the newsroom and took on a life of its own.

Now Womersley set to work on his investigation, convinced it would take a great deal of time and painstaking effort to establish the truth. But on the contrary, he was surprised by how quickly he was able to show that the key piece of evidence in the exposé, a letter allegedly sent by Lord Ryder to Alex Park, was a forgery. This was the letter that discussed at length the setting up of 'Special Account Arrangements'. Said Womersley,

> It took just *two days* to establish, independent of the NEB and British Leyland denials...
>
> Handwriting experts challenged the signature. The letterhead didn't ring true. Typewriter specialists ruled that the letter was a concoction. Even my secretary spotted three spelling mistakes. A police contact reported, 'Not only is it a forgery but a pretty amateur one at that.'

But if that was true, how could Stewart Steven and his investigative team have been so completely taken in? Years later, in ruminating as to the reasons, Steven chalked down the whole fiasco to an atmosphere of arrogance that had permeated every level of operation at the *Daily Mail*.

> There was unquestionably an arrogance at the *Daily Mail* at that time. We were so successful and had run so many wonderful investigations that

almost all of us believed that we could do no wrong. The *Daily Mail* has never been as hot as it then was. So I think that was part of it.

But there were other reasons why the letter seemed genuine. Steven and his investigative team had been given access to a special internal report that purported to detail the workings of the secret slush fund. The informant who was offering the material wanted to refer to himself as the 'White Rabbit', refusing to give Steven his real name. Later, under pressure, he revealed himself as Bart. But the team's checks of incidents in the report showed verification for each of them.

Eventually, it became clear that the informant was himself working for British Leyland, and he had been put in charge of writing a report on the topic. Once the team established that fact, they believed they were on safe ground. According to Steven,

> Therefore, we had every reason to believe that the document was a correct document because he [the informant] had absolute access to it because it was a report. So at that point we thought, 'Well, it must be right, everything must be right.'

But to John Womersley, 'the investigator of the investigation', it seemed another phenomenon was at work. 'Where did the whole of British Leyland go wrong?' he asked years later.

> It went wrong in my opinion because the experienced news and investigative journalists on this story believed that it was true from the very beginning... Once you start down that path, then all the pitfalls, all the stones you can trip over, all the signposts you should look at, all the cautionary warnings you should be seeing – you become blind to them.
>
> I think the facts we had... maybe they were investigated to stand them up, maybe they were not investigated to knock them down.

Stewart Steven had seconded three reporters for the British Leyland story: Dickie Herd, Frank Thompson and Peter Cliff, all of them experienced, capable newsmen. Herd said,

> Stewart Steven was running this investigation. We were doing the legwork and he was saying, 'How are you getting on?'
>
> And we would answer, 'Yeah, we saw this guy today.' We kept Stewart abreast of what was happening. It came to the time we were 100 per cent certain.

One morning I typed a note...'We are happy there is a slush fund, and this proves it, and now we are at the stage *where we must confront the boss* [his emphasis].' We'd got all the proof, and now we have to ask him about the letter and what had he got to say in answer to our allegation that there had been a slush fund operation. And we sent it up. Stewart said, 'Sure, go ahead.'

And twenty minutes later, he came running down and said, 'Don't worry about the confrontation, the editor will do that.'

We splashed it and had the centre spread the following night.

It was true that David English had made the decision to confront Lord Ryder himself. But when Ryder was unavailable to answer his calls, English began to worry that British Leyland were on to the investigation and were preparing to get an injunction against the publication of the story. With pressure mounting to publish, he decided to go with it. That was one version of events.

Inside the newsroom there was another. It suggested that David had acted in haste because he was angry at a scoop the *Daily Express* had got, and had decided to run the story to regain the news initiative.

Whatever the case, the *Mail* rushed ahead to publication on a Thursday, which surprised most of the old hands on the newspaper. For it was customary to start an exposé like this one on a Monday in order to derive the maximum attention throughout the week. To Dickie Herd's mind, the haste to publish, without the customary confrontation in which the subject of the investigation has a chance to deny the charges against him, lay at the heart of the disaster.

One of the great ironies of the fiasco was that during their investigation, Stewart Steven and his team were holed up in secret headquarters in Northcliffe House. No one knew where they were and no one had access to them. Their headquarters? Room One.

Room One was the spacious office the legendary Viscount Northcliffe had specially designed and constructed for his use over sixty years before. It was a beautifully appointed office space, with an impressive library shelving handsome leather-covered volumes. Sage inscriptions were embossed in gold leaf above the glass-fronted shelves that held the most hallowed works of Western Civilisation. It was here that the great Northcliffe received his visitors. 'Big rooms for big ideas,' he would explain, as he welcomed them into his inner sanctum.

Within three days, the letter from Lord Ryder to Alex Park detailing 'Special Account Arrangements' was exposed as a forgery. The *Mail*'s informant was identified as Graham Barton, a British Leyland executive, and under enormous pressure he publicly confessed to the forgery. Embarrassingly for David English, it was also widely reported that the *Daily Mail* had paid him with a suitcase full of money, in small bills, variously said to be between £15,000 and £17,000.

Now the fraudulent exposé was taking on new life as the *Daily Mail* became the focus of the story. The press was having a field day, but instead of British Leyland executives in the hot spot, that chair was occupied by the editor of the *Mail* himself.

Calls for English's resignation were mounting, as the *Daily Express* and other competitors gloated over the increasingly sticky situation the *Mail* now found itself in.

In Parliament, Labour MP Ian Wrigglesworth gained the support of 115 Labour Scottish Nationalist and Liberal MPs in calling for English's resignation. In his public statement Wrigglesworth said,

> No figure in public life could stay in office following an incident such as this.
>
> Whether Mr English or Mr Steven were politically motivated is irrelevant. The central point is that the editor made a gross error of judgement which damaged the public interest.

The Labour MP for Luton West, Brian Sedgemore, entertained motions, one of which was to petition the Attorney-General to ask whether he intended to prosecute David English for criminal libel, or sedition, a legal concept long discredited in the civilised countries of the world. It held that some actions of libel involving the intent to overthrow the government were so heinous they had to be punished as criminal acts. In England the law was in disuse but remained on the books. Now it was being dredged up again.

Pressure was mounting on David English, but he took the view that if heads rolled on this one, the survival of the *Daily Mail* itself was in question. In the uphill battle for survival since he had taken over the *Mail* in 1971, his name had become so closely identified with the newspaper that if he went, the newspaper might follow in his wake.

Thus when Stewart Steven offered his resignation, David refused it. Years later, in explaining his generosity to Steven, he would say that, as editor, the final responsibility was his own and that was another reason why he had not accepted Steven's resignation. But refusing to pass the buck resulted in David's facing more heat himself.

And face the heat he did. Only his closest associates realised it, but when David came under stress he lost his voice. Now he became subject to a massive throat infection, was unable to talk and had to go home to recover. But even there he found no respite.

The *Daily Express* and the *Mail*'s other competitors were highlighting obvious mistakes in the letter, and the pressure on English to resign was becoming irresistible.

Many years later, having survived the fiasco and prospered, David English put his particular spin on the events surrounding the Leyland affair. It was typical of him to treat the matter with levity, converting it into the kind of psychodrama that motivated him to overcome his enemies and prevail throughout his career. It became one of David's great set pieces, in which the possibility that he might have been indicted for criminal libel and sedition was played for humour and hilarity:

> Under this law you could be arrested and you were taken to this cell under Big Ben at Parliament's pleasure, and the theory is the constant bonging which is right next to you sends you crazy and you never recover...
>
> Their argument was that I had deliberately done this forgery in order to bring down the Labour Government.
>
> I began saying, as all people under pressure say, I was beginning to crack. I had said to Vere right at the beginning, 'I will resign because I've cocked this up,' and he is the one who said, right at the beginning, 'No, you mustn't resign because that will destroy the paper. We won't be able to find another editor. You made an honest mistake, and I won't let you resign.'
>
> But this night I was getting near cracking, and I said to Grover, everyone was around at my house, I said, 'I can't take any more. I shall clear off to America and that's it. I've had it.'
>
> So Grover called Harmsworth in the South of France, who had gone to a restaurant, and when he rang, they said, 'Well, Mr Harmsworth is sitting down to supper.'
>
> So he came to the kitchen phone and he said, 'I'm just having my dinner, is it important?'
>
> Grover said, 'Well, yes, it's very important, David wants to resign.'
>
> 'Resign?' Vere said, 'Absolute nonsense. You tell him he can't resign.'
>
> 'Look you've got to talk to him.'
>
> 'No, no, just tell him he can't resign.' And I got on the phone. 'Look I'm having my supper,' he said. 'I can't have it disturbed. No, no, no, I don't want those potatoes.'
>
> And then the phone hung up, and there I was left. So that was that. It kind of brought me down, and I was able to take a few more days of it.

The story took on legendary status inside the *Daily Mail*, as it was told and retold throughout the newsroom.

But if the anecdote told a great deal about the workings of David

English's mind, it also showed a great deal about the strange relations between Vere Harmsworth and his editor. For one thing, David throve on dramatic situations, being theatrical and histrionic by his very nature. It was like him to take the entire crisis upon his own head because, ultimately, he had great faith in his ability to survive.

Vere, on the other hand, was more stable and perhaps more stolid, but he too had a colourful side and didn't particularly like being upstaged by his editor. *He* enjoyed centre stage. But he stopped short of taking crises upon his own head because he had no interest whatsoever in exposing himself to danger. His way of resisting any onslaught perpetrated by David English was to step up his eccentricity, becoming more and more like Colonel Blimp, a character he referred to often in his everyday conversations. He was quite a showman in this role.

But David had no stop mechanism in trying to influence Vere and he would drive him to the very edge in order to get his own way. Eventually, although Vere could be evasive and tricky, in the long run he always gave in. But somehow Harmsworth always got his way as well.

David English never intended to resign over British Leyland and Vere Harmsworth never intended him to. Said Harmsworth many years later,

> It never *entered my mind* to let David English go, *not for a solitary second.* There was a great furore in the House of Commons demanding that David English should be dismissed. But they could demand whatever they liked. It wouldn't get anywhere with me...
>
> It was a good news story. And if British Leyland hadn't been bribing the Arabs or whoever, well, then, they bloody well should have been, like everybody else has to do. You can't do business in those parts of the world if you don't.

The reporters on the *Daily Mail* considered David English infallible. The catchphrase that David could always do your job better than you could continued to circulate among staff members. And it was not an empty recitation; *everybody believed it.*

It was not surprising, then, that political editor Gordon Greig later remembered British Leyland as

> the worst blow to the collective confidence that the *Mail* has ever been through in the twenty years of my career.
>
> I mean, we were absolutely terrified and didn't know where to look. Before he left for the South of France, Vere had called us all in and he said that Stewart had offered his resignation. Stewart was there and he walked out of the room. I think he was suspended for three to six months.

In a sense, in reporting, there are always all sorts of things that go wrong, but in terms of all the reporters thinking, 'God, what have we done?' and 'What's going to happen?' this was quite the worst.

'How could we have been so slipshod not to have checked and checked again?' That was the question. It was like an enormous attack on our competence.

Even though David English assumed responsibility for the fiasco and volunteered to go, nobody on staff wanted him to and a round robin quickly circulated to prevent him. Many believed that the evidence unearthed by the reporters pointed to the underlying truth of the *Mail*'s allegations, but the forged letter, 'the poison cherry on the cake', destroyed their validity.

Despite the faith of his colleagues in the facts of the story, Dickie Herd, the chief investigative reporter in charge of the case, was to become increasingly embittered over the events that followed the affair. While he and the other reporters on the investigative team were exonerated in formal terms by the administration of the *Daily Mail*, and 'no heads rolled', he believed each of them felt subtly pressurised afterwards. So far as Herd was concerned, his residual bitterness grew into outright anger after David English appeared on *The Editor's TV Programme* on the BBC a month later. David had obviously prepared a scenario he believed would satisfy everyone.

'Looking at it generally,' the presenter asked, 'in terms of investigative journalism, are there any safer ways, less hazardous ways, of confirming the authenticity of documents which you wish to produce in evidence?'

English's answer haunted Herd until his death in 1995. David began by saying that true investigative reporters were few and far between. They were 'a very special breed of person, a very particular type of reporter'. David said that their procedures were greatly different from 'ordinary' reporters'. English then held up for emulation Harry Longmuir, who had formerly worked for the *Mail* but who was now reporting in the United States.

We had a very distinguished and very talented man called Harry Longmuir who did all our investigations and won a number of awards for them. And he was very thorough. And he had a particular mind, more like a policeman's mind or a lawyer's mind, I think, than a journalist's mind. He never rushed into things. And he was an expert in checking things...

We never made any mistakes with Longmuir. And I think I now realise that you do have to pick a very special person. You can take an excellent reporter and you can't necessarily make him an investigative reporter.

He continued to praise Longmuir's 'scientific' methods, saying, 'If you're Longmuir, you check through sources, you use all sorts of scientific means and you approach it like a lawyer.' As to other reporters, they *should* be acquainted with these methods, but too often weren't and, essentially, their journalistic training was inadequate.

Herd believed this left him and his team carrying the can. Even though publicly they had been supported, everyone who watched television that night understood the subtext of what David was saying. 'Everyone in Fleet Street knew', Herd said later, 'that, in short, the reporters weren't sufficiently thorough.'

Throughout his life, Herd prided himself on never publicly refuting David's statement. At the time, he refused to answer any questions from anybody about what had happened. But in his own mind his investigative team had 'got more material than the *Washington Post* had with "Deep Throat"'.

But it's an ill wind that blows nobody any good. One effect of David English's appearance on television that June was that Vere Harmsworth personally contacted Harry Longmuir in the United States where he had worked for several newspapers including the less-than-prestigious *National Enquirer*. Harmsworth had seen David English on the programme and he asked Longmuir to return, with a significant increase in his salary.

It was an offer Harry couldn't afford to refuse.

But insofar as the *Daily Mail*'s investigative reporting was concerned, that was placed on the back burner. It was expensive. It played havoc with work schedules. It could result in enormous libel damages being paid out in cases when things went wrong.

Slowly but surely, the tone of the *Daily Mail* changed and intensive investigations slowed to a trickle. It was cheaper and easier to fill the paper with celebrity hype and the reading public couldn't get enough of it. In the same way that the *Sun* piggybacked on the working-class heroes of television and films, the *Daily Mail* began picking up on the celebrities that were the favourites of the middle class it catered to. In a way, the move was inevitable. But the Leyland scandal hastened it.

Those on the staff who were perceptive monitored another change after British Leyland. In the face of the beating he had suffered at the hands of his competitors and the government, David English hardened. His openness was eclipsed and he ceased putting his trust in those around him. As the years passed, the private man disappeared behind an image of public success.

The old David was no more.

ELEVEN

BETTER THAN THE LOT OF THEM

When Vere Harmsworth refused to accept David English's resignation he made the right decision. He wasn't likely to see the likes of David's mercurial talent again and he knew it. Not only that, but it would have been unseemly to let David go when he had given six years of his life in backbreaking labour to rebuilding the fortunes of the ailing *Daily Mail*.

Then, too, the relentless calls for David's resignation and the venomous attacks he sustained over British Leyland were a direct outcome of his incredible success on Fleet Street. David English was outstripping the competition to the extent that bringing him down, by any means, was highly desirable in the eyes of the cut-throat competitors of the Street.

Vere understood as well as anyone how all this worked. He had himself been forced to learn how to roll with the punches. He would have been a fool to give in to the *Daily Mail*'s rivals and get rid of David.

There was also the question of the survival of the newspaper. If Harmsworth had accepted David English's resignation, *would* the *Daily Mail* have survived? It might have. But it would have been chancy. Why should Vere take that chance if he could simply hold tight?

Another phenomenon was also at work. The dichotomy between the Right and the Left in Great Britain was and remains a massive divide, where men intent upon defeating the opposition take no prisoners. When David English returned from the United States where he had been the American correspondent for the *Daily Express*, he had been appalled by the backwardness of the British economy. All his life he remained starstruck with the progressive, 'go-ahead' attitude of the Americans. At that time Britain's workforce was showing its disaffection with industry and commerce by participating in frequent paralysing strikes and the country seemed on its way down. English saw the American way of life as an exit from hard times.

Thus did he defect from the left-wing background of his youth, becoming the leading newspaper advocate for a more entrepreneurial England. His new belief system tallied increasingly with the Conservatives, with whom the Harmsworths had always been identified.

David had found his natural home on the historically right-wing *Daily Mail*.

But in so doing and by his own admission, David was rapidly becoming a 'demon figure' for the Left, and when the Left caught him in an untenable position they were relentless in their savagery. No matter if Parliament believed David English *was* trying to bring down the government, in truth a patent absurdity, Vere would have had to take leave of his senses to give in to his traditional opponents in the Labour Party.

Defying the criticism was the only course he could have followed. But Harmsworth could make an art form of doing nothing. Phlegmatic and eccentric, difficult and impenetrable, he was beginning to emerge as a figure of emotional stability. He had strength of character that belied his playboy antics and those who dismissed him as a dilettante were in for a surprise. He was a determined character, stubborn in the extreme, and he could take the heat.

That heat intensified when Labour politicians publicly remembered the flirtation of Vere's grandfather Harold with Oswald Mosley during the 1930s. This was inevitable and, whenever a row erupted, it was typical of Harmsworth's opponents to recall the famous headline, HURRAH FOR THE BLACKSHIRTS, that was published in the *Daily Mail* on 8 January 1934.

Going back even further to 1924, Labour seized upon the *Mail*'s publication of the Zinoviev letter, an infamous forgery that had prevented the first Labour Government from gaining power in the election campaign that year. According to Labour, the British Leyland fiasco had to be a like attempt to bring down the government. Stopping short of accusing the *Mail* editor and proprietor of actual sedition, the Prime Minister, James Callaghan, did call the *Mail*'s journalism 'contemptible', saying the newspaper had 'reduced journalism to a lower level than I can remember for many years'.

But now Vere, always slow to anger, was roused and he quickly countered by referring to the recent press row over the appointment of Callaghan's son-in-law Peter Jay as ambassador to the United States. 'I reject utterly Mr Callaghan's allegation of vindictiveness,' Harmsworth said, 'despite my understanding of his feelings, as this deplorable but honest mistake has followed so closely upon the furore occasioned by the appointment of Mr Peter Jay.'

It was 25 May and Charles Wintour happened to be listening to the radio that morning. There he heard a complete report on this angry exchange between the Prime Minister and the proprietor of the *Daily Mail*. 'I thought it was very unfair that the *Daily Mail* had attacked Peter

Jay in this way, considering the origins of the proprietor,' Wintour said later.

> It was just very fortunate that on that particular day I was billed to address the AA in tribute to the retiring Secretary General, and it all fitted in rather well. The press table was actually cheering every word. I felt very worked up, and I was, about the *Evening Standard*, of course, and Vere, because of his inheritance, was attempting to kill the *Standard*.
>
> And it was a direct attempt on my part to damage Vere.

Wintour told the AA that Vere had been right not to accept the resignation of David English over the Leyland affair. But, he continued, in trying to answer the Prime Minister's condemnation of the *Daily Mail*'s journalism as 'contemptible', Vere had 'dragged up the appointment of Mr Peter Jay as ambassador to Washington'.

> In other words he is smearing the charge of nepotism against the name of the Prime Minister. Why is Mr Vere Harmsworth chairman of Associated Newspapers? Why is he in a position to squander millions of his shareholders' money in an effort to force the *Evening Standard* out of business? ...
>
> May I suggest that the only reason why Mr Vere Harmsworth is chairman of Associated Newspapers is that he is the son of the second Lord Rothermere. And the second Lord Rothermere had the job because he was the son of the first Lord Rothermere. And the first Lord Rothermere had the *Daily Mail* because he was the brother of a real newspaper genius, Lord Northcliffe.
>
> Mr Jay is acknowledged by all to be a most brilliant man who is earning large sums entirely as a result of his own talents. Mr Harmsworth however is in a position to endanger the jobs of 1700 people in Fleet Street purely through a mere accident of birth ...

Years after the speech, Charles Wintour remained highly satisfied with himself for what he said about Vere Harmsworth that lunchtime at the AA: 'After I sat down, the chairman of the meeting said it was the best speech they had ever had at the AA lunch.'

Wintour went on record as saying that he had little or no respect for the type of journalism David English produced and found it personally distasteful. He thought he detected a nasty edge to the *Mail*'s style of journalism and that was one of the things that motivated him to act so forcefully in defence of the *Evening Standard*.

He was quick to admit, however, that he did 'get into a lot of hot water with Max Aitken over this. And at a board meeting, he censured me for not telling him about my speech at the AA in advance.'

Max had two reasons for resenting Wintour's comments. The first, of course, was that he himself had inherited the chairmanship of Beaverbrook Newspapers and the same charges that Wintour had levelled against Harmsworth could be levelled against *him*.

The second was more serious. He had worked hard to bring Associated Newspapers back to the negotiating table as bidders for Beaverbrook Newspapers and now his position was compromised.

Indeed, although Vere did eventually return, his heart was no longer in it. By now, Goldsmith was back in and, more dangerously, Rupert Murdoch had made a £10 million offer for Beaverbrook Newspapers, with considerable extra sweeteners for Max Aitken as well. But in the end Trafalgar House, run by Victor Matthews, won the corporation with a bid that amounted to just under £15 million. Before Aitken accepted their offer, he gave Associated Newspapers the chance to respond. Their response was silence.

It was speculated afterwards that Vere had become indifferent to gaining control of his old competition, that the attack waged by Wintour and the near riot at the Bonnington Hotel had taken away his desire to own Beaverbrook Newspapers, or the *Evening Standard*. But that was not really what was bothering Vere.

He believed that any attempt on his part to take over Beaverbrook Newspapers would inevitably meet with defeat at the hands of the Labour Government. Since British Leyland, the government made no secret of their animosity towards the *Daily Mail*, its editor and its proprietor. And Vere's chances of getting any kind of deal through were virtually nil.

Charles Wintour apart, the British Leyland affair had taken a terrific toll at Associated. There were no two ways about it, Vere Harmsworth had suffered a terrific defeat.

If the repercussions from the British Leyland affair had done serious damage to Associated Newspapers, David English was more than compensating for his lapse in another arena.

As everyone on the editorial staff knew, David was particularly astute at picking talent. It was one of his greatest gifts. When he turned this skill on to the national political scene, he realised he was witnessing an outstanding talent on the rise. It was David's genius to back this talent, making the *Daily Mail*'s aims and political goals if not synonymous with those of Margaret Thatcher, then very much allied to them.

For the past twenty years this attractive and intelligent woman, often derided for her humble beginnings as a shopkeeper's daughter, had been steadily working her way up the political hierarchy in the Conservative Party. Her rapid-fire style of oratory; her strongly held beliefs in thrift, independent thinking, hard work and the other homely virtues; her fearless criticism of the welfare state; all these characteristics made her a perfect candidate for the *Daily Mail*. It was David English's shrewd assessment of the unfolding political scene that led him to back her in her fight for the Conservative leadership against Ted Heath in 1975.

Stewart Steven, who was there when David decided to back Margaret Thatcher, said that at the beginning the decision had been strictly a journalistic one. 'David was first and foremost a newspaperman,' Steven said, 'and he saw Margaret Thatcher's bid for leadership as a great story.' Steven continued,

> Here was a woman going up the ladder and he wanted the *Mail* to support her. At first he had no real deep knowledge of her political stance, he just saw it as a great story.
>
> So Peter Grover and David and I went to Vere and suggested that the *Mail* put its entire support behind Margaret Thatcher, not on the basis of her 'right-wingedness' but because she was a woman and therefore somebody we should support.
>
> Vere immediately agreed and the *Daily Mail* put its support behind Margaret Thatcher instead of Ted Heath. At the time, it caused real consternation.

Over and above the story, however, was a philosophical likeness between editor and politician. David felt a personal kinship with Thatcher as someone not unlike himself. He had been raised in Bournemouth with middle-class values,* and here was someone who had made the same difficult climb he had. Margaret Thatcher was against the increasingly paralytic power of the trade unions, in favour of small business and shared the highly ethical background David had been raised with in his youth. It was little wonder he felt a sense of empathy with the woman and her goals.

Peter Wright, then a junior on the news desk, believed that 'David and the *Daily Mail* had a big personal influence on Thatcher and helped to create the climate that made her possible'. He said,

---

* See chapter 7 in *The Reluctant Press Lord* for an account of English's life.

David believed if you had a problem, you should fix it. And that applied to everything. But people didn't think that at the time. Britain was in the doldrums and people thought you couldn't do anything about it.

In Thatcher's camp, it hadn't escaped the notice of her advisers that their candidate seemed tailor-made for the *Daily Mail*. Bernard Ingham, Margaret Thatcher's press secretary during her eleven years as Prime Minister, said, 'She was so glamorous, and a star, and a female as well. All David's instincts were with her.' Ingham believed that English's experience in the United States had made him extremely receptive to the 'Thatcher Revolution'. There was a political match, yes, but there was also a philosophical match.

The *Mail*'s editorial staff went to work dressing Thatcherism up. 'The more she succeeded,' Peter Wright said, 'the more we could sell our newspapers.' English developed a line wherein he showed how prosperity could be linked to Thatcherism. 'David made it seem like Thatcherism wasn't just about hard work. You could live like a king. And the more we dressed it up, the more sales we had,' said Wright.

Around the office it was 'David and Margaret', with the relationship taking on legendary status. David's leader writer Chris Nicholson conjured up a homely image of David dropping in on Thatcher late at night and the two of them conferring on the *Mail*'s next editorial as Margaret Thatcher prepared ham sandwiches in her kitchen for the two of them.

David's deputy Peter Grover also referred to David English's frequent trips to Downing Street late at night. In Grover's words, David lived 'just round the corner in Cowley Street', so such visits came about naturally:

> David would go round to Number 10 late at night for a chat. Then he would come in to work and say to me, 'I've had an idea.' And I would instinctively know that he had been with Margaret Thatcher.

David himself never confirmed that these visits had, in fact, taken place. It was up to the observer to deduce where he had been. He always said he couldn't possibly comment on any such conjecture. Was this a sign of his loyalty to Thatcher? Or was there another reason for his discretion?

Tim Bell, the PR guru who masterminded Margaret Thatcher's three election triumphs, admitted that there were some limitations to the friendship between 'David and Margaret':

> The Prime Minister was in no position to forget that English was a journalist, and for his part, David had no wish to appear to be in her pocket.

He was an independent man, whose success was measured by circulation, readership and ad revenue, and he cared about that.

Although David English did appear at Chequers on rare occasions, he was not one of the 'inner circle' who was present on Christmas Day, when Margaret Thatcher entertained her closest friends.

But David was very close to Gordon Reece, who was adviser to Margaret Thatcher and director of publicity in the Conservative Central Office during her three terms as Prime Minister. He was also a good friend of Tim Bell. It was often surmised that much of David's special knowledge of Thatcher probably emanated from these sources.

Nevertheless, ethically and ideologically, they were on the same wavelength. Bell believed English understood Thatcher better than any other editor in Fleet Street, probably because of their shared sense of values. 'David was an intensely decent man who hated indecent behaviour,' and Margaret was like this as well. 'His readership and editorial posture, anti-trade union stance and opposition to state dependency – all the things she cared about – conspired to bring them together.'

But if David English genuinely liked and enjoyed Margaret Thatcher's company, his proprietor didn't share his enthusiasm. Grover was fond of recounting a story about a luncheon that Vere was to have hosted in the boardroom, where from time to time the proprietor invited important political figures of the day:

> Vere wouldn't agree and wouldn't agree to a date, because he didn't like her. He obviously didn't want to do it at all. Vere finally did agree very reluctantly, and Margaret was duly invited, along with Bernard Ingham. We all assembled in the boardroom at about 12.30. We had a drink and chatted, waiting for Vere to arrive, time ticking away, no sign of Vere. Margaret arrived, with Bernard Ingham, by now it was five to one and no Vere.
>
> David whispered, 'We have to go to the anteroom and call Vere's secretary.' We call her and David says, 'Where's Vere? Where's Vere? It's nearly one.' And back came the answer, 'Oh, he's in Paris, dear, he left on the twelve o'clock plane.'
>
> What could we say? We went back to Margaret Thatcher and apologised to her, saying a relative had been taken suddenly ill and that he had to fly off to Paris. She said, glaring, 'Well we'd better get on without him.' At the earliest possible moment, without even waiting for coffee, she left. And on her way out she said, 'Do tell Vere I hope his relative gets better.'

One of David's colleagues speculated that Vere believed Thatcher had actually done little for the *Daily Mail*, but had done much for his competitor Rupert Murdoch, and this formed the basis for his dislike. Another simply thought Vere disliked her forthright personality.

Whatever the case, Bernard Ingham believed that the *Daily Mail* was in the long run probably more useful to Margaret Thatcher than the other newspapers that supported her because it was 'more balanced'. It was, in his words, 'more capable of being critical'. David English didn't slavishly support Thatcher and in a way that gave the *Mail* more credibility.

One of the issues to which the *Mail* took exception was Europe. Both David and Vere were very much pro-Europe, and especially in terms of *Daily Mail* policy David was at pains to distance himself from Thatcher's views on the topic.

Otherwise, it was widely believed among the staff that David English was playing a high-profile role in some of the events of Margaret Thatcher's tenure as Prime Minister. Just before Nigel Lawson resigned as Chancellor of the Exchequer in October 1989, David had launched a front-page story that Lawson must go, causing a terrific furore. When Nigel did go, Stewart Steven speculated that he and Margaret Thatcher had perhaps put their heads together on the earlier story. In the event, David was skiing in Switzerland when Lawson actually resigned and he rushed back, giving substance to the rumours that he had been instrumental in some part in deposing him.

Then, too, a legendary interview between David and the Prime Minister gave credence to the view that the two of them were closely allied. Gordon Greig, the *Mail*'s political correspondent, was present at what he called 'an astonishing interview' that proved to him how comfortable they were in one another's company.

About two years after the Falklands War, rumours were circulating that the United States was going to rearm Argentina, and Margaret Thatcher agreed to give David English and Gordon Greig an exclusive interview on the subject. Greig said,

> It was the end of the week, on a Friday, when she was generally exhausted and more run-down than on Monday, when she was sharp as an eagle. And she had had an operation on her eyes that added to the exhaustion, and she just talked for twenty minutes non-stop.
>
> She was saying things like 'I hope Reagan sees sense', and 'I hope the President doesn't do it'. And ten or twelve minutes into the interview, she suddenly turned to David and said, 'David, you know where to put the

questions, don't you?' And then she just plunged ahead without waiting for an answer.

David and I both came reeling out on to Downing Street in a state of disbelief.

Gordon Greig subscribed to the 'David and Margaret' theory, crediting David generally not only with having a great deal to do with her success, but also with helping her achieve certain political aims. But if he did, David English remained silent about it.

The unofficial but mutually beneficial relationship between him and the Prime Minister continued until she was deposed in 1990. Then, according to legend, 'There was a falling out.' Some speculated that this resulted when Thatcher refused to resign after the first ballot went against her. According to this theory, English thought it was unbecoming for her to continue fighting a battle she could not win and he had told her so. Others believed that the disagreement had resulted from David English's enthusiastic support for Tony Blair and that was what drove them apart. But if indeed such a falling out had occurred, David himself never referred to it.

Whatever the case, a few years after he had been named managing director of Associated Newspapers, David English confirmed confidentially that he had plans to write a book about his relationship with Margaret Thatcher after his retirement. He died before he could carry out his plans.

'He understood her better than any other editor on Fleet Street,' Tim Bell believed. 'And when she was ousted, he said in his editorial, "She was better than the lot of them." He gave her the plates afterwards and she was very pleased.'

As to Margaret Thatcher, in reference to their parting, she said, 'David may have had a falling out with me, but I never had a falling out with him.'

TWELVE

TRIAL BY MENU

Vere Harmsworth was, as John Winnington-Ingram often said, a good man and a nice man. But he was also a complicated man. His thinking was complicated, his relationships were complicated and he was attracted to complicated personalities, both in the workplace and in his personal life.

In modern parlance, Vere showed the ability to tolerate a high level of ambivalence. That turned out to be fortunate, because the men he employed sometimes entertained highly ambivalent feelings towards him. Many of them were jealous of the power he wielded and he never permitted himself to forget, not for a moment, that their loyalty depended solely on who he was. Early on, he accepted that much in his life would have an unreal quality. Genuine relationships would be few and far between. Even as he was surrounded by people almost every minute of the day, he remained a lone and much misunderstood figure.

On one level, and especially in the mythic tales of the journalists, he was often portrayed as a figure of fun. Anecdotes abounded about his eccentric behaviour, greatly exaggerated in each new telling, until he emerged as a character not unlike the Wizard of Oz. He was the man behind the helm who wasn't quite sure what he was doing. He was a bumbler and an eccentric, a kind of idiot savant whose innocence accidentally carried him, time and again, to good fortune. This was the image the journalists wanted to believe.

Probably the most famous anecdote showing Vere in this role involved gossip columnist Nigel Dempster.

In the story an angry Nigel storms into Vere's office to complain that he is not receiving enough money. His editor David English won't give him a rise, so Dempster is going over his head and coming straight to Vere. He states his business and Harmsworth listens intently. Then, as if thinking it over, he goes over to his window, pulls the blinds open and invites Nigel to join him as he stares out across the Thames. 'Isn't the river beautiful today?' he asks the famous gossip columnist.

'Yes, very,' Nigel responds, slightly nonplussed.

'And look,' he continues, 'there's a gondolier going past on the water. It's so wonderful to see them churning along at this time of year.'

Nigel Dempster can see no gondolier on the Thames. He doesn't have any idea what the proprietor is talking about. But he carries on doggedly about his rise. Vere keeps his eye on the putative gondolier, saying nothing. After sputtering for a few minutes, Dempster sees that Harmsworth isn't listening. He is transfixed by the invisible gondolier. Nigel tries to continue, but he can't see the gondolier and he can't get Harmsworth's attention. He eventually leaves his office. Without the rise.

Here is poor Vere Harmsworth, in a hallucinatory sequence about a gondolier on the Thames, so out of it he cannot muster the focus necessary to talk to an employee about a rise in salary.

Did this really happen? Well, sort of. Nigel Dempster said later he did once go to Vere Harmsworth's office and ask for a rise and Harmsworth replied by saying he wouldn't override Nigel's editor. Harmsworth himself reported much the same thing. He remained baffled but amused by the addition of a gondolier to the story. 'I think I hear the voice of David English in the telling of the tale,' he said later, completely unperturbed.

This was the journalists' classic caricature of their proprietor. To the managers it was a different Vere, one who brooked little opposition. But his means of thwarting deviant thinking was subtle. It was this version of Vere Harmsworth that had the ring of truth.

In a story told by Stuart Martin, who was financial director of Associated Newspapers at the time, a group of managers met with Vere in Paris to discuss Associated Newspapers' continuing involvement with *Esquire* magazine. Martin said that one of those present liked to give the appearance of high style and he was staying at the Hôtel Crillon on the Place de la Concorde. It was here that the group gathered in the lounge for a preliminary meeting. This man began by criticising Associated's involvement with *Esquire*, saying it was merely a publication for an élite upper-class minority. He seemed completely unaware of the fact that the American magazine was 'Vere's baby'. During his tirade, Harmsworth's eyes began to glaze over in anger. At last Vere interrupted his critic saying, 'I believe we should dine here.' He asked the man who had been so critical of the investment in *Esquire*, 'Don't you agree this is the most convenient place?'

The Hôtel Crillon is not an inexpensive venue. The group nevertheless trooped into the restaurant and there, Vere proceeded to make his way straight down the menu. 'He had his soup,' said Stuart Martin. 'He had his hors d'oeuvre. He had his main course. He had his sorbet. He went through the lot. Then he addressed the man who had criticised *Esquire* suggesting, "Why don't *you* pay?"'

The bill was exorbitant, greatly in excess of his credit card limit or his cash advance, and the hapless man was reduced to going round the table, collecting francs from whoever happened to have any as he tried to accumulate enough money to pay. In retrospect, Stuart Martin called the episode 'Trial by Menu'.

'So you could cross Vere,' Stuart said later. 'But he had ways of getting back.'

Vere was, as Winnington-Ingram said, a good man and a nice man, but there was a serious 'at your own peril' principle at work if you did happen to cross him. And he could be so subtle that, on the managerial side of the company, he became known as the 'Delphic Oracle'. The truth according to Vere came down in complicated riddles; your job could depend upon correctly interpreting them.

Just to confuse matters, Vere might not be communicating a secret message about work. He might simply be discussing a historical event that interested him, nothing more. But most of the time the subject under discussion carried an ulterior meaning. If you weren't paying close attention you could miss something important. An alternative nickname for the eccentric proprietor was 'the Sphinx'. Harmsworth deplored both these names, but they stuck nevertheless because each captured a singular aspect of his personality.

When Vere's eccentricity became the focus of his employees' imagination, he enjoyed exaggerating his natural propensity to be slightly daft, either to camouflage his intentions, or simply for the fun of it. He possessed considerable *joie de vivre* and carried on a number of jokes for his own amusement.

But there were times when he showed a darker side. He had a foul temper and, when he gave into it, could be menacing and sometimes hurtful. When in this mood he could and did reduce people to tears. And when he was angry, he would take it out on anyone who happened to be around him. He was usually sorry afterwards and in the calm after the storm he might carry out one of his 'good deeds', whereby in some subtle way he let the person know he had meant no harm. But that was small comfort to anyone who had been confronted by his unbridled fury.

Another dark feature was his tendency to be highly suspicious of almost everyone around him. He desired loyalty and would very much have liked to believe in it, but he was too cynical to think anyone was capable of being loyal. Everybody, he thought, was on the take and he chose to be amused by what he imagined to be almost universal dishonesty. In fact, he masked his true feelings of hurt by expecting the worst in everyone. That way, he couldn't be disappointed. Sadly, he was often right.

Everywhere Harmsworth looked he saw conspiracies and, when he was right, it confirmed his worst prejudices. In some ways his was a self-fulfilling prophecy and it certainly didn't leave a lot of room for manoeuvre for those around him who did try to conduct themselves with integrity. Then again, integrity wasn't always rewarded. Nor was goodness. As Vere frequently reminded everyone, often lacing the statement with a heavily ironic tone of voice, 'And of course, virtue is its own reward.'

At the office Vere often found himself in the middle of jealous plottings. Perhaps the most prevalent belief among the staff was that David English could do no wrong. What David wanted, he got; that was the perception. Said Winnington-Ingram, 'It would have been better at times if David English had been brought more under control. But then, a David under control might not have stayed. At the end of the day, there was only one person who could control David – and that was Vere. Even David would have to toe the line if Vere so decided.'

But not everybody was as philosophical about David's privileges as Winnington-Ingram. Mick Shields openly resented the editor and competed with English for Harmsworth's attention, Vere taking a kind of covert delight in playing one against the other. This infuriated Mick.

At home during this period, his son remembered that his father tended 'to rant and rave about how Vere drove him mad, how he let him down, how he used to give in to David English. He was the despair of my father.' As Tom Shields said later,

In fact, in the end, my father viewed his job as little more than providing the funds for David to dissipate, because my father always felt, up to his death I'm afraid, that journalists were given far too preferential treatment in the company.

My father used to feel that throwing away money on bingo games and other promotions, apart from being demeaning, was unreal when compared with the fact that they were prepared to squander in one weekend on advertising all which was earned by NOP or another company in the commercial organisation.

He thought that was grotesquely unfair, grotesquely uneconomic and he thought that it was demoralising for the morale of those people who worked in the other companies.

Vere's attitude was, 'You will always get people to work in our non-newspaper companies, but getting good journalists and good editors was extremely difficult and you must therefore be prepared to pay them a premium.'

Vere made no secret of favouring the editors over the managers. He had seen his father Esmond and grandfather Harold go the other way, bringing the *Daily Mail* to the brink of disaster. On a more personal level, David English invariably won any contest over money and privilege because Vere considered him irreplaceable. Outside the firm, David was wont to brag that the *Daily Mail* was 'a money tree'. The money just kept raining down, he would say. But in Vere's mind, at least, David English was the most valuable member of his staff and he wasn't about to quibble with him.

Although David could occasionally be brought to return Mick's resentment, it didn't happen very often because, as he put it, he considered Mick Shields a colourful character and he enjoyed him so much as a person. He also knew he had the upper hand. He won practically every inter-corporate contest, to the extent that it wasn't necessary for him to take Shields on as a major competitor and 'cat's-paw him to death', as David did to so many.

As the victor in every contest, David English could afford to be generous. Indeed, he usually was when dealing with his peers. He basked in being the golden boy who always got his way.

Beyond that, as a collector of interesting people, David recognised that 'knowing Vere was one of the great experiences. He was larger than life, astonishingly complex, a complete character. Anyone who knew him was enriched by the experience. I don't mean money, although that too ... something else ... a fabulous character.'

The stakes increased when Vere's wife Patricia entered the picture. Patricia got on with David and she believed he was an able editor. But the fact that he had her husband's ear could irritate her and then she would use her influence with her husband to try to bring a little misery into the editor's life. Such was the case when Barbra Streisand was a guest at her Eaton Square apartment.

In March 1975 the Hollywood star had a new film out and the *Daily Mail* ran a less than favourable review of it, only days after Patricia had given a party in her honour. Patricia hit the roof, she was absolutely furious and she pressurised her husband to sack David for causing embarrassment to the two of them.

Harmsworth duly wrote David an accusatory letter asking for his resignation and David shot back the requested resignation in high dudgeon. As usual, he took full responsibility for the bad review, which had been written by a member of staff, although he had actually been away on holiday. David wrote,

> The dismissal of [the reviewer], totally unjustified on any professional
> grounds ... would have become a cause célèbre in and outside Fleet Street
> and would have destroyed for all time the new *Daily Mail*'s reputation for

objectivity and excellence. The morale of the first-class staff we have built up would have been damaged to a disastrous effect...

Naturally, it makes me extremely upset that our partnership has come to an end in such a tragic and sad manner...'

But of course the matter came to no such 'tragic and sad' ending. Vere could afford to threaten to fire David because he knew David knew that he would never actually let him go. The two could afford to indulge themselves in histrionics because the relationship was completely secure. Nobody was going to fire anybody and nobody was going to quit. In this case Vere allowed the affair to subside into silence and David carried on as usual.

But one thing was clear, Vere was at his worst when taking the advice of his wife or of close friends who were angry about some story that had run in the paper. He was very likely to make a fool of himself, or help David make a fool of him, when he gave in to their demands.

In the meantime Patricia believed that David had it in for her. Vere shared that belief, for he later said that David often made Patricia's life a misery, paying her back for her interference with traps and tricks. For his part English maintained that Patricia was constantly trying to interfere with the content of the newspaper, as if this excused any retaliatory measure he decided to take. The net result was a series of border wars between the two with constant sniping that made Vere's life a misery.

One of Patricia's ways of getting back at David was by showing favour to Mick Shields. She praised him highly, frequently referring to him as 'the most brilliant man in the company', most often to David himself. 'Mick made this company what it is today,' she would comment. But it was more than something she said to get back at David. She did believe Mick was a genius and, for his part, Mick was pretty well devoted to Pat.

He was also a close friend of Mary Rothermere, Vere's stepmother – as was David. David genuinely liked Mary and said he enjoyed her company. 'She was very positive and bubbly, with a lot of steel in her personality,' he said later. 'She wasn't a snob, like a lot of Texas millionaires. And she could be very funny.

'When she married Esmond, she revitalised him. She softened him in a way and he got jollier. He even had some small talk. Mary gave office lunches and parties. She made it fun for him.'

But if Mary Rothermere happened to have a drink or two too many, David said, she was apt to become rather sharp-tongued and difficult, and then he quickly made his apologies and left. All said and done, David wasn't particularly close to Mary.

But Mick made it a point to see her whenever he found himself in the

United States. He would stay with her and Esmond, usually at the couple's impressive mansion in Newport, which was one of the famous houses on 'Millionaire's Row' in that exclusive New England preserve. Robert Morrow, who was suspicious of Mick's intentions, used to say, 'Mick was always too close to Mary Rothermere for my taste.'

What Morrow was referring to was the gap that had widened between the two wings of the family that were separated by the Atlantic and his implied criticism of Mick Shields wasn't entirely fair since it fell to Mick to harmonise the two factions.

The divisions between the family came to a head when Esmond died in July of 1978. About ten days before, a strange event had occurred. Esmond was travelling home with his wife Mary from a holiday in Monte Carlo when he suddenly disappeared at the airport. He was missing for quite some time before he was found in a ditch nearby, in pretty bad shape. His daughter Lorna, as well as Vere, flew out to be with him, but he died soon thereafter.

Some of the family blamed Mary, saying he hadn't been well enough attended considering he was in the latter stages of Alzheimer's. Putting it baldly, they believed Mary had neglected him. The incident got into the London papers, along with a comment made by Ann Fleming, Esmond's second wife, who had left him for the novelist Ian Fleming. Never short of salt to pour on wounds, Ann was quoted as saying, 'At least I never lost Esmond at the airport!' This embarrassed everybody, heightening tensions.

The stage was set, then, for an out-and-out family war and when the will was read the situation became particularly explosive. According to Vere,

Up until near the end, I and my sisters were in the will. Then, in the last version, we suddenly were not in it. Funny, it completely changes and *we all vanish*.

I was asked to contest the will and I decided no. It would have been very expensive, with the lawyers' fees and everything else, and it would have caused very bad feelings.

I did dispatch a representative to my father's doctor to determine whether, in his opinion, my father was competent to undertake the will at the time it was written, and he said Esmond was in his right mind and perfectly capable of writing his will. So that was the end of it.

Vere was also disinclined to make public private family matters. For quite some time Mary Rothermere had been a major player in the Harmsworth family's finances. Ever since his father Esmond had stepped down from the chairmanship of Associated Newspapers and Vere assumed the reins of the company, he knew that when he was conducting business with his father he was actually dealing with Mary. This was because Esmond, as his Alzheimer's progressed, relied more and more upon her opinion.

Then again, Vere's stewardship of Associated was greatly limited by the rather unusual tiers of company control. Vere's father continued to retain the chairmanship of the Daily Mail and General Trust. For all his seeming power, Vere knew only too well that technically his every action as head of Associated was subject to his father's scrutiny, at least in theory. In practice, that meant to Mary's. Mary wasn't a particularly easy woman and Vere had come to dread what he considered to be her interference.

There was the earlier schism between Vere and Mary, stemming from the rivalry between her and his wife Patricia to bear a son and thus become the line of the family to carry on the title. On New Year's Day in 1967, Mary wrote to Patricia, informing her that she was pregnant and that 'she wanted Patricia to be the first to know'. That was her way of saying that if her pregnancy resulted in a male child, according to the outdated but still applicable practice of primogeniture, the title and control of the business would pass away from Vere and Patricia, returning to Esmond and Mary through their son.

Patricia chose to interpret Mary's pregnancy as a challenge and, although she and Vere were already having trouble in their marriage, Patricia became pregnant again. This was a dangerous matter, for Patricia had been told that if she had another child she would be seriously endangering her health. She had nearly died in giving birth to her second daughter by Vere, Camilla, and it was not an exaggeration to say she was risking her life by becoming pregnant again.

But the stakes were high and Patricia decided to risk it. Of course, the title was in question. But, much more important, the business was at stake. And then there was the money.

In the late 1920s and early 1930s a complicated set of trusts had been set up by Harold, first Viscount Rothermere. Harold intended them for the benefit of his grandchildren and great-grandchildren, and they were Canadian in origin. Of course, by having a child, Mary could succeed in having the trusts redivided because any son she had would naturally be entitled to his share as one of Harold's great-grandchildren. But the title was also at stake, as well as control of the company. Whoever was the viscount would eventually control Associated Newspapers and its parent company, the Daily Mail and General Trust.

In June of 1967 Mary gave birth to a son, Esmond; in December of the same year, Patricia gave birth prematurely to a son, Jonathan. If he had been born only a few months later, the entire trust would have devolved upon the offspring of Esmond and Mary, so Vere said much later. But Jonathan *was* born and so, by the complex terms of the trust, he and Esmond divided the proceeds and, in fact, these shares would enable his father Vere eventually to pass control of the company down to him.

Now, eleven years after the strange competition between the two women, Esmond Rothermere was dead. As a result, Mary was effectively in control of a very large block of shares. Although she had lost her chance to control the company, she was still a very influential stockholder.

Thus, Mick Shields's many visits to see Mary were highly appropriate, given her position as a major shareholder, and actually these visits had been authorised by Vere. Vere saw Mick as the man most likely to be able to bring harmonisation between the two sides of the family and their mutual interests.

But secretly David English's continuing friendship with Mary galled Vere, and he criticised David for it time and again. Said David,

> Vere called Mary 'the adventuress'. She was great friends with the Hollywood actress Gayle Hunnicutt, and Vere often saw the celebrity at Daylesford when he went to visit his father. She seemed to him to be there all the time.

David speculated later that this was the real reason Vere never wanted Simon Jenkins to become editor of the *Evening Standard*. Jenkins was close to Hunnicutt, whom he married in 1978, and Vere was probably suspicious of the connection, David surmised.

It was necessary for Mick Shields to see and deal with Mary, Vere would stress to David, but not for David to, and Vere said he saw it as a form of disloyalty. Years later, David still remembered those times with bemusement.

But feelings were running high between the two families and there was an almost palpable sense of antagonism between them. Part of the problem was a lack of recognition on the part of the British family as to Mary's social standing in the United States. In fact, it was very hard to understand, because it entailed a grasp of a social and cultural system entirely foreign to the British side. When Mary came to England to marry Esmond, she was very much aware of the fact she was marrying a viscount and a publishing scion who controlled one of the foremost newspapers in the world. The Harmsworth family had a number of illustrious members and for generations they had been pre-eminent in many facets of English life.

But a great deal of prestige also attached to Mary's background. She came from a family that had been largely self-made only a generation before and although she wasn't a member of the East Coast establishment, self-made men have always been highly regarded in the United States. If not as illustrious as the Harmsworths', her background was colourful and controversial as a member of the Murchison family, one of the richest in Texas and indeed in the United States.

The family's fortunes had been made by Clint Sr during the twenties and thirties. A bold and freewheeling character, he was possessed of a wildcat mentality that led to his making hundreds of millions in the oil fields of Texas and passing it down to his family, who lived high and hard.

Mary was Clint Sr's niece and her father Kenneth was the black sheep of the family, wealthy at one moment, bankrupt the next. Throughout her youth her family flirted with poverty, the bailiffs actually coming to the house at one time. However, Mary did come into her share of the Murchison wealth and when she married Esmond she was independently wealthy – by any *normal* standards of wealth, her son Esmond said wryly. The family wielded enormous political power as conservative Republicans, not only in the state of Texas, but also in the nation. They were pre-eminent in the affairs of state.

Indeed, it had been through Mary's connections that Esmond and Associated Newspapers became involved in Blackfriars Oil Ltd, a foray into oil drilling in the North Sea that ended up paying great dividends to the newspaper company. Mary's sister Jane was married to oil man Fred Hamilton, who had formed Blackfriars with Esmond. That investment contributed directly to Vere's ability to expand his newspaper empire in Great Britain.

So, although Esmond's late marriage to Mary Rothermere had created a number of complications for the Harmsworths, there were benefits derived as well.

For her part, Mary Rothermere could be, in the words of one of her American family members, 'a very difficult woman'. She was capable of acts of enormous unkindness that some of the elder Harmsworths could not forget or forgive. In one incident Mary sent presents to the children of one of the Harmsworths, but when Christmas came and the children opened their presents, the boxes were empty. A call was made in good spirit, to tell Mary she had forgotten to include the presents. But Mary said, 'I didn't forget. That's what your children will be getting when Esmond dies.'

So Mary, who could be completely charming, had her problems too. She was an exceedingly complicated woman who had many conflicting sides to her personality.

When Esmond died, David English and his editors naturally concluded that Vere would not particularly wish to see his father's achievements lauded in the newspaper and made plans for a scaled-down obituary. Peter Lewis, who was put in charge of the story, said,

> None of them really knew Lord Rothermere, Esmond, very well, and they were terribly flustered and worried about the story, saying, 'Of course we don't want you to go into all the details of his time as proprietor of the *Daily Mail*. And on no account must you look up people like Noel Barber. I don't think anyone wants you to go into interviewing people of the old days. Just do the best you can.'
>
> I thought, 'Well, this is weird,' and I was nonplussed by this job and I thought, 'Well, there's only one man who can really talk about him and that's his son.'
>
> I rang up Vere and he said, 'Well, I want you to go into the great days of his stewardship, especially get in touch with Noel Barber. He knew my father very well. They were great mates.'

In fact, Vere himself wrote a tribute to his father, an almost wistful remembrance that touched on his father's 'particular greatness'. Here was a man, Vere wrote, of 'deep sympathy and understanding of the human predicament'. He spoke of his 'infectious humour and irresistible charm'. And he pointed to the moment when his father had lent him his greatest support:

> The decision of mine which so deeply affected his beloved *Daily Mail* must have caused him many anguished hours of doubt in the early days.
>
> Nonetheless he supported me loyally and totally, never wavering.
>
> He was a man in a million – a lovely man – a man of great strength and a father to love and respect.

There can be no question that Vere believed every word he had written. But like all Vere Harmsworth's relationships, his relationship with his father was far from simple. He certainly loved his father and, on one level, very much wanted his achievements to be published and remembered. But on a more subconscious level he remained confused all his life about his father's undeniable ambivalence towards him.

Throughout the literature that accumulated about Vere over the years there were stories about his heritage. It was widely assumed Vere's father set him up. In particular, Charles Wintour claimed that Esmond settled £2.75 million on Vere when he married Patricia in 1957. But this was untrue.

Vere's fortune emanated in large degree from the trusts his grandfather had settled upon his grandchildren in the 1920s and 1930s. But Esmond had also set up a trust to provide for his children and those trusts were

David English (left), Vere Harmsworth and his wife Patricia. The editor of the *Daily Mail* and Chairman of Associated Newspapers look singularly relaxed about the fate of their new 'compact' newspaper. Behind the scenes, English and his staff were putting in nineteen hours a day in a ferocious battle to survive.

Vere and David celebrate the first birthday of the new compact *Daily Mail*. In a letter to staff, David told his key people, 'Now we're only working fourteen hours a day! I told you it would get better.'

The controversial ad campaign launched by a young 'in-your-face' agency in Soho—Saatchi & Saatchi. Hired by Vere to boost the *Mail*'s advertising revenue, a young Bill Muirhead came up with the idea of a fictional agency—Conwell, Smarm and Drone. The old-style media director 'Reg' constantly upbraids his assistant 'Eric' whose statistics tell him the *Daily Mail* is a rising star. When it turns out Eric is right, Reg takes the credit.

Below: 3 May 1971, David's first editorial conference. Twelve grimly determined men begin the task of saving the *Daily Mail*. Left to right: Bob Findlay, Sports Editor; Michael Borrisow, Night News Editor; Brian Freemantle, Foreign Editor; George Elam, Deputy Picture Editor; John Lyth, Picture Editor; Gordon MacKenzie, Assistant Editor (Features); Ted Jeffery, Night Editor; Peter Grover, Associate Editor; John Jinks, Deputy News Editor; Jack Crossley, Assistant Editor (News); Dennis Holmes, Managing Editor; John Womersley, News Editor; David English, editor. Not pictured is Louis Kirby, deputy editor. He was closing down the *Daily Sketch*, whose last issue was published that morning.

Every woman needs her Daily Mail.

Above: The ad campaign that put on 85,000 readers for the *Daily Mail*. Created during a tense 24 hours when it looked as if Foot, Cone and Belding might lose the *Mail* account, American Bill Jenkins came up with the slogan, 'Every woman needs her Daily Mail. And every man knows why.' Jenkins went on to several more advertising triumphs, before the pressure got to him and he took his own life.

The young and flamboyant Nigel Dempster. He won international fame for his exclusive interview with Richard Burton just after the star had left Elizabeth Taylor.

John Edwards. He was going *into* Saigon as the rest of the world press was scrambling to get out.

Ann Leslie. Caught up in the euphoria when the Berlin wall came down, Leslie didn't sleep for 48 hours. English ran her prize-winning dispatch word-for-word as she dictated it, exhausted and barely coherent—but jubilant.

Ian Wooldridge. He covered the Black September assassination of the Israeli Olympic Team in Munich, 1972, calling the brassy memorial service thrown together afterwards 'the sorriest moment I ever had to report in my career. All it lacked were the drum majorettes.'

Brian Vine. Zola Budd's keeper while she trained to represent Britain in the Olympics, Vine said of the stunt, 'And the *Mail* received more brickbats for that than anything else we ever did.'

The classic cartoon by Mac (Stan McMurtry) on the Casino fiasco in February 1982. When the computer hit a glitch and over 100,000 people won the promotional game, each ended up receiving a cheque for 50 pence.

Yes, I'm a Casino winner, but I won't let it change my way of life

The brilliant and quirky *YOU Magazine*, edited by the brilliant and quirky John Leese. Many at Associated believed it was *YOU Magazine* that saved the *Mail on Sunday*, after its relaunch in the autumn of 1982 by David English and his go-ahead task force.

Charles Sinclair, Chief Executive for Daily Mail and General Trust. The architect of what the *Financial Times* termed 'an elegant transaction,' the take-over of Associated Newspapers by its own holding company, Daily Mail and General Trust. Vere said of the take-over, 'It's supposed to be theoretically impossible to devise a deal that benefits everybody . . . but this one did.'

Genevieve Cooper, Deputy Editor of the *Evening Standard*, and John Leese, Editor, at Leese's leaving party on 1 March 1991. The headline refers to Leese's victory in the famed 1987 newspaper war between the *Evening Standard* and the London *Daily News*. Seven months later, John Leese died from cancer. Nine years later, Genevieve Cooper succumbed to the disease.

Left to Right, Roger Gilbert, Managing Director of Harmsworth Media; Geraldine McKeown, PA to Rod Gilchrist; Gilchrist, Executive Producer of Kensington Film and Television and Deputy Editor of the *Daily Mail*; Julian Aston, head of Channel One. 10 a.m., 20 January 1992, the team who won the franchise for ITV's teletext service, after an exhausting overnight session putting finishing touches on Associated's bid. They personally delivered the application documents to the IBA Headquarters in London's Brompton Road by the 12 noon deadline.

Left to right, John Bird, Managing Director of Harmsworth Quays Printing; Jonathan's wife Claudia; Ian MacGregor, Launch Editor of *Metro*; Jonathan Rothermere, Chairman of Daily Mail and General Trust; Alistair Sinclair, Deputy Editor of the *Daily Mail*; Paul Dacre, Editor of the *Daily Mail*. 16 March 1999, the first issue of *Metro*, London's first free London daily newspaper. It was Vere's last legacy to the firm, carried out after his death by his son Jonathan.

The men who saved the *Daily Mail*.

dismantled in 1971, when Vere took some capital and gave up his interest in the remainder.

Vere could hardly say his father hadn't been generous and he was always grateful for Esmond's help in setting up a portfolio, showing Vere which stocks were best and explaining the reasons. This resulted in Vere's making a great deal of money. But there had been no fabulous settlements such as Charles Wintour claimed in his book *The Rise and Fall of Fleet Street*. Indeed, at times Esmond was unkind to his son.

As far as Esmond was concerned it was possible, even likely, that he associated Vere with his mother Peggy and took out some of his unconscious anger towards his first wife on his son. Otherwise it would be difficult to explain why Esmond believed Vere never measured up to his expectations. Then again, Esmond was, despite his own rather colourful personal life, very much a Victorian father. It would never have occurred to him that his actions could result in lasting unhappiness for his son. In his own mind he could bear no responsibility for any such thing.

As to Peggy, her feelings towards Esmond were bitter to the very end. When Esmond died she called her youngest daughter and said she wanted to go to the funeral. 'Let me give you a lift,' Esme said. Her mother then proceeded to criticise her former husband continually the entire way to Daylesford, Esmond's country home.

'Come on, Mummy,' Esme said jovially. 'If you don't stop, I'll put you out of the car.' What happened next was so shocking that Esme had to check out her actions with her sister Lorna and her brother Vere. She told each of them what she had said and they both saw the comment as Esme intended, a humorous aside to break the tension. But her mother did not see any humour at all, and *she never spoke to Esme again*.

In dealing with parents so difficult, it could certainly be an emotional roller-coaster for the children, right into maturity. Vere's relationship with his mother remained cordial, although she was a less than loving mother to him in many ways. It was said she and Vere were attached to one another 'by a silver cord'. Possibly. A more accurate description might be that she never ceased interfering in Vere's affairs and her interference always cost her son dearly, in one way or another. His father was remote and often critical. And all this took a toll.

His confidence was impaired to the extent that after his father died, Vere wasn't altogether certain he would be appointed in his place to become chairman of Daily Mail and General Trust. Vere's lifelong friend and solicitor John Hemingway had at that time just gone on to the DMGT Board, and he remembered that Vere gave him a phone call in France, where John was doing some business, and said, 'You had better come back for the vote,' which Hemingway of course did. In the event, Vere was voted into the position with no trouble at all.

But Vere did leave England to go to live in France from 1978, becoming an expatriate, and for a complex set of reasons. It was true that at the time the income taxes payable in France were somewhat less than in the UK. But it was less a matter of savings on Vere's income tax than to do with inheritance complexities in the United Kingdom. According to John Hemingway, Vere had been anxious 'to arrange his affairs so that family control of DMGT was unlikely to be put at risk by the impact of English estate taxes on his eventual death'. In short, Vere intended to leave control of the company intact to his son Jonathan and moving to France helped facilitate this.

On a more emotional level, there were complicated psychological reasons for his leaving England and in some ways Vere's life came apart the year his father died.

From the outside, 1978 was a triumph for Vere Harmsworth. By now, it had become apparent that the *Daily Mail* he had sought to save would not only survive; it would prosper. When his father died, Vere not only succeeded to the title, becoming the third Viscount Rothermere, but he also became chairman of the Daily Mail and General Trust. All the power devolved to him and now he had everything. At least, that was how it appeared from the outside looking in.

But psychologically things were very unhappy. It began in January when the country house where he and Patricia lived at weekends and during holidays burned down. Then, in July, Vere's father died. Most significantly, this was the year when Vere and Patricia signed a legal Agreement of Separation, effectively ending their marriage of twenty-one years. Again, 1978 was the year Vere left England to live in France.

Years later he tried to explain the forces behind his going. 'I was disillusioned with my father,' said Vere. 'If you are disillusioned with your parents, then you find yourself disillusioned with your country. And I went to live away. I had other reasons to go, certainly. But it was still a strange thing to do.

'The truth was, I just wasn't happy here any more.' And for Vere, the reason he left, at bottom, was largely because of this estrangement from his father. It was the closest he ever came to admitting how unhappy his father had made him when he was a boy and even when he was an adult. In the end, on some indistinct level he could never understand, he believed that he had been betrayed.

And somehow, to alleviate his own pain, he made an important promise to himself at that time: that he would never betray his own son.

THIRTEEN

TWO PATRICIAS

Richard Compton Miller met Patricia Harmsworth in the early 1970s at one of the many parties she gave in her Eaton Square apartment. Compton Miller had just joined Paul Callan, Nigel Dempster and Jack Tinker as the youngest reporter on the *Daily Mail*'s new gossip column, but it was an unusual job for someone with Compton Miller's background.

He had attended New College, Oxford before studying law, eventually becoming a barrister in the Inner Temple. In this, he was following in the footsteps of his father, Sir John Compton Miller, who was a judge. But Richard was secretly disenchanted with the legal profession. When he was at Oxford, he had edited *Cherwell* and had loved it. He had always wanted to be a journalist and, more than that, a journalist with flair. So when he was offered the chance to go to work for David English's new tabloid he jumped at it.

His new job entailed his living 'the grand life' and for the next few years he attended the most glamorous events on the London social scene. He liked the work and was good at it. Soon he was offered his own column on the *Evening News*. It was called 'In Town', and he quickly became accustomed to his newly found role as a kind of authoritative voice on the new, hip London scene.

There was no doubt in Compton Miller's mind that Patricia Harmsworth was *the* society hostess of her era, as Lady Cunard had been in an earlier generation. The only real rival to Patricia for this role was Lady Hartwell, Pamela Berry, who was of an older generation and who had always been more inclined towards gatherings that were of a political nature. Patricia liked a more eclectic crowd. It included the café society of her age, but with a touch of class. And the word was quickly out that she was a social catalyst who had a knack for introducing the right people to one another. Relationships seemed to make a beginning at her parties.

'Patricia introduced me to my then girlfriend, Sue Lloyd, and for three or four years we were together,' Compton Miller said later. But it was amazing for him to see the mixture of celebrities Patricia was able to attract. It wasn't unusual to see David Frost, Peter Sellers, Andy Warhol or even Princess Margaret at one of Patricia's parties, along with aristocrats, tycoons, businessmen and Hollywood stars. There were always a number of young, socially élite men and women in attendance, who gave the parties a youthful buzz.

'The Honourable Mr and Mrs Vere Harmsworth' were featured in the glossy magazines as social gadflies who attended the most important charity dances and dinner parties of the London social season. Many people on the scene were envious of Patricia's success. When Patricia entertained, she frequently sat thirty, with others arriving later in the evening. 'Vere was much less stuffy than people thought,' said Compton Miller and the social events Patricia hosted were always exciting and 'rather fabulous'.

But many of these events were actually fund-raisers for one of the many causes Patricia supported. After her marriage to Vere she set about with characteristic determination to raise money for a number of charities, most especially the NSPCC, Old Ben (the News-vendors' Benevolent Institution) and the United Nations. During these halcyon days she gave unstintingly of her time. Over many years she gave many thousands of hours. She became the first woman chairman in the 133-year-old history of Old Ben. She was also the first Englishwoman to receive an American Woman of the Year award, given to women of achievement in a wide range of activities. Honoured for her work with charities, Patricia had raised over £1 million for her causes, an astonishing sum in 1977, the year she received the award.

She always looked for the practical side in everything she did, even her social activities and she was indefatigable when it came to raising money. A genuine asset in such an environment, she could always be depended upon to bring a lively and witty presence. In her own words, Patricia was 'doing what I like best, which is living life to the full and making people happy'.

But there could be a tricky side to being with someone so lively. One story that Vere recounted showed the problems that sometimes accompanied Patricia's colourful imagination. At her height, she attended a gala dance with her husband, and was asked to dance by an influential gentleman who could have opened up an entirely new social world to Pat and Vere. Patricia afterwards said that the man told her during the dance that he alone controlled access to this highly desirable group, and he could be persuaded to see that Patricia and Vere were included. But she had to do whatever he said.

'And what did Patricia answer?' Vere asked rhetorically, much later. 'She told him to *fuck off!*' In retrospect, it seemed that Vere believed this obviously apocryphal story. Even years later he was amused by his wife's spirit and in some ways proud, still taking pleasure in her rebellious nature. He then darkly added the rider, 'But from that day to this, we were never invited to another party by anyone in the group.'

Another story about Patricia that made the rounds occurred when she was much older. A member of the royal household was visiting Hollywood and she was to be fêted by one of Hollywood's premier hostesses. But Patricia, who was staying in Los Angeles at the time, was not included on the guest list. Patricia rang the hostess and said, 'There must be an oversight. I wasn't included on the guest list for your party.'

The hostess replied that there had been no oversight.

Said Patricia, 'Well, it's an astonishing omission, seeing as how I'm the only genuine viscountess in this goddamn town!'

Patricia was never short on spirit and that was one of the reasons so many people found her irresistible. But on the other hand she usually put herself at the centre of her stories, sometimes to the detriment of others.

She was fond of recounting how she had 'put the stuffing into Vere' during the time in 1970 when his father Esmond was about to merge his newspaper empire with his traditional rivals at the *Daily Express*. In Patricia's lively version: 'Vere was fed up with newspapers and Fleet Street, the trade unions had made business impossible. But I stopped him quitting. And the rest is history.'

Few people questioned this version of events because Vere never contradicted her. She told the story to her children and they too pretty much accepted her line. Their father had lacked confidence; their mother had helped him overcome that. Vere, on the other hand, while giving his wife a great deal of credit, later indicated that the story was one of her great exaggerations. To a large extent Vere had found his own way. But he was still grateful for all she did do. She endangered her own health to present him with the son he had longed for all his life and indeed had planned for, and he honoured her for it and her very real support and loyalty until the day she died.

So this story, like so many others, was one of the more fanciful flights of her imagination, much like the overblown stories she told when she was a child. In most of these childhood tales Patricia was at the centre, saving the day. It was an endearing trait, part of her lively personality, to spin these stories. When she got older and became an actress, moving into the entertainment world, she immediately grasped how important good publicity could be. After that she became her own best public relations representative and there was no stopping her.

Whereas most people put a limit on how much credit they are willing to claim, Patricia understood intuitively there didn't have to be a limit. She also understood that people loved exciting and melodramatic stories with a fetching heroine and dramatic outcome. And she was quite clever at casting herself in the lead role as she recounted some event that might have made a good film or West End play.

But despite these flights of fancy, what was absolutely undeniable about Patricia was her intelligence, along with a high degree of 'woman's intuition'.

She was also a good judge of people. It was Patricia, for example, who first 'discovered' Vere's lawyer and lifelong friend John Hemingway. The couple met John at the Lyford Cay Club, which had been developed by the Canadian Brewer Eddie Taylor. The secretary of the club, Henry Montgomery, was a friend of John and the Harmsworths were staying with Montgomery. They all decided to go over to Windermere Island one day for lunch, and Hemingway got on very well with the Harmsworths. Later, he helped them sort out a few trusts they had in the Bahamas and eventually Hemingway helped them buy 960 5th Avenue, their Manhattan penthouse.

It was obvious to John that Patricia had a kind of star quality that was usually reserved for Hollywood celebrities and she adored the limelight. But did she 'push it' with Vere, just to see how far she could go? John Hemingway thought that 'she got a certain energy out of it'.

But some of it Vere caused himself. Because Vere indulged her far too much in the early days of their marriage, she never really understood the importance of giving him credit for what he was achieving and for the pressures he was facing. Eventually, her own need for attention and her unwillingness to extend a small part of the credit to anyone else would become more troubling. But for now, she was a dazzling figure on the London social scene.

Her eldest daughter Sarah Holcroft, who was the child of Christopher Brooks, Patricia's first husband, was old enough in the sixties to remember 'the swinging parties' she gave in her penthouse flat opposite the church in Chester Square. Years later when she was an adult with children of her own, Sarah still remembered the excitement of having famous people come to their house, even though she was just a child in the nursery.

In those days Vere and Patricia often enjoyed breakfast in bed, while the children remained in the nursery 'in the self-contained, old-fashioned way that Vere was brought up in', said Holcroft later. Patricia loved babies, but didn't care much for the nappy side of child rearing.

Sarah remembered early holidays the family took, when they went to the South of France and rented villas, usually near St Tropez. Vere had a great passion for sailing and bought himself a small sailboat. He also loved yachting, and when Sarah was about six or seven he got a yacht with three cabins and a sitting room. He used it to go round the islands in Greece, sometimes joined by Howard French, his great mate from work, and Howard's charming wife Erma.

But Patricia didn't like staying on the boat at night, so Vere would have to moor it in the bay and rent hotel rooms in the nearby village. Then, too, he always spent a lot of time mending the boat and pottering about, fixing it, before he would take it out. So in the end it became more hard work than holiday, and 'Vere gave it up as a bit of a lost cause', said Holcroft.

Later on, in the early 1970s, Vere began to favour holidays in the American West. He liked riding holidays in Wyoming, where the family could go on the trail and cook out around a campfire. His wife found these holidays dreadful because when she was a child, she had been thrown from a horse and had broken her back. She spent a long time recovering in hospital and never got over her fear of horses.

Sarah's younger half-sister, Camilla Yeates Cameron, also remembered the first riding holiday. It was such a success that it would lead to many more like it.

It was in Wyoming, and it was just one of these fantastic holidays where we were all together, which was very rare. My sisters Sarah and Geraldine sometimes didn't come, and my mother often took a separate holiday.

And my mother, who was frightened of horses, in the end got on a mule, because she was the quietest thing they had in the stable and my mother was still nervous. She went with us, and it was dead funny because the mule wouldn't move. It ended up dragging her through a bush. My mother wore hairpieces, and her hairpiece got stuck in the bush and was dragged off her head. We were all in tears from laughing so hard.

When we got to the camper, where you have the campfire and cookout, Mother decided she'd had enough. And she radioed for the ranger who came and picked her up in a Land Rover and took her back to the ranch. She'd done her bit...

When we went on these holidays my father always made sure that there was at least one telephone in the complex. He had to find a phone. He didn't make it a big chore. He just went off quietly and made his business call. He never tried to ruin our holiday by bringing business into it.

Sarah Holcroft also remembered a wonderful holiday in Sardinia, where the family rented a villa and Vere took his boat along as well. Peter Sellers was there with Britt Ekland and Lord Snowdon was also around. They had their yachts as well and when the three went out for a day, Peter Sellers would sit there with a megaphone and shout in an Indian accent at smaller boats in his way, 'My God, my God, what are you doing? How dare you get in the way?'

Later on, Patricia began collecting the property that would give her the reputation for being very shrewd at investing in real estate. She acquired Greta Garbo's famous villa in Monte Carlo that was built on a rock overlooking the sea; an old hunting lodge in Los Angeles; a house in Round Hill, Jamaica; the apartment in Manhattan.

Patricia loved music and loved to dance, and she tried to teach all the children. So later, when they ended up in discos during their teenage years, they were all able to dance tolerably well. She also painted, as did Vere, who was very good at it, and occasionally, the two of them painted together in the conservatory. 'They played chess as well. Then Patricia beat him for the first time,' said Sarah, 'and they never played again!'

Camilla also remembered her mother's love of music, and her 'tremendous power and force for life'.

She was so much fun at parties. She had tremendous zest and a tremendous sense of humour.

I remember one particular moment, when I was about eighteen. I had been in hospital and I had come out, and they said I had to convalesce. I went back to my mother's house. While I was in hospital she had accidentally sat on the bed with a pot of tea, and the bed had tilted and all the tea had spilled down the base of her back, causing terrible burns. She was laid up with these, and we lay beside one another in her bed. And she got the video for *That's Entertainment*.

We would watch it for hours. She would know all the words to all the songs, bouncing around on the bed, singing at the top of her voice, then rewinding the tape and playing it again. It was terrific fun.

But memories like this one were in large part missing on an everyday basis. Patricia was frequently absent from home pursuing social activities and the gap she left was filled by her mother. Mrs Matthews often came to the Eaton Square flat to take care of the children. The children also stayed in their grandmother's big country house where she made homemade dinners and became a second mother to them.

But even Doris Matthews had to conform to Patricia's rules. Patricia's younger sister Jenny Willis remembered the three of them taking a taxi when her mother and Patricia were going to meet Vere. Patricia was giving her mother minute instructions as to how she should act in front of her husband, what to do and what not to do.

This didn't at all bother Doris Matthews. It was Patricia's mother, after all, who had wanted a wonderful life for her daughter. She had encouraged Patricia to marry well, meet interesting and important people and move up in the world. And now it was Patricia's mother who took care of her children, providing them with a home away from home. This was an obvious solution to the problem of leaving the children too often with a nanny and it had the advantage of giving them an old-fashioned home life. In the meantime Mrs Matthews tended to live vicariously, basking in Patricia's incredible social success.

But glittering as things were on the surface, there was a dark side to Patricia's life. She often slept much of the day away, a sign of serious depression. As late as three o'clock in the afternoon she would still be asleep. When she did wake up she was constantly on the telephone to the extent that it became a kind of diversion, perhaps from less pleasant realities of living. To family members who cared about her, it was apparent she wasn't happy. Her behaviour seemed evasive, as if she was trying to cover over something.

One of Patricia's most winning traits was a kind of childlike vulnerability. But it sometimes seemed as if she was truly vulnerable, in a way that suggested something had gone wrong in her life.

And whereas she had sometimes been very generous with her family during the early years of her marriage, later on she became stingy, counting out every penny. She delayed in paying her bills, so that people who worked for her often had to use subterfuge to get their money. This was at direct odds with her generosity in conducting charity work. It appeared as if money had become the focus of a larger question in her life, perhaps symbolic of what was missing. In moments of clarity she would say that money was less important to her than power.

Patricia appeared to believe that power was a kind of make-believe quality that having money automatically conferred. If she got enough money, she would have power; it was a simple matter. The heavy responsibility and constant pressure that accompanied power were beyond her reckoning. Vere understood this only too well. In fact, Patricia enjoyed Vere's power more than he did and that seemed to be having a negative effect on the relationship.

When Patricia married Vere she set aside her own ambitions to become a successful actress, subverting her goals and ambitions to his. She was in essence living Vere's life. It was a fairy tale ending that wouldn't end.

Patricia had to live the fantasy, a difficult proposition. And she wasn't always steady enough for the task. She was much admired by the men on the staff, one editor saying frankly, 'Patricia was both beautiful *and* sexy.

It isn't very often women manage to be both.' But she was also feared. One oft-repeated story had her criticising the mistake of one of the managers at Associated Newspapers. 'That man should be fired,' she told her husband. Several other employees were in hearing and not only did they fear for their colleague's job, they feared for their own. If Patricia had been the powerful one instead of Vere, they speculated, any one of them could suddenly find himself out of a job.

But they needn't have worried. Vere blithely ignored her advice on staff. It was as if he didn't hear her. But it would have been a mistake to think he disregarded all that she said. The pair were on the telephone to one another two or three times a day until Patricia's death. Vere always wanted to hear her ideas, which he took seriously. He knew she was intelligent and that her motivations were for the good, and he never forgot her loyalty over the years. He had a great deal of respect for his wife, added to the fact that he loved her dearly. As more than one person close to Vere said, 'Woe betide anyone who spoke ill of her in front of him.'

Vyvyan Harmsworth, who was director of Corporate Affairs at Associated Newspapers and also a member of the family, came as close as anyone to describing the nature of the relationship between Vere and Patricia. 'Whereas during the bad moments in their marriage, Charles and Diana were the kind of couple who might have come to a party together and left separately, Vere and Patricia were the kind who might come to a party separately and meet up later.'

Still, it would be hard to deny that Patricia was envious of Vere. One episode that caused him pain occurred when she joined an investment club in New York City that promised fantastic returns on a 'minimal investment' of several hundred thousand dollars. Patricia joined without telling him and lost the money when the financial officer absconded. Vere did everything he could to clean up after the fraudulent deal, but years later he still had trouble understanding why she did it, especially when she had everything she could possibly want. 'She wanted to make her mark as an investor,' he said later. 'I don't know why.'

Jenny Willis had her own ideas. 'Patricia never really developed,' she said. 'She wasn't motivated to develop. She got too depressed to develop. She didn't have the courage to do anything besides what she was doing and it depressed her. She didn't have anything of her own.'

Her daughter Geraldine Maxwell said, 'She was an extremely intelligent woman who had to pretend to be a pretty little thing. It was her generation, but also her.'

Patricia *was* envious of Vere and she wanted to live her life vicariously through him. Later on she started to identify with her son Jonathan, whose birth had been her great achievement in life. She began to phone both Vere and Jonathan frequently and sometimes rather desperately, trying, as one of her children put it, 'to get a pick-me-up'. When she did get a buzz she was delighted. Her mood would suddenly change and she would be great fun to be with. But when she failed to get the response she needed at that moment she tended to sink more into the depression that was manifested largely by self-destructive behaviour.

When all was said and done, Patricia had very few inner resources. As time passed, more of her friends, family and acquaintances began to realise that, despite her confident manner, she was actually too vulnerable to criticism and to rejection for her own good. While her vulnerability had an appealing side, it was becoming increasingly apparent that she was deeply unhappy and dissatisfied with herself.

It seemed almost as if the gayer and more outgoing she became, the more she was haunted by self-doubts. In addition her depression was becoming a shared problem. Everyone who knew her well began to recognise that Patricia had become an extremely volatile personality. She grew increasingly difficult to be around, to some extent because of her growing reliance on prescription drugs – especially sleeping pills. If one doctor would no longer give them to her, she would go to another – and another and another.

John Hemingway saw that Patricia's increasing need for medical attention was getting out of hand. 'She was seeing doctors night and day,' he said. 'It was almost pathological, the number of doctors she was seeing.'

Like so many others of her generation, Patricia entered willingly into the prescription drug culture. Relying on sleeping pills and tranquillisers seemed a quick fix for a multitude of ills. But Patricia routinely mixed homeopathic drugs with prescription remedies. Her judgement, which had been astute, now became less reliable. She could be unduly sharp, unkind and sometimes shrill. Among family members she could be cruel in a care-less way, almost in passing, completely unaware of the hurt her words caused. Yet she showed such profound affection for all her family that they were constantly confused by her mercurial nature. A sharp criticism would emerge quickly, seemingly from nowhere and with little rhyme or reason.

At the same time she was still a shimmering personality. No one could remain oblivious to her appeal, her point of view or her opinions if she made the decision to be charming. She was a star. Although she often dis-appointed her family by showing little interest in what they were doing, they always ended up overlooking it because of her star quality.

'In a way, I was always puzzled by her,' Jenny Willis said.

She was such a huge influence in my life.

I grew up thinking she was the best thing since sliced bread. I was bursting with pride when I saw her on the stage at the Edinburgh Festival. That was before she met Vere. After she married Chris Brooks, she went to the Royal Academy of Dramatic Art. And after that, she did a lot of stage work, and she had always modelled. She had just started in the movies when she met Vere, and she was having a bit of success at it. And she couldn't do both. She couldn't marry him and continue with her acting career.

And although he was rich, and our mother had encouraged her to be with someone rich, she was attracted to Vere right from the start. He was the love of her life. She wasn't wholly closed to affection.

It makes me feel so bloody sad. She was in a position to do so much and she got stuck in a time warp. Her highlight in life was when she was the darling of London society. But being married to money stultified her because she thought she could be everything to everybody and she never developed herself.

Richard Compton Miller said he had always thought there were really 'two Patricias'.

The first was the bubbly, fun, social Pat, who was the life of the party. And then there was 'the second Pat', an altogether different person who struck people as a rather sad character.

This description was probably more astute than Compton Miller realised. And those few people who did understand the extent of the 'rather sad character' couldn't guess how deep it went. But Vere knew what outsiders were only trying to guess, that the flip side of Patricia, the side she tried to keep private, the side she *denied*, was dominating her personality more and more.

Vere knew that Patricia was suffering, almost unconsciously, from a nervous ailment known as trichotillomania, where tension is relieved by pulling hair out. None of the people Patricia knew socially were aware of it, because she wore wigs most of the time. But as she grew older the tendency worsened.

Decades later, when another member of the family became seriously depressed after childbirth, Vere saw the syndrome again in this young woman. And something about that triggered his memory. 'It was Patricia all over again,' he said later.

She had been very depressed, unable to come out of it and eventually I asked Patricia's doctor about it. And he said it was quite possible Patricia suffered lasting effects from post-partum depression.

Vere's generation of men had no idea of the adverse effect that sometimes resulted after childbirth. But he certainly realised his wife had suffered a serious depression after the birth of her third daughter Camilla in 1964. It was nearly thirty years later that he began to discover the effects that very long depression might have had on his wife's continuing mental health.

His reaction was absolute fury: that he had not been told she was seriously ill, that her doctor at the time had not given her the treatment she needed, that her health might have been permanently damaged. But it was much worse than he imagined.

In 1964 the condition Patricia might feasibly have had was not generally recognised by the medical profession. It would therefore have been impossible to diagnose or to treat Patricia. She might have been diagnosed for generalised depression, but even the treatment for that would have been fairly primitive. Besides, to admit to having emotional difficulties after the birth of a child was at that time considered a source of shame, for Patricia and for the family. Traditionally, it should have been the happiest time of a woman's life, when she should be overjoyed with her new baby. Anything else would have seemed unnatural.

So was it likely that Patricia's behavioural changes resulted from a disorder stemming from childbirth? It is not only possible; many of her symptoms match closely with the onset of the condition.

Puerperal psychosis, a term stemming from the *puerpereum*, that is, what obstetricians call the 'lying-in period', occurs in two to three cases per thousand after childbirth. It does not refer to the post-partum 'blues', which 60 per cent of all women experience between the third and fifth days after the baby is born. This condition entails tearfulness and emotional volatility, abnormal anxieties about the child's welfare, sometimes accompanied by sleeplessness and loss of appetite. But these 'blues' are fleeting and transient, and usually settle within a few days.

Nor does puerperal psychosis refer to post-natal depression, a second common condition which sometimes appears about six weeks after childbirth, wherein the new mother suffers from a deep depression. This is an ailment lasting nine to twelve months in which the new mother can lose her pleasure in living, her libidinal drive and her depression can become chronic.

Instead, it is a psychotic reaction that advances rapidly after childbirth, within about a week, with the symptoms resembling either classical schizophrenia or manic-depression.

If Patricia did in fact suffer from puerperal psychosis, her behaviour most closely resembles the manic-depressive manifestation of the disorder. In this case the sufferer goes through a profound psychotic depression, wherein the baby is often rejected, or the woman herself feels suicidal. On the other hand she may feel elated, distractible, with grandiose delusions about the baby's status in the world. Significantly, the condition is sometimes accompanied by a morbid fear of bad health or preoccupation with physical appearance.

In both the depressive and the manic phases, the symptoms closely parallel clinical secondary narcissism wherein self-absorption is taken to an extreme. There is an inability to imagine what others may be feeling, or to empathise with what others are going through, or a willingness to do so. Instead, there are frequent attempts to elevate or glorify the self by humiliating others.

But unlike secondary narcissism, puerperal psychosis stems from physiological causes, and this can seem particularly cruel in light of the effect upon family and friends. The condition is disruptive, particularly upsetting and confusing to children who can carry the effects of the ailment without understanding its source. Most poignantly, as in physical injury or other cases where psychotic symptoms result from physiological sources, the very traits that make up the most desirable parts of the sufferer's character become distorted, so what the family loved most about the person now can cause revulsion. Family members and friends can be left in a state of perpetual confusion about the woman's motivations and actions as she tries to interact. The condition also accounts for a high number of marital breakdowns. Ironically, there are periods of tremendous lucidity, causing added confusion to those around the affected woman.

If, in fact, this was the condition affecting Patricia's behaviour, her dependence upon prescription and homeopathic drugs might very well have been a subconscious attempt at self-medication. In the event, there is no question that the reliance upon drugs would exacerbate the condition.

In a particularly weak moment Vere once told one of his employees that life with Patricia was intolerable, life without her unthinkable. It was a much-quoted sentiment, but few realised then how much Vere genuinely loved his wife, and it was a very apt statement to describe the difficulties he was encountering more and more as Patricia changed.

Patricia began dressing more extravagantly, favouring opulent Zandra Rhodes designs. But at the same time she was putting on weight and these creations were not the most flattering she could have chosen. She took to carrying her own pink champagne with her to parties, with the result that she was given a nickname she came to hate. Gossip columnist

Nigel Dempster had called her 'Bubbles' because of the champagne and also because of her bubbly personality.

What no one knew was that Patricia prepared herself for the parties as if she were going on the stage. She felt genuine stage fright beforehand, even taking pills to shore up her courage. Then she would dash to as many as half a dozen parties in an evening, trying to turn in a credible 'performance' as a woman who was enjoying herself. As for the nickname 'Bubbles', which stuck, Patricia resented it because 'it doesn't make me seem a very serious person'.

The truth was she wasn't considered by the outside world as a serious person or an intelligent woman. She was mostly identified as a social butterfly, with no more serious purpose in life than to go to a lot of parties and have a good time. Patricia longed for people to see her as a more involved personality than that, to recognise her charity work and her intelligence, but it was not to be. Her style of living didn't lend confidence to an image of reliability and maturity.

Then, in 1978, she shared a profoundly upsetting year with her husband and one that would end up bringing an end to the marriage. It started on 13 January, a Friday, when Patricia's country house, Stroods, caught fire. Patricia was staying in Eaton Square at the time and her daughter Sarah was with her when they got word. Patricia was so upset that Sarah had to drive her down to the estate in East Sussex. Vere was in New York, but he returned immediately.

Patricia suffered a devastating loss: all her family memorabilia and her personal belongings, including photographs and cuttings that went back for years. She had kept private diaries since her childhood and these were lost along with the photo albums with pictures of her children growing up. To the *Daily Express* she made a formal statement, 'The house is mine, and it has been a great shock to me.' She complained of losing all her old theatrical mementoes, including dresses she had worn on the stage. There were rumours of arson, but Patricia told her daughter Camilla that the Christmas tree had been left with all the decorations still on it and it had gone up in flames. In all, over £250,000 worth of damage was done.

It was also the year that Vere left England, renting an apartment on the Ile St Louis, where he was to stay for over two decades. But at the bottom of everything was the fact that his marriage to Patricia had fallen apart.

Now there was much talk of a divorce and lawyers began 'circling round' Patricia, as one family friend put it. For a time, she had as her counsel Roy Cohn, who had been counsel to Senator Joseph McCarthy during the notorious hearings of the House on Un-American Activities Committee in the United States Congress. John Hemingway was asked to speak with him at his house in New York and was somewhat surprised to find him in his dressing gown. At that time Cohn kept saying, 'We just must have a meeting, we must have a meeting.'

Then, when John was in the South of France at the Hôtel de Paris in Monaco, Roy Cohn made good his plan for the meeting. He and one of his law partners took Concorde from New York to Paris where they stayed the night. The next morning they flew to Monaco, took a helicopter from the airport and met John for a one-and-a-half-hour lunch at the Hôtel de Paris. That evening, they returned by helicopter to the airport, took a flight to Paris and returned on the Concorde to New York from there. Recalling the episode Hemingway said wryly, 'I can never remember who paid for lunch.'

It was a good example of the kind of legal advice Patricia was getting.

In the end, however, the couple did not divorce. Vere didn't believe in divorce, having lived through the ravages of both his parents' divorces first-hand. So when he and Patricia decided their marriage was over, they worked out a unique agreement, one that would be misunderstood for as long as Patricia was alive. They separated legally, Vere settling an immense annual allowance, a seven-figure sum, on Patricia, ironically, one that she was never able to live on.

Whenever he was in London he escorted Patricia to any social events she wanted to attend. For her part she became especially well known for her annual Christmas Party at Claridge's, given for the employees of Associated Newspapers. She also continued to support the Evening Standard Drama Awards.

But the separation did result in a great deal of confusion, perhaps even causing harm in the long run. Because Vere never made a formal announcement of their separation so that Patricia could continue to enjoy the social position she had occupied since marrying him, people never really knew they were apart.

So when Patricia started dating other people, it looked improper and seemed to reflect badly on Vere. In fact, both of them were free to see whomever they pleased. Beyond that, the couple remained best friends, enjoying one another a good deal of the time. In a strange way they were closer once the separation was agreed. Under these singular circumstances it was a marriage that lasted until Patricia's death.

FOURTEEN

DAVID AT HIS BEST

David English had witnessed at first-hand the immense pain that could he caused by 'the Holy Spirit Foundation for the Unification of World Christianity', otherwise known as the Unification Church. Led by its South Korean 'Messiah', the Reverend Sun Myung Moon, the organisation attracted much of its membership from well-meaning youths who could be easily swept away by their idealism. Moon's followers were called 'Moonies', a nickname springing from the word 'Zombies', because of their trance-like obedience to their leader's dictates.

When David worked in the United States, a son of one of his neighbours had been taken by the cult and the family suffered terribly when it became apparent the boy was not coming back. Then, later, David saw a British family go through the same thing when their son was taken by the church. David described the phenomenon in highly emotional terms – how the boy became intrigued by the group outside a railway station in San Francisco as he was hitch-hiking across the United States on holiday. He never again emerged to rejoin the outside world. David described the promising young man as 'coming under their complete control'. He later wrote,

> In the weeks that followed, I saw the seeds of disintegration take root and tear that family apart. Michael, the son, stopped writing to his family after one missive telling them he had found a new kind of life. His father, with some help, traced him to a Moonie settlement in New York.

But when the boy's father went to see him to try to persuade him to come home, 'the boy was cold and indifferent, he refused to stay in the same room with his father alone'. The father returned to the UK without his son, 'shaken and disturbed'.

David then traced how the event affected the family. They began to fight among themselves, blaming one another for the loss of their son, the mother taking heavier and heavier doses of tranquillisers in order to cope. The family literally fell apart as they began to realise that their gifted boy, who had been headed to Oxford on a scholarship, was working ten-hour days on buildings sites for churches and offices needed by the cult.

But it wasn't only this experience that drove David to write the first of his attacks on the Unification Church in the *Daily Mail*. It was a series of letters from readers begging the *Daily Mail* to help them get back their children. 'That is one of the things a newspaper is for,' David wrote later, 'to fight for its readers.'

So began the *Daily Mail*'s exposé of 'The Church that Breaks Up Families'. The Unification Church was popularly known as the Moonies' Church because of its methods of enlisting young people from around the world. The particular type of brainwashing used by the group was called 'love bombing', wherein the person being inducted is never left alone for a moment to think things through for himself. Scholars who make a study of this kind of group said that the church made simplistic, frequently repeated appeals in a language of idealism that would be typical of students and young adults who wanted to help humanity. Once inside, these young people were constantly surrounded by like-minded individuals who reinforced the beliefs of the cult.

Another of the mind control methods of the cult was sleep interruption. It was common for the inductees to be awakened in the middle of the night with sermons and repetitions of the church's goals and aims. Fed a high-sugar diet, called 'sugar-buzzing', this, along with sleep deprivation, would usually render an inductee amiable to the suggestions of the church. The acolytes took on 'zombie-like' characteristics, becoming eager to obey their superiors. They were then set to work doing either menial labour or begging on the streets for as many as fifteen hours a day. The money they received was recycled for use as the leadership saw fit, which, unsurprisingly, included the support of a lavish lifestyle for Moon and his wives and children and the upper administration of the church.

The *Mail*'s publication of 'The Story of David' was what actually brought about the church's charge of libel. In the story headlined THEY TOOK AWAY MY SON AND THEN RAPED HIS MIND, a moving account of a family's loss of their son was told by the boy's father Warren Adler, who was a writer. His son was eventually repatriated to them, after his father almost literally kidnapped him. Adler wrote afterwards, '[The cult] operate on deception through idealism and their credibility is enormous.'

But even before this article and several others were run, David English knew the opinions of the lawyers at Associated Newspapers. They had predicted the Unification Church would bring a libel action if he went ahead with the story and, if they prevailed, the damages could be ruinous. This kind of legal assault was possible because of the archaic libel laws of the United Kingdom that permitted, and continue to permit, suits that would be considered frivolous in most other civilised countries of the world. In the case of the Unification Church the leaders inevitably would claim, said Associated's lawyers, that the *Daily Mail*'s allegation saying the church broke up families was untruthful. They would defend the church by saying that their followers entered the cult voluntarily. And if they were able to prove that, the damages could reach millions.

Moreover, the church was conducting its law case through its UK spiritual director Dennis Orme. He was a virtually penniless individual, backed by the church, who was claiming that, as the church's UK director, *he* had been subjected to humiliation and embarrassment by the untruthful article. But because he, Dennis Orme, had no assets, it would be a practical impossibility for the *Mail* to collect its own costs.

The lawyers also advised that defending the case would be incredibly costly. Witnesses would have to be brought in from around the world and their testimony carefully co-ordinated in order to achieve a favourable outcome. Again, recovering the costs of their air fare and lodgings would be almost impossible. And defending libel suits in general was always a minefield; there was never any guarantee of success, because of the potential emotionality of the jury, even in a case like this one, where the Unification Church's unpopularity was manifest.

On the other hand the plaintiffs in the case, if they were given good legal advice, would probably be content to accept a public apology for the *Mail*'s allegations, their full withdrawal and a small emolument, given to a charity of their choice.

But despite all these arguments David English, Mick Shields and Vere Rothermere all agreed the *Mail* should run the article and, if need be, defend the case. The questions at stake were of such importance that none of them felt they could do otherwise. In the first place, the cult had brought so much misery to families in America who had lost their sons and daughters that it seemed a small price to pay if this lawsuit could prevent the same thing happening in England. In the second, the freedom-of-speech issue at stake was very basic – whether a newspaper has the right to criticise an organisation it believes guilty of heinous misbehaviour.

The barrister selected to defend the action was Peter Rawlinson QC, a former Attorney-General with a distinguished legal and political career. He was an expert in libel who had defended many cases for the *Mail*. But this case was like no other. It was destined to last longer than any libel case tried until that time in Britain, over a hundred days, six months actually in court, and with 117 witnesses called from all over the world.

In his autobiography, *A Price Too High*, Rawlinson would later describe what he called 'this mammoth operation'.

> Vast files of documents were built up as we scoured through all the writings of the 'Messiah' and his lieutenants. The business and corporate affairs of the captive companies in which the proceeds of the street begging had been invested were analysed. Psychologists and psychiatrists were sought for their advice and if possible their agreement to come to London to testify at the trial. For it would be necessary to show to the jury the effect of the methods used to recruit and then indoctrinate and then retain the young people who had been sucked into the organisation, and to explain how there had been achieved the bitter alienation from their families whereby the Moonie neophytes became convinced that hitherto loved parents were now evil creatures of the devil. Theologians had to be canvassed so that they might come and tell the jury that a faith that elevated the South Korean into the Messiah and denigrated Jesus Christ could hardly rank as a Christian Church. All this demanded a supreme effort…

One witness travelled from South America after he was persuaded to testify about the production of the barrel of an automatic infantry weapon in factories owned by the Rev. Moon. Others agreed to come only if they were housed in certain hotels or flown on Concorde. The *Daily Mail* reported later,

> Of vital importance to the case was Dr Margaret Singer, who was professor of psychology at the University of California. She was one of the United States' leading experts on cults, having conducted specific research into the mind control methods used by the Moonies.

Given the enormous costs being accumulated, the managerial staff on the *Daily Mail* became more and more concerned with cutting expenses. During the conduct of the trial it did begin to look as if the *Mail* would win. But at the end of the day, would the church actually pay up? Eventually the idea was hit upon to name Dennis Orme as a 'nominal witness', that is, a witness whose reputation has not actually been damaged, but who is in truth acting on behalf of others. In this capacity, the defence side was able to have paid into court security for libel costs in several stages. By the end of the lengthy trial, the amount that had been paid in was £215,000.

The final result was a triumph for the *Daily Mail*. On 1 April 1981 the jury brought back a verdict that justified all the efforts of the last six months. The *Daily Mail* story was headlined: DAILY MAIL WINS HISTORIC LIBEL ACTION: THE DAMNING VERDICT ON THE MOONIES.

> The *Daily Mail* was RIGHT to expose the Moonies quasi-religious sect as 'the church that breaks up families', a High Court jury decided yesterday.
>
> As a result, the Government is ordering a review of the Moonies' activities, including the effect of their psychiatric techniques on young members.
>
> In the High Court, the jury delivered its verdict for the *Mail* after the longest and costliest libel case in British legal history, ruling that the Moonies' UK leader Dennis Orme had not been libelled by this newspaper.
>
> And the six men and five women added two riders to their verdict: They urged that the charitable status of the Unification Church – the Moonies' official title – should be examined by the Inland Revenue on the grounds that it was really a political organisation; and they expressed their 'deep compassion' for all the young people still members of the sect.

This was a great victory for freedom of the press. It was a complete vindication of the right of the *Daily Mail*, or any newspaper, to criticise the activities of a suspect organisation, no matter how rich or powerful.

As it turned out, the Unification Church retained its charitable status in the United Kingdom; the newspaper did not succeed in changing that.

But the newspaper did succeed in keeping the Moonies out of the country. And later on, the *Mail* was able to provide authorities in the United States with evidence that would prove helpful in showing the Rev. Moon's tax evasion in America. In terms of acting on behalf of the interests of its readers, and of the interests of the nation, this was arguably the *Mail*'s finest hour.

Twenty-four hours before the Moonies case was decided, David English was hosting a party for a visiting journalist from the *Los Angeles Times*, Tom Plate.

David had met Plate at the 1980 Republican Convention in Detroit, seeking him out at the suggestion of a *Times* editor, Jim Bellows. By Bellows and later by Plate, David English was seen as a priceless character and talented journalist, well worth the effort of getting to know. As it turned out, Tom Plate and David hit it off as personal friends, with Plate somewhat in awe of David's ready wit.

At the convention Tom was running splash pieces for his newspaper, and one day he wrote a piece predicting that George Bush would be the vice-presidential nominee and explaining the reasons he believed that.

But over the television, at 6 p.m. that evening, a network broadcaster said that Gerald Ford would be the likely nominee. As Tom Plate later recounted, English looked at him and said,

'Oh, Mr Plate, you will be sacked.' He needled me relentlessly and I said, 'David, it's true I may be sacked. But I'm telling you Bush is going to be the nominee.'

Then Bush was nominated. David looked over at me and said, 'You look like you've swallowed a thousand cats.'

As David sat there, he spun out a scenario in which the American journalist would come to London to work for a while and before the Convention ended he had talked Plate into doing just that. Plate was invited to become a guest editor and writer for the *Mail* for several months. The American journalist duly turned up in the winter of 1981, just when the Moonies trial was at its height, so he was able to see for himself how David handled that challenge.

But overall, the experiment of having a visiting journalist proved so successful that David decided to throw a party for Tom and his wife at his Westminster home. Plate said later,

Of course one of the things that was so much fun was David's conviviality. He worked hard and he played hard.

So this was a typical British party in that there was a lot of drinking, so it was loud and boisterous and a great deal of fun and very lively.

What we didn't know was that, while we were sitting there having a good time, back in America, President Ronald Reagan had been shot by a twenty-five-year-old college drop-out named John Hinkley.

David's deputy editor Peter Grover tried to call David's house to inform him of what had happened so they could remake the newspaper. But the party had become 'so loud and raucous' that nobody heard the telephone ringing. According to Plate,

So Peter wrote a little note, put it into an envelope and gave it to one of the *Mail* drivers. He drove across town at the speed of light, was pounding at the door, and finally someone heard it! So the note is delivered to the table, and David opens it and it says, 'President Reagan has been shot. Extent of the injury is unknown at this time. It would be helpful to me if you and Mr Plate could return to the office. *But the one I need most is Mr Plate.*'

Nothing Peter Grover could have written, Tom Plate said later, could have made more certain that David English would be in the car going back to the *Mail* that evening.

> So David and I got in the car and were going across London. And it's raining and it's dark and the driver is running late and as we're coming across David doesn't say a word. And I don't say anything, realising he's thinking of how he will remake the newspaper. I had told him that I had won a major American journalism award for deadline writing. I am sitting in the back seat and I hear this voice of doom coming over, 'OK, Mr Deadline Writer, now we will see how good you really are.'

What Plate wrote was a think piece and it was carried in the *Mail* beside the leader. David was pleased with the work.

So David told Plate that he believed he should come back to work for the *Mail* every year for his 'Fleet Street Booster Shot', an immunisation to prevent him, as a typical American journalist, 'from coming down with the disease of taking myself too seriously! And it worked! It really worked!'

Plate wasn't David's only friend among the press corps in America. David actually enjoyed something of a following there. His friendships multiplied and eventually Jim Hoge met him through a mutual friend. Hoge was the golden boy of newspaper publishing, a young and handsome publisher who took New York by storm when he left Chicago and moved up to become the publisher for the *New York Daily News*. Hoge had long admired David English's work, so when he took over in 1983, he asked David to come in and make some suggestions.

'David worked as an unpaid consultant on the *Daily News*, as a friend,' said Jim Hoge later. 'And he was very, very helpful, as he always is.'

As was customary with David, he brought in an entire team of his own men, taking the place by storm with his usual powerhouse approach. But he fell foul of Gil Spenser, the famed editor of the *News*, who was a powerful force in his own right:

> David was in New York and he and I met, and then he brought over some people who had worked with him to show us some of the things that they might do with the paper. This was working in England but it just wouldn't work for the *Daily News*. They were going to bring over a whole group of people, technicians etc., to put this into action, a whole redo of the design of the newspaper. At that point, I asked him to forget about it, and we did it another way.

But if Gil Spenser wasn't enamoured of David's efforts, Anthea Disney remembered how skilled an operator he was. At the time, she was working on the *Daily News* as features editor.

> One day I was walking through this gigantic features room and I called my secretary, who was this girl from Queens, and she said, 'There's a guy here—'
>
> And I heard this voice going, 'Anthea, Anthea, look!' And I looked up and I went, 'Oh, my God, it's David.' It was such a pleasure to see this person who was on the money, who knew what he was doing. He put a big picture on page one and a big centre spread with big pictures going across in the style of the *Daily Mail*, and of course they didn't do things like that.
>
> David was a brilliant layout man, I think a much more talented layout man and headline writer than he was a writer or editor of words. I think that was David's great strength – presentation. He was a great showman. That's what made him fun to work with.

But the Americans would have no part of it. They took themselves far too seriously to go with a layout that jumped out of the page at the reader. Anthea had her own take on it:

> …all these dreadful American journalists, they had no idea what tabloid meant. They had no idea what having fun meant. Here was this person… David didn't believe it had to be all life or death, he believed you could have fun. We stayed in touch ever since.

It was true that, along with driving his staff harder than any other editor, David also knew how to have a good time. And his editorial staff loved him for it. They worked hard and David often rewarded them with terrific parties 'where champagne flowed like water'.

At one unforgettable party, a news editor was retiring. One of his favourite stories was the one of the corpse that suddenly comes alive in the mortuary. Peter Grover later told the tale:

> This chap was always presenting stories of this kind. Where he got them from, I don't know. So for his party, David got a skeleton and a trolley from the hospital. And he put this skeleton on it with a sheet over it. And David trundled it in and said, 'This is your latest scoop' and whipped the sheet off.

Then, when Brian Freemantle, the foreign news editor, decided to quit, he had a marvellous going away 'do' as well. For many years Freemantle had travelled by rail from his home in Southampton to work and back again. While he was on the train he wrote books – seventeen of them. All of them failed to be published. But finally he got a film based on a character in one of his novels, Charlie Muffin. After that his books took off and he became a best-selling author.

To celebrate his great success and early leave-taking from the *Daily Mail*, David English and Peter Grover and a couple of others got into harness and carried Brian Freemantle to Waterloo Station by rickshaw.

Much later, when Peter Grover himself and Ted Jeffery retired, David actually hired a train to take them to a secret destination. It began its journey at Blackfriars Station and proceeded south on to Lingfield. When the train stopped for a few minutes at Croydon, people waiting to go home actually tried getting on David's train, but stopped when they saw the carriages full of men in black tie with party hats on, alongside their wives. One of the carriages had a band going and couples were dancing, at last convincing those who tried to join them on their journey that this was a private party.

Once they arrived, a coach and horses were waiting for Grover and Jeffery and their wives, and it carried them to the racecourse just outside town and did a lap round the track. Grover again:

We ended up at the Banqueting Suite, and David stood up and said, 'Now I'd like to introduce our special guest.' On walked Mrs Thatcher, not the real Mrs Thatcher but this wonderful woman who did a perfect imitation of her, handbag and all.

Later on, when David retired as editor of the *Daily Mail* in order to take over as chairman of Associated Newspapers, he gave a party wherein he and all his editorial staff dressed up like Hitler and various members of the Third Reich. A memorable appearance of the newspaper's drama critic Jack Tinker as Goebbels brought the house down.

But David English wasn't the only one who hosted parties. After Vere had secured *Esquire* magazine and *SoHo News* in New York City, he gave a terrific party at the MGM Grand Hotel at the American Newspapers Proprietors Association held in Las Vegas in 1978. Over at Caesar's Palace, Frank Sinatra was giving a performance, so Vere told Norman Heath, the promotions director, to get tables for twenty-five people. But the performance had already been sold out long in advance. Alwyn Robinson reminisced later,

Norman just kept calling me, saying, 'Bring more cash, bring more cash!' And we kept taking down more money and more money and more money. And eventually we got the tables, but it took a whole day and a whole lot of $50 bills. But Vere hadn't cared what it cost. He expected we would get the tables.

The following year the American NPA was held in Los Angeles and David English, John Leese and John Winnington-Ingram came out along with Alwyn Robinson and Vere. David said, 'We have to have a toast-master.' But in the United States, there were no toastmasters to be found.

So Norman Heath enlisted an out-of-work actor and sent for a suit that was flown in the next day. Thus it was that Norman found himself teaching an American actor how to be a British toastmaster. *Washington Post* proprietor Katharine Graham and media mogul Sy Newhouse attended, as did every major proprietor of every national newspaper. Norman arranged to have that day's issue of the *Daily Mail* flown in by Concorde and Norman remembered it as one of Vere's greatest moments. 'He was over the moon!'

Promotions manager Norman Heath, whose enthusiasm was legendary, was the man put in charge of one of the *Daily Mail*'s most famous, or notorious, promotions – Casino. The whole thing started when other national newspapers in London were beginning to see their circulations slide, and suddenly the *Mirror* started Bingo to try to retain their reader-ship. Although the *Daily Mail* wasn't actually losing sales as the game got underway, it became apparent that it would be, if somebody didn't think of a retaliatory promotion. Said Norman,

So David and Vere put their heads together and said, 'Let's launch Casino. It has to be upmarket and we have to have a winning number every night. There was only one place to go and that's Monte Carlo.

'So get going, Norman. Get down there and start this game up.' I jumped on a plane with photographer Monty Fresco and flew down. I talked with the man who ran the casino there and he said, 'You'd better talk to the guys who run our American Room. If those guys are in agreement, we'll do it.' We met them, and they were a couple of East Enders. And they said, 'Don't worry about paying us any money, we'll do it. Just bring us back some cockles and whelks when you come down here next time.'

We established a telephone link. Every night they spun the wheel and sent the winning number to the editorial, and it was published the next morning. It was very popular.

Then one day, every telephone line in the south of England was suddenly blocked. All the telephones went down and suddenly it was 'Fortress Northcliffe House'.

The computer had made an error and we had 100,000 winners! People were on their holidays, and they turned around and came back. And the telephone lines just jammed up.

A lot of the winners, when they couldn't get through, lined up in front of the building. And I had to go out and tell them there were too many winners and it had all been a big mistake!

The *Daily Mail* already had forty or fifty phones being manned for the normal work day and promotions activities. But they were swamped in minutes when the contestants who believed they had won began phoning in to claim their prizes. Thus were the telephone lines across the country blocked.

The damage control for the embarrassing episode fell to Norman Heath. He quickly got together with some of his colleagues and they cooked up an idea that if the prize was split, everybody would get 37p. Armed with this knowledge, Heath went to Coutts Bank and said to their banker, 'Can you do a hundred thousand cheques and put "Pay the Bearer 37p" on all of them?' The banker assured Norman that he could do this, but it would have to be for 50p. Norman believed people wouldn't actually cash their cheques, but instead would frame them as a kind of joke. And that was what happened. All around the country, people were waking up to find they had a cheque for a windfall of 50p.

The morning the cheques arrived, the cartoonist Mac, without telling anyone, showed up with a marvellous cartoon of people lined up in front of the *Daily Mail* with their cheques for 50p. The caption read, 'Yes, I'm a Casino winner, but I won't let it change my way of life.'

Inside Associated Newspapers the matter was allowed to drop and Norman Heath wisely formed the habit of never referring to it himself. Better, he reasoned, to let sleeping dogs lie. This continued until many years later, at his retirement party, suddenly the entire Casino affair came back to haunt him.

Heath retired in 1983 and in honour of the occasion David English published a four-page 'Special Edition' of the *Daily Mail*. Across the top was the streamer, 'Norman Heath (Mr Fixit of Fleet St) retires.' Beneath it, in screaming 180-point type, was the banner headline 'A LEGEND IN HIS OWN LUNCHTIME'.

The story explained how restaurateurs and head waiters throughout London were going into mourning at the announcement of Norman

Heath's retirement. Yes, 'Mr Fixit of Associated Newspapers was finally folding up his napkin'. As a result, 'the cry of "Have some more champagne, old boy, it's all on the house" will no longer ring out with the same joyous insistence,' the parody continued. With tongue firmly in cheek, David English stood up to toast the departing promotions director and said that no other promotions man in Fleet Street 'could match his genius at crowd-pulling'. David continued,

> This culminated in his greatest triumph in assembling a queue of 187,000 people outside Northcliffe House for seventeen hours to cash in their chips.
>
> This event produced more publicity for the *Daily Mail* in rival newspapers and on TV than any other daily newspaper promotion. It was indeed Heath's finest hour. And it might have been his last!

It was typical of David to give the well-liked Norman Heath a great send-off. This was David at his best. He was a fountainhead for wild and zany ideas like this one, where everybody had a good time.

It was the David English who had ideas for madcap features that made people laugh at the same time as he made a point. One of his most outlandish features occurred after he received a number of complaints about the Royal Mail. Somehow David came up with the idea that he would mail three letters: one by first class, one by second and one, no kidding, by pony express.

For this stunt he hired John Evans, an assistant instructor at Windmill Hill Riding Academy, near Stratford-upon-Avon. Evans was to ride from Elstree directly to Kenilworth, being timed against the two other letters. Some thirteen hours and fifty-seven minutes later, riding on a horse called True Blue, John Evans delivered his letter to the town council office, where he was greeted with a bottle of champagne. The first-class letter arrived the same day, two hours later. As to the second-class letter, it came twenty-four hours later.

David had made his point but he was not content to stop there. For his follow-up he wanted to give the new courier services competing with the Royal Mail a chance to show what they could do. So he drafted Colin Reid, crated him up and had him delivered by the SkyPacket Courier Service to Toronto. Reid was Job No. 3328, with a freight weight of 176 lb, and a bill of lading that listed the reporter as 'Livestock–homo sapiens'. More like 'homo-nutcase', Reid's wife said as he was carried out of the house.

In Toronto Colin Reid's brother was celebrating his birthday. So in his hand, Colin held a bottle of champagne. As Reid put it later, 'I was sending my brother a bottle of champagne to help celebrate. I just happened to be attached to it.'

There were only two close calls for Reid in his quest to get to Canada by courier. The first was when a customs' official in Canada asked whether he had been treated for 'Foot and Mouth Disease'. But here Reid was saved by the courier, who talked him through.

The second was something he didn't anticipate. It was twenty-three degrees below zero, 'despite assurances that Canada was having a mild winter'. So Reid was nearly frozen through by the time he arrived. But he did arrive in Toronto in time for his brother's birthday, one day after he started.

Perhaps the most successful of all the *Daily Mail* stunts, however, came in 1987, about four years after Des Nichols took over from Norman Heath in the Promotions Department.

On Monday, 30 March, Rod Gilchrist, deputy editor of the *Mail on Sunday*, was leafing through a Sotheby's catalogue of the jewellery that had once been owned by the Duchess of Windsor. It was being sold for an AIDS charity. Rod called Des Nichols over, suggesting they get some of the jewels and create a competition for the *Daily Mail*. Later that day, when Des suggested the idea to David English, he jumped at it in his 'marvellously enthusiastic way'. He immediately got the catalogue, went through it and told Des exactly what he wanted.

By 2 April Des Nichols was sitting at the 9 p.m. auction at the Hôtel Beau Rivage in Geneva, alongside celebrities like Shirley Bassey and Joan Collins while Elizabeth Taylor opted to put her bids in by telephone. Nichols later said,

> The whole problem with this was we had to do it in a very cloak-and-dagger way because of the threat of a spoiler from another newspaper. So out I went with a cheque for £126,000 ... and I actually did a deal with a chap from the auction house named David Bennett who was bidding for me.
>
> I wouldn't be bidding on the floor. I would just be indicating what I wanted to David Bennett who was sitting with a telephone to his ear pretending he was taking a message from America.

Despite the fact that he was bidding against some very determined celebrities, Nichols managed to get a compact with sapphires, rubies, emeralds and amethysts on the front with a map of Europe on the back.

Various locations joined by ruby, sapphire or emerald stones outlined a 'love-cruise' taken by the couple on the fateful trip where the two of them fell in love.

But Des's £126,000, which seemed such a lot back home, didn't go very far once he got to the auction. The jewelled compact set him back £65,843, although it was actually a bargain at the price. He also managed to get an 18-carat gold, enamel and diamond clip in the shape of a panther for a mere £26,748. When he got the Duchess's trademark pearl necklace, with 15 rows of pearls twisted with a diamond clasp, he actually did have to go over his allocation. In fact, Des was later to discover that he had paid a world record for artificial pearls.

With all his jewels tucked safely away in a plastic bag in his pocket, Nichols flew home at 4.30 the next day, where he was met by Rod Gilchrist. Typical of Rod, 'he grabbed the jewels, patted me on the back and carried them away to put in a television commercial. The way it worked out,' Nichols said later,

> *News at Ten* had an enormous feature about the auction and the sale and how the prices had gone through the roof. We actually had an ad in the break, saying 'Win these Jewels'. We had an incredible response to this, well over half a million entries for each item they were trying to get, and the readers even had to collect tokens to enter!

The public was wildly enthusiastic about owning something previously owned by the glamorous Duchess of Windsor. But when all was said and done, and the jewellery had been awarded to the winners, Des Nichols was surprised to find out that, despite the 'tender sentimental story' attached to each piece of jewellery, practically every piece found its way back to Sotheby's to be sold. Sentimental they may be, but the readers liked the cash better.

Somewhat anticlimactically, Des was the man put in charge of seeing that the jewellery attracted private buyers – and of keeping the matter out of rival newspapers.

FIFTEEN

UP THE DOWN ESCALATOR

It was not uncommon for Patricia Rothermere to ring David English direct, especially when she was seeking information. But one particular morning she seemed slightly rattled when she called, which was out of character.

'I was going through Vere's suit pockets,' she said candidly, 'when I found a telephone number.'

'Yes?' David said.

'I think he must have a girlfriend, and you must find out who she is.'

The *Daily Mail* editor agreed to do what she asked, because he really had no choice. He hung up the phone, picked it up again and dialled the number. To his surprise, a man's voice answered.

'Who's speaking?' David asked.

'This is Bernard Shrimsley.'

David quickly hung up without speaking. He sat at his desk for some few minutes, putting two and two together. It didn't take long to figure out that Vere had hired Shrimsley as the editor of his new venture – the *Mail on Sunday*. Feeling the full irony of the situation, David realised that, after all, Vere wasn't being unfaithful to his wife.

'No,' said David several years later. 'He was being unfaithful to *me*!'

Just after he left the *News of the World*, where he had been editor for five years, Bernard Shrimsley received a confidential telephone call from Mick Shields, managing director of Associated Newspapers. Vere was going to start a Sunday newspaper, Shields confided, and he wanted to meet secretly with Bernard at a suite at the Savoy.

A few days later, on 12 June 1980, Bernard met with Rothermere, where Vere described to him at length the details of his plan for a Sunday newspaper. It was to be a middle-market tabloid, aimed at ABC1 readers between the ages of fifteen and forty-five, its biggest potential market the young married couples who had moved into the new private housing estates that were springing up around the country. Vere paused a moment, looked straight into Shrimsley's eyes and asked, 'Would you like the job of editing it?'

Shrimsley gave his answer succinctly: 'Yes.'

Rothermere then uttered three words that very much surprised Bernard. '*Don't tell David!*' he said.

But Vere was wasting his breath, because David, of course, already knew.

There were many theories about why Rothermere chose Bernard Shrimsley to edit his new Sunday tabloid, leaving David entirely out in the cold. One that appeared frequently in print was that Rothermere was jealous of David and wanted an achievement all his own. Another more political take was that David and Vere had discussed the issue privately, and David had actually taken a hand in the selection The most Machiavellian version was that David himself had nominated Shrimsley, knowing that his type of journalism was bound to fail and he could eventually take charge, winning the day.

Even though Fleet Street was awash with such rumours, it was not very likely that David English had a clue as to Vere's intentions until he learned about them from Patricia. Certainly, Bernard Shrimsley didn't put much credence into what was being said.

But he had been actively discouraged from taking on the job by John Junor, who said, 'The whole thing is only a game, laddie. It will never happen.' Junor theorised that the *Mail on Sunday* was little more than a subterfuge to destabilise the already shaky *Express* management.

But Shrimsley knew for a fact that Rothermere's intentions were very serious and he was beginning to get a feel for how difficult his plans would be to put into practice. It was going to be an uphill battle to wrest readers away from the *Sunday Express*, a strong rival. And there was going to be a great deal of internal resistance. Nevertheless, Shrimsley still entered into the deal with the highest optimism and couldn't wait to get started.

But only a few weeks after he arrived at Associated, a major distraction occurred. The *Evening News* merged into the *Evening Standard*. In practical terms this meant the *News* was closing and the agenda for the new Sunday tabloid began to get lost as all the management energy went into the deal. Even Shrimsley himself got drawn in when Vere asked him to interview all the *News* journalists to see if he could find a place for any of them on the new paper. This entailed about a hundred interviews and Bernard couldn't help feeling bogged down by the task.

Then again, there was the ambience of the place. For the many years he had worked for Murdoch, where there were no familial feelings whatsoever, it had been all business and no sentiment. Here at Associated,

The Young Vere. Shy, introverted, unhappy, Vere showed few signs of the Harmsworth genius in his formative years. His mother Peggy over-protected him. His father Esmond told friends, 'Don't bother with him.' Against Vere's mother, he instigated the longest divorce proceedings in the history of English jurisprudence. Vere later said, 'I spend the first 45 years of my life getting over my childhood.'

Patricia Matthews. As a young Rank Studios starlet, Patricia was named by the photographer Baron as one of the top ten beauties in England. But Vere's attraction to Patricia was less a matter of her looks than of her vivacity and enthusiasm for living.

2 November 1978, memorial service for Vere's father Esmond. Front row, left to right, Vere's sister Lorna; Vere; his son Jonathan; his half brother Esmond Jr.; Esmond's wife Mary. Behind, Vere's mother Peggy, Patricia, daughter Camilla; above Camilla, partially shown, stepdaughter Sarah; left, daughter Geraldine, Lorna's son Esmond. A fraught year for Vere, he and Patricia signed a Legal Agreement of Separation, effectively ending their marriage of 21 years, and Vere left England to live in France. He said later, 'I was disillusioned with my father, and I went to live away. I had other reasons to go, certainly. But the truth was, I just wasn't happy here anymore.'

Jonathan, Patricia, Camilla, Geraldine, Vere, Sarah – at Jonathan's 21st birthday party at Claridge's.

Above: 15 July 1993. Jonathan and Claudia Clemence marry at the Church of the Immaculate Conception, in Farm Street, Mayfair. The couple moved to Glasgow, where Jonathan went to work at the *Scottish Daily Record* and *Sunday Mail. Below:* 18 May 1997. Christening party for Eleanor Patricia Margaret Harmsworth, second child of Jonathan and Claudia. Jonathan, cutting cake; Camilla; Claudia; Lucinda Murray (godparent); Vere's second wife Maiko. Behind, Esmond Harmsworth (godparent); Fidelma Cook (godparent); Vere; Geraldine, with daughter Alfreda Harmsworth Maxwell; Claudia's mother Patricia Clemence; Geraldine's husband Glyn Maxwell; Claudia's father Terence Clemence; and Claudia's brother-in-law Richard Pilkington (godparent).

Above: Salzburg, 1995. Hamming it up with Jonathan and his Japanese Akita Ryu-ma.

Below: On the job.

Above: With Ryu-ma on his estate in the Dordogne.

Opposite top: Budapest, December, 1996. President Árpàd Göncz invests Vere with the Order of Merit of the Hungarian Republic, Middle Cross with Star—the highest honour that can be given to a foreigner who is not a head of state. The award reflects his grandfather Harold's involvement in Hungary in the late 1920s and Vere's commercial interests in Hungary's emerging economy, including the regional newspaper *Kisalfold* and the radio station Danubius.

Opposite below: Oxford, September, 1993. Vere and his sister Esme, the Dowager Countess of Cromer, are admitted to the Oxford University Chancellor's Court of Benefactors in recognition of significant contributions to the university's development and strength.

Farewell

Bernard felt the setting was like Ancient Rome, where his boss was surrounded by courtiers, all of whom seemed to represent vested interests. As far as the *Mail on Sunday* was concerned, there was a big effort afoot to resist the project, or at least to keep the costs down.

Mick Shields made no bones about his opposition to the project. He showed Bernard statistics proving that the new Sunday tabloid had no chance of succeeding. There was no way, Shields told Shrimsley, that the paper would be able to make a profit. 'You're trying to go up the down escalator, Bernard,' he concluded. It was the first of many demoralising interactions Shrimsley would have as he prepared for the launch of the *Mail on Sunday*.

The most upsetting was the Board of Directors' refusal to have a free colour magazine with the newspaper. They believed such a supplement was too expensive, considering the high costs they were incurring in the launch of the newspaper itself. Shrimsley believed it would be the deciding factor, but the best he could get was Vere's personal promise that he could have a magazine the following year.

For his part, Rothermere knew better than anybody that he was the only wholehearted supporter of the new project at Associated. It had been a highly controversial decision, and his alone. If it failed, Rothermere's continuation as chairman of the company would come under intense scrutiny. Yes, Vere's intentions were serious, deadly serious. Nobody knew better than he that the new tabloid was nothing less than a life-and-death matter.

Rothermere had wanted this paper since 1978 when his father died and he became chairman of Daily Mail and General Trust. And he had been actively involved in planning it for at least three years, and probably longer.

The history of Vere's involvement was dotted by numerous attempts on the part of Mick Shields to thwart him and bring a halt to the project. Shields had earlier reckoned that he could divert Rothermere from the idea by getting hold of the *Sunday Times* and with this in mind he entered into talks in 1979 with Harold Evans, the editor, about securing independent ownership.

But of the seven different potential buyers, who were referred to by Evans as 'the seven dwarfs', Rothermere was viewed with the most suspicion. Looking at the matter dispassionately, it was difficult to say why Rothermere struck such terror into the hearts of the general workforce at the *Sunday Times*. As history would show, the other contenders were not altogether sanguine in temperament. They included Rupert Murdoch, Robert Maxwell, Lord Matthews of the Express Group,

Jimmy Goldsmith, Robert Anderson of ARCO, which then owned the *Observer*, and a 'City consortium' associated with Australian Robert Holmes a Court.

But by Evans's estimation, Rothermere was the chief villain. During the shutdown of the Sunday title, NUJ members met with the controversial proprietor at the Howard Hotel. There Vere promised non-interference so long as Harold Evans remained editor. But something in his speech hit a sour note with the union officials: 'The *Daily Mail*', he said, 'is us and me, so to speak, it is our right arm and leg.' Evans reported later that the *Sunday Times* staff had no intention of becoming 'the left arm and leg'.

At the time of the discussion Mick Shields was quite open with Evans about his strategy of getting the *Sunday Times* in order to divert his employer from taking on 'a risky project, the *Mail on Sunday*'. For his part Evans believed the deal with Associated Newspapers fell apart because of Shields's desire for total control of the Sunday newspaper. Citing the desire of Associated to move its printing operation to Gray's Inn Road, Evans believed all Rothermere was interested in was 'a sordid property deal'. He opined that this arrangement would free Associated to sell Carmelite House on the open market. History would show that Evans was wrong.*

As to Thomson's reaction, they favoured Rupert Murdoch's bid because Associated was reluctant to take *The Times* along with the *Sunday Times*. Vere Rothermere said later,

> I didn't want *The Times*. I wanted the *Sunday Times*. What we wanted to do was somehow shunt off *The Times* where it would survive as a parish newspaper of the élite. So it would remain that way at a minimum loss situation because none of us could see how it could ever be made commercially viable. I couldn't see it and I don't think anybody else could either. And Rupert wasn't able to do it either. He came fairly close to it from time to time, depending on how you apportion the overheads.
>
> But the *Sunday Times* could become a very valuable newspaper. At that time it had all the potential for domination, if it was handled properly.

When the bids were submitted, Associated still had the *Evening News*. It was an open secret in the organisation that it wouldn't be long before it folded and when that happened the redundancy payments would be immense. Shields feared that *The Times* could also fold and, if Associated owned it, the company would face still more ruinous costs. But Rothermere saw it another way. He said later,

* Carmelite House and Northcliffe House were not sold until 1998. See chapter 22 for the details.

We needed three papers. It was the most efficient way of running this business. But that's not the first reason I wanted a Sunday newspaper.

The first reason was that there was a market. And it so happened that it would be very efficient for us to exploit the market because we had the equipment. Had we not had the equipment, we would have got it somewhere else. You start with a market and then you produce.

So first of all, I was absolutely convinced there was a market. The *Sunday Express* had become so out of touch, nothing had changed there, an antique product. And to my mind there was an opportunity.

If I had got the *Sunday Times*, I would have had the production equipment and the product. And if I had got it, I suppose I would have done both the *Sunday Times* and the *Mail on Sunday*.

In the end, Rothermere did not get the *Sunday Times* – and for two main reasons. The first was Rupert Murdoch's absolute determination to have it, to the extent of taking on the problems of the rudderless *Times* in order to secure its sister publication.

The second reason was that the offer made by Rothermere was adjudged by Thomson Newspapers to be 'fluffy' – a result of internal resistance inside Associated Newspapers.

'Associated's offer to Thomson Newspapers was fluffy', Rothermere said, 'because my managing director, Mick Shields, made it fluffy ... because in his heart he didn't want a Sunday newspaper at all!' So Shields, according to Rothermere, unconsciously sabotaged his own company's offer.

But even if he had got the *Sunday Times*, Rothermere wouldn't have abandoned his plan for a Sunday *Mail*. In Rothermere's scheme of things, there was never any alternative to launching a Sunday tabloid, which his intuition told him would not only survive, but prosper.

Even before the talks took place with Harold Evans and the *Sunday Times*, Vere had demonstrated his commitment to the project. He had recruited David Kirkby, who had spent many years as general manager of the *Sunday Express*, as well as ten years on *Time Out*. With 'no clearly defined role', Kirkby came aboard in 1978, working for a time as PA to Mick Shields, and he also carried out little jobs for Rothermere. But one day, he was put to work on a secret assignment, the *Mail on Sunday*, and as Kirkby put it, 'It became quite clear that, all along, I had been recruited for my Sunday newspaper experience.'

From the early studies he did on the *Mail on Sunday*, Kirkby knew the cost of the launch would be enormous, probably around the £50 million mark; in the event, the costs went higher still, something around £60 million. And Kirkby estimated the newspaper had no chance of coming into profit in the first three years.

These early estimates must have gone a long way towards convincing Mick Shields that this must be Rothermere's most harebrained scheme and, as Mick himself so often put it, his first, last and best duty was to protect the chairman from himself.

Despite the objections of financial management and the statistical evidence showing it was a bad investment, work on the *Mail on Sunday* went ahead.

Bernard Shrimsley's very first decision wreaked more controversy upon the already controversial project. He decided that the *Mail on Sunday* should not be a seventh-day *Daily Mail*, but instead should take on a personality of its own. The decision caused a great deal of comment in the company, many believing it was a matter of ego with Bernard that his paper had to be different from David English's paper. Others thought it was simply a stupid decision since the new newspaper should be taking advantage of the greatest asset the company had – the success of the *Daily Mail*.

The truth was that Shrimsley made the decision in consultation with Vere. Their combined wisdom led them to believe that readers wanted something different on a Sunday. They were basing this on the experience of the *Sunday Telegraph*, which twenty-one years before had tried to launch a Sunday edition that was an extension of the *Daily Telegraph*. It hadn't worked. The new *Sunday Telegraph* had to be retooled to become a distinctive voice on the basis that people wanted something different on a Sunday. Anticipating that, Shrimsley and Rothermere decided against having too much overlap.

But of course, Shrimsley didn't want a complete departure and with this in mind he tried to recruit several stars from the *Daily Mail*. Ann Leslie seemed very enthusiastic when Bernard took her to lunch to ask her to do a column for the new tabloid.

'I'll have a word with David,' she told Shrimsley. But in the end she had to bow out. She said David wanted to be able to send her to Hong Kong or wherever, whenever, and so she was not, as she had earlier thought, available.

It went very much the same with Patrick Sergeant, whom Bernard wanted for city editor. Of course, Sergeant preceded David on the *Daily Mail* and was very much his own man, and even a director on the board of Associated, but when push came to shove, he didn't come to the *Mail on Sunday* either. As for Peter McKay, whom Bernard wanted to recruit to do a gossip column, David English actively discouraged the new editor. McKay, David told him, was too close to *Private Eye* when that magazine was writing unpleasant things about the proprietor's wife Patricia.

By the same token David advised Bernard not to take too many people from the *Express* for fear of a retaliatory raid on the *Daily Mail*. And so far as the 'popular tabloids' were concerned, he thought it wouldn't be a good idea to have too many of those on the Sunday newspaper either.

Now Bernard felt he was relying too heavily on the broadsheets for recruitment. 'Too few of them had had directly relevant experience,' he said later. 'The people I put together were a good team, but they weren't as strong as I would have liked.'

But the other things holding Shrimsley back were his own personal foibles.

I had a chance at Chester Stern, the chief press man at Scotland Yard. He would have been brilliant. But I thought it was too uncertain a venture for him to leave a good job and pension.

Then, too, I only recruited people I liked and that was a problem. And I know I'm over-ethical. I can't really fire people and I've never been able to overcome it. When I was a Murdoch editor I fired only one person in eight years.

So I didn't have the right person in every job on the *Mail on Sunday*. And I wasn't ready to sack people who weren't swift enough.

These were the bare bones of Shrimsley's assessments of where the *Mail on Sunday* was falling short. But as he came to realise later, these were only the beginning of the problems.

Associated Newspapers had been printing the *Sunday People* from the early 1970s and now the irony struck everyone that if they could drop the *People*, they would have sufficient press capacity to print the new *Mail on Sunday*. But Associated was contractually obliged to continue with the job.

It fell to John Winnington-Ingram to assemble the press capacity to print an estimated 1.5 million copies of the *Mail on Sunday* each week, the sales figure needed to bring the *Mail on Sunday* into profit.

Winnington-Ingram had been general manager in Manchester before 1971 and he had created the joint printing company that printed the *Guardian*, the *Manchester Evening News* and the northern edition of the *Daily Mail*. At the time it was considered revolutionary. Now he was being asked to work an even larger miracle. Later he said, 'Vere took an immense gamble that I would be able to find the printing capacity we needed.'

As part of his search, Winnington-Ingram went to every single provincial newspaper, including Northcliffe Newspapers, asking them to print for the new Sunday tabloid. There were no takers. They all showed stiff resistance to becoming involved in printing a national newspaper because they were frightened of becoming engulfed by the union problems of Fleet Street that, up until now, they been able to avoid.

Under enormous pressure, John came up with a plan. He persuaded Douglas Long, managing director of the Mirror Group, to free some of the presses being used for the *People*, whose circulation was down, for use by Associated. These were six 1938 presses that were something less than state-of-the-art. For the northern editions they would be able to use one high-speed press the company owned in Manchester. But for London and the Home Counties, things weren't so orderly.

In Carmelite House, Winnington-Ingram commandeered three abandoned 1928 presses that hadn't been run since the heyday of the *Evening News*. The brass fittings for this ancient machinery had been stolen and all the reels had to be handled manually. They didn't even have conveyer belts and arrangements had to be made to install them.

Just to make matters a bit more complicated, new photo-type computer methods were to be used for the typesetting, while still retaining traditional cut-and-paste techniques for the actual layout of the newspaper. Shrimsley was familiar with cold type, but only just. He had used it for special projects before he took over the *Mail on Sunday*. But this would be the first time he used it to produce an entire newspaper. He was advised to use as few pictures as he could, substituting line drawings wherever possible, because in the joining of the two methods, degradation would occur on the reproduction of photographs.

All things considered, the whole production side of the new tabloid was, as John Winnington-Ingram put it, 'a wing-and-a-prayer operation'. But on it depended the success of Rothermere's new Sunday middle-market newspaper.

In order to give it every chance for success, the management instituted four weeks of practise runs for the crews and special training on how to handle the presses. But since the crews were on loan from the *Daily Mail* and therefore always changing, these training sessions turned out to be less helpful than had been hoped.

'Even those who were close to it were astonished at how difficult it was for the crews to handle those ancient presses,' said Bill Pressey, who was, as one of the general managers of the *Mail on Sunday*, responsible for the smooth running of the operation. 'On the actual night, we were down in the machine room,' he went on. 'We knew how many we had printed, we knew what we had printed each hour and how many we could print before the night was out, and we knew it wasn't enough. The decision was taken in the middle of the room: OK, something has got to go.' It was down to two men – Pressey and John Winnington-Ingram, the managing director of the *Mail on Sunday* – and they decided coldly and without emotion. They would blitz London 'to the detriment of the Home Counties'.

As circulation representative for the South Midlands and Western Home Counties, Graeme Thomson bore the brunt of that decision. He was responsible for the delivery of the first new Sunday newspaper in twenty-one years to the wholesalers and retailers in his area, and during the past two months Thomson had personally visited each of them, explaining the newspaper's policies and goals.

The public relations team came up with the idea of a promotional train that carried *Mail on Sunday* executives from London to Bristol and on to Birmingham, Manchester, Sheffield and Cambridge to meet the men and women who would sell the product to the public.

At each stop the wholesalers had been given a lavish lunch, the retailers afternoon tea. There were special *Mail on Sunday* pens and pencils, pads with the newspaper's logo at the top, promotional posters, special discounts for regular *Daily Mail* readers – and plenty of promises. So by the morning of the newspaper's launch, expectation was great and enthusiasm had reached a high pitch.

The train scheduled to carry the first copies of the *Mail on Sunday* to Thomson's area had departed right on time at fifteen minutes past midnight – empty. Since then, Thomson had not seen a single copy of the paper. He wasn't exactly panicking, but if the distribution had been switched from rail to road, he wanted to know. It was not until 4.15 a.m., however, that Thomson managed to break through the busy signals on the Sunday newspaper's switchboard and speak personally with the circulation director, Mike Newman. 'I hope you're not going to tell me it's a total disaster,' he said.

'It's a total disaster,' Newman confirmed.

It took a minute for this to register. 'Right, I'm coming down.'

Thomson looked round the office that was located in his house for his car keys. There might be copies of the newspaper kicking around and he intended to pick up a few.

Making his way to his car Thomson, who actually lived in one of the new housing estates where he had planned to pick up his main customers, jumped into the front seat, started the engine and began backing down the driveway. At first he couldn't hear his wife Jill calling to him. Then he saw her standing in the headlights at the top of the driveway. She was wearing her pyjamas and running to catch her husband before his car pulled away.

One of the wholesalers was on the telephone asking for compensation, Jill told him breathlessly. She was laughing, but Thomson couldn't see the humour of it.

'At 4.25 in the morning?' he asked.

'He said he hung up posters, canvassed his customers and participated in various promotions, and now he wants compensation.'

'Tell him I'll call him later,' Thomson muttered and pulled out of the driveway, directing his car towards the M40.

A little over an hour later, when Thomson arrived at Carmelite House, he found himself viewing a sorry sight. There were no copies of the nascent *Mail on Sunday* for him to retrieve. As far as the eye could see, there were only empty vans and what seemed to him a sea of waste paper rolling gently in the early morning wind.

At the time Graeme Thomson was surveying the scenes of disaster at Carmelite House, another man was walking the length of Kensington High Street. Bernard Shrimsley went from one newsagent to another, only to find there were no papers to be had. It wasn't that they had sold out. They had never arrived.

It was a walk Shrimsley would make the next week and the next and the next. He was never able to buy a copy of his own newspaper.

The other general manager of the *Mail on Sunday*, David Kirkby, had suffered through a difficult evening the night before, as he stood in the foyer of the Howard Hotel located on the Embankment. Kirkby looked calm, but he was actually in a state of near panic.

Kirkby had been put in charge of organising the launch party, and in honour of the occasion he had hired a coach drawn by four horses to deliver copies of the new newspaper to the expectant party-goers. The idea was that the bells on the coach would 'jingle-jangle' to announce its happy approach.

Rothermere was standing by and, more daunting even than that, so were at least fifty top advertisers for the newspaper, along with their wives. Embarrassingly, Kirkby had scheduled a series of short speeches by key staff members, but none of his speakers had yet turned up – leading Kirby to deduce the worst.

As he stood entertaining the wife of his boss, Patricia Rothermere, Kirkby was increasingly aware of the absence of the much longed-for jingle-jangle.

When at last the coach appeared, and copies of the newspaper were distributed to the guests, a new problem arose to haunt the harried executive. The new paper seemed to lack the punch of its sister publication, the *Daily Mail*.

To the practised eye of many of the professional journalists at the party that night, this first issue lacked sufficient white space. 'It looked a bit grey,' said one of them.

Indeed, the word 'grey' took on tremendous significance in the criticism that followed concerning the *Mail on Sunday*. Bernard Shrimsley had selected a small point size for the body type, more appropriate for a broadsheet than for a tabloid. In ordinary circumstances the choice might have remained unremarkable. But with the lack of clarity in impression caused by the older presses, the small point size gave a 'grey' cast to the new Sunday tabloid. This alone might have accounted for the impression the newspaper gave of dullness.

But others believed it was purely a question of direction: with the highly successful *Daily Mail* setting the pace for readers' expectations, it was thought the *Mail on Sunday* veered too far from that successful model.

It was up to one advertising executive to find the silver lining in the black cloud that was settling upon Associated Newspapers that night: 'The good thing was that we didn't get out as many papers as we wanted to get out. Had more people seen it … who knows?'

The *Mail on Sunday* had been launched by a team of absolute professionals each of whom had risen to the top of his profession by dint of intelligence, competence and hard work. In the wake of the paper's lacklustre launch and during the weeks that followed, the heat on them was turned up.

The fledgling paper was plagued by editorial and production problems, circulation began a rapid decline, morale was plummeting. Rivals were hopeful the new paper would sink without a trace.

It is only in such a situation that the will of the team and each man's ability to improvise is tested.

In the ten years before the launch of the *Mail on Sunday*, sales of Sunday newspapers had slipped from 23.4 million to 17.5 million, and as a result many in the industry believed there existed 'a market gap' waiting to be filled.

But where was the gap? Was it among the 6.6 million readers in the desirable ABC1 category who already read newspapers? If so, they must be peeled away from their accustomed Sunday title. But it was a well-established fact in the newspaper business that it is easier to get a man to change his cigarette brand than it is to get him to change his newspaper.

Or could the gap be among the desirable 3.6 million readers who at present read no Sunday newspaper at all?

If that was the case, the readership included a large percentage of those who read the *Daily Mail* during the week and who presumably were in the market for something like it to read on a Sunday.

The question could be stated more simply. Should the new newspaper have patterned itself after the *Daily Mail* or not?

The *Mail on Sunday*'s editor Bernard Shrimsley, a respected journalist with a long track record, had made the decision on the basis of the *Telegraph*'s earlier experience. He had made it in consultation with his proprietor. The conditions of the launch had been difficult. But none of that made any difference. The fact was, with sales plummeting lower and lower – down to about half of the first-day sale, the editor had to go.

At the end of ten weeks Bernard Shrimsley was called to Room One where Vere Rothermere was waiting for him. Shrimsley said later,

> Monday is the traditional day of rest for a Sunday newspaper staff, but when Vere called me in on a Monday morning I knew why. It was difficult for him and I tried not to make it any more difficult.
>
> Vere was very nice about it. It was a good, fair, no-hassle ending. He said he wondered if he could find a place for me in one of his publications in America. I declined.

For Bernard Shrimsley it was all over.

SIXTEEN

EDITOR-IN-CHIEF OF WHAT?

Some time before the launch of the *Mail on Sunday* a different drama had been playing out. Having succeeded in getting the *Sunday Times*, Rupert Murdoch began casting around for an editor with the kind of star quality he wanted for his new newspaper. The name he came up with was David English. It was the logical next step. He had beaten Rothermere to the draw in getting the *Sunday Times*; now he would help himself to his talented editor.

But English declined the offer – without even bothering to consult his boss. Later on, when he did tell Rothermere, the press baron was greatly impressed by his loyalty and insisted on rewarding English.

'He gave me a rise and made me editor-in-chief. But I was already editor-in-chief of the *Mail*. And I said, "Well, editor-in-chief of what?"'

Now, with the launch editor of the *Mail on Sunday* suddenly gone and the company on the brink of a disastrous loss, English was about to find out.

David English's version of how he became editor of the *Mail on Sunday* goes down as one of his typical set pieces about his relations with his proprietor.

Vere rings David from New York and asks him to fly over and have lunch.

When he arrives at the designated restaurant, he finds Vere ranting and raving about the *Mail on Sunday*. 'It's a grey newspaper put out by a grey editor and grey journalists,' he says. And he is eating. He is eating enormous amounts of food, as he does when he is upset. David, on the other hand, can't eat a morsel, because the conversation is upsetting him. David, Rothermere argues, is the only man who can save the new newspaper and he must give it a go. David doesn't want to give it a go, but he must. His proprietor needs him. So goes the story.

This may have been what happened. Or it may have been that Rothermere revealed to David English some of his actual feelings about the launch of the *Mail on Sunday* and the two men never told the truth to an outsider. But there is still another version, one that comes from a source close to Rothermere.

To this source Rothermere revealed his suspicions that the *Mail on Sunday* was being sabotaged – and the saboteur was none other than David English himself. Rothermere had somehow become aware that David was resisting giving any real assistance to Shrimsley and, perhaps even more problematically, denying him access to any *Daily Mail* talent.

Shrimsley had not himself reported this to Rothermere, but where Shrimsley believed English was simply resisting giving any help and perhaps being a bit awkward, Rothermere believed it was out-and-out sabotage. And Rothermere wasn't the only one. A rumour to that effect was making the rounds on Fleet Street.

In the strange but strict Harmsworthian logic of Vere Rothermere, that meant the only man who could save the *Mail on Sunday* was the man who was out to get it. Why? He wouldn't sabotage his own effort. So Vere determined that David English should be the new editor of the *Mail on Sunday*.

But what, if anything, did David have to gain by taking over the failing newspaper? By now, trying to save the *Mail on Sunday* was an impossible task. Anyone in the business knew that once a newspaper's circulation began a steep decline, it could not be halted. Anyone who tried would inevitably suffer ignominious defeat.

Why, then, did English allow himself to be persuaded to take on the absurdly difficult task of trying to save the *Mail on Sunday* – while at the same time continuing to edit the *Daily Mail*?

English himself counted out five reasons.

'First of all, I was enormously flattered by the offer, and that was very ego satisfying,' he said later. Second, he hadn't thought the product was right and he was sure he could improve it. If he could make a better product, he believed, the newspaper would not fail.

Then again, he had the power to bring all his staff to the task and he knew, given the internal competition in the company between titles, 'the *Daily Mail* journalists would just give their lives to come and do this job'.

'And fourth, I thought I would succeed and, rather than diminish my reputation, this would enhance it.'

But this wasn't the whole story. David English had a secret weapon. Whenever he took on a new project, he actually mesmerised himself, wilfully altering his perception of reality, and this was how he succeeded time after time. 'I never let failure get into the front of my vision,' he said – although he admitted that it sometimes lurked about 'at the back of my mind'.

In English's self-constructed world, at the centre of the serious issue of whether or not the *Mail on Sunday* could be saved, was the irrepressible idea that trying to save it would somehow be, well, fun.

Converting tragedy to comedy was an unconscious goal in almost everything English did. Faced now with sacking the staff of the *Mail on Sunday*, English remembered that twenty years before, almost to the day, he had been among the journalists made redundant when Associated Newspapers closed the *Sunday Dispatch*. He was at the time the American correspondent for the *Dispatch* and, called back to London for his dismissal, he was given a redundancy cheque by the managers.

It was £658 short, English pointed out. 'And they said, "No, no, no, no, no," and I said, "Yes, it is." And it was. And I said "I'm going back to New York, and I either want this cheque changed, or I want the money."

'And I went to the Cashier's Department, and they had this machine that counted out money, and it counted out 658 one-pound notes. And I stood there, and these pound notes spewed out, and I counted every one myself, and I put them in great big bundles.'

The machine was next to the newsroom and the reporters watched as English counted out what was owed him. He then hopped on a plane back to America and went to work for the rival *Express*. That was in his early days.

Now he wanted to save the *Mail on Sunday*, in a way to make up for the closing of the *Sunday Dispatch*. So his last and most important reason for wanting to save the newspaper was a sentimental one.

It was only about a year after the Iranian embassy siege when the SAS, in a controversial attack, overpowered a group of terrorists who had seized the embassy. Now, in the same spirit as the SAS attack, English fashioned his so-called 'Task Force'. Their mission? To save the *Mail on Sunday*.

For the next three and a half months English would sleep on a camp bed in his office, working from 9 a.m. until 1 a.m. the next day – half his time on the *Daily Mail*, half on the *Mail on Sunday*.

When his staff assembled for news conference, English would stand in the doorway, sorting them like sheep, some to the *Daily Mail*, some to the *Mail on Sunday*: 'You in there, and you and you and you in there.'

In the first week he redesigned the entire make-up of the *Mail on Sunday*, rewriting copy to give stories by his daily staff a longer run, appropriate to a weekly publication.

He cajoled the writers from the successful television series *We'll Meet Again* – now in Hollywood working on other projects – into continuing the saga for the pages of the *Mail on Sunday*.

And yes, he enlisted Peter McKay who was in Washington. David said, 'I'll be needing a column from you for the *Mail on Sunday*.'

'What about a contract?' asked McKay.

'There's no time for that,' English said. 'I'll be needing it in an hour and a quarter. And ... it had better have four or five short pieces.'

And yes, Ann Leslie also wrote for the new *Mail on Sunday*.

And yes, Chester Stern did eventually come aboard.

But Shrimsley's city editor, Christopher Fildes, who by everyone's account was doing a tremendous job, remained in place for only a relatively short time before leaving the position.

Fildes later said of the swift changeover of editors, 'It was rather like being on a plane and a voice comes on and says, "This is your pilot speaking. The plane has got stuck on the edge of the runway." And then a pause and another voice comes on and says, "This is your *new* pilot speaking..."'

Ian Pay joined the *Mail on Sunday* on 6 July 1981, when the idea of a Sunday newspaper was still a shadowy one known only to Lord Rothermere and the handful of men he had hired to work on the project. Secreted away on the first floor of Northcliffe House, they were heavily into the planning of every aspect of the new newspaper when Pay walked through the doors.

Pay had come from the *Express*, hired to be advertising manager by a man he much admired, Bruce Olley, the new advertising director at the *Mail on Sunday*. Only three weeks before, Pay had had dinner at the RAC Club at Epsom with Olley who was just about to go on holiday.

'I really hope while I'm away', Olley said, 'I can clear my sinuses. My doctor said, "Get some sea air and maybe they will clear. Otherwise, you'll have to have surgery."'

Olley went on his holiday while Pay prepared to go to work and when Olley came back the pair again went out for lunch. 'Tomorrow', Olley told him, 'I'm playing golf at an advertising agency golf day and on Wednesday I'm going to Epsom Hospital to have these sinuses looked at because they still haven't cleared.'

Bruce Olley, it turned out, had cancer, and Pay ended up doing his job by proxy. For the next three months he visited Olley every evening in hospital, telling him whom he was thinking of hiring and what his plans were. Olley would agree or disagree, explaining his reasons.

This was how Ian Pay received his training to become advertising director of the *Mail on Sunday*, because, by the time Olley died in September of 1981, Pay was literally carrying out all his duties.

Predictably, during the first ten critical weeks in the life of the *Mail on Sunday* the steady decline in circulation had given the advertising department plenty of problems.

Pay, taking on duties far beyond his early brief, had decided to be conservative in his new position. Although it had been quite realistic to suggest sales of 1.5 million for the new newspaper, he and his sales team had played it safe, suggesting to advertisers that the *Mail on Sunday* would sell only 1.25 million copies.

It turned out to be the right decision, because within six weeks, the paper's circulation had made its steep decline to 712,000. This was the twilight zone when many advertisers could be expected to drop out. And certainly it was true that Pay had to renegotiate many of the rates. 'But', he said later, 'an awful lot of the advertisers just believed we would win through and make it work.' It wasn't only that Pay's original sales estimate had been sensible. It was also the reputation of Associated Newspapers in the marketplace that was helping. The advertisers seemed to believe that the teamwork they had seen at Associated many times before would carry the day.

In the next three and a half months, that teamwork did pay off. David English managed to halt the decline and had actually increased the circulation to 840,000.

There were to be three new sections: first, a sponsored partwork, the initial one to be a cookery book; then a coloured comic supplement, an innovation in the Sunday market; and last a magazine.

For Ian Pay the magazine presented a special problem. For it to be of any reader value, the bare minimum of pages had to be twenty-four, or, even better, thirty-six, to make it thick enough to be an attractive feature. In order to produce a thirty-six-page magazine, it needed some eighteen pages of advertising. It was up to Pay and his sales team to go back to the advertisers, asking them to buy adverts in a magazine none of them had seen, in a newspaper whose circulation was only now recovering from a spectacular crash.

'The reason that we succeeded', Pay said, 'was that the editorial were part of the management team. And I think that, more than anything else, sustained us during those awful three to four months.'

The magazine would be *You*, the brainchild of John Leese, and many believed that its verve and flair was the main contributing factor in bringing the *Mail on Sunday* into profit.

Genevieve Cooper was late in applying for the position of commissioning editor on *You* magazine, and this was probably the reason she got the job, because a box full of applications had been accidentally left on the floor and the janitorial staff had thrown them away. So getting the job was simplicity itself. 'I came for an interview,' Cooper said later, 'and John Leese hired me.'

The magazine was housed in temporary quarters in Temple House near Carmelite Street. Except for the *You* staff, the building was ramshackle and empty, and there was mouse poison in every corner.

Cooper had been working in the 'swisher offices of *Cosmopolitan* and I had this rather gloomy office, attractive in a way, I quite liked all that sordidness.

'There were eight or nine of us on the magazine to start, a strange crew,' Cooper said.

John liked to talk about what made a perfect office. To him, it was a certain mix: a very eccentric person, a very nasty person so everybody could hate him and a funny person to keep everybody happy, and he liked to hire people who were a little bit odd, not predictable, and he would hire people other editors wouldn't.

He didn't have time for a slick person who might impress an editor. John liked idiosyncrasy and he thought out of it he would get unpredictable copy. He liked, wanted, intelligence. He didn't like clichéd journalism.

He hated that pretension that characterised the other Sunday magazines, he hated worthiness, stuff about the rainforest. His style was to treat trivia intelligently and get a much more interesting article from that.

He once twisted up a piece of copy, a trendy social commentary, and threw it across the room. He thought it was pretentious and shouted at the person who had brought it in to him.

In some ways, he was that northern character, gruff on the surface, but incredibly deep and emotional. A lot of people were very frightened of him. And he could be sharp and angry when it was needed.

But he also liked the chatting, he liked to talk, he was not a silent man. But he was quite shy in lots of ways – an odd mixture.

He was just his own man, that's all.

Leese loved all the outrageous American headlines, like 'Headless Body Found in Topless Bar' and 'Ford to City: Drop Dead'. One afternoon he mentioned to his staff what a lovely word 'lovenest' was.

That week in *You*, there was a story about a new motorway, and how, for environmental reasons, the engineers had built a little tunnel for toads to travel when they crossed over to the other side of the road. So Leese stunted up a picture, with a toad in the foreground illuminated by the headlights of an oncoming car and the headline was FATHER OF FIFTY, SLAIN ON WAY TO LOVENEST. He liked treating animals like people, and he treated the people he featured in the magazine with humour and affection.

He told his son Michael, who eventually went into the news business himself, that journalism was about people – and he cautioned him 'never to forget somebody is involved there'.

You magazine was built on that idea, of ordinary people caught in extraordinary situations, and it flourished because ordinary people wanted to read it. It was an entirely new genre from the other magazines that were being published in Fleet Street, and some believed that it was Leese and *You* that carried the *Mail on Sunday* through its crisis.

Leese himself was a strong personality channelled by force of will into extraordinary repose, a thoughtful man with an irrepressible sense of humour. His staff remembered him for lauding the American shoeshine boy – and dressing down anyone who came to work with dirty shoes.

His son and daughter, Julie, after they became adults, remembered him for throwing open their bedroom doors at 6.30 every morning to wake them up, and carefully placing a freshly made bacon sandwich at the foot of their beds while quoting from 'The Rubaiyat of Omar Khayyam': 'Lo! The Huntsman of the east has caught the Sultan's turret in a noose of light.'

It was on the shrewd observations of such an outwardly whimsical man that *You* magazine was built.

The struggle of the *Mail on Sunday* for survival was notable for the camaraderie of the staff as they fought to make the newspaper live. From the first days, the involvement was intense, so much so that the families of staff members became vicariously involved. When it had appeared at the outset that the newspaper would fold, it was like a family sorrow. Then, as the newspaper began to rally, it turned into a family triumph.

David English had control of the advertising budget for the relaunch and he determined that the entire country would wake up on that day knowing about the *Mail on Sunday*. The campaign, run by Saatchi & Saatchi, pictured four dogs with the motto, 'the complete family paper'.

At the end of his three and a half months at the helm of the *Daily Mail* and the *Mail on Sunday*, English admitted to being completely exhausted. He had never worked so hard, he said later. In a promotional film, asked whether he would be able to continue the two jobs or whether he would drop dead, he bluntly replied, 'I'd drop dead.'

But he must have taken some comfort from the fact that he and his task force were being paid double salary for their work. Known within the company as the 'double bubble', the second salary that David had demanded remained highly controversial. Some within the management team deemed it ridiculous, or as one manager put it, 'totally crazy'. They grumbled privately that they had been forced to put in hours as long as

David and his team had throughout the first launch *and* the relaunch, but they had not received extra compensation. Nor had they asked for it – or expected it. Nevertheless, in this as in most other things, David was triumphant.

At the end of the day, however, English was glad to get back to his *Daily Mail*. Despite his momentary exhaustion, he still craved the excitement of a daily newspaper. In his place on the Sunday newspaper he left the permanent editor, Stewart Steven. Now, with *You* magazine, the comics and the partworks, the newspaper was set to succeed.

In the meantime, Bill Pressey and John Winnington-Ingram had been pushing their production crews to reduce the time necessary to print the newspaper. To give the staff an extra hour, they chose 24 October, when the country changed over from Daylight Savings Time, for the relaunch date. By 11.30 on that morning the *Mail on Sunday* was sold out. The circulation topped 1.3 million, practically doubling the sales at the paper's lowest point.

But the push wasn't over yet.

Production problems still plagued the newspaper and, in particular, the difficulty now lay with *You* magazine. The only organisation free to print the magazine on short notice was Robert Maxwell's British Printing Corporation.

'We had to do a deal with BPC,' said John Winnington-Ingram,

'to make a contract with Maxwell, and it turned out to be a nightmare. He would ring me saying he refused to print another copy of the magazine unless I agreed to overtime, and I would say, 'It's not our overtime.' We were arguing the whole time. Then he said, 'I'm revising the contract,' and I said, 'You can't revise a contract.' Then he said, 'The contract was based on a million plus.' Then I said, 'It wasn't, the contract was based on a million copies with a run-on figure. And there was no upper limit on the run-on figure.'

What had happened was we had become so successful that he was having to employ additional labour to print the magazine and it was actually costing him money.

We agreed to go to arbitration. And every time I spoke to him I had to tape-record my conversations and I used to say to my wife, 'Tell him I'm in the bath.' So he must have thought that I was permanently washing while I went to switch on the tape recorder! We finally reached settlement an hour after we were intended to see the arbitrator, we paid a little more money and he agreed to print.

In the meantime, Winnington-Ingram prevailed upon a friend of his at Watmough's in Bradford to change over from being catalogue printers to magazine printers. 'They did a superb job,' he said. 'We saved over a million a year on the contract, there was no hassle, it was a joy, they did a brilliant job.'

For the management team, then, the battle was virtually over. But editorially the struggle to consolidate the newspaper's gains had only begun.

Stewart Steven, the man whose job it was to edit the Sunday tabloid, began the job on the crest of a wave. But it would soon flatten.

The week after he took over, the circulation of the *Mail on Sunday* soared to 1.5 million. 'We thought it was amazing!' he said later, and staff began to congratulate themselves. What had happened was that a main competitor, the *People*, had gone on strike and as soon as the strike ended the *Mail on Sunday*'s circulation slumped to 1.25 million.

In Steven's mind it was not until eight months later that the *Mail on Sunday* would be truly safe, and what established it once and for all was a single story.

West Yorkshire's Chief Constable was retiring and he had written his memoirs which explained why the Yorkshire Ripper had escaped detection for such a long time.

'I bought his story for about £40,000 and I knew it was a controversial thing to do, although I didn't quite know how controversial,' Steven said. 'I actually wrote the whole thing myself. I interviewed him at enormous length.'

Saatchi & Saatchi then produced a highly dramatic advert for television. It showed a man walking down a dark street with a bowler hat on and beside him on the ground was a chalk mark of one of the victims of the Ripper. A voice-over explained that in the next morning's *Mail on Sunday* West Yorkshire's retiring Chief Constable, Mr Ronald Gregory, would tell why he thought the Ripper had not been caught. Stewart later said,

This caused in Yorkshire unbelievable fury because at that time people's emotions were still very raw about the Ripper. They saw Gregory as the policeman who failed to catch the Ripper, making money out of the Ripper.

I always remember I was sitting on the backbench on a Saturday night. In those days we had old-fashioned boxes with a switch where all the lights go on for the telephone and I was looking over at the news desk and I suddenly realised that every light was on. These telephone boxes were alive.

I said 'What's going on?'

The calls were from outraged television viewers from Yorkshire who had seen the advert and were calling to protest against the next day's story. Along with these calls were requests from television and radio outlets in Leeds for Steven to appear the next day on their shows.

Steven slunk to his office, badly shaken. He wondered whether he had 'gone over the top', whether he was a purveyor of Yellow Journalism. 'Am I right? Did I get this right?' he asked himself. For Steven, who had made his share of mistakes on the editorial floor, it was a crucial question ... and these callers hadn't even seen the newspaper.

He began to realise the kind of power he had and the emotional reaction of the public. Steven said,

> I thought, 'Well, Gregory was the man whose job it was to catch the Ripper. Therefore, what Gregory has to say must be in the public's interest to know. And if we had to pay to interview him, so what?
>
> 'If we say as journalists that certain things in our society are so shocking that we can't write about them properly and honestly, then you won't report them at all, and then you're in trouble. You've got to tackle these things even if it offends people.' So I worked all this out in my mind, and I knew I was right.

Steven went back on to the editorial floor, rang all the shows in Yorkshire that had requested him to appear and accepted. He then drove to Leeds, and the next day appeared on every radio and television programme, and defended himself.

The gist of his argument was that nobody could be hurt by knowledge or by the words of a man who tells the truth as he saw it, which was what Gregory had done.

When Steven returned to London, he did the same thing all over again, accepting appearances on radio and television, and explaining his viewpoint:

> I got to the office on Tuesday, and I looked at the circulation figures and the circulation had gone up from 1.25 to 1.4 – a huge jump. And nobody called me. I sat there and nobody called me. Silence.
>
> Wednesday morning my secretary said to me, 'The chairman's on the phone.' So I thought to myself, 'The fury is such that I am going to be fired.'
>
> Rothermere came on and said, 'I understand that you got yourself into some hot water.'
>
> I admitted that I had, then 'explained the situation properly'.

Rothermere said, 'Are you sure that you are morally in the right?' So I said, 'I'm absolutely sure. I've got no problems with it whatsoever.'

So he said, 'I've read all the criticisms and I entirely agree with you. If you're sure you're morally in the right, then you've got nothing to worry about. I believe you're morally in the right, so I don't feel I've got anything to worry about. So very good. Congratulations. Wonderful story. That's what journalism is all about.' And he rang off.

About a quarter of an hour later all my lights were going, ringing up again. By now various people in the management had realised that I was going to survive, so therefore they could call me and say, 'Very good. The circulation is up wonderfully.'

And Rothermere gave me that support when he could easily have pulled out the rug from underneath me.

The next weekend circulation went from 1.4 to 1.45 and it never fell back. Readers had suddenly realised that it was a good paper. And we never fell back.

Inside Associated Newspapers was a political system of resist and obey. Too much obeisance could be as dangerous as too much resistance and key staff members discovered that their proprietor was expecting these two very opposing poles of behaviour from each of them at varying times.

No single one of them fully understood what was on the mind of their proprietor because, as much as anything, Vere Rothermere proceeded by a progression of strict logic and Harmsworthian intuition. Hence, while an employee might grow to understand the logic, practically no one had an inkling of what being a Harmsworth entailed.

But in the early days of the publishing empire, before he became Viscount Northcliffe, Alfred Harmsworth once gave one of his editors a single weekend in which to launch a magazine he believed would sell. The editor was literally sick in his waste-paper basket the entire weekend, but the magazine was launched on schedule and it flourished.

In the case of the *Mail on Sunday*, Vere Rothermere had been actively planning it for four years before its launch. Given this, any opposition was futile – although each member of staff played out his part of opposing or supporting without knowing how useless any objections would be.

By some estimates the cost of the *Mail on Sunday* topped £60 million before it eventually reached profitability. It was nevertheless Vere Rothermere's intention to relaunch the newspaper after its shaky beginnings and to prevail in the Sunday market, and to this end went all his energy.

He believed that a coloured comics section in the newspaper would be attractive to children. He had in addition read research from the United

States showing that every single successful Sunday paper published there had a colour supplement. In the relaunch of his newspaper, then, he insisted that these two components be included. Rothermere said later,

> John Leese was in New York. He had turned around the *SoHo News*, a rival publication to the *Village Voice* that was owned by Associated Newspapers. But our studies showed it would be four years before it came into profitability. And we were wondering whether it would be worth it.

Rothermere was introduced to the *SoHo News* in 1976 by Clay Felker, who was then editing *Esquire* magazine for Associated Newspapers. But the *Village Voice* was in the dominant position, both in circulation and advertising. The *Voice* was then owned by Rupert Murdoch, who had ousted Felker from the magazine he founded, *New York Magazine*, after a daring buyout. So it was possible Felker was seeking to gain revenge on Murdoch through Rothermere. Whatever Felker's motives, the investment in *SoHo* had been less than stellar.

But it did serve one very important purpose: showing John Leese's unique talents to advantage. So Rothermere brought him home for *You*.

But that wasn't all. Rothermere wanted the American comic strips. He said later,

> Not a single Sunday paper in London had comics, but all the American Sundays had comics. I told Leese to buy all the top cartoon strips in America and bring them back here. The Americans were delighted to have an opportunity to sell them and we got them at low rates. We got an artist to change them editorially for British readers, then we had them printed at Watmough's.
>
> We had the newspaper first by David, then by Stewart. We had the magazine by John Leese. We put in the children's section of cartoons, with a few for adults. And we had a terrific package.
>
> And of course, the children all made their parents buy the paper.

Today, the *Mail on Sunday* has a circulation well in excess of 2 million, with the largest share of ABC1 readers of any Sunday newspaper. It is a tribute to the teamwork and professional expertise that the staff members on Associated Newspapers were capable of.

But it is also a reminder of the Harmsworthian determination of Vere Rothermere, who refused to take no for an answer.

SEVENTEEN

THE 'LEAD-THE-HORSE-TO-WATER' FACTOR

Mick Shields was to money as David English was to news. As managing director of Associated Newspapers, Mick's ability to assess financial opportunity was as astute as David's in assessing breaking news. The question then arises whether Shields knew ahead of time about the Reuters windfall that would result if the international news agency went public.

In his comprehensive history of the Reuters agency, Donald Read reported that Mick Shields was one of only two men on the Newspaper Proprietors Council 'who fully understood the financial complexities' of the revolution taking place inside Reuters. But did Mick actually anticipate what that revolution could mean to Associated in terms of hard, cold cash? Indeed, to the British press at large? The answer, as rumoured on the management side of Associated Newspapers, was 'yes'. Or, as John Winnington-Ingram put it, 'We all knew ahead of time. It depends on *how far* ahead you're talking. Some knew further ahead than others...'

Far enough ahead to launch a new newspaper?

Persistent rumours held that Victor Matthews, chairman of Fleet Holdings and proprietor of the *Sunday* and the *Daily Express* newspapers, launched the downmarket *Daily Star* on the back of his expectations of a massive Reuters windfall. According to the point system upon which membership in the news agency was based, the *Star* would become worth between £20 and 30 million from the bonanza. In Fleet Street lore, where swashbuckling tales of pirate proprietors abounded, exaggerations were the norm and that rumour, though mistaken, was perpetuated by news hounds at the *Express* who loved the idea of their proprietor outwitting his razor-sharp rivals on Fleet Street.

Certainly, Matthews did at one point instruct his managing director Ian Irvine, a distinguished and aggressive accountant, to look into the matter. But according to one *Express* insider, Matthews had resisted paying the *Star*'s subscription to Reuters when he launched the *Star* in 1978: 'He saw the Reuters shares as a liability. In the end he had to be persuaded.' There is every probability that when he launched the *Star*, a title not noted for its coverage of international events, Matthews was simply maximising time on his presses and he actually had no idea how much the new tabloid would soon be worth.

It was Rupert Murdoch, owner of the *News of the World*, the *Sun*, and *The Times*, and a director of the Newspaper Proprietors Association, who first alerted Matthews. 'This Reuters business is very useful,' Murdoch told him. 'It's going to make a lot of money.' This, in conjunction with an unexpected and unprecedented £1.9 million dividend paid in 1982, was enough to send Matthews scuttling to Ian Irvine with a directive to check it out. According to a *Sunday Times* article,

> Matthews and his new chief executive pulled out every available document on Reuters; annual reports of the company's articles of association and the Trust agreement. At first, neither was sure whether it was feasible for the news agency to go public.

Eventually, however, Matthews became convinced and as a result he became the prime mover on the Newspaper Proprietors Association Board of Trustees to try to convince the others on the board that the hundred-year-old news agency should be allowed to float on the stock market.

Reuters was founded by Julius von Reuter who came to England from Germany in the wake of the widespread economic depressions of 1848. In England, he began collecting news items from continental newspapers and submitting them to the London press. These he copied out by hand, delivering them himself to the various London newspapers. Then, after expanding, he used carrier pigeons to transport stock market prices from Aachen to Brussels and from there to England. Eventually his firm grew into the great Reuters Agency, with correspondents posted in the most far-flung corners of the world. His firm quickly gained the reputation of being the most reliable news-gathering organisation in the world.

The Duke of Saxe-Coburg-Gotha conferred a barony on the enterprising young man, who took his place in English society in style, dispensing lavish hospitality from a mansion he had built in Kensington Palace Gardens.

But by 1941, at the height of World War Two, the firm had fallen into financial disarray and was very nearly dismantled. It was rescued by a consortium made up of the national newspapers, through the Newspaper Proprietors Association, the British domestic Press Association, known as the PA, and the Australian and New Zealand Press Agencies. A point system was created whereby a daily paper received six points, a London evening three points, a weekly one point. The national titles, through the NPA and the British Press Association took 'shareholdings' of 41 per cent each. The Australians took 14 per cent, the New Zealanders 3 per cent.

These shareholdings came by way of a trust rather than an investment and the articles of association were clear in their admonition that the company required unanimous agreement among members for any significant change. Thus the owners quickly came to the conclusion that the Reuters shares were a continuing liability since, the larger their share and the more they used the service, the more they had to pay.

The tables turned radically in the mid-1960s when Reuters spotted a gap in the marketplace for computerised transmission of financial information. Reuters began by putting out a range of data on video screens. Then, in 1973, the news agency started its breakthrough Monitor, offering the Money Rates Service which dealt in information about currency. By 1982 these rates were available globally, as well as information on 'shares, commodities, gold, shipping rates and oil'. By using satellite transmission, the data could be called up faster than by phone or telex; the system was said to be a crucial eleven seconds faster than any other means of communication. Thus the company ushered in a new age of profitability for subscribers and, indeed, for Reuters.

For shareholders, the first tip-off of the changing status of the company was its 1982 dividend – the news agency's first for forty-one years. Based on an unprecedented profit of £16 million, Reuters issued the dividend at £1.9 million. At this point the value of the company became apparent to all and the thought occurred in the minds of the many that getting some of their investment out would be a good thing. Unsurprisingly, it was Victor Matthews who first leaked the idea of Reuters being floated on the stock market.

There was no secret about the fact that the share price of Fleet Holdings, the holding company for *Express* newspapers, was on the slide. Anxious to keep his institutional investors on board, Matthews let it slip during question time at his company's AGM that Reuters had 'a new look' and he expected a public quotation for the agency 'within twelve months'. That was in the summer of 1982.

To Nicholas Gold, who was then a thirty-one-year-old lawyer at Freshfields attending the AGM on behalf of Associated Newspapers, Matthews's comments seemed very well prepared, perhaps too well prepared, and he suspected that the original question about Reuters was a plant. But at the time, Matthews's comment aroused little or no reaction.

By the spring of 1983 the topic was high on the agenda of the Reuters board. But although the move was taking on its own momentum, egged on by Matthews, there were several substantive objections still to be dealt with, not least of which was the question of whether or not the trustees could actually themselves take a hand in breaking the trust.

On 10 June 1983 the matter came to a head. On that day, when the Reuters trustees were meeting before their AGM, a major disagreement broke out between the chairman of Daily Mail and General Trust and the chairman of Fleet Holdings. Vere Rothermere objected formally to Matthews's forcing of the issue of flotation.

> MATTHEWS: As Trustees we would not be opposed to a public flotation in some formal manner provided the safeguards of the Trust were there, and you suggested obviously that proposals have to be put forward. But by whom? Would it be improper for a Trustee to put them forward, or would we look to management to initiate that proposal, or otherwise we remain silent on it? There is a distinct feeling that, while everyone is rather shy of saying too much about it, I have a feeling that no one would be really opposed to it because obviously there is substantial money involved...
>
> ROTHERMERE: I think the Trustees only come into this at a considerable remove. Their fundamental duty is not to the shareholders and their profits but to uphold the objectives of the Trust, and I don't think in that connection that this Board of Trustees should take the initiative in anything. We should be fully informed, and we should contemplate and make our decision on whatever is put before us to ensure that it is in accord with the Reuters Trust...
>
> MATTHEWS: I would also suggest we have a responsibility not only for the Trust but for the shareholders as a whole. It is implied.
>
> ROTHERMERE: I don't think so.
>
> MATTHEWS: That is my view, that it is our duty to look after the Trust and the shareholders.
>
> ROTHERMERE: I think that is the duty of the directors.

This dispute, though fundamentally procedural, underlined a more serious rift between the owner of the *Mail* and the owner of the *Express*.

Even though Matthews was relatively new to the media scene, the *Mail* and the *Express* were long-term rivals, and there was no sign of this rivalry abating. Even if Matthews wasn't consciously aware of the long history of competition between the two middle-market newspapers, Rothermere *never* let the fact slip from his mind.

There was also the more serious question of the split of the shareholdings, Rothermere holding out for his firm's advantage. One especially bitter argument followed the disclosure that Matthews had not, as an *Express* insider had earlier indicated, paid his full Reuters subscription when he launched the *Star*. There were other complicated questions about the amount Matthews might personally gain from the flotation. At this point agreements that were on the verge of being completed collapsed and the proprietors adjourned the meeting, back at square one.

One participant said, 'Until then, one had only seen [the proprietors] in their glamorous roles having tea with the queen or out at a gala. Now, for the first time, one saw men like Murdoch, Rothermere and Matthews in their business roles. They were very fast on their feet, very rough and bloody impressive.'

There was a great irony in all this. Only six years before, Max Aitken had been eager to sell out to Matthews's Trafalgar House. Now, if the Reuters flotation went ahead, the *Star*'s share alone would be twice as much as Matthews had paid for the entire buyout of Beaverbrook Newspapers.

Vere Rothermere's first direct encounter with Victor Matthews had been in 1980 when he was forced to close down the *Evening News*. This was a highly emotional moment for Vere, because the *News* occupied an historic place in the saga of the Harmsworth dynasty.

It had been the first newspaper that Vere's great-uncle Northcliffe, then the struggling young Alfred Harmsworth, had purchased. That was in 1894 and Alfred's brother Harold, the future Viscount Rothermere, took over the financial side of the ailing evening broadsheet. Significantly, he also took over distribution.

It was Alfred's genius that transformed the newspaper into a going concern, pricking up the ears of Fleet Street to the arrival of a new competitor who might very well pose a threat. But Harold's distribution was as important in the success of the *Evening News* as Alfred's editorial. Now, years later, Harold's grandson Vere was very much aware of the important role his grandfather had played in the success of the *News*, even if the world at large was only apprised of Northcliffe's genius. In the name of family pride, closing the loss maker was almost impossible for Vere to accept.

But the costs were escalating out of control. In 1980, the projected losses were put at £20 million and despite Vere's sentimental attachment to the *News*, that amount was simply unsustainable. Vere at last agreed to do what his managing director Mick Shields had been advising him to do for years: close down the newspaper – albeit reluctantly.

At the same time the *Evening Standard*, now owned by Victor Matthews's Trafalgar House, was making the same kind of losses. The trouble was, shutting down these evening papers was an expensive business, mainly because of the gigantic redundancy payments that would have to be made, not only to editorial staff but to the print unions as well.

Vere had the dubious honour of being able to *afford* to shut down the *News*. Matthews was between the proverbial rock and hard place. If he kept running the *Standard*, his losses would spiral out of control. If he shut it down, he would accrue expenses he really couldn't afford.

Surveying the situation objectively, Mick Shields saw the opportunity to benefit both companies, while dealing a winning hand to his own. He came up with the idea of calling the shutdown of the *News* a 'merger' with the *Evening Standard* and Matthews bought it. Mick's son, Tom, later said,

> The most spectacular deal my father ever pulled off was when they closed down the *Evening News*. They did a deal with Trafalgar House whereby they closed the *News* in return for half the *Standard*. The *Standard* got rid of its competition straight away and Associated became half-owner of the *Standard*. Both sides went from losing millions every year to making millions.
>
> But the great part of the deal was that if either party wished to sell its half-share, it had to offer it to the other one first. So when Trafalgar House wanted out, they sold their half to the *Daily Mail*.

It was left to Nick Gold to draft the agreement. 'We drafted it so that even *if only one share changed hands*, control would shift to the other party,' Gold said later. 'In this case, the devil *really was* in the detail.'

Thus the deal that Mick Shields envisaged had its benefits for both parties, because, along with the closing of its major competitor, Trafalgar House inherited not only a major market position but it also gained a lot of other advantages. There was, for example, the advertising revenue of the *News* to be gained and, perhaps the most helpful bonus, the expertise of the distribution team at the defunct *Evening News*.

Since Harold had devised the distribution of the *News* some eighty-six years before, it had evolved into a highly sophisticated method of delivery, in the main because of a harrowing set of deadlines. Saturday nights provided a good example of how the deadlines worked. Bill Pressey, then in charge, explained what the team was up against.

> On a Saturday night, we would produce the football classified edition. It had all the football results in a classified form. You had a short window of sale. The last result was in at five minutes before 5 and the last classified was finished at 5.10, and you couldn't start printing until then. And you

had to get in the region of 250,000 copies of the classified edition with all the Football League results out to the shops by 7 or 7.30 when they shut. So that was done with over forty-two-odd presses running.

So from about 1976 to 1980 when we closed, there were some 260 men on the inside, publishing in the warehouse, but there were 600 people on the outside distributing. So we had to finish our printing by 5.45 and get them out, or we missed it. When we shut, I went across and spent three months on the *Evening Standard*, handing over information about our depots and distribution system. And then the *Standard* took the best of both systems.

Certainly, part of the bargain envisaged by Mick Shields was the incorporation by the *Standard* of the first-rate distribution system of the *Evening News*. So on the 'horse-trading scale', the *Standard* not only got rid of its greatest competitor, but it avoided paying out redundancy moneys and it also benefited from the defunct *Evening News*'s advertising and distribution departments.

When Mick was calibrating the deal, perhaps the results of his internal 'monetarising' audit of Reuters was also resonating in his mind. Said one insider who was watching Mick Shields spin this deal, 'I don't know whether or not he had insider information, but he was very perceptive. He reckoned that Reuters would float, so we did a deal that turned out to be very good.' That was in 1980.

So the answer to the question of whether Mick Shields had known ahead of time that Reuters would float was that he knew *far enough* ahead of time. He was even ahead of the 'some' that John Winnington-Ingram was referring to when he said, 'Some knew further ahead than others.' That was Mick's contribution. But why was Vere so seemingly opposed to the flotation?

From those who observed the sharp clashes that took place over Reuters at the meetings of the NPA, there was no question where the major altercation lay: between Rothermere and Matthews.

But why were they at one another's throats? A lot of credence was put into the idea that the two men were like 'chalk and cheese'.

Matthews had been raised by his mother after the death of his father in World War One. He had experienced the privations of the 1930 depression personally and it was said he never forgot them. He served in the navy during World War Two, taking part in the Dunkirk and Dieppe operations. A self-made man, he had made a success of construction work, until he came to the attention of the head of Trafalgar House, who recruited him in 1960. The press liked nothing better than calling him 'a rough diamond' and contrasting his background with the patrician upbringing of Vere Rothermere. It was inevitable that the press would contrast the backgrounds of the two men in explaining the enmity they appeared to have for one another.

But the matter was far more complicated. Matthews must have remained slightly chary of Rothermere and his management team in the wake of the 'merger' between the *News* and the *Standard*. Despite the obvious advantages Trafalgar House had gained from the deal, anyone could have seen that the *News* was going to shut whether it 'merged' with the *Standard* or not, and Trafalgar would have gained most of these advantages without giving half-ownership of the *Standard* to Associated.

On Rothermere's side there were also reasons to be suspicious. In searching for an editor for the *Evening Standard* who was acceptable to both parties Bert Hardy, then managing director of Associated Newspapers, had 'lobbied hard' for Max Hastings to be recruited for the position.

> Max had come back from the Falklands and was extremely well regarded, and I approached him and he was enormously keen, and I was then shuffling between Rothermere and Matthews because they both had to agree. They both did agree that Max should become editor.
>
> Unfortunately, Matthews then tried to poach Hastings to become editor of the *Sunday Express*. This had the effect of upsetting Max who felt that he was being used. Indeed, he then resigned from the company altogether and joined the *Sunday Times* as a writer, so we lost that opportunity.

If Hastings was upset, Rothermere was less than overjoyed.

So the history between Rothermere and Matthews was a bit longer and more involved than a superficial glance at the two proprietors' backgrounds might at first indicate.

Then, too, Matthews was not aware of the 'lead-the-horse-to-water' factor that governed many of Vere Rothermere's actions.

Inside Associated Newspapers it was said that Vere argued with his managerial and editorial teams more often than not, too often, it was thought. And they were spending a great deal of energy 'leading the horse to water'. Vere was truly not an easy horse to lead because of his basically suspicious nature. But also Vere put forth a barrage of objections that could only be dismantled by an extremely logical explanation. He very stubbornly took a sceptical view of the greatest of plans.

Only after the passage of an unconscionable amount of time would Vere allow himself to be persuaded to go in the direction his managers wanted ... and drink the water.

The difficulties Victor Matthews encountered in persuading Vere

Rothermere to agree to the Reuters flotation were vast. Vere was his own usual stubborn and difficult self. It was not unlike the situation his managers so often encountered when putting forth a new idea. But it was exacerbated by Vere's suspicions about the motives of his Number One Rival, the owner of the *Express*. Matthews had little feel for the history of this rivalry. Vere did.

Using all his persuasive abilities, Matthews eventually agreed a deal with Rothermere about how the money would be split, taking into account that Matthews had not paid his entire subscription for the *Star* when it was launched. Matthews was also instrumental in helping the head of Reuters, Denis Hamilton, devise a method of leaving the essential principles of the trust intact. In this way the flotation could proceed properly.

For his part, Vere reluctantly agreed.

Thus it was that Victor Matthews led Vere to water and convinced him to drink.

The top three winners in the Reuters bonanza were Victor Matthews's Fleet Holdings, whose 12.1 per cent holding was said to result in a windfall in the region of £120 million; Rupert Murdoch's News International, realising some £90 million; and Associated Newspapers. Although Associated had only one national title in the NPA at the time* – the *Daily Mail* – it had a percentile holding of 12.2 per cent and was entitled, roughly, to £122 million.

In fact, Associated received a larger allotment than any of the other Fleet Street giants because it was the only firm in London that held newspapers in the provinces. Northcliffe Newspapers, at the time a subsidiary of Associated Newspapers, was the highly profitable chain operating across the country that in 1971 had helped Vere to finance the relaunch of the compact *Daily Mail*. As subscribers to Reuters as members of the PA, those newspapers were entitled to a substantial allotment in the Reuters bonanza.

But the story of how Associated came to own such a highly profitable chain had often been misrepresented. The brainchild of Vere's grandfather Harold, the first Viscount Rothermere, Northcliffe Newspapers had been founded in 1928 at a cost of £3 million. At that time Harold had believed the ownership of a newspaper chain could become a lucrative business. So he invaded what was clearly the territory of the Berry brothers who, until then, had enjoyed a primary position in the market.

The result was one of the roughest newspaper wars England had ever

---

* Although the *Mail on Sunday* was launched in 1982 and had applied for its Reuters shares, they had not yet been allocated any when the news agency floated.

experienced, and as usual, Rothermere was publicly demonised as an interloper and ridiculed for his stupidity. The war reached across most of England and Scotland, with Rothermere gaining the upper hand in Gloucestershire, Staffordshire, South Wales and Hull. In Bristol and Newcastle, the competition from the Berrys was much stiffer.

These rivals eventually resorted to give-away promotions in order to increase circulation, causing ruinous losses to both sides. At last an agreement was reached. Rothermere was to leave Newcastle and not to start papers he had planned in Cardiff, Sheffield and Aberdeen. The Berrys left Bristol and Rothermere took over the *Derby Daily Express*, which he merged with the *Derby Telegraph* to form the *Derby Evening Telegraph and Express*. At last, in December 1932, Northcliffe Newspapers was wound up and its remaining provincial papers passed to the parent company, Associated Newspapers.

This action was interpreted as a total defeat for the press lord, and that was how his attempt at establishing a chain of newspapers came to be known as 'Rothermere's folly'. But at the end of the day Associated Newspapers had gained a foothold in the provinces and decades later Harold's actions would be recognised as a brilliant investment.

In perhaps his most successful contribution to the company, Harold's son Esmond renewed Associated's interests in Northcliffe Newspapers. Adding to the newspapers his father had established, Esmond acquired papers in Hull, Grimsby, Derby, Stoke, Gloucester, Cheltenham and Swansea. The provincials, uncontaminated by the union action that plagued the national press, made good profits; labour relations were generally smooth and co-operative, in marked opposition to those in Fleet Street.

In fact, so strong were the provincials that Vere never failed to reiterate that he would have been unable to relaunch the *Daily Mail* in 1971 without them. For many years they accounted for more profit than the nationals, providing a support to the company during the years when the national unions were eating it alive.

Now they accounted for the largest part of the proceeds that would fall to Associated Newspapers from the flotation of Reuters. That money was to fund the modernisation of Associated, bringing in the new computer-based technology that would lead to a complete overhaul in the methods of news gathering and production. Vere would be able to rehouse his editorial department and build vast new presses south of the River Thames.

In fact, Reuters provided the base that enabled the national press to leave Fleet Street, the very words becoming an archaic term that properly belonged to the past but was retained because there was nothing to replace it.

It was an environment that had already been transformed by the arrival of Margaret Thatcher at 10 Downing Street to head the government in 1979. A new age of deregulation and privatisation was about to begin, an age when tax reductions increased real income significantly and entrepreneurial activity became an item high on the government's agenda.

Most important to the national press was the effect upon the unions. A series of industrial relations acts greatly reduced their power and, for Fleet Street, it meant a lessening of the stranglehold the unions had held on production.

The new era provided the impetus for the national press not only to survive but to prosper and in this new environment the Reuters moneys laid the foundation for a revolution in working practices. It was the vehicle by which Rupert Murdoch undermined the unions, when in 1986 he opened Wapping. His brutal methods would shock the nation, dismantle the unions and disillusion his journalists. But for this he would make no apologies.

In a manner of speaking, Murdoch had to destroy Fleet Street to save it.

The deal that Mick Shields had originally envisaged when the *Evening News* merged with the *Evening Standard* was not completed until December of 1985, when Trafalgar House sold the remaining half of the *Standard* to Associated Newspapers.

To David English's mind, this was one of Vere's greatest achievements, his watching and waiting until he could at last get the newspaper he had wanted for nearly a decade. But Vere could not have done it without Mick Shields's incredible financial sophistication.

For Shields planned that the buyout of the *Standard* would be completed only a little before an expected sharp rise in the Reuters stock. In this way, Mick was fond of explaining to his more literal-minded colleagues, the second half of the *Evening Standard* came to Associated free of cost.

The newspaper had paid for itself.

In 1990, the book *Editor in Chief: Fleet Street Memoirs* by Denis Hamilton was published posthumously. On page 188, Hamilton had written:

> Gradually, then, I managed to persuade the owner-members of Reuters that there was a way in which they would retain control of the news agency, and yet benefit from this windfall...

> One of my worst difficulties was to get Lord Matthews and Lord Rothermere to attend a meeting together. Matthews was using the *Daily Express* to attack the *Daily Mail*, and they didn't get on. Rothermere regarded himself as an aristocrat, and I felt objected to Matthews because he'd been a Brixton bricklayer. So if I wanted to move the Board of Trustees in a certain direction, I had to give lunch to Victor Matthews one day and Rothermere the next – but never together.

The passage rankled Rothermere and he engaged Peter Carter-Ruck as his lawyer to sue the publishers of the book for libel, because the statements labelling him an aristocrat were false and misleading. 'Lord Rothermere has never regarded himself as an aristocrat', Carter-Ruck said in his 'Statement in Open Court'.

> [He] has never declined to meet Lord Matthews and their relations are, and always have been, one of friendship.

The defendants' solicitor confirmed Carter-Ruck's statement, apologising for any distress and embarrassment caused to Rothermere. They agreed to pay an appropriate sum for damages and all Rothermere's costs.

The damages were donated to the News-vendors' Benevolent Institution, the Newspaper Press Fund and the St Bride's Fund.

And thus the matter ended.

But not quite. Still outstanding when this book went to press was the question of the taxation on the Reuters windfall. By now, Associated Newspapers was in receipt of some £300 million from the news agency.

Associated had no objection to fair taxation on the windfall. Its only question was in regard to *when* the levy would be agreed to be properly calculated. To the way of thinking of the managerial side of Associated, the most appropriate tax point to make the levy come due would be as of the year 1982, when the first dividend was declared and Reuters became a fiscally viable company.

As to the distribution system, that came back to Associated when they acquired full ownership of the *Evening Standard* in 1986. It was widely acknowledged that when Robert Maxwell launched his rival publication to the *Evening Standard*, the London *Daily News*, the distribution expertise of the team at Associated played a major role in that entrepreneur's defeat.

EIGHTEEN

WAR

Magnus Linklater's first clue that he was to play a central part in the biggest British newspaper war of the century came in April 1986.

The son of the Scottish novelist Eric Linklater, Magnus was an Old Etonian whose education had included sojourns at Freiburg University and the Sorbonne before he gained a Second Class Honours degree in modern languages at Trinity Hall, Cambridge. Something of a patrician in style and substance, Linklater had nevertheless prospered in the grimy atmosphere of Fleet Street, advancing steadily during fourteen years on the *Sunday Times*'s editorial staff. At the time he received the telephone call that would change his life, Linklater was managing editor of news at the *Observer*.

The call was from Charles Wintour, Linklater's editor from his apprentice days on the *Evening Standard*. The older man had been something of a mentor to Linklater and a legend in his own time to the young and talented staff he had enlisted during the glory days of the *Evening Standard*. Much to Wintour's chagrin, Vere Rothermere had managed at the end of 1985 to gain full ownership of the *Evening Standard* and what Wintour was about to propose to Linklater no doubt had something to do with his desire to strike a blow at the heart of his old rival.

But later on, in reflecting upon events, Magnus Linklater would say that Wintour's personal agenda mattered less to him than the opportunity to work with a man with such high journalistic skills. So when Wintour asked him to discuss 'a matter of extreme secrecy' at the American Bar at the Savoy, Linklater was in a receptive mood.

But Linklater privately thought the American Bar 'a rotten place to discuss a secret project', since it was nearly always 'crammed with journalists'. He nevertheless agreed to the venue.

Once there, Wintour asked him if he was interested in editing an evening paper, but he declined to identify the group. Linklater said he would have to know who it was, 'because for all I knew it might have been Colonel Gaddafi or someone worse, so Charles went off and made a telephone call and came back and told me it was Robert Maxwell. And that seemed almost as bad.'

Robert Maxwell had two years before taken over the Mirror group, with its six titles and weekly sales of 3 million. In this role he had taken up cudgels for the British Left, although Maxwell was anything but British and his left-wing credentials were belied by his ostentatious show of wealth.

Maxwell had been born in Solotvino, in a mountainous region on the eastern Czechoslovakian border with Russia and Romania. He had worked his way up from gruelling poverty and although this attracted the admiration of many, Maxwell had never been able to shake off his reputation for shadowy business dealings. He was born Ludvik Hoch, but reinvented himself under several different identities, taking among other pseudonyms Leslie Jones and Ivan Dumaurier. A shameless self-publicist, he sought the public eye in ways that had become, by the time he stormed into view as a press magnate, increasingly cringe-making.

But despite his serious misgivings, Linklater agreed to talk over the proposal with Maxwell in his offices. In his mind, he was carrying a set of resolutions 'about what I was going to say and about how he had the reputation of being an interfering proprietor and about how I insisted upon certain conditions'.

But when Linklater arrived, Maxwell bolted forward from behind his desk, grasping Linklater's hand warmly in his own and saying, 'Welcome aboard. This is a decision you will never regret.' Simultaneously, Linklater admitted, his prepared text 'rather crumbled'. Maxwell nevertheless agreed that Linklater should write out his conditions and he would sign them. One of these had to do with a settlement, in case the paper folded, but Maxwell signed it without complaint, even ostentatiously, with a flourish.

So Magnus Linklater signed on. It was, after all, the chance to create a newspaper from scratch, 'a fantastic opportunity', and in the general excitement and enthusiasm his initial reservations fell away.

In 1960, the sale of evening newspapers had hovered around the 2 million mark. By the time Maxwell enlisted Linklater to edit the London *Daily News*, the evening market had declined to half a million copies. In large part this was the result of the broadcasting media; the attrition had been slow but steady. This had forced Rothermere to shut down the *Evening News* with massive losses in 1980 and since then the market had only become more difficult.

But now that Robert Maxwell was willing to invest seriously, the question was being cast in a different light. Could a dying market be revived by dextrous and intelligent editing such as Linklater would bring to the task?

Linklater was willing to try and, to begin with at least, it looked as if he had made the right move To his gratification, Magnus found his early plans for the paper became the object of Maxwell's close scrutiny. He appeared to be endlessly fascinated by Linklater's ideas.

> He was terrific. We had a famous weekend at some smart hotel in Staffordshire, where we met to work out the shape and philosophy of the paper, and Maxwell arrived by helicopter for lunch, expressing his approval for all the ideas that we were working on.

Thus sustained, Linklater prepared and submitted dummies for the paper, and 'we did a lot of market research, and they went down like a bomb. The readers' response was fantastic. The market researchers were saying, "Wow, we've never known this kind of response to a product. They love it."'

But then, shortly after Linklater signed on in the summer of 1986 the Commonwealth Games, awarded to Edinburgh in 1980, came under threat from inadequate funding. After a series of appeals to the government, then to private individuals, the chairman of the organising committee announced on 19 June that Maxwell and a team from the Mirror Group would take over the responsibility for the games' finances. In the mad scramble that followed, and during the games themselves, Linklater watched Maxwell's interest in the new newspaper flag. Approval for important decisions as well as vital expenditure ground to a halt and gaining access to Maxwell became a hit-and-miss affair, with the London *Daily News* running a distant second to the games.

By the time Maxwell again turned his attention to the newspaper, Linklater had reached the conclusion that it was necessary to postpone the launch from the original September starting date. This was because no agreement on distribution, printing, or even on the computing system had been reached, mainly as a result of Maxwell insisting on negotiating all these contracts himself. After shuffling to October, then November, a more realistic date in February 1987 was agreed. This delay would turn out to be crucial.

Linklater had been recruited on the brief that the London *Daily News* would be an evening paper and the clearly delineated competitor was Rothermere's *Evening Standard*. But, alarmingly, when the launch was postponed, a new concept had entered into the mix, an idea that turned out to be dear to Maxwell's heart – the creation of a twenty-four-hour paper. To Linklater, it seemed 'a pretty hazy notion' but sufficiently interesting for a hastily organised visit to the United States to see how such newspapers were run.

Two trips later neither Wintour, who had gone to Detroit, nor Linklater, who along with other staff had toured Florida, managed to locate anything that nearly resembled a round-the-clock newspaper.

The only paper that might minimally have fitted the bill was the New York *Post*, owned by Rupert Murdoch and managed by the energetic Roger Wood and Steve Dunleavy. During the heydays of the well-publicised newspaper war with the New York *Daily News*, the *Post* was revving up to as many as nine editions each day. But because Murdoch was seen as a competitor who might revive earlier plans of his for a London *Post*, his New York newspaper was omitted from the itinerary of Linklater and Wintour.

If they had visited the New York tabloid, what they would have found was a twenty-four-hour staff to go with the twenty-four-hour paper. Gripped by war fever, editors and reporters sustained themselves with cases of beer, as often as not sleeping on the floor of the building as they fired off volley after volley at their competitor. When Murdoch was finally forced to sell the *Post* under a complicated legislative catchment twelve years after acquiring it, there was also the matter of an overall loss of $150 million – a seemingly significant deterrent to others who were considering following the *Post*'s example.

As to Linklater, he swore he would never have accepted the editorship if he had known and understood 'what the hell a twenty-four-hour newspaper was and the full implications of it'.

If Magnus Linklater was a product of the establishment school of newspapering, a member of the Old Boy network and a gentleman to boot, his opposite number on the *Evening Standard* was anything but.

John Leese was the hero-editor of *You* magazine, an integral part in the successful effort to relaunch the *Mail on Sunday*. Many at Associated believed it had been Leese and not David English who had insured the success of the *Mail on Sunday* with his brilliant version of *You*.

Now he was the man Rothermere chose to spearhead the battle between the London *Daily News* and the *Evening Standard*.

John was part and parcel of the old school of journalism, one of the unwashed few who came up the hard way. He had started on the *Birmingham Gazette* as a copy boy, then moved to the *Coventry Evening Telegraph*, making his start as a sports reporter because 'it was easier to become a journalist in sport than in news and in those days there was no formal way in to journalism'.

An admirer of Ben Hecht's wickedly funny play *The Front Page* about over-the-top Chicago journalists of the 1930s, Leese was the kind of editor who wasn't ashamed to be labelled 'an old-time, shirt-sleeved newspaper thug' by enthusiastic staffers who worked under him. At the same time he was a strangely calm and philosophical man, the sort to whom Henry James's directive 'to try to be a person upon whom nothing is lost' certainly applied.

It was highly ironic that in taking his stand against the Rothermere type of journalism, Wintour had drawn Leese, because John Leese was the most original mind in the Harmsworth editorial stables, as distinct from David English's voice as Linklater himself. Throughout his career, Leese had been his own man, no mean trick in an organisation dominated by English.

But Leese was the right man for the impending war. It had been Leese whom Rothermere had chosen 'to see the old *Evening News* through to its death'. This 'melancholy task' was particularly instructive to Leese because it gave him the chance to see for himself 'how people behave differently in adversity from how they behave in the good times'.

Even more important, overseeing the shutdown of the *Evening News* gave Leese first-hand experience in understanding exactly how limited the evening newspaper market had become. He knew it was not a matter of healthy competition between his own newspaper and one edited by Magnus Linklater, but a bloody fight to the finish.

Only one paper would survive this war and he intended to use any means necessary for it to be the *Evening Standard*.

Poignantly, Leese was late in taking over the *Evening Standard* because he had to have surgery on his cheek, where doctors had discovered a growth. This was John's first intimation of the cancer that would take him in only five years. Even as he fought the war, he was painfully aware of his own mortality. But he thrust the thought aside as he turned his attention to the urgent matters at hand.

The *Standard* was still a hot-metal newspaper and the first task facing John was to convert to photo composition before his competitor's launch. 'We did it on the run, so to speak,' he said, 'so that one page was hot metal, one photo-composed, converting it almost page by page. We didn't have any choice.' He finished the mammoth task only three weeks before the first issue of the London *Daily News* hit the news-stands.

It was one of the great ironies of newspaper history that had Linklater managed to keep to his original launch date, he would have caught John Leese and his staff right in the middle of the process. It would have given him an enormous advantage in the newspaper war to follow. Leese knew this, as did Linklater. But somehow the fact could not be brought home to Maxwell, who was a genuine innocent in the ways of the newspaper world.

As to the market research conducted by the *Daily News*, Leese was less than impressed. He had managed to learn of some of the results that were creating such a furore of enthusiasm at his competitor's camp. 'There were questions like, "Do you think it's time there was some competition for the *Evening Standard*?"' Said Leese, 'The obvious answer to this would be yes. Or whether there should be a paper which represents the Labour Party. Again, yes is the only obvious answer.' To Leese's mind the research was tainted. Indeed, he gave short shrift to this kind of market research in general. 'People buy papers because they like the product,' he argued, 'not because they want a particular political bias.'

This was a shared belief of Rothermere's. 'If you can't sell the newspaper,' Rothermere said, 'you can't sell anything else. A newspaper sells on its words and packaging and style – its essential ethos. If you can't get that right, there's not much point being efficient about business, because you've got nothing to sell. You can sell the advertising, but you must first sell the newspaper.'

In Rothermere's view the *Standard* had grown lazy. The words, packaging and style had grown stale. It was Leese's mission to change all that – and in view of his new competition from Magnus Linklater it was necessary he do it literally overnight.

But it was Leese's particular inclination that whenever this could be accomplished at cost to his competitor, it should be. Thus a special kind of psychological warfare evolved within the higher echelons of the *Evening Standard*.

It began with the public image of the proprietors themselves. Maxwell loved arriving by helicopter to meetings, often a couple of hours late. He loved speaking publicly. It was even planned, for a time, that at the launch party for the London *Daily News* he would descend from the ceiling of the Albert Hall, hidden from view inside a globe adorned with flashing lights. When it reached the ground, it was to break into segments, like an orange, and out Maxwell would step, to the admiration of all.

But whereas Maxwell actually enjoyed a veritable frenzy of publicity, Rothermere had always shunned it. It was decided to emphasise this natural tendency: that as many steps as Maxwell should take forward, Rothermere should recede – until, to the public's eye, he would become a shadowy figure of mystery and stealth, in contrast to Maxwell's propensity for overexposure and braggadocio. Rothermere and Leese decided he would seldom break his self-imposed silence and the only photographs released of him were to be taken in profile, preferably among the shadows.

Who was this man? the public would eventually want to know. It would be a long time before they found out.

A second spearhead for Associated Newspapers' attack came from the title of Maxwell's newspaper. It was named after the *London Daily News* which had been founded in 1845 by Charles Dickens and which, before its death, had swiftly become 'the largest half-penny morning paper in Great Britain'.

But much opposition existed within the Maxwell camp to the name. For one thing the title, along with the other options – 'The Londoner', 'London Newsday' and 'Newsday London' – had been tested by the agency conducting the market research. They found that the most popular name among potential readers was 'The Londoner'. For another, the word 'daily' generally means 'morning' to British newspaper readers. Yet both Maxwell and Linklater preferred to call the paper the London *Daily News*. Charles Wintour objected. He grimly pointed out that it would be very much in character for Rothermere to launch a spoiler under the title of the now-defunct *Evening News*. Wintour's astounding act of clairvoyance, however, was lost in a welter of other issues that were quickly piling up.

Not only was the spoiler in character for Rothermere, he had been planning the details of it since shortly after Maxwell and Linklater began planning their launch. The thing was 'only a question of timing', Rothermere said later, and he told no one about his plan, because 'there are no secrets in Fleet Street that you don't keep to yourself'. He explained it this way:

By choosing the name *Daily News*, they made it a gift. They made it a logical step. It was quite obvious that having launched the *Daily News* as a twenty-four-hour paper, the afternoon section would be called the *Evening News*. Under the law, if we weren't using the title, they could have appropriated it, and therefore they could have had a *Daily News* and an *Evening News*. To protect our title, we had to launch. It seemed quite obvious to me.

And it was great fun. It was an enormous laugh. I had asked the Board of Directors to raise the matter at a meeting on the Monday before the London *Daily News* came out, in order to plan it, and they had decided against it. They didn't think it was a serious proposition.

Then, on Wednesday, I rang Bert Hardy who was the managing director of the *Evening Standard*, and John Leese, and said, 'Let's get this going. We've got five days to do it in and I'm sure you can manage it. My grandfather launched the *Sunday Pictorial* in a week and I'm sure you can launch the *Evening News* in five days.'

Rothermere's call, Leese remembered, came from Tokyo, and after he and Hardy put their heads together they assembled ten journalists, mostly seconded from the *Evening Standard*. As each of the team was told, in greatest secrecy, about Rothermere's plan, they broke into a huge grin.

'They were smiling in delight,' said Leese. 'And the paper was assembled over the weekend before the launch of the London *Daily News*. It was a terrific kick, the adrenalin charge of producing this thing in only about five days.'

The journalists on the spoiler had no plans to go out and pursue any stories; they simply relayed *Evening Standard* copy. Leese said later,

> We supplied fresh feature material and they got a very good gossip column. But news and sport was *Evening Standard* material, so it was very cheap to do. We thought if we distributed it in our own vans, we would just about make enough to cover the cost.
>
> The point was to allow the *Evening Standard* to take a lofty tone and say, 'Well, they're fighting it out for second place,' and meanwhile, we could sail on unperturbed by the vulgarities taking place at our heels. It was the best Fleet Street spoiler that there's ever been.

One of the advertised features in the pre-launch publicity for the London *Daily News* was that contemporary short stories would appear in the pages of the paper. On the staff of the spoiler, it was thought the best way to counter the appeal of such stories was by running their own short stories. They fell back on the classic writers, like W. Somerset Maugham and Guy de Maupassant, and because the copyright had run out they were free and, as Leese put it, 'readily available'.

> People were cutting up books and pasting them right up on the pages. And the main purpose of that was to enrage the staff at the London *Daily News*.

It did enrage them. The first edition of the *Evening News* came out during Maxwell's celebration luncheon at the Savoy and, when it was delivered to the table, it is said that Charles Wintour, who had predicted the move, turned ashen. For his part Robert Maxwell denounced the publication as 'an obvious spoiler'. It was, he said, an attempt to confuse customers with a similar title. 'But', Maxwell was quoted as saying, 'you and I know that Londoners are streetwise. They will know the difference between the "Gold Top edition" of the London *Daily News* and the leaden coffin of the *Evening News*.'

Perhaps they should have. But they didn't.

The London *Daily News* was launched with a fireworks display over the Thames and the first issue was published on 24 February 1987. The front page led with the story of a new AIDS danger: 'A London man has become the world's first known victim of AIDS contracted through a skin graft.' There was an impressive photograph of the fireworks display the night before which, as the paper put it, 'heralds the birth of Britain's first 24-hour paper'. The diamond-shaped logo looked very metropolitan, with a splash of red and a graphic of Big Ben superimposed over it.

Inside, the paper was strictly a class act, with special appeal to its projected eighteen-to-thirty-five-year-old ABC1 readership. There were features on food, wine and the restaurants of London; and a daily recipe by the principal of Leith's School of Food and Wine. Later in the week the paper launched *Metro*, billed as 'London's only Daily Independent Guide to the Arts and Entertainment' – an exhaustive listing of opera and concerts, cinema and theatre, with ample attention paid to fringe productions. The review pages employed well-known names from literature and the arts who produced dazzling critiques of what was on in London. It was a frontal attack on the upmarket readership of their competitors, a highly readable newspaper with a gratifying appeal to the intelligence of the readers.

The appeal of Rothermere's spoiler was straight nostalgia and the paper was riddled with clichés that went right over the top. 'Good Evening, London,' the *Evening News* proclaimed. 'Tonight, joyfully, we announce our rebirth...Once more we shall seek to mirror the many-splendoured life of London and the world, and as we helped to shape its history, so we shall help to shape its future. We trust you're glad to see us.' The lead story was about an opera star who 'flew in to save the show' at Covent Garden the night before and was headlined TO THE RESCUE!

Meanwhile, over at the *Evening Standard*, Leese was deliberately purloining the ideas from the London *Daily News*, in his words,

> to blunt their promotional activity. We learnt that they were calling their entertainment section 'Metro' so we called ours 'Metro'.
>
> It was good old-fashioned stuff. And particularly amusing to us because they were being produced from a rather grand and glamorous office and the office we were in was at the back of the old *Daily Express*. They were coming out rather like Lou Grant, and ours was something straight out of Ben Hecht in the 1930s. We thought we would respond to that time as well, with some rather full-blooded, cut-throat competition. Because seriously, it was a question of them or us.
>
> And then Bert Hardy pulled off a brilliant promotional stunt. It was at

the height of the property boom when everybody was talking about buying property. So he planned a competition for London property that lasted thirty days. Maxwell retaliated with a pay-off-your-mortgage competition, but it was really too late. The first strike is always more effective.

While all this was going on, Rothermere was having fun 'reading Maxwell's temperament', as he put it. He had decided to bring out his spoiler, the *Evening News*, at 15p – 5p below the cost of the London *Daily News*. In swift retaliation, Maxwell immediately cut the price of his paper to 10p, against the advice of almost everyone around him. It was done, Maxwell said, 'to encourage newsagents and news-vendors to resist the *Standard*'s intimidation and to sell our newspaper. He, Lord Rothermere, has sought a price war and he can have it.'

The effect of such a cut, just as Rothermere had planned, was to devalue the London *Daily News*, both to customers and to advertisers. But by now, Maxwell was on a roll. 'I warned him a week ago', he said during the second week in March, 'that I would not allow this tactic to succeed and that the London *Daily News* would not be undersold. I meant it.'

Said Rothermere, 'I then cut the price of the *Evening News* to 5p and he just went berserk.'

Maxwell now accused the *Evening Standard* of falsifying its circulation figures and refusing to supply the vendors of the London *Daily News* with copies of the newspaper. In addition, he said that Rothermere had banned many independent news-vendors in the City of London and the West End from handling the rival newspaper. 'I intend to test in the courts the legality of this restraint on trade,' Maxwell loftily declared.

But by 13 March, Maxwell had been forced into an about face. 'Publisher Robert Maxwell', his own paper wrote, 'was ordered by a High Court judge here today not to repeat allegations that the *Evening Standard* had lied about circulation figures.'

'It was a silly allegation to make,' said Rothermere, 'because our figures are all audited by an outside body. Even if we had wanted to falsify them, we couldn't have got away with it. And at the time we had a very few sellers who worked for us – perhaps a dozen people. The rest were independents.'

The *Evening Standard* won 'substantial' libel damages from Robert Maxwell and the London *Daily News*. All that remained for Rothermere to do was discreetly to release a copy of his formal reply to Mr Robert Maxwell's apology:

Thank you for your letter of 11 March. I am pleased to receive your unconditional admission that your allegations of intimidation and harassment against the Evening Standard Company Ltd and myself were quite false and without foundation.

As to any suggestion from Maxwell that they now halt the price war, Rothermere said he preferred free competition. He had no desire to participate in an action that could be interpreted as price fixing. 'That', wrote Rothermere blandly, 'would be a flagrant breach of the law.'

Over at the offices of the London *Daily News*, Magnus Linklater found himself treading an uphill path. If his inability to gain access to Robert Maxwell had prevented the early launch of the paper, he was now suffering from 'a surfeit of access'.

'My problem now is that I can't get away from him,' Linklater told colleagues. Maxwell, who was described by one of his journalists as 'the most top-of-the-head guy you've ever met', had immersed himself in the everyday business of newspaper production, taking over the most minute of editorial decisions. At one stage he instructed Linklater to pick up all the stories in the *Sun*'s first edition because 'the *Sun* picked the best stories'. When Linklater brushed this suggestion aside, Maxwell said, 'You are perilously close to dismissal.' As Linklater was to put it in his wry manner, 'as far as the organisation of producing a newspaper [is concerned]', Maxwell left 'something to be desired'.

But besides this there were other more terrible problems besetting the paper. The staff of the London *Daily News* no longer knew who the enemy was. 'We knew exactly what we were doing in the evening market,' says Linklater. 'We were positioned, we thought, perfectly for that. It was a straight battle with the *Evening Standard*.

'But the morning was more difficult to determine. Were we competing with the *Mail* and the *Express* on the one hand, or the more upmarket papers?

'In theory,' Linklater continued, 'a twenty-four-hour paper is great. But the practice was a nightmare.' The London *Daily News* – billed as 'the paper that never stops, for the city that never sleeps' – was now being produced by a staff who never left work. According to Linklater,

We never had time to stop. We would be prepared from early morning, news pages made up for the first edition, but with feature pages prepared the afternoon before.

Was the newspaper too upmarket? Too left-wing? Some on the staff thought so, but there was no way to test it out, because we were too exhausted. Throughout the day we would be responding to events like an evening paper with the kind of instant reaction that is needed.

At some point in the afternoon where in normal circumstances we might start to sit back and think in terms of the next evening paper, we were in fact having to gear up to producing a morning paper for the next day. A new production staff would begin to come in and we would begin work on the next morning's paper, in half a day – a paper that other morning papers had been working on *all* day. It was tremendously pressurised and the pressure was relentless.

And all day we were changing those pages as an evening paper changes through the day. The test of an evening paper is how fast it can respond to the news and get it out on to the streets. Part of the battle is actually responding journalistically to the news, but at least as important is getting it out on to the streets on time.

That was just what the London *Daily News* was unable to accomplish. Maxwell knew nothing about distribution, but he wouldn't listen to people who did know. He had entrusted the distribution to a new non-union organisation unfamiliar with the traffic patterns of the city. In any given twenty-four-hour period, some 17,000 deliveries were to be made by 200 vans to 6000 retailers from five printing plants that ringed the city.

But evening circulation carried its own specialised problems, requiring expertise and knowledge of traffic and routes through the city, as well as enthusiasm and commitment from the managerial staff to the men who drive the trucks. It would not be an exaggeration to say that the *Evening Standard*'s distribution system had been perfected over decades.

But from the beginning the *Daily News* experienced a whole series of production disasters having to do with their facsimile transmission of the paper to the five printing departments. And with a delivery staff untrained in newspaper distribution, there were reports filtering back to the editorial staff that whole areas had failed to receive their newspapers. Said Linklater, 'We had stories of lorry loads being tipped in a field because they couldn't get to the right place on time.' Years after the event, it would still pain him to think of it. He continued,

And a lot of people were working between twelve and fifteen hours a day. It may sound macho, but really it's just bloody exhausting. And while we did get more staff, about 180 in all, and could divide the rota between the evening people and the morning people, there were some like the features editor and the news editor, the editor himself and his deputy – chief executives – who felt the need to stick with it all the way through.

We couldn't just wash our hands of the morning paper or of the evening paper. Then we brought back a special late sports edition, the pink edition, on Saturdays, so we were doing a six-day week.

I didn't actually loosen my tie, but metaphorically speaking, I was in my singlet. It was not the sort of situation where as an editor you could be remote and hope that everybody else would get on with it. It was all hands to the pump. It was sandwich-on-the-desk stuff.

I found that I was working eighteen hours a day, and I was driving home very late one night and I felt a sort of tingling all up and down my right-hand side. And I thought, 'My God, this is it, I'm having a stroke.'

I had a check-up with the *Mirror* doctor the next day and he said, 'You're perfectly all right. It's a syndrome that is perhaps unique to the *Daily Mirror*. That is that Robert Maxwell, who works twenty hours a day, expects everybody else to be able to do the same, and the fact is that they can't.'

The paper promoted the idea that it would change 60 per cent during the course of a day, and as a result there was a general expectation on the staff that people would buy the paper twice – once on their way in to work and then again on their way home.

And lo and behold, they didn't. Their response was that 40 per cent of the paper remained the same.

One newspaper pundit set out to read every edition from the 'Gold Top' morning edition to the late evening edition, but found himself 'surfeited in early afternoon and still two more editions to go'.

Sales began plummeting and, as the drift downwards turned into an avalanche, the management from the *Daily Mirror*, kept at arm's length in the early stages, began to become involved. It was generally felt that the paper was too upmarket, and 'tremendous recriminations' over editorial content began surfacing.

'And', says Linklater,

there were some ludicrous ideas about how the paper should become, which mainly consisted of making it more like the *Daily Mirror*, and there was a phrase that we coined, behind their backs.

They insisted there was too much to read in the paper and they kept on saying, 'We want you to produce more bite-sized chunks, that is to say, easily digestible snippets of news.'

And we coined the phrase, the 'Macnugget complex'.

The London *Daily News* had aimed for a circulation of between 500,000 and 600,000 within a year. But by July the paper had only

100,000 buyers, about half of them for the morning edition, half for the evening. Confidential papers leaked to the *Sunday Times* showed that in late July it was costing 29.5p to deliver every copy of a paper that was retailing at 20p.

On 24 July at 10.04 a.m. everything was normal at the offices of the London *Daily News*. Some time in between that time and noon, a message appeared on the computers saying, 'a week in Tenerife, with jacuzzi' and at 12.01 a message appeared that Maxwell would soon address the staff. Finally, at 12.15, the message 'goodbye' appeared on staffers' screens and the paper was no more.

The London *Daily News* had lasted five months and in that time amassed an estimated £50 million loss. It went down as one of Fleet Street's most expensive failures ever.

At Associated Newspapers Rothermere responded to the demise of the London *Daily News* by sending each of his employees a bottle of champagne and the victory celebration began.

A few days later, at the Maxwell camp, a gloomy Magnus Linklater knocked on the door of his proprietor's office, proffering the crumpled agreement that Maxwell had signed on the day he had recruited Magnus. 'You will remember the deal we signed, Bob,' he said. 'I think the time has come for me to go.' Maxwell did not even glance at the document. 'If you think I'm going to honour that, you don't know me very well,' he said.

It was to take Linklater several weeks to negotiate a severance package in light of Maxwell's resistance and when he did get it the sum was considerably less than originally agreed.

The demise of the London *Daily News* was commemorated in *Private Eye* with a cartoon that unknowingly anticipated events still to come. For in November 1991 when, discredited and at the end of his rope, Robert Maxwell would disappear over the side of his yacht, also missing was the *Mirror* pension fund.

But for now, *Private Eye*'s jab at Maxwell carried no deeper meaning, just honest ridicule. It pictured Rothermere out on the high seas, relaying a message from his yacht to that of Maxwell. 'Ahoy, Cap'n Bob! This is Rothermere speaking. Since you launched your new paper the sales of my *Standard* have soared.

'Would you like to launch another one? Haha.'

NINETEEN

AN ELEGANT TRANSACTION

On an overcast Saturday morning in August 1988, four men gathered in a loft in Clapham, laying secret plans for a financial revolution that would transform the Daily Mail and General Trust and its subsidiary Associated Newspapers. The men were meeting in Winsham Grove at the family home of Charles Sinclair, who only six months before, on 4 January, had been named managing director of Associated Newspapers.

Sinclair had taken over the position from the colourful Mick Shields, who had died on Christmas Day 1987. Shields had been grooming Charles from the time he was a young man, sending him to New York at the tender age of thirty to sort out Associated's complicated financial affairs there. For the past nine years Charles had shown himself capable of performing at the hectic pace Mick Shields had set for him in those early days, but his style was very different from that of his predecessor.

For one thing Sinclair was a worrier, and the first thing he found to worry about in his new position was the relatively weak control that DMGT exercised over Associated Newspapers. It was common knowledge that the break-up value of Associated was higher than its share price. 'So when I became MD,' Sinclair said later, 'I realised somebody could take over Associated and the DMGT could do little about it.'

Part of the problem was the family ownership of the company, which was viewed with suspicion in the City. Various members of the Harmsworth family held stock in the company and, although Vere Rothermere was in the dominant position, chairing DMGT as well as Associated Newspapers, Mary Rothermere, Esmond's widow, also owned and controlled a great deal of stock.

All through the 1970s neither side had absolute control and, in the popular imagination of many, Mary Rothermere represented a threat. Vere shared that view. He made no secret of his suspicions about Mary. She was a looming presence: a kind of silent partner whose views were nevertheless put across quite clearly. This seemed to suggest that Mary was the single person capable of overthrowing Vere and wresting control from his capable hands.

But although the scenario had much to recommend it in terms of sheer theatricality, nothing could have been more removed from the realm of possibility. Mary could be highly critical, but no one could accuse her of being stupid. To take over the firm, she would have had to have the co-operation of the Harmsworth family and there was no likelihood that they would voluntarily exchange an American woman with no background in the business for a British man who had been steeped in it practically from birth. Just as important, Mary had no inclination to take over. She wasn't a businesswoman and she knew it.

She was a well-connected socialite living in her native country, with homes in Newport and Palm Beach, prominent in East Coast Society and occupying a place on the fringes of the American intelligentsia.

But since Esmond's death in 1978, Mary had become more and more restless. 'When my father died,' her son Esmond said later, '*that day*, life changed completely for my mother.' In his words, that was the day 'all the glamour and beauty ended, and she was never really centred again'.

Mary began to travel constantly, from Newport to Palm Beach to Monaco; she went twenty times to China to pursue her love of Chinese society. She made friends with experts in the field of Chinese studies and even started a small Chinese jewellery business in New York City. Her son Esmond remembered a time when he was a boy at Eton and his school fees were unpaid because his mother had moved around so much that the bill couldn't catch up with her. When the school authorities asked him where she was, he said he didn't know and got into trouble because they assumed he wasn't telling the truth. Eventually he had to telephone to find out where his mother was so the bill could be paid.

To an outsider, Mary's nomadic lifestyle might have looked highly enviable and glamorous, but her family knew it evolved out of loneliness.

As to designs upon the Daily Mail and General Trust, Mary had none. She lost no more love on Vere than he did on her, but she wasn't about to try to unseat him. Still, Mary occupied an important symbolic role as a kind of 'external focus' for the company, as one executive at DMGT put it. 'Every fighting machine needs an enemy,' said Charles Sinclair, trying to explain why Mary came to be so regarded, 'and in the case of the DMGT, Mary was it.'

She sent her representative, Ned Ram, to sit on the board, and he turned out to be unfailingly supportive of the aims of Vere and the company. But he didn't keep her informed on some of the most important aspects of the business because it contravened the laws of confidentiality as they applied to board directors in England. Ned Ram even took the trouble of consulting an English lawyer to try to find out whether he could break the confidentiality code in order to keep his client informed of what was going on. He was advised he could not. As a result, Mary received no more information on DMGT than the average stockholder. This infuriated her and she wasn't shy about letting Ned Ram know it.

But in fact, in later years it became apparent that Mary had been of inestimable value to DMGT. A realistic assessment of her contribution to the firm came from Vere's son Jonathan.

> Mary had under her control 20 per cent of DMGT at a time when 50 per cent were voting and 50 per cent were non-voting. Vere had 30 per cent. But she backed him. She kept her shares and supported him. Shares and little else were the basis of her personal income, and during that time there was a low dividend yield. It was risky for her because Dad kept investing the proceeds back into the company. But for many years she kept her nerve and *backed him*.
>
> Without her backing he would have had to sell the company.

So, as Sinclair had suggested, Mary's role as an 'enemy' was largely symbolic, with little basis in reality.

But now a new focus of danger had to be identified to keep everyone in fighting fettle. Obligingly, the scenario shifted to Vere's son Jonathan. According to one insider – and this is the romantic version –

> Vere was consumed with the notion of Jonathan running the company after his death. And in turn that Jonathan would marry and have a son who would eventually run the company after his father's death. Most of Vere's motives, you will find, [were] geared towards protecting the Rothermere fortune and insuring the dynasty.

In this plot, Jonathan was pitted against Esmond, who was about the same age as he was. It was naturally assumed that the son of Mary and the elder Esmond would want to usurp power in the firm, and a great deal of speculation was given over to considering which of the two boys would turn out to be the more able. Never mind that they were both children while all this spinning was going on, it made a good story.

As for Vere, he was always taking into account any possible threat, no matter how unlikely. It was in his nature to be suspicious and he was capable of taking it to extremes.

But after growing up, 'Little Esmond', as he was sometimes called to distinguish him from his father, had gone into the book publishing business in the United States and owned his own literary agency in Boston. He had no designs on the company in England, although he believed it represented a good investment opportunity. He also thought leading the company was a difficult task and one of the advantages of his situation was 'he could sleep easy at night'.

Vere himself knew at heart that the only genuine threat which could arise to his leadership, or later to his son Jonathan's, would have to come from within the firm. The family was an unlikely source of trouble. Though unwieldy and full of random forces that could come into prominence at any time, the members had shown through the years an impressive ability to stick together when the going got rough.

Although various members could at one time or another behave in a dysfunctional manner, the term 'dysfunctional' could not be extended to the family as a whole.

But Vere remembered only too well that his father had fought off a major attempt at overthrow in 1944, which emanated from his managing director, Stanley Bell, perhaps in collusion with his American business associate, Frank Humphrey. At that time Esmond had defended himself ruthlessly, demanding Bell's resignation without delay.

Again, in his early years at Associated, when he was twenty-five years old and a minor executive, Vere was approached by a cabal that wanted to install him in place of his father as chairman of the company. He dealt with that threat by going to the very man who had fomented the plot and returning the incriminating evidence to him. It was a way of rejecting the plan and affixing blame without making outright accusations.

Most significantly, Vere never forgot how close a thing it was in 1970, when his father Esmond nearly merged with Beaverbrook Newspapers, in effect destroying Vere's birthright.

So, while there was no direct threat to Vere either from Mary or anyone else in the family, or from anyone on his management team, he knew the only real method he had of securing his leadership was to make sure the firm prospered. If their investment were seen to languish, his shareholders would quite sensibly sell their stock and invest elsewhere.

By now, Vere had managed to put the firm on a new footing. Not only had he saved the *Daily Mail* but he had also launched the *Mail on Sunday* and that Sunday middle-market tabloid was beginning to show the first signs of success. The provincials, always a mainstay of the company, were also doing well and, in large part, the American investments were sound. It was also clear, of course, that the Reuters bonanza was going to be gigantic.

So in the face of all this success and the lack of a realistic threat either to his leadership or to the dynasty, why was Vere so worried?

It was the very wealth of Associated Newspapers and its holding company, the Daily Mail and General Trust, that was causing the problem. DMGT owned 49.95 per cent of Associated, both companies being listed on the stock market. This division in itself represented a structural anomaly that had the effect of artificially depressing the price of their shares. The split in ownership acted to diffuse the value of Associated Newspapers' underlying assets and to keep the price of its stock low. From the point of view of a predator, this made the company particularly ripe for takeover. In the case of the holding company, DMGT, the price was languishing for a slightly more complicated reason.

The Daily Mail and General Trust held a portfolio of blue chip investments that, since their purchase in the 1920s, were now valued in the region of £70 million. If DMGT wanted to sell these stocks even to reinvest them more favourably, the company would be hit by a capital gains tax that had gone into effect in 1965. That meant effectively that an enormous amount would go to settle taxes, a drain on the capital of the company it could hardly afford. It was also viewed as a heavy drag on the assets of the company, as explained in an article from the *Daily Telegraph*:

> Since it assumed its present form 60 years ago from the profits of dealing in the *Daily Mail* [the DMGT] has sat on a portfolio of British shares, just like an investment trust.
>
> But because of the holding of 50 per cent of Associated Newspapers, the trading arm of the group, the Trust has never secured investment trust status. Should those British shares, now worth £71 million, be sold the capital gains would total £25 million, on which tax would be due.
>
> This is reflected in the rating of the Trust shares. They stand at a discount of 38 per cent to asset value, against 22 per cent for large investment trusts.

But these challenges, serious though they were, were as nothing compared with a much larger issue that threatened the very lifeblood of Associated Newspapers and its parent company. And if Vere didn't get this right, none of his triumphs of the past fifteen years would count for anything.

The decisions facing Vere Rothermere as a newspaper proprietor were extremely high-risk, amounting to expenditures that ran into the hundreds of millions of pounds. The major issue, modernisation, was fraught with pitfalls, any one of which carried the potential to bring the company to its knees. Yet evading the issue was impossible. The competition among the Fleet Street rivals was unrelenting, colour and computer-based technology being the most important buzzwords of the race towards technological supremacy.

Re-equipping the national titles alone would cost Associated in the region of £320 million, if the price of Harmsworth Quays, the modernisation of the editorial offices of the three national titles and labour expenses were included. If the provincial titles were also switched over to computer-based technology the sum would be larger still.

It was generally agreed that some of the funding for the new technology would eventually come from a decrease in manning. But, predictably, the print unions were committed to rejecting any change that could lead to a loss of jobs. So before the company could succeed in persuading them to co-operate, there would have to be massive redundancy pay-outs. Perhaps even more significantly, the journalists themselves were resisting. They were demanding extra pay if they took over the duties of the printers by inputting their stories themselves on the keyboard. Added to which David English, usually a force for progress, was showing little enthusiasm for the new technology.

But even if these impediments could be overcome, where exactly would the capital the company needed come from?

The simple answer was that some of it could come from the £70-million-plus portfolio held by DMGT in blue chip stocks. But how could the company realise the value of these investments without the capital gains tax kicking in?

In 1986 an initial finance package was decided. Said Peter Williams, group finance director, later,

> We decided a one for ten rights issue, raising £30 million. This was a gesture, really, to show that the family were behind the ... re-equipping. Of the £30 million, DMGT had to provide £15 million, which it raised by selling shares with the lowest capital gains tax bill. We did not then sell any of the large holding in Marks and Spencer which had been held for years.
>
> Second, we opted for lease finance to pay for the new Koenig and Bauer presses at Harmsworth Quays. This amounted to £35 million, came from the TSB and was signed up in March 1987.
>
> Third, a £120 million bank facility to pay for the rest.
>
> Last, sale of assets, notably Blackfriars Oil and Gas.

But one other, if controversial, avenue ripe for investigation seemed to be for DMGT to exercise the 'freedom of movement' guaranteed to members of the EEC under Common Market law at the time by emigrating to The Hague for the express purpose of tax efficiency. In Holland, new companies were enjoying much lower capital gains taxes than in Great Britain and this seemed a marvellous time to go. Accordingly, the company wrote a letter to the Treasury requesting permission to emigrate, stating clearly its intention to attract a lower rate of capital gains tax.

But, surprisingly, the letter remained unanswered. A second letter was sent. It also remained unanswered.

Speculation at the company maintained that the reason the Treasury had not replied, simply rejecting the request, was that they had no grounds in law for doing so. After two years DMGT decided its only recourse, in the absence of a defining answer from the Treasury, was to ask the European Court to rule.

The matter became something of a cause célèbre among similarly situated businesses who were watching closely for the outcome of the case – if the DMGT succeeded, they might be tempted to try the same thing. But when the decision finally came down on 27 September 1988, the finding seemed to fly in the face of the EEC Treaty and its 'guaranteed' freedom of establishment.

As Clive Schmitthoff, honorary professor of law at the University of Kent, was quick to point out in the *Business Law Journal*, the finding against DMGT was disappointing. It had succeeded in making 'the relocation of UK companies into another member state of the Community dependent on Treasury approval'.

In a decision that Schmitthoff said 'did not advance the objectives of the Community', the idea of freedom of movement relating to companies was 'honoured more in its disapplication than in its practical effect'. Schmitthoff wrote,

> The European Court of Justice is a very distinguished and highly regarded tribunal. It has done much to give practical reality to the provisions of the EEC Treaty. It had performed the same political function in the development of Community law as the Supreme Court did in its early interpretation of the US Constitution. An English lawyer is naturally reluctant to criticise such an eminent tribunal. But it must be said candidly that the judgement of the European Court in the *Daily Mail* case is totally wrong.

Although business lawyers generally agreed with Schmitthoff's assessment, it was cold comfort to DMGT. No matter how resourceful the company's Board of Directors, unlocking the capital and asset value of either of the two companies was proving to be easier said than done.

Associated Newspapers has always been a combat zone where constant sniping among high-level executives continues endlessly from day to day. This state of affairs was no accident. It was carefully engineered by Vere Rothermere, who believed that truth emerged from diversity, prosperity from competition. Once asked by a friend why there were so many differ-ent companies under the general umbrella of DMGT, he answered, 'So the managing directors can fight with one another.' It wasn't a joke.

In the days when Mick Shields and David English each represented a powerful constituency, the two men were often at each other's throats over budgetary matters or policy decisions. Occasionally, John Winnington-Ingram could be drawn in and he usually sided with Mick, whom he believed to be one of the most talented and creative executives in the newspaper business. David, he believed, too often went 'over the top'.

But the old regime was ending. About the time Winnington-Ingram was thinking of retiring, Shields underwent surgery to halt the advance of a brain tumour. But although the operation slowed the process, Mick was worsening to the extent that it became plain he was dying. Vere knew that Mick wanted 'to die in the harness' and supported the decision, although it was very painful for people in the office to watch Mick's decline. There was tremendous affection for him and he had earned the respect of the staff. Now it would be up to Charles Sinclair.

In June 1988 Simon Borrows had recently joined Baring Brothers and Charles Sinclair acted as one of his referees. Borrows knew Sinclair's input had been crucial, and he dropped by Sinclair's office at Northcliffe House one afternoon to pay his respects and to let Charles know he appreciated his efforts on Simon's behalf.

Sinclair had just finished reading an article in the *Financial Times* by a Harvard professor suggesting companies should 'do unto themselves' before they were beaten to it by outsiders and the two men got to talking about it. At the same time Borrows was aware, as were most people in the City, of the problem Sinclair was facing with respect to Associated Newspapers' exposure to the possibility of a takeover. In one of those rare leaps of logic connecting the article they were discussing with the poten-tial takeover problem, Simon suggested, 'Well, why don't you take over yourself?'

Charles looked at him sharply and Borrows enlarged upon the subject. 'Associated is an asset-rich, undervalued company,' he continued. 'Had you considered buying out the public shareholding from Associated in order to extend the control of the Daily Mail and General Trust?'

It was an outrageous idea, a conversational novelty, and after a few smiles the subject was allowed to drop. But later on the prospect of such a takeover began to preoccupy Sinclair's thoughts. So much so that later that week he awoke suddenly in the middle of the night, turning on the light and waking his wife Nicky. 'This is how we're going to solve the problem,' he told her as she groggily tried to imagine what in the world he was talking about. 'We're going to take over ourselves.'

Thus did Sinclair unknowingly initiate eight months of highly charged executive activity, the pace of which would energise the corporate climate of the Daily Mail and General Trust, changing it for ever.

In a series of simultaneous and overlapping deals, a small team of DMGT executives would develop a plan to buy out the public shareholders of Associated Newspapers, at last selling the company's by now infamous portfolio of shares. Not only that, but the team would in quick succession sell Blackfriars Oil, the company's holdings in the Canadian firm Consolidated Bathurst and half its holdings in the American firm Whittle Communications.

At the end of the day this rapidly paced reconfiguration would result in sales in excess of £500 million.

'And that was big money to us then,' said Sinclair years later, in what was perhaps one of the most unwitting of testaments to the success of his startling decision many years before.

The theory behind Charles Sinclair's midnight vision was that such a takeover would unlock the value of the Daily Mail and General Trust shares. At that time they were valued at £2.50 each. Who knew how high they might go in the aftermath of such a deal? Indeed, who knew if the theory would work at all?

That was the purpose of the highly private meeting in Charles Sinclair's loft in August 1988. The four men who were there would determine whether the numbers worked sufficiently well to warrant proceeding with the notion. Present were Nicholas Gold, Simon Borrows, Christopher Steane and, of course Charles himself.* They were all young men. Charles had just turned forty in April, Nicholas Gold and Christopher Steane were in their thirties and Simon Borrows was an astonishing twenty-nine years old. The tension in the loft that morning

* 'The fifth man', Peter Williams, was not at the meeting in Charles Sinclair's loft, but was certainly a member of the 'cabal'. At the time of the takeover Williams was thirty-five. It was said in the City that Williams was unlike any other executive who acts as the public face for a major company. He was lacking in the sometimes flamboyant ego many display and his honest commitment to the long-term value enhancement of DMGT was at direct odds with the short-term goals that often typified other firms.

was so all-consuming that when one of Charles's young sons came up to offer the men biscuits, Charles couldn't remember which one it had been. Nick Gold would remind him twelve years later that it had been Robert, who by that time was a student at Bristol University.

Sinclair was nervous as he prepared for the meeting with Rothermere in which he would present the details of the plan worked out by himself and his colleagues. At the time, he thought,

> This is such a radical idea I will have only one chance to present it to Rothermere. So I wrote it all down on two sheets of paper with all the figures, a kind of crib sheet for what was to us then an enormous deal.
>
> I started out by saying to him, 'This is the most difficult presentation I'm ever going to have to give in my life.'
>
> All Lord Rothermere said in return was, 'Continue.'

Simon Borrows, who was at the presentation, reflected later than on the one hand, Charles Sinclair seemed calm and rational, representing the kind of sound financial intellect that typifies men who are responsible for other people's money. Rothermere, on the other hand, had the more intuitive intellect. On this occasion, he went into his 'Delphic Oracle' mode as he sat there silently weighing the idea of the takeover of one of his firms by another. After a very long pause he surprised the two men by saying, 'Well, let's *do* it!'

'He was very emotional once he had decided,' Borrows said later. Since the younger men had been holding themselves in check, it seemed a source of relief that Rothermere could show so much outright enthusiasm.

Rothermere's own take on the deal was that it solved a lot of problems the company had been facing for a long time. He said later,

> The ownership of the companies was too untidy. It needed cleaning up, really, and this transaction provided a situation in which everybody benefited. It was one of those rare occasions when everyone did well. It has been described as 'an elegant transaction' and that's just what it was.
>
> The money was freely available and I saw this window wouldn't last very long, and if we were going to do it, then we had to do it quickly before the window closed again. So we did.

'It was good fun,' Borrows said later. 'There was a great sense of camaraderie, of enthusiasm. Of course, the entire project was conducted in the utmost secrecy.' He continued,

Nick and I gleefully gave the project the code name 'Salmon and Trout', because Charles was keen on fishing. Later on I was flying back from a business trip to New York and I happened to see that you could buy a smuggler fly-fishing rod at the House of Hardy on Pall Mall. I thought we could give those to everybody involved with the deal if it worked out. And that's what we ended up doing.

We were breaking new ground. Until then the DMGT had been conservative and then this *bold* move.

It was the largest ever buyout of public shareholders in a company in Europe at that time and, as a result of that deal, I was put on the board at Barings when I was thirty. On 29 December 1988 Charles Sinclair was made managing director of Daily Mail and General Trust and chief executive of the group. This when he was only forty years old.

Using a loan facility in excess of £530 million from Citibank, the DMGT offered £7.65 for each Associated share, putting a value on the entire publishing company in excess of £1.02 billion. Considering the debt the group was already carrying, the company was now carrying a load of nearly a billion pounds.

But as everyone at DMGT knew, Vere hated debt and would carry it only very reluctantly, Indeed, if Associated Newspapers and the Daily Mail and General Trust hadn't had a number of assets to realise he wouldn't have done the deal. The first move therefore was to realise the value of the portfolio of investments held by DMGT.

To some extent this was helped by a change in the capital gains tax procedure itself. An article in the *Financial Times*, written by Raymond Snoddy and Nikki Talt, explained how this could help:

> ... the situation has been complicated by a possible tax bill faced by DMGT if it realised any of the [*sic*] its long-established non-Associated holdings ...
>
> However, the last Budget has eased the Capital Gains Tax position, and yesterday DMGT estimated a tax bill of about £12 million if – as now planned – it eventually liquidates the non-Associated Holdings.

But that was not all. When he and his committee of four were 'doing the numbers' for the deal, Charles Sinclair reckoned that the high interest on the loan and the cost of the redundancies the company would pay during modernisation would offset the capital gains tax due when they sold the £70 million portfolio. And that is how it worked.

Peter Williams later spoke about the sell-off, which had its moments of drama:

DMGT's investment portfolio did get sold quite early in the bid process. It was vital that we could achieve 100 per cent ownership to get access to the cash flows of Associated to pay off DMGT's debt.

For technical reasons, this meant that we had to get approval for the bid from 90 per cent of the shareholders (excluding DMGT).

Soon after the bid, one shareholder holding 5 per cent rang to say that they would sell to us, but only if we would pay immediately. That was the point of no return. Until then, we were merely seeking approvals and, if we got enough, we would draw down on our loan. To meet this request we needed cash and the available source was the portfolio.

If that 5 per cent stake had been sold to someone else, it would have been a major problem. The decision was therefore made and I gave the order … to sell the portfolio, which was done within twenty-four hours.

Rod Marten, who had looked after the portfolio for nearly twenty years, was very upset!

The short-term effect on the company of the buyout was an immediate surge of the Daily Mail and General Trust shares on the stock exchange. But the long-term effect has been nothing short of miraculous. The real value of the stock has increased twenty times in eleven years. There have been two share splits and in January 1999 DMGT joined the ranks of the United Kingdom's top hundred quoted companies when its shares were admitted to the FTSE 100 Index.

The success of the company is the result of the high level of expertise and capabilities of the men Vere put in charge of DMGT. But how was Vere shrewd enough to attract such innovative executives to a relatively small company? First, he rewarded them fulsomely, with high salaries and all the trappings due a high level of competence and creative thinking.

Herein Vere differed from many other company chairmen. He provided an atmosphere distinctly at odds with most corporate environments where innovation is regarded with suspicion. Vere was that rare creature, a man who was able to support the creative thinking of his subordinates. In many ways they were a hard-to-handle bunch, but he had the mastery of them. 'Better wolves than sheep,' he was wont to say on the rare occasions they got out of hand. He remained unintimidated by their most radical schemes, thus giving their creativity uninhibited range.

And he had other virtues as well. As Padraic Fallon, the chairman of *Euromoney*, put it, 'Vere was like a block of granite. You could stand on top of him and fight markets and the competition and nature itself. He was stalwart in his support.'

He showered his executives with personal attention. He coaxed them.

He nagged them. He irritated them and he criticised them. But in the end he listened to them and when their advice warranted it he acted on it. In the long run it was this constant interaction between staff and proprietor that brought forth the best creative efforts of his team. Vere was born into a privileged world where rank and station were all, but in running the company he made a commitment to unencumbered interaction.

Thus freed from the straitjacket mentality imposed by most corporate environments, Vere's people gave him their all.

Just prior to the buyout of Associated in October 1988, the company took the first of several steps to realise its assets, exposing the true value of Associated's assets to the City.

In August that year the Board of Directors announced it was selling its shares in its oil and gas subsidiary Blackfriars for £110.2 million in cash. The amount implied a total value of £143 million since the deal involved Ultramar's assumption of £31.4 million of Blackfriars' net liabilities. As always with the firm where tax efficiency was a byword, the agreement had been organised to minimise the company's overall tax liability.

For Sinclair, who had joined the firm on the same day that the first oil from Blackfriars went on sale in Great Britain, the sale to Ultramar was the end of an era. As a young accountant he had handled Blackfriars' tax affairs, delivering the first royalty cheque the government received personally to the Bank of England. Then again, he remembered the excitement of visiting the Esmond, Forbes and Gordon fields by helicopter in the early days. In one episode, arriving last in a group of men going by helicopter out to a North Sea oil rig, he had had to wear the last safety suit available, one designed for a man five feet six inches tall. Sinclair is six foot two and he rode the entire distance hunched over double.

Less nostalgically, he worked with the well-known Peter Burt, then the general manager of the International Division of the Bank of Scotland. The International Division encompassed the Oil and Energy Division, and it was through Burt that Sinclair hoped to arrange a new kind of debt that would cover Blackfriars' part of the rigging expenses, some £30 million. Burt, who twenty years later was destined to be the catalyst in the failed but famous hostile bid for NatWest Bank, agreed to help the young accountant. In so doing, he set up the first non-recourse bank financing in the North Sea. It was ground-breaking finance, in the North Sea, yes, but also in the United Kingdom as a whole. But Burt was known for continually pushing back 'the frontiers of financing'.

Charles Sinclair would later reflect that this was the beginning of his skills in financing what he would come to call 'interesting debt'.

In this effort he was assisted by Richard Kent, then of Morgan Grenfell, later Deutsche Bank. Kent said,

> It was the first syndicated non-recourse financing in the North Sea where the banks lent the funds before the facilities were built and installed with no recourse to the parent company.
>
> In one way it was a natural progression of the market in that the banks had been gradually taking more risk in the North Sea.

But the decision of Peter Burt was based on his own bank's expertise in the field of petroleum engineering. He said later,

> Non-recourse financing, or limited-recourse refinancing, which is a better term, had been around for a long time in America. It was the first and is still the only deal where the shareholders didn't have to put up any money.
>
> We had our own reservoir of expertise at the Bank of Scotland. We had set up our own Oil and Energy Division in 1972, and we had our own Petroleum Engineering Department. British Gas held the monopoly right to buy all the gas found in British Waters, so Blackfriars had this contract in place. From there it was a matter of simple arithmetic. Our own engineers told us how much gas there was in the field.
>
> The good news was that it was a robust development. There was a lot of gas there, in shallow waters, so development costs were easily manageable. But it wasn't a conventional deal and our biggest problem was persuading other banks to come in. They expected to see the borrower put his money in first, not second. Any precedent causes problems and so it was with this. So we charged more.
>
> But for Charles it was well worth it because it freed his money to do other things. Had I known about the phenomenal success of the *Mail on Sunday* I'd have charged him even more.

This, then, was the debt that was discounted from the sale price of Blackfriars, good debt for Ultramar to assume and a tax-efficient method of selling for Associated.

When the time came actually to negotiate the sale it was, fittingly, Sinclair who handled the final negotiation. He had returned to London from his family home in Cornwall on Friday, 19 August 1988, and he and Richard Kent, working at Morgan Grenfell, opened all the sealed bids. The highest bid at the time was £120 million from Ultramar in the United States.

The next morning, Charles boarded the 10.50 return train from

Paddington. With him he carried one of the earliest mobile phones, which was about the size of a brick. At about 1.30 British time, he and the Ultramar representative, who was playing golf on a course in Poughkeepsie, were just concluding the deal when the train went into a tunnel.

Five minutes later, as it emerged, the men, who had both instinctively stayed on the line, concluded the deal at £144 million, the delay actually lending them both manoeuvring room.

In evaluating the sale some time later, DMGT managers viewed the sell-off as having been particularly timely in terms of achieving the best price possible on the sometimes volatile oil market.

But good as the deal was, the sale of the Canadian firm Consolidated Bathurst eclipsed it. Stone Container Corporation of Chicago ended up offering DMGT Canadian $25 a share, amounting to a consideration of $378 million in Canadian currency, some £180 million in sterling.

This, then, was the last chapter in the story of the 'overnight deal' that Bob Morrow had engineered during one freezing weekend in Montreal in November 1974. The panic that characterised the agreement then culminated in the biggest takeover in Canadian history – the giant firm of Price Brothers by Abitibi. Morrow managed to bail DMGT out of Price Brothers in the nick of time with a hastily organised shares swap with Consolidated Bathurst, a subsidiary of Power Corporation. Morrow, a long-time friend of Paul Desmarais, the chairman of Power Corporation, worked frantically alongside Bill Turner, the president of Consolidated Bathurst, in arranging the deal that stupefied the Canadian financial world, with little word of its magnitude ever making its way to the British Isles.*

An ironic aside to the story was that at the time this deal took place, Charles Sinclair was a very young man who had just joined Associated Newspapers as an accountant. He remembered later that in the first few weeks of his employment he had been invited to a dinner in Dorset where a Canadian woman stockbroker from Richardson Greenshields and Co. told him, 'You've just joined the company that lost out in the reorganisation of the Canadian newspaper business.'

Charles had no idea that by bailing out of Price Brothers and into Consolidated Bathurst, Associated had pulled off a coup unimagined by either the Canadian financial community or by the Canadian press. His reaction to his dinner partner's acerbity then was to wonder whether he had joined the right company.

---

* See chapter 5 for a full discussion of the deal.

He wasn't the only one who didn't realise how shrewd a deal Bob Morrow had pulled off. At the time Vere's father, Esmond, then still alive and involved with decisions, had roasted his son for getting involved with controversial Canadian financiers – 'people we don't know', he called them.

But Vere defied his father and proceeded to completion of the deal through a welter of contradictory advice. His decision to finish the deal turned out to be one of the most successful of his career. It permitted DMGT to avoid triggering British and Canadian tax laws that would have cost the company millions of pounds sterling from double taxation. It also permitted the company to retain its high profile in the Canadian investment community, something it would have lost if the swap had not taken place.

Now further rich dividends were resulting from that cold winter weekend fifteen years before. At the time Paul Desmarais and Bill Turner masterminded the sale of the Consolidated Bathurst shares for Canadian $25 on behalf of Power Corporation and DMGT, a highly satisfactory price, the Canadian paper milling industry was at an historic high. Not long after the sale, the industry began showing signs of a slump that many believe will prove to be a terminal decline.

Charles Sinclair was present the night the deal was done, having flown over in February 'in rotten weather' to oversee Associated's interests. At 3 a.m., just as the lawyers were completing the essentials of the sale, the phone rang in the conference room where they were all working. Without a thought, Sinclair picked it up. 'Anyone here with a Christian name of Richard?' he asked the gathering of men.

One of the lawyers smartly quipped back, 'Anyone here with a Christian name?'

Only a short time before the buyout of Associated Newspapers by Daily Mail and General Trust, another major asset was sold: Associated's share in the American magazine *Esquire*. It resulted in a profit of around $25 million for the company. At the same time Associated was in the process of selling half its share in 13–30, for $125 million.

But another investment didn't fare as well. Vere and Mick Shields had earlier become enamoured of a legal newspaper called *American Lawyer* and a handful of similar legal journals, which had been losing money ever since. With the costs running at something between $4–5 million a year, Charles Sinclair believed it was far too expensive a drain on the company while it was carrying the debt load created by the takeover of AN by DMGT.

American Lawyer was edited by the flamboyant New Yorker Steve Brill. Brill was a friend of Clay Felker, who had introduced Vere Rothermere to *Esquire's* innovative young legal columnist in 1978. Known later for his founding of Court TV, Brill had originally attracted Vere and Mick to the *American Lawyer* project and the legal journals with a well-written prospectus, which worked very well on paper. The projects, however, consistently generated losses while Associated was involved and by 1988 it became apparent that selling out would be the best move.

Over the years, there had been little love lost between Brill and Sinclair. Said Brill of Sinclair, 'He's the kind of guy who, if he won the lottery, would say, "*Damn*, it's the wrong tax year."' Sinclair's retort was, 'You don't pay taxes on lottery winnings.'

Sinclair personally negotiated the company's exit from the *American Lawyer* project with Ed Aboodi, who worked specifically for Steve Ross, the controversial chairman of Warner Brothers. Aboodi was an Israeli whose reputation for being a tough negotiator was internationally established, especially after the merger of Warner and Time Inc. Ed Aboodi negotiated that deal alongside Gerald Levine, who later emerged as head of Time-Warner and eventually Warner Brothers and AOL.

Sinclair nevertheless came out with $29 million and that sum, as well as the yearly loss that had been going to help finance *American Lawyer*, all went to lessen the debt load of Associated, as it moved tentatively, but optimistically into the last decade of the millennium.

TWENTY

FLEXO-FURY

Bert Hardy knew the ropes because he had been on them himself. The basic rule of thumb? When buildings costing in excess of £125 million go up, tempers flare and heads roll. Said Hardy,

> I'd been with Murdoch for about ten years and then he fired me. I'd built Wapping and he decided it was a monumental disaster and so he fired me and the building became known as 'Hardy's Folly'. He fired me – I had built for him two factories, one in Glasgow and one in Wapping – we were friends and anyhow he fired me.

When Bert Hardy took over as managing director of Associated Newspapers, replacing John Winnington-Ingram who was retiring, he had no illusions about what would happen to him if he didn't get the problems with the new flexographic printing plant solved – and speedily.

On 15 May 1989, a new state-of-the-art printing and distribution centre, Harmsworth Quays, had been opened by Prime Minister Margaret Thatcher. Built on a twelve-acre site at Rotherhithe in London's Docklands, the centre was the world's biggest flexographic newspaper production plant, built for the purpose of publishing the *Daily Mail*, the *Mail on Sunday* and the *Evening Standard*. Manning had decreased from 1687 in 1985 to 486 and that figure included the production needs of the *Evening Standard* which, prior to the opening of Harmsworth Quays, had been printed in the *Express* building. The achievement was immense and, from the outside at least, it was all very impressive.

Behind the scenes chaos reigned. The new presses from Koenig and Bauer, which cost Associated Newspapers £35 million, could print only two colour photographs per section. The photographs themselves were often out of register, meaning they were blurred and unclear. This caused both rage and grief among the editorial staff, tempers were flaring and the fight, as they say, was on.

The brief three-year history of Harmsworth Quays was fraught with controversy. In one telling, by the time Associated Newspapers committed to building the facility, the company was already behind the other national titles, most notably the *Telegraph*, in the race to modernise.

The primary reason given for the delay was that Associated had been waiting for the *Mail on Sunday* to take hold with the public and show conclusively that it would succeed. By the time that happened a whole host of new safety regulations had come into force and the 'cellars of Fleet Street', that is, the vast printing facilities beneath the buildings owned by Rothermere, were no longer acceptable. The company needed an entirely new printing plant. And since the *Mail on Sunday* had recently come into profitability and the *Evening Standard* was now up and running as an Associated title, the massive investment required to build a new printing plant had for the first time become practical.

Said Winnington-Ingram, who had been responsible for all aspects of production,

> We couldn't afford to be left behind. We had to persuade the unions, who were beginning to be humbled by Thatcher's new labour regulations, the full weight of which hadn't taken effect. But the unions were now willing to begin to talk.
>
> More and more our own staff were showing a certain amount of flexibility and support for what was inevitable, and we began to make the deals.

The first state-of-the-art facility was built in 1985 by the provincial newspaper publisher Eddie Shah, in order to launch a new national title, *Today* newspaper. Shah had centred the production of his national in Nottingham, sidestepping the print unions in Fleet Street. The newspaper's use of satellite printing plants, colour and the direct input of type by journalists instead of specially trained typesetters presaged the long-lasting and bloody battle that would take place in Fleet Street later.

Then Rupert Murdoch's shock transfer of News International from Fleet Street to Wapping witnessed eleven months of picketing and violence. The ultimate fate of Murdoch's workforce held a lesson for any of the unions who still believed they could halt the changeover of national news production facilities from hot to cold type. As Linda Melvern, author of *The End of the Street*, put it:

> Rupert completely outmanoeuvred the unions. And they totally lost all their power. He offered them very little money compared with what he would have had to pay, if they had accepted his ultimatum earlier. In the end he did pay them something only because he felt so terrible. And it was

a way of getting rid of the pickets. They would have been there for ever, they would have been there today.

But had Eddie Shah and Rupert Murdoch had any effect on Associated Newspapers? 'We had deals on the table before *Today* and before Wapping,' said Winnington-Ingram.

> But the influence of *Today* was alone quite powerful with our workforce because they suddenly realised that the old days were over. The new technology was here and it was going to happen, and their whole attitude changed. Then Wapping happened and it really did make a difference for us. It really did.

But the modernisation programme carried out by Associated Newspapers was not characterised by the kind of acrimony and bitterness between the unions and the management that had characterised News International's move to Wapping. Bill Pressey, general manager in charge of production at Associated, said:

> We started seeing our chapels before Wapping happened. We had established the redundancy payments. We had established the levels we wanted. We had not reached agreement but discussions were going quite well when Rupert suddenly shut the place down and moved to Wapping. That in itself was a great help to us. When that happened, if there was any reluctance of our people to come along with us, it disappeared.

In all, in three years the number of employees shrank from about 5800 to 2800. There were massive redundancy costs, but Associated Newspapers was on target for modernisation. Pressey said, 'So as we came to the end of 1986, 1987, staffing levels were very much in hand. Then we were able to implement what we wanted.'

What they wanted was flexographic. It was a highly controversial choice, but there was, as one executive put it, 'an astonishing degree of unanimity' among the staff that 'flexographic offered the highest quality printing'. Stuart Martin, who would become project director for Harmsworth Quays, said:

> Offset as a printing process had been in operation for thirty-odd years, and had developed pretty well and to the point where metropolitan papers could use it.
>
> But although it had been around, it had never been used in British

national newspapers. But there was also this new technology of flexographic and it appeared to be developing well.

Lauded for its 'non-rub quality', flexographic printing produces stock that doesn't come off on the hands because it uses clean, water-based inks. It is a kind of printing where only a kiss impression occurs between the rollers and the paper and the ink. So it is possible to use it with coated stock. Perhaps the most distinctive advantage of flexographic is the high quality of colour it offers, especially in the reproduction of photographs.

Originally developed for the food industry, flexographic printing was just beginning to surface as an acceptable method in the production of newspapers when it caught the eye of Associated. In the United States, the *Miami Herald* was using it and sections of the *Washington Post* were printed by 'flexo', as it was called. Inside Associated Newspapers, technical director Tom Garrud was conducting extensive research into as many new developments in the field of printing as he could discover. Eventually he decided that this new method was the right one for the company.

John Winnington-Ingram described the process in a speech he delivered later, in 1989, before a group of international professionals in the field, the FIEJ Marketing Seminar that was being held in Austria that year. The company had been 'experimenting with a small flexo unit in a factory in Oldham', he explained, 'as early as 1980'. Winnington-Ingram continued,

> We were very concerned, producing a newspaper in the middle market, that our quality of colour should not detract from the product and give us a downmarket appearance, either in its use for advertising or particularly editorial purposes. At the time of the decision, where colour was being used, it was not of a particularly high standard and it tended to be associated with provincial and downmarket newspapers. So we had to have quality.

By adopting flexo, Associated would steal a march on its rivals, who were still opting for offset. The company would become a pioneer in the field, bringing the most advanced printing technology to its titles.

No one could deny that the quality of the printing was superb, and the costs overall of the process were lower than other methods. But one of the overriding problems was that, once you had committed to flexo, it was practically impossible to change.

This was the first setback for the managerial staff who had to determine that the decision to go flexo was the right one. In the end, Vere Rothermere himself decided it was too risky simply to install flexo without a fallback position. The idea of re-drilling special sets of holes in the floor of the new plant and in the machinery gained favour, as a means of allowing the switchover to another type of process if, for some unanticipated reason, flexo turned out to be an unmitigated disaster. This entailed an extra expense of £200,000, but it was thought to be a nominal amount to pay for insurance to give the company an 'out' – if it ever came to it.

Later, the drilling of the extra holes would in itself become a controversy, fuelling criticism of the choice of flexographic. The logic was, if they had so little confidence in the system that they anticipated its failure even before they installed it, why install it at all?

Some time around late 1988 or early 1989 Murdoch MacLennan, who was production and technical director at Express Newspapers, conducted a tour round the new premises at Blackfriars Bridge. Both David English and Vere Rothermere were scheduled to attend, but at the last minute English cancelled. Vere came on his own and MacLennan showed him around the new facility. 'In some ways', MacLennan said later, 'we had got ahead of Associated and actually surpassed them.'

Vere must have realised this because a short time later Bert Hardy contacted Murdoch MacLennan, saying that Vere had asked him to see if he would join the staff. Murdoch as a result became managing director of Harmsworth Quays in 1989. He was just in time for the free-for-all. As Bert Hardy said later,

> We had a lot of headaches and a lot of fights, and papers were being delayed and the results were not very good. The fights were among ourselves.
>
> The editorial people were furious with the bad printing and terrible photo reproduction. They were shouting and screaming. The fights were hugely fierce and, I think, there was even a bit of fist fighting here and there.
>
> So it was every day. It wasn't a question of having a board meeting once a month and saying, 'Ah, yes, what do we have on the agenda today? Ah, yes, let's discuss the bad printing.'
>
> No. This was our life, every single moment of our day.

The facility itself was nothing short of fabulous. Stuart Martin had three years to finish Harmsworth Quays and a budget of £124.5 million. He said, 'We came in one month late and completed £300,000 within the budget, and part of that was re-drilling the holes.'

Much of the credit belonged to a chartered engineer named Michael Rush, who had been hired by John Winnington-Ingram as a consultant, but who ended up working full time on the project. There was no doubt that by the time the plant was up its value was already a great deal more than the original allocation.

So what MacLennan found when he arrived at Harmsworth Quays was a very valuable installation. He also found the man he was replacing still on the job. It was a fairly awkward situation.

But it was as nothing to the fury he witnessed between various factions fighting it out over the printing problems. Murdoch had been warned from the start by a friend of his who was familiar with flexographic that it would be next to impossible to solve the problem, because, as the friend put it, 'it was like trying to print from wine gums'. The printing plates were made of polymer plastic and it was very hard to stabilise them.

When Murdoch tried to discuss the problem by talking to various staff members one manager, who, in MacLennan's words, 'thought he had a special relationship with the proprietor', implied MacLennan himself was on thin ice and should watch his step. He was one of the managers who had been instrumental in bringing in flexo. Murdoch said later,

I said to the man, 'I'm fed up. I'm sick to death of the argument. What can you offer me to make this system work?' And he answered, 'I can offer you constructive criticism!' And I said, 'I don't like criticism of any kind!' And he left my office in a fury.

As far as Hardy was concerned, he considered himself in a good political position to solve the problems because he had not originally been part of the group who brought in flexographic.

In the politics of the thing, I was standing above, involved with it when we started trying to find the solutions, but standing above it...

I didn't have to defend anything. All I had to do was find a way out of it. And one way was to sack the people who had made the decision...

I had been aware of the work with the prototypes and I had come to the conclusion, like others, that the plates were the problem and not the original presses made by Koenig and Bauer. So I had to persuade everyone to write off the plate-making part of the investment, it was millions, close to five. But it wasn't just that. It was also the people running the plant because they were refusing the solution.

The man who actually found how to solve the plate problem was Peter Highfield who was, in the words of Murdoch MacLennan, 'an unassuming guy who was just good at his job'. Highfield was on a fact-finding trip in California when he discovered a plant that was making a metal-backed plate that could hold in register because it could be locked into position. But that company, NAPP, was thinking of pulling out of the manufacture of flexographic altogether. MacLennan explained:

> We persuaded them of the potential, that we could give them an order that was worth more than all their other customers put together.
>
> What we had to do was to replace nearly 1000 plate lock-ups in order to move to steel-backed plates, a major engineering expense, while maintaining full production.
>
> But in the end it was thanks to Rothermere, who made the decision to write off £5 to £7 million plus to invest in the operation.

In Bert Hardy's own estimation, Rothermere's decision was the key to the successful adaptation of flexographic to Associated's needs.

> There's a touch of steel about Rothermere which he doesn't look as if he's got and people underestimate him. They look at Vere and think he's a bit of a softy. So when I went to him and asked for the money, it was *big* money. He saw instantly there was no way of going to the board and asking permission. When you're in a situation like that, you've got to act. So he acted.

Yes, Rothermere acted, but he regretted his part in the gamble to go flexographic. 'We made a big decision,' Rothermere said,

> and it was made by myself and the then management of the company to buy this flexographic equipment from Koenig and Bauer. And they were guaranteeing that this was going to work beautifully, so we took a chance on it in the end. I wouldn't do it again, literally regretted doing it, because it was a disaster to start with, it could have ruined us. We really were on the razor's edge.

But was that the whole truth? Probably not, because in the years to come, nobody would take more pride in the success of flexographic than Rothermere. Moreover, had he really wished to get out of flexo, he did have the chance.

Just after the problems with the process were solved, Murdoch MacLennan invited Vere for a Chinese lunch at Wapping. There, to Rothermere's surprise, he offered the press lord 'a good price' for Harmsworth Quays.* (*See footnote p. 251*)

Vere's question was immediate: 'Who else is involved?'

MacLennan was coy, admitting only to 'corporate financing'. In the end it wouldn't have mattered how he was financing the deal – Rothermere intended to keep Harmsworth Quays and along with it flexographic.

But that didn't save the people Hardy wanted to sack. According to his logic, the fighting had isolated two distinct camps and it was necessary for him to get rid of the people who were *in situ*. Hardy said later,

> They had built the bloody place. It's no small achievement to get the thing up and running. Suddenly these newcomers come in and say the problem is the plates. And they are going to wipe out the decisions you've made.
>
> So what I had to do was to sack them, get rid of them and I did that.

But there was another point of view, this one about Hardy. It was that he had to have his own men in order to achieve maximum efficiency. Rothermere had to choose. He could stay with the old guard, or he could go with his new manager. He chose Hardy.

For those who were to go, Rothermere's reaction must have seemed a shock. Vere had always been considered to be 'the gentleman proprietor', but that was changing. In the words of one of those who ended up biting the bullet, 'It was a very pleasant gentlemanly company to work for as a group, but then there were changes in the group in the last two or three years.'

But a great deal was at stake. If his new staff hadn't solved the problem of the plate-making, the firm would have been down over £125 million in mid-1980 money. The result would have been ruinous. When faced with the decisions that needed to be taken to insure the survival of his company, Vere emerged as a man quite different from the popular conception of him as a well-meaning bumbler:

> The decision was to go with the new technology. But it was the old management and the time had come when they were redundant. They really had the wrong mentality for this brave new world.
>
> They were all very nice people and good company people for many years, but they found it hard to adjust to the ruthless demands of this new world. When you're in business, too bad, you've got to take decisions in the real world, otherwise you're not going to survive. Hardy and his people could carry things out on that level and they survived.

So who had been in the right in the flexo wars? Was it the managerial

---

* MacLennan was reluctant to reveal the amount he offered Rothermere for Harmsworth Quays, but did admit it was in excess of the £124.5 million the facility cost.

team at Associated who first made the decision to pioneer flexographic? Or was it Bert Hardy and his managerial team who fought to the bitter end for a new plate-making facility?

Everybody was right. They were all part of the process and, if blood was shed, well that was part of the process as well.

Hardy may have been the survivor of the flexo wars, but the fight was only just beginning. Now he found himself facing a new challenge, this one from the journalists. Aware of the vast savings that would be made to Associated when the old-style linotype printers were discontinued, they now staked a claim for more money. Their argument was that they would be the ones inputting the type and for this they should receive compensation.

Hardy refused outright, but in return he made the less than salutary discovery that the whole of editorial was dragging its feet in accepting the new technology at all. It was something he hadn't expected.

The only editor willing to co-operate was John Leese, who had recently taken over the *Evening Standard*. Leese was fascinated by the new technology and, in particular, believed that an evening paper would derive incredible benefit from the sheer speed of delivery it offered. He welcomed electronic page make-up and story-setting because it had the potential of getting his newspaper out on the street faster.

Hardy brought in Allan Marshall to facilitate the process. Marshall was an Australian national who had been systems editor on the *West Australian* in Perth. By chance he met Craig Orr and Rob Nevett at a conference in California and, impressed by Marshall's use of editorial systems, the pair urged him to come to London to help with the changeover at the *Evening Standard*. Marshall was flattered, but thought little of it. Within a day of his return to Perth, however, Bert Hardy had him on the phone inviting him out for an interview.

It was an instant hire and from 1987 Marshall was working directly with Craig Orr and Antony Hilton on electronic page make-up for the *Evening Standard*. For them, the big day was 8 December, the first day of live transmission. This was initiated by Tony Hilton at the City office, and the successful transmission of the City pages led to the same method being employed on features and eventually on the sports and news pages.

But Leese was outside David English's fold and it now appeared to Bert Hardy that Leese's enthusiasm hardened the resistance of the editorial staff of the *Mail* and *Mail on Sunday*. There was a lot of talk about 'what was going on down at the *Standard*', said Hardy,

and people came to resent Leese's attitude. I always regarded these other editors as a bit of a club that didn't want me for a member. I think, eventually, David English called a meeting of all his editors of the *Mail* and the *Mail on Sunday*, and we had a face-to-face, if you like. I addressed them and told them what we were doing and why. This took place in David's conference room.

It was Bert Hardy's first experience with the David English phenomenon and until that moment he hadn't fully appreciated the power English held over all aspects of newspaper production at Associated. For Allan Marshall, who was also at the meeting, it would be remembered as a highly political affair, with the various editorial staff openly showing their reluctance to adopt the system Marshall and Hardy were recommending.

For one thing, Marshall was very much viewed, in his own words, as 'the evil one', and for a variety of reasons. First, he favoured a system that the editorial staff was resisting. They were expecting a 20 per cent pay rise for a labour-intensive system and Marshall wanted a simpler system that could be run, literally, by anyone. So compensation was very much an issue on everyone's mind and if Marshall got his system there would be no extra compensation.

But Marshall was also an outsider, new to London and new to Associated, and therefore he was viewed with suspicion. To top it off, he was many years younger than the people who were resisting and it must have been galling to them to have a younger man telling them what to do.

As expected, the meeting produced a high degree of resistance to both Hardy and Marshall. But in Marshall's mind the moment of opportunity came when Stewart Steven commented that he believed this system was the way forward. Some things were still wrong, Steven said, but if these things could be fixed, he believed it would work.

A test was arranged and, after much humming and hawing, it was settled that Allan Marshall and his team would use his electronic system on a Sunday night edition of the *Daily Mail*. This would be carried out parallel to the traditional system as a back-up in case of the failure David English still believed was inevitable.

English had privately told Allan Marshall that electronic page make-up would never happen. But on that Sunday evening he said that if, in fact, Marshall and his team succeeded in finishing at the same time as the old-time practitioners he would send a crate of champagne to Allan.

Marshall did succeed and David English's attitude changed overnight. Bert Hardy explained:

There was this sort of shift in the direction the papers had been taking and

I must say the *Daily Mail* went ahead at one hell of a speed. Once having got the sign from David, once he had made *his* decision, everybody moved.

Marshall's take on the situation was a little more ambiguous. English, he knew, subscribed to a kind of editorial philosophy that could be termed 'survival of the fittest':

> If I was strong enough to survive, well, then I could get my system. David had a lot of the old guard saying this was not the right path to go down. But I always wondered if David himself was not in some way behind Stewart Steven's endorsement at the meeting.
>
> Conversely, I couldn't help wondering if Lord Rothermere wasn't the powerhouse behind the change in attitude.
>
> Well, I never found out.

Thus did Associated make the changeover to the new technology. It was not a wholly smooth operation, but it wasn't marked by overt hostility. In the final analysis Allan Marshall got his system. He never did get that crate of champagne David English had promised him.

Even as the drama over Harmsworth Quays was playing out, another flashpoint for conflict emerged. Although the move from Fleet Street to Kensington did not have the life-and-death urgency of the flexo wars, neither was it a meeting of the minds between management and staff. Just as they had been in charge of putting up Harmsworth Quays, John Winnington-Ingram and Stuart Martin had put in motion the move to Kensington, having conducted the meetings with the owner, Mohammed Al Fayed.

But despite the fact that the new atrium located behind Barkers department store in High Street Kensington was a light, airy and glamorous new setting for Associated Newspapers, according to Tony Gamble, who was in charge of the move, the transfer was marred by 'aggravation and bad feeling'.

The company couldn't hide the fact it was trying 'to squeeze a quarter of a million square feet into a new office complex of 180,000 square feet', said Gamble and at the time renovations began on the leased building no one knew the *Evening Standard* would be coming along as well. Space was at a premium, even though many service staff were going because permanent staff were being replaced by contract workers. Gamble added, 'Most didn't want to leave Fleet Street at all. So with that not too promising premise, the move began in earnest in December 1989.'

But Rothermere was pressing ahead. One of his biggest concerns was the famous Room One, where Northcliffe had greeted visitors during his heydey. It was dismantled and reconstructed in the Kensington offices in mint condition. The bronze front doors, depicting various means of transporting newsprint, were also reassembled as a decorative feature in the reception of the sixth floor.

It had almost become a matter of company policy that David English would get first choice of the premises. He took what was considered the best floor of the new building for the *Daily Mail*, even as the top executives of the company vied for the offices surrounding the atrium.

Gamble again: 'Many of the secretaries would now be housed in open-plan offices and there were some hard feelings. Most of the staff simply did not want to go.'

Another point of squabbling turned out to be the new security system. Because the company was moving to new premises, Gamble believed this gave him the opportunity he needed to get the system right. As he later said,

All staff were issued with security identification passes which also gave individuals access through the turnstiles. Without these passes, staff could not gain access unless a security guard vetted them and allowed them to pass.

Because there were initial difficulties, we put in a test: Bert Hardy gave instructions to program the DMGT chief executive, Charles Sinclair, out of security. 'What better way to test the system?' Hardy asked.

The following morning there was a commotion in the atrium when Sinclair could not get into the building. The conversation that took place then between these two top executives may be left to the imagination. Suffice it to say, Charles Sinclair's security pass was quickly programmed back into the system.

The fact was that it didn't matter what the employees thought about the move. It didn't matter what the journalists thought about the new technology.

Despite the squabbles over office space, despite the flexo wars, despite the sackings and despite the setbacks, the company was moving forward. There was constant rivalry between Associated's national titles and their competitors, between the titles themselves, and between the managers of various branches of the company. And all along the way the rank and file employees of the firm were locked in mortal combat. The place was alive with it – competition, the fight to survive, the fight to excel.

TWENTY-ONE

DAVID'S VERSION

In David English's version of events he was always the chief protagonist of the play, the initiator of the action – the star of the show. So when the *Sunday Times* elevated him to the rank of KING DAVID in one of its headlines, it must have pleased him enormously.

The news story topped by this 200-point tribute came complete with a photograph of English wearing a paper crown made of a folded *Daily Mail*. It covered the legendary editorial reshuffle that took place at Associated on 10 July 1992. As in a game of musical chairs, two editors jumped places and two others came out of the ranks to take over prime positions in the editorial line-up at Associated Newspapers.

It was an event unprecedented in the history of British journalism.

Stewart Steven left the *Mail on Sunday* to take over the *Evening Standard*, while Jonathan Holborow, deputy editor on the *Mail*, transferred over to fill Stewart's shoes. Dee Nolan became editor of *You* magazine, replacing Nick Gordon, who was unceremoniously ejected from the position.

But by far the most surprising outcome of the reshuffle was Paul Dacre's shift from the *Evening Standard* to the *Daily Mail*, where he took over as editor. Incredibly, David English relinquished the position willingly. It was a situation inconceivable to anyone who knew David well. Why did he do it? What could have initiated such an unpredictable move?

The answer was complicated but no one doubted for a moment that the entire scenario had been finessed by English who had brilliantly turned what could have been a terrible blow to the group to his advantage. It was a testament to his hold on editorial policy at Associated.

As if that weren't triumph enough, even as David's people slotted into position, he took over from Vere as chairman of Associated Newspapers, a role so highly regarded in Fleet Street that it brought about the KING DAVID headline. For a time, most people believed David had supplanted Rothermere himself who, it was assumed, had stepped aside for English because of his dazzling talent.

The misunderstanding was partially the result of the complex structuring of the family of companies under Rothermere's control. It took a little time for the pundits to realise that Vere Rothermere was still in control of Associated Newspapers since he remained chairman of the Daily Mail and General Trust, its holding company. And in fact, David wasn't invited to join the board of DMGT until 1996.

For a time, among those with only a rudimentary understanding of how the company worked, David English was considered to be 'Supreme Being' at Northcliffe House, with many outsiders believing he had taken over from Rothermere. Even the internal mail system began delivering Rothermere's mail to David's office, much to the chagrin of the proprietor's office support team.

Meanwhile the director of Corporate Affairs, Vyvyan Harmsworth, was informed that the new chairman would be taking over his offices. Harmsworth was away from work on jury duty and found out about this only later. But in the event, English did not take over the Corporate Affairs offices, only a part of them. The rest of the suite he deemed too small. Instead, he instructed staff to construct a new office complex over the weekend.

So when David assumed his new duties on the Monday after the Friday when Rothermere offered him the job, he and his secretarial staff occupied an entirely new suite, custom-built to his specifications.

David English had always assumed Paul Dacre would become the next editor of the *Daily Mail*. In fact, he had nurtured Paul for years in the belief that he was the only man with the right mix of skills and temperament to take over from David himself. English was Dacre's mentor and benefactor, and it was he who put the younger man's name up for editor of the *Evening Standard* in 1991. In David English's words,

> There had been a lot of opposition because the *Standard* people did not want a *Mail* man down there and everyone had a view on it. But I really persisted and Vere was very supportive, and Paul went to the *Standard* and I thought, 'Well, he'll be five years on the *Standard*, and that will be just the time for me to go at the time of the next election.'

English's plans were proceeding very nicely – until the night of 9 July 1992, when the well-known correspondent Ann Leslie produced a very good contact for the Prince of Wales. The informant was insisting on speaking directly to the editor as well as to the reporter in order to be certain his disclosures would be handled responsibly. 'So,' said David English later,

I had this meeting, this incredibly important meeting, when Paul Dacre said he had to see me urgently for a drink. So I had the meeting and Paul came in at the end of it, and we went to the Kensington Garden Hotel and I thought, 'What on earth can it be?' When we sat down he said, 'I've been offered *The Times*,' and he said, 'I've got to take it.'

I said, 'Have you spoken to Rothermere? You have to speak to Rothermere. It's common sense and it's common courtesy.'

He said, 'I can't get him, nobody will tell me where he is, I don't know where he is.' So I said to let me speak to him. So I then went on to try to get Vere. And I couldn't get him. Somebody had arranged for him to go on a salmon fishing trip with Charles Sinclair and Peter Williams, and he was in the middle of bloody Iceland. There were only emergency telephones there. I was told they called in once a day and I said, 'I've got to be on that call.'

But it was a two-way phone. I finally got on to Vere and I was talking, and it was 'over and out', and he was pressing the wrong button. He obviously didn't want to be disturbed.

So at last he said, 'You'll have to wait, David. I'll be back. I caught a wonderful salmon today. Goodbye.'

And I saw in a blinding flash that we could not lose Dacre, because you can't lose the next generation. It was absolutely vital to hold him. So I went back to Dacre and I said, 'You can't go because your destiny is to edit the *Daily Mail* and you must edit the *Daily Mail*,' and he said, 'Yes, but –' and I said, 'I don't mean in the future, I mean now. I will stand down for you.'

He said, 'That's incredible. I can't take your job.'

I said, 'It's not my job. It's the paper that matters.'

And I convinced him not to take *The Times* job until I could go over to Paris and see Rothermere.

It was only right that Paul Dacre should wait to see what the offer from Associated Newspapers would be, because Dacre – and he was the first to admit it – owed English a great debt.

Paul had been working for the *Express* when David lured him away with a high salary and career offer that Dacre couldn't afford to refuse. He had gone to the United States to cover the presidential election in 1976, when Jimmy Carter defeated Gerald Ford, and as a result of his coverage he was named New York correspondent for the *Express*. His office was in Room 402 on the fourth floor of the *Daily News* building and the *Daily Mail's* office was in Room 403, creating a frenzy of competition between the two rival newspapers.

Unexpectedly, David English rang him one day, inviting him to a confidential lunch where, to his amazement, he offered Dacre the job of running the *Daily Mail*'s New York bureau. Paul Dacre was a young man in his early thirties, an accomplished writer and reporter, very much aware that the *Daily Mail* was mopping up the middle market while his own paper was nosediving in terms of circulation. But more, since Paul joined the *Express* it had gone steadily downmarket until he was forced to admit that it wasn't the same paper he had gone to work for. Dacre said,

> I knew I was a pretty good writer and a pretty good reporter; I had embarrassed the *Mail* on more than a few occasions over the last few years, but I still knew I was very lucky that I got this call at this time. The offer was marvellous.
>
> I went back to my office feeling absolutely over the moon and the phone went and this man with a kind of disguised voice said, 'If you go down to the foyer of the *Daily News* building to the magazine stall, something will happen.'
>
> So I went down there. I was just looking at a magazine and this must have been about half an hour after leaving the man. I felt something being slid into my pocket. I turned round and saw David English scuttling off into the crowd. What was in my pocket was a full, typed contract, with David's own kind of typing mistakes, outlining the terms of the job and the offer. I was totally impressed by this.
>
> He gave me what I thought was a fantastic salary then. It was only after I signed the damned thing that I realised a huge union rise was going through in England that didn't make it quite so attractive!

The plan was for Dacre to take over the New York bureau for three or four years, develop it and more or less take the worry of it off David's mind. But only a year later English insisted that Dacre come back to England to become his deputy news editor, 'which I didn't want to do, of course'.

Dacre resisted until David said, 'I promise if you do this for me, you'll never regret it.' So Paul finally gave in, having rationalised with his wife Kathy, who was teaching drama at Vassar at the time, that they would have to come back some time and it was better to come back inside a career structure. Thus began Paul Dacre's apprenticeship to become editor of the *Daily Mail*.

Without realising it, Dacre was about to embark on one of the most intensive training courses that any newspaperman could envisage. Dacre worked up the ranks, first as deputy news editor, then as news editor, then as assistant editor in charge of foreign news, then as features editor and finally as executive editor. He said,

> I learnt news, I learnt the backbench, I learnt feature editing, I learnt layout, I learnt politics and I suppose throughout all that the exemplar was David English, who has always worked on the philosophy that you lead from the front. I don't know if he was training me, but I was certainly doing the crash course.

In 1991 when John Leese was seriously ill with cancer, English called Dacre in and told him he believed he could get him the *Evening Standard* editorship, and within two months, by February, after several talks with Vere, Paul Dacre was named to the position. It was a great opportunity for Dacre, but a positive triumph for David English, since the fierce, dog-eat-dog competition that prevails on Fleet Street is only outflanked by the internal competition that exists between titles at Associated Newspapers. The *Mail* was considered to be dominated entirely by 'David's people', but at the *Standard* especially, where John Leese had very much run his own ship before he became ill, a special kind of atmosphere prevailed. It was thought one of David's people would trample on the particular independence of mind Leese had fostered.

Those fears were justified. Paul Dacre turned the evening paper on its head. His view of the *Standard* was that John Leese had produced a very good paper, having turned it around into an upmarket publication that was supplement-led. But in Paul's mind the focus of the paper was becoming too narrow:

> It was now in danger of becoming just a little too twee and its appeal was to too narrow a social band of people, too Fulham orientated. I was aware that the recession was savage in London and a lot of commuters were no longer coming into the city because they were being made redundant. And I thought we had better broaden our appeal if we were going to combat the effects of the recession in London.
>
> So the challenge was to keep up circulation in light of this. I'd also noticed there was a huge imbalance when I arrived, in that the paper had a heavy predominance of male readers. And I went for women readers in a calculated way. To my great delight, within six months, I'd increased the women's readership by 60 per cent against a lot of resistance from people on the paper who thought the women's pages were sexist and old-fashioned. Well, I didn't call them women's pages. I made them life pages.
>
> After I'd been on the *Standard* for fifteen or sixteen months, it had

become a much talked-about paper, and we were taking on the national newspapers and breaking stories. The features were excellent, plus circulation did well and readership went up 25, 26 per cent consistently during that period. I suppose inevitably Rupert Murdoch noticed those things because I suppose they coincided with a rather bad year for *The Times*.

Dacre was quick to exploit the new technology that he had inherited from Bert Hardy and John Leese. He found he was able to change eight to ten pages, even on the last edition, where previously the paper had only been able to change two. The morning newspapers were just about to make up their pages as the last edition of the *Standard* was hitting the streets. So Paul Dacre was setting the news agenda for the next day's national publications in London.

When Paul had the fateful dinner with Rupert Murdoch that was destined to change for ever the editorial face of Associated Newspapers, he was pressed hard for an answer. But he held back, believing it would be dishonourable to accept without talking to his mentor. Secretly, he was very attracted by the challenge presented by *The Times*. 'I think any human being would have been,' he said later.

So in Dacre's mind, at least, by the time he and David English sat down for their drink at the Royal Garden Hotel it was a foregone fact that he would go.

From David's viewpoint the scene at Vere Rothermere's offices in Paris the next morning was pandemonium. Rothermere, on the other hand, viewed the dilemma with his usual detachment.

David told Vere, 'This is terrible, terrible, terrible. We mustn't let Rupert take our best man. We've clearly got to have a shake-up.' David said,

So we went off to lunch, and I had no appetite and I couldn't eat anything. But when he gets nervous Vere eats, so he was gobbling like crazy. Then he said, 'We'll have to have a complete change-around, you know.' I said, 'I know, and I have a pad here with several scenarios.' And he said, 'Before we start, I've got a very good idea for the *Evening Standard*.' And I said, 'Well, I have a very good idea too.' So he tore off the menu and said, 'You write down your idea and I'll write down mine.'

We both wrote it down, folded it and handed it to one another. And we'd both written 'Stewart Steven'. He said, 'He won't want to go.' And I said, 'No, he won't want to go.' I had had a disagreement with Stewart and he viewed me with suspicion, so I didn't think I'd be able to persuade him. So I said to Vere, 'That'll be you.' He said, 'What will we do about the *Mail on Sunday*?' And I said, 'You know my deputy Jonathan Holborow is absolutely right for the *Mail on Sunday*.'

He said, 'I want Dee Nolan for *You* magazine.' And it was true, he'd told me months before that he wanted Dee Nolan to take over *You*.

Then he asked, 'What will you say to Dacre to persuade him to stay?' And I said, 'I'll use the phrase you used when you were trying to buy the *Sunday Times* without being forced to buy *The Times* as well.

'I'll tell him *The Times* is a death ship.'

It was a clear-cut simple strategy, but things didn't turn out quite the way the two men envisaged.

That weekend was the Bastille Day holiday in Paris and Rothermere, who always planned an escape route at that time of year, had decided to take his mistress Maiko Lee to the Loire Valley to look at a chateau there. So Vere called Paul Dacre and told him he would see him in London on Tuesday.

But Dacre was still in a state of shock and he said, 'Not until Tuesday! I can't wait until Tuesday. I've promised Murdoch a decision by then. I've put him off long enough. He wants me to fly over and see him in America. I think I'm going to accept *The Times*. It's essential I see you before Tuesday.'

There was a long pause and Vere said 'OK. I'll see you in the office on Monday.'

Right to plan, Rothermere was there in the morning, and he and David English saw Paul Dacre together, offering him a substantial improvement in salary and terms. Paul said he would like an hour to talk to his wife and think things over.

After the hour, Dacre still hadn't returned and now it was Vere's turn to become nervous. So it was agreed between the two men that David would find Dacre and Vere would inform the other editors of the change in assignment. Eventually David returned, along with Paul. David reported what happened then.

'I'm going to accept, Lord Rothermere,' Dacre said. 'I'm honoured to accept. I'm doing it for David, and I'm doing it for the *Daily Mail*, and I'm doing it for you.' Rothermere grabbed his hand and said, 'Thank you very much.'

And we had him.

That evening, Dacre called Rupert Murdoch and told him he wasn't going to accept the editorship of *The Times* after all. 'Well, there you are,' the press magnate replied. 'You're making a mistake, but that's life.'

But Dacre wasn't making a mistake. Tempting as the offer to edit *The Times* was, that newspaper was no longer the pace-setter of a modern England. It was a vestige of the past, the newspaper of record for a dwindling number of older readers. The *Daily Mail* was the paper of the present and the future, and Dacre was the right man to edit it.

While these dramatic events were taking place that fateful day, Rothermere had been having what he reported to David as a 'terrible scene' with Stewart Steven.

Steven didn't want to take over the *Standard* and he wanted to stay at the *Mail on Sunday*. According to Vere, Stewart had hummed and hawed, saying that he would have to get up early in the morning to do the *Standard* and besides, he was a weekly man. He was making excuse after excuse, Vere told David.

But Vere assured Steven he would be getting a big increase in salary and an important venue where he would strike a London figure with great power and influence. English recounted what happened next:

> Stewart paced up and down, then he said, 'Very well, I'll do it on one condition only.' So Vere says, 'Y-e-e-e-s-s,' and Stewart says, 'That you are personally asking me to do it.' So Vere said, 'What do you mean? I've just been personally asking you to do it for an hour and a half ... *Yes, I Vere Rothermere am personally asking you to do it.*' 'Very well, then,' said Stewart, 'I'll do it.'

Then Vere had the formidable task of letting *You* magazine editor Nick Gordon go, albeit with a good pay-off, and hiring Holborow and Nolan, both of whom were in and out of his office in no time, accepting the deals as they were offered. Then the two men, former editor and proprietor, sat down with one another, emotionally exhausted.

Rothermere, as a kind of afterthought, brought up the question of David's future and, according to David, said,

> 'Look, I want you to be the chairman of Associated Newspapers. We need someone there to work in all these new editors. We need someone to deal with the management. I'm in France and I'm less and less involved. And quite frankly, I don't want many more days like today.'

This was David's version. But both Paul Dacre and Vere Rothermere remembered it differently.

In the first place, when David first proposed giving up the editorship of the *Mail* to Dacre, the only way he was able to persuade the younger man to take his job was to tell him Rothermere had the chairmanship in mind for him. Otherwise, of course, Dacre would never have considered replacing English on the newspaper he had built almost from a dead stop.

And Rothermere remembered the offer of the chairmanship to David as being the redemption of a pledge he had made to him years before. Rothermere explained it like this:

> David said to me, 'I think I can get Dacre to stay if I give up the *Daily Mail* and offer him the editorship.' I said, 'That's a noble sacrifice.' He said, 'Yes, I love the *Mail* so much. I trained and have brought Paul up to be my replacement. He is the one to take over.'
>
> I said, 'Well, that's very fine of you. It so happens that for the last two years I've been thinking that when you did come to retire from the *Mail* I would make you chairman of Associated Newspapers. In fact, if you recall, I actually mentioned it to you.' He said,' Yes, I know you did.' And I said, 'Well, now's the time to do it.'

The colourful story of the changeover took on a life of its own, and in the telling and retelling of the story many embellishments were added. But at the heart of it was David who, in nearly losing Dacre to Rupert Murdoch, saw his chance to advance early to the chairmanship and negotiated until he brought it to the conclusion he desired.

Estranged from David English and isolated from the seat of power, Stewart Steven would have been within his rights to see the hand of treachery in his move to the *Evening Standard*. Indeed, in some ways the transfer was actually a demotion.

Editing an evening title is that most demanding of editorial jobs, not only because of the early start and late ending the job requires, but also because enormous amounts of physical and mental stamina are needed to produce a revolving layout for the multiple editions the paper will go through. It's a never-ending task.

Certainly, a rumour quickly made the rounds that Stewart's move was intended as a punishment from David English. It was widely known that the two men had had a falling-out, but no one seemed to know why. It was quite obvious to almost everyone, however, that they now maintained a healthy distance.

But Stewart chose to put a different spin on the matter. 'The fact is, I was very lucky to be able to take on another newspaper, to have a second editorship. Very few editors have two newspapers. They have one and that's it.'

But the day Steven found out what was in store for him was a tragic one, because Ian Walker, the executive editor, had the previous week accidentally died in a fall while mountain climbing. His body was being cremated in Scotland that Friday and the ashes would be brought down to Purley in Surrey where he and his wife Clare lived. Stewart said afterwards,

> That Friday couldn't have been a worse day for the Sunday newspaper. On Friday everybody is working, as you can imagine, incredibly hard, very long hours. But I said I had to go up to this cremation and take a half-dozen people from the paper with me.
>
> So I laid on an executive jet to go up there. I came in wearing my dark suit and black tie, ready to go to the plane at Heathrow at 12.30. I was due to leave the office at twelve.
>
> But David English called me in and said, 'I understand you're going up, you've got a plane. But you've got to see the chairman before you go, and he won't be in before twelve.'
>
> I said I had to go. He said, 'I'm terribly sorry. But it is some very serious business here. Vere is flying in. It's absolutely essential that you see him. You simply can't go.' And he said he couldn't tell me what it was about. He just said, 'It's incredibly serious.'
>
> So I couldn't go.

Rothermere didn't see Stewart until 12.30 and when he did, according to Steven, he began by saying he had a terrible problem that only Stewart could resolve. He needed to fill the editorship of the *Evening Standard* and Stewart was the only person in the company 'with the experience, the intellectual capacity and the knowledge of politics to do the job'. For a moment Stewart believed that Vere was exchanging him with Dacre and he would never have agreed to that because it implied the *Mail on Sunday* needed some kind of rescue operation. Rothermere had to assure Stewart this was not the case, although he said he couldn't tell him more about what was happening. Stewart then agreed to the job change, went back to his office, and within the hour it was all settled with Dacre and Holborow, and Stewart at last told the staff.

What happened then, Stewart explained, was straight out of an episode from *film noir*. It was about two in the afternoon and in Dundee, people began pouring out of the church, emotionally upset from the cremation of Ian Walker. The journalists were standing in the churchyard when their mobile phones began to ring:

> The news then came through and there was this wonderful moment which actually worked to transform the funeral into a wake. Clare Walker, who is this most wonderful woman, realised the phones were ringing and asked, 'What's going on?'
>
> They told her, Stewart Steven is leaving the *Mail on Sunday* and Jonathan Holborow is going in. Now Ian Walker didn't particularly get on with Jonathan Holborow or with any of the *Daily Mail* men, and Clare Walker looked to the heavens and said, 'Ian! *You knew!*' And somehow this broke the oppressive mood of the funeral and people collapsed with laughter.

Stewart believed that the special and close relationship that existed on the *Mail on Sunday* didn't just end that day; it exploded. Ian Walker had died. Political editor Alan Cochrane left the job. That meant that two Scotsmen were gone. The staff that had worked together to take the newspaper from failure to success was breaking up and it all came to an end. Stewart said,

> There's this thing called 'banging out'. When the old-time printers used to retire, colleagues would take up these great metal plates and bang them, making an enormous noise. It's something that has disappeared into the Fleet Street past, really.
>
> Suddenly that Saturday night, everybody began banging as I left. They presented me with a present; it was incredible and I felt overcome. They were banging me out just like they used to in the old days. And I actually cried.

Dee Nolan had been persuaded by David English to leave the *Sunday Express Magazine* and go to work for him. He offered her the chance to launch a new magazine, *Metropolitan Home*, a joint venture between Associated Newspapers and American Corporation. But in September 1990, when she brought out her first issue, the economy was sliding into what was to become a major recession. The magazine closed and Nolan was given a job on the *Daily Mail*. So at the time Nolan received her offer to edit *You*, she was assistant editor at the *Daily Mail*, working temporarily on 'Femail'.

Dee had come to Rothermere's attention when she played a winning game of golf as his partner at Hardelot, France at the *Daily Mail's* annual golfing event. There had been champagne at every hole and Dee had assured victory by sinking a putt that became legendary in the annals of the Northcliffe Golfing Society.

So when Rothermere decided to change *You* over to a women's magazine, he naturally thought of Dee Nolan.

Jonathan Holborow was on holiday at his home in Kent when David English rang him to say he would like him to come into the office the following day. Holborow was surprised, but since he often edited for David, he assumed he had to be out of the office and needed him to fill in. But when Jonathan turned up for conference that morning, it was obvious that David was editing the paper himself. That was the first clue Holborow got that something was up.

As he sat there eating lunch at his desk, he got a call from Kathy Campbell in Rothermere's office, asking him to come up. When he got there, he was ushered into the chairman's office and Holborow remembered later that Vere said to him,

'There have been one or two changes and I'd like to offer you the editorship of the *Mail on Sunday*.' And he proceeded right into salary. Then he paused for a moment and looked at me, and he said, 'How do you feel about that?' And I said, 'I accept,' and he said 'Good' and shook my hand, and that was it. That was totally it.

But by the next week things had become more difficult. On his first conference he immediately decided to change the typography on the paper to give it a different, more readable typographical weight. He put several staff members on it who worked hard to accomplish what he wanted.

But he was still reeling from the fact that Alan Cochrane had left the paper on the previous Friday, almost as soon as he heard that Jonathan was taking over. 'So I had a difficult situation.' Later on, Holborow remembered how they made it, though:

Sue Reid was amazingly helpful, she was the Number Three, and John Ryan, he helped a lot and no one except me knows how much they did help. They were wonderful.

It was a difficult few days but we got through it and we got through it on pure professionalism. It was a hell of a week, frankly.

It was a hell of a week, because on the Friday night, at just about seven, Holborow received a telephone call from a consultant at the hospital where his wife was having a battery of tests. He broke the news to Jonathan that his wife had cancer. The cancer was extensive, it would require chemotherapy and a long rehabilitation.

Bravely, Holborow went back to work. He worked until about eleven that night, then went straight to the hospital where his wife was staying. From now on he began working a schedule wherein he put in long hours at the *Mail on Sunday*, then went to the hospital to be at his wife's bedside. As far as possible, he now became accustomed to a new work pattern, wherein he put in the hours necessary to get out the Sunday newspaper, then went to see his wife. He had two young children and there was the need to help them through the crisis as well.

Then, on his first Sunday when Holborow was still reeling from the unbelievable events of the week, the *People* broke the David Mellor–Antonia de Sanchez story.

> We did pick it up on the second edition and got it on the front page. We didn't do a very good pick-up to be honest, but we had it on page one.
>
> The following week, after days of difficult negotiation by Sue Reid, we got Antonia de Sanchez's story. It didn't arrive at the office until about 2.30 on the Saturday. So I had to edit it right there on the stone because our deadline was at 4.30.
>
> That Sunday we ran the story on page one and it worked out quite well. So we had a rough July and then Rod Gilchrist joined as deputy editor, thank God. And slowly, slowly, we began to pull upwards and improve the paper.

Jonathan Holborow was only able to make it through that time, he believed, because of the support he received from everybody at the newspaper and in particular from David English. He said later,

> He was an old, old friend and he said, 'I know what you're going through but you've got to plough on.' And he was truly wonderful. What happens is you compartmentalise your mind and you get on with it.

Eighteen months later Jonathan's wife Susan died on 27 January 1993, at the age of forty-eight. A true newspaper wife, Susan Holborow continued to worry, right up to the end, that she hadn't been able to provide her husband with the kind of support he needed during the difficult time when he took over the *Mail on Sunday*.

TWENTY-TWO

MURDERERS

It seemed a foregone fact that Paul Dacre would become the pre-eminent editor on Fleet Street. Rupert Murdoch tried to poach him. David English gave up his own editorship to keep him. Subsequently Dacre was offered and turned down the editorship of the *Daily Telegraph*.

But what was so special about Paul Dacre?

He was a workaholic, OK. A lot of people on Fleet Street were work-obsessed. But Dacre worked fourteen to sixteen hours a day in pursuit of excellence. The eighteen-hour day was not unknown. Said one colleague, who in the early days turned down the chance of becoming Dacre's deputy news editor, 'Paul didn't balk at working an eighteen-hour day. I did. It was that simple.'

Dacre was determined to ride out the whirlwind of his own talent, no matter what the cost in personal terms. A man of simple tastes with none of the vices so often associated with editors of the national press, he astonished his wordly-wise colleagues with a strong commitment to his family, and his hobby gardening made them shake their heads in wonderment.

Whereas David English had used his talent to widen his power, Paul Dacre seized power primarily for the purpose of exercising his talent. The key to his personality was talent; it was so potent a force that Dacre himself was caught under its sway.

'But it's bloody hard work as well,' he would say, pointing to the '95 per cent perspiration rule' of success, trying to prove that talent wasn't everything. In Dacre's case it was. He and everyone he worked with felt the oppression of that talent as well as the thrill of the adrenalin surge that went with it.

Paul referred to the eighteen months he spent editing the *Evening Standard* as the most exciting time of his career.

> Bert Hardy gave me the technology, a creative tool for a newspaperman. He speeded up the process. And in that context I arrived at the *Mail* coiled up with energy.

Once there, he astonished the management by informing them he planned to do the paper 'on the edition', meaning he intended to have 96 pages of 'raw, live copy' that was produced on the very day the paper went to press. For that, he would need them to speed up every aspect of the technology.

This must have been a shock for Hardy. David English had been suspicious of computers and it was only at Hardy's insistent pushing that the *Daily Mail* was modernised at all. Paul's attitude was the exact opposite. He wanted to be able to push pages 'down the wire' and across the country in two minutes, not the twenty it was taking. 'And Bert Hardy and Allan Marshall solved that problem,' Dacre said. 'This kind of speed was Hardy's *vision*.'

So beginning at 5 p.m. on the *Daily Mail*, virtually all the copy of the day comes in, is edited and mechanically laid out on pages and zipped to the presses. Dacre believes implicitly this is the secret of the *Daily Mail* – that the paper adapts instantaneously to the tone created by the breaking news of the day.

The newspaper's supplements – 'Self', 'Money Mail', 'Femail', and 'Good Health' – were intended, theoretically at least, to be completed before the day. 'But in reality,' Alistair Sinclair, deputy editor, said, 'much of it is still being finished on the day. And if there is a burning issue we'll get it in.'

But creating an entire paper from a full stop wasn't the only thing Dacre intended to do. From the beginning, he planned to change the public perception of the *Daily Mail*. He knew that the newspaper was alienating the young and they looked at it as a rather boring, slightly racist publication that was Conservative to a fault. For his part Paul was bound and determined to end 'the slavish mindless appeasement of everything Conservative' that had come to represent the *Daily Mail* in the minds of the public.

Dacre believed Margaret Thatcher was great and that David English had been right to support her. But by the time Paul came in as editor in 1992 that dream was gone. 'You could actually smell the decadence and weakness of the Tories then,' he said. John Major was 'a weak chap', as Dacre put it, and the successive scandals that beset the Tories were making the sleaze factor into the Conservative Party's most prominent characteristic.

At the same time Paul believed he was witnessing a kind of social revolution, wherein the Asian community was taking its place at the top of the ladder of achievement and an increasing number of bright decent black men and particularly women were looking for a newspaper that reflected their aspiration. He wanted those readers. The political tone of the entire country was changing – 'You could feel the excitement,' he said – and he intended to put the *Mail* at the centre of those dynamics.

His first big challenge was the newspaper price war initiated by Rupert Murdoch. It ran for over five years and, at its lowest price, *The Times* was selling on Mondays for only 10p a copy. It was a slug-out mainly between *The Times* and the *Telegraph*, but the *Sun* and the *Mirror* were drawn in as well. As he watched the *Telegraph* 'dumb down' in order to compete in this widening field of contenders, Dacre saw his opportunity to pick up some of the *Telegraph*'s high-quality readership. He said,

> We didn't cut our price. And while everybody else was involved in cutting theirs, we went the opposite way giving more and more value-for-money content and improving our quality. We had a major serialisation every week, outbidding everybody to get it. We provided more long reads, more supplements like 'Self' and 'Good Health', new part works, and we kept driving our circulation forward. Vere totally backed us and at a time when everybody else was reducing their price we were actually raising ours. We were giving value for money.

One of Dacre's most successful innovations during the price wars was *Weekend Magazine*. It became possible after the government ended the *TV Times* and *Radio Times* duopoly on weekly TV listings in 1991. David English had in 1988 tried to publish a Saturday magazine to accompany the publication of the *Daily Mail*. Entitled *Male and Femail*, only seventeen issues of the fortnightly magazine were published before, in May of 1989, it folded with a statement from Associated that the magazine had not attracted enough advertisers. The price tag topped £6 million.

Now Paul, realising the dream of his father, decided to produce the best TV listings magazine in the business. Dacre's father had been the foreign editor on the *Daily Express*, working for a time as the Diary editor before ending up Show Business editor on the paper. At one time 'the editorship of the *TV Times* was held out to him, but he didn't get the job'. Now Paul adapted his father's idea for excellence in a weekly television listings magazine for the Saturday *Daily Mail*. Paul intended to produce a magazine with emphasis on 'family, warmth and happiness' on serviceable paper, and he took this idea to David English. He met with unexpected resistance.

At the time David was planning *Night & Day*, a magazine for the *Mail on Sunday*. David's idea was that it would consist of brilliant writing on provocative topics and include the review section for the Sunday newspaper. But in a way what David intended was unsuitable for the style of magazine he was publishing – a big, high-quality publication with paper more suitable for photographs than copy. Nor was English's idea particularly commercial, as Peter Wright, who was then assistant editor, pointed out. 'And reviews always sit better on newsprint,' he said.

Paul Dacre made his pitch for *Weekend* at a hastily convened 'summit' made up of David and Bert Hardy, that had been called, Paul believed, 'to shut me up'. Hardy said outright he didn't believe Dacre's idea was commercially viable. He told him he could have a small square magazine, about 5 x 7 inches, and that was all.

'But I knew I was right,' Dacre said later. 'I knew it would be a success. And I said to the two of them, "I want as much as *Night & Day*, the same page size and quality, and if I don't get it I'm quitting." And I would have quit!' Paul got what he wanted.

Weekend Magazine is now 104 pages and regarded in the industry as the best of its kind. It has been a huge success, with circulation for Saturdays climbing from 1,693,107 at the magazine's inception on 16 October 1993 to 1,954,000 by the following December. And circulation has continued to climb. The average Saturday sale for September 2001 was 3,317,850 copies. And in 2002, *Weekend* was voted Supplement of the Year in the British Press Awards.

But *Weekend* was only the start. Inside the pages of the *Daily Mail* other changes were taking place. Dacre and his editorial team were pioneering a set of formulae that created a force-field of reader interest. By using easily recognised symbols and pictures of well-known personalities and events, Dacre and his staff produced a kind of visual shorthand that created a set of outside associations, enriching the text with visuals and references from the popular culture of the moment. These were eschewed by high-toned broadsheet editors, who nevertheless immediately seized upon them and adapted them to their own readership. Indeed, today it would be difficult to find a tabloid or a broadsheet in Fleet Street, and even further afield in the United States and elsewhere, that hasn't in one way or another aped the innovations brought in by Dacre and his team.

Otherwise, throughout the paper, topics are cast with an argumentative edge, so that it is impossible to read without formulating an opinion, pro or con, on the subject at hand. Celebrity debates figure prominently in the *Daily Mail* and the rhetorical question comes into its own in the headlines. These techniques conjure up a surge of reader interest, increasing involvement, and pushing up circulation and readership.

But other than this there were several defining moments in Dacre's race for higher circulation. One of the most important occurred when, on 17 November 1995, *Today* closed. Said Dacre,

> They closed at two or three in the afternoon, and within hours the editorial staff had rebuilt themselves into a war machine. We'd hired their astrologer, Jonathan Cainer, their cartoonist, Peter Plant, and several of their listings people. I wrote the bloody TV adverts directed at *Today's* readers as we were holding a news conference and we adopted an aggressive promotional campaign that involved offering ex-*Today* readers eight weeks of discounted copies of the *Daily Mail*.
>
> In the meantime we calibrated the newspaper slightly downmarket for about nine weeks and we creamed off those *Today* readers.

The result was a 4.92 per cent rise in sales, taking the *Mail* to the brink of two million. In contrast, the *Express* captured just 35,000 former *Today* customers.

Following on the heels of the *Today* triumph was the launch of the Scottish *Daily Mail* in January of 1995, another of Dacre's innovations. It had an initial sale of 37,000, but by December 2001 it had climbed to 122,000.

In the years of Paul Dacre's editorship *Daily Mail* campaigns have included a stand against genetically modified foods, mixed wards in the National Health Service, pornography on TV and highlighting the terrible plight of the mentally ill released by hospitals, but still a risk to themselves and the community. A campaign to aid Kosovan refugees resulted in reader contributions of £5 million, the largest amount ever raised by a newspaper in such a short time.

In the GM campaign the *Daily Mail* took on the industrial giant Monsanto and succeeded to the extent that a frustrated Prime Minister Tony Blair complained to Dacre, at a dinner at Number 10, 'I believed in it. You've halted it.' Dacre had devilishly coined the phrase 'Frankenstein Foods', which was later to appear in the United States under the rubric 'Frankenfoods'. The readers got the message.

Eventually, the fight against mixed wards and other failings of the NHS, such as better care for patients and a reduction in waiting lists, especially for operations to alleviate life-threatening ailments, led the *Mail* to coin the phrase 'Third-World Hospitals' – still a sore subject in government circles. And in September 1998 the *Mail* launched its campaign for higher nurses' salaries under the headline NHS FACING STAFF CRISIS.

Readers were urged to cut out a front-page sticker saying '*Daily Mail* Campaign – TIME TO PAY OUR NURSES MORE' and put it in their front windows. By January of 1999 nurses had gained a salary increase of just below 6 per cent, while new nurses would get 'an inflation-busting 11 per cent'.

But of all these campaigns for better health for the nation, perhaps the most important was the campaign to warn readers of the dangers of prostate cancer, an illness that had been cloaked in secrecy and shame, and thus accounted for the death of 'one British man every hour'. Headlined as 'THE CANCER THAT NO ONE TALKS ABOUT', the first article of the campaign that eventually raised £1 million for research on the disease was sub-headed, 'Dying from Embarrassment'. It was the first time a British newspaper had taken on a subject as taboo as this.

Dacre himself is a workaholic whose drive for perfection can make him difficult to work for. But it is hard to fault a man who, night after night, stays on the editorial floor until the last edition is put to bed, obsessing over each issue of the newspaper until it meets his near impossible standards. Even though he has a hard exterior, his subordinates invariably feel protective of him, perhaps because at a certain level he remains vulnerable to criticism and open to change.

There is also the sheer excitement of working for someone so dedicated to his job. One columnist on the *Mail* believes that newspapers as independent entities are falling by the wayside one by one and that Paul Dacre is one of the last editors for whom the news is something more than a marketing exercise. Under Dacre, marketing is a matter of common sense, a matter of knowing the readership, a matter of experience. Under Dacre there is no brand advertising, but tactical commercials based on serials, exclusive stories and promotions. This gives a sense of urgency and professionalism and even unpredictability to the product. It goes a long way too, towards explaining how successful the *Mail* has become.

How successful is that? The *Mail* won Newspaper of the Year in the British Newspaper Awards in 1995, 1996, 1998 and 2001. Dacre himself is the longest-serving editor on Fleet Street.

'Paul is a thinker,' says Peter Wright, who along with Sinclair has worked with Dacre for some twenty-one years. 'His views are unpredictable but strongly felt. He thinks long and hard about what he believes, and seeks our opinions. These he discusses at length. Then, when he does formulate an opinion, he does so with utter determination and conviction.'

Such was the case on a night in February 1997, and perhaps what happened next was the result of a crescendo of interest in the murder of a promising young black man named Stephen Lawrence that had been downplayed by most news outlets and neglected by the Metropolitan Police. According to Peter Wright,

> My modest part in what happened that night was to say to Paul in earlier discussions that there was something wrong with the Stephen Lawrence case. He had been murdered and everybody apparently knew who had done it. No one would come forward with the evidence. It was injustice by intimidation. People were terrified to say what they knew.
>
> At this stage the issue didn't seem as much racial as a gross miscarriage of justice. But it was Paul who saw it. It was Paul who drew it up in one page.

What Wright was referring to were the events that took place on the editorial floor on the night of Thursday, 13 February. The inquest on Stephen Lawrence's death had been reconvened on Monday of that week. Since the original hearing had opened and closed in April 1993, five suspects had been charged with murder. But two of them had walked free from the charges. A trial of the other three had collapsed after identification evidence from a friend of Stephen Lawrence who had been with Stephen when he was murdered was ruled inadmissible. All three were officially acquitted.

When the inquest reopened, all five original suspects had appeared but refused to answer the questions. They were Neil and Jamie Acourt, Luke Knight, David Norris and Gary Dobson. Hiding behind 'a wall of silence', they cited their legal privilege not to say anything which might incriminate them. The *Mail*'s crime team had carried out an intensive investigation into the men and were convinced they were guilty. But the catalyst that caused Paul Dacre to lock into his opinion was the sight of these five young men on television news that night, in his words, 'swaggering out of the coroner's court'.

Dacre was horrified and, thinking what good and attractive people Stephen's parents were and how they'd been betrayed by British justice, he began drawing up a few front pages. He came up with one that pictured all five suspects with the scored block headline: MURDERERS, using the sub-heading 'The *Mail* accuses these men of killing. If we are wrong, 'let them sue us.' When he started drawing it up, it came more under the heading of what he would like to do rather than what it was possible to do. After all, it is the gravest of charges to call someone a murderer who hasn't been judged so by a court. But after he had drawn it

Dacre wondered why he couldn't do it. 'About half my staff thought I was mad,' Dacre said later, 'and the other half said, "Why not?"'

Eddie Young, Associated's specialist on libel, had earlier been given intimations that something quite strong might be coming as regarded the Lawrence case and he had made it his business to familiarise himself with the facts of the case by reading all the background he could lay hands on. By 8 p.m. he had covered reams of copy, including statements from police officers and neighbours that gave him a feel for the story. 'The atmosphere in the newsroom was electric,' he said,

> the best I've ever worked under, and Paul called me over and showed me his dummy for page one. They were all looking at me and asking my opinion on whether the suspects would sue or not.

At that moment Peter Wright was just coming back into the newsroom from handling another crisis and he saw a small group of people forming around Paul and Eddie,

> And they had this front page. Paul asked what I thought and I said, 'It's powerful, but do you think we can do it?' And Paul said, 'I've asked Eddie Young and he thinks we can. Some have been tried once and they can't be tried again.'
>
> And usually in a case like this, we can think of a lot of reasons against carrying on. But this time we couldn't think of a reason *not to do it.*

Eddie Young went over and over the headline in his mind. He considered the fact that the suspects had very little reputation to defend, such as is required in a libel case, some had records and came from notorious criminal families with long histories of appalling violence, so if the *Mail* lost, the damages would not be high. And even though the *Daily Mail* would have to prove they did commit the murder of Stephen Lawrence, since it was a civil case, they would only have to prove to the standard of a balance of probabilities. Legal aid was not available for libel cases, but if the suspects tried to sue for malicious falsehood, for which they *could* receive legal aid, they would have to go into the witness box, something Young felt sure they would not be eager to do.

Over and above all this legal reasoning, however, Eddie Young had 'a gut feeling' that they wouldn't sue. He said to Paul, 'I am totally unfazed by this.' Paul, who had rung his wife to warn her how violent the men were, said, 'OK, let's go with it.'

That night, Eddie Young was on an adrenalin high and he had trouble getting to sleep. In his mind the events of the evening were what made his job worthwhile and as he lay there, open-eyed, he planned out his next legal moves if they turned out to be necessary. 'It was like a chess game where you are ten moves ahead,' he said later. Some time between 3.30 and 4 a.m. he fell asleep.

At about the same time that Young was falling asleep, Paul Dacre was waking. It was something that often happened to him. After an exhausting day he would wake up at 4 a.m., his whole mind rerunning all the downsides of what he had done during the day. This morning he snapped awake, drenched in sweat, and thought, 'You're going to end up in jail for this. You may have struck a blow for justice, but you've destroyed your career.'

Peter Wright was the only one of the three who slept soundly, which turned out to be lucky because, the next morning as the deluge of e-mails, phone calls and faxes started pouring in, it was Wright who was elected to go on all the television and radio news shows to discuss the matter before the startled international media.

The results of that unprecedented front page (never before has a British newspaper called unconvicted individuals 'murderers') were momentous. There was huge national sympathy for the Lawrences combined with outrage over the inadequacies of a judicial system that had failed them. The next day, Saturday, former Master of the Rolls, Lord Donaldson, said he reacted with 'surprise and horror' at the front page, accusing the editor of contempt of court. But since there was no trial pending he was referring to contempt of court at common law, an archaic concept that dated back hundreds of years. 'It was an historical anachronism,' Eddie Young said. Nevertheless, the Attorney-General considered the suggestion seriously.

Then, on 5 March, a fax came to the *Daily Mail* offices from the Attorney-General's office to the effect that in considering whether 'articles published by the *Daily Mail* following the inquest into the death of Stephen Lawrence might constitute a contempt of court at common law', the Attorney-General had concluded that such proceedings 'would not be justified'.

But Paul Dacre had ceased to worry over the matter since the morning after the headline appeared, when 'the phones went into meltdown in my office'.

We held our nerve. And God bless our readership. There was not one dissenting voice. To the last one they supported us. And it was proof the *Daily Mail* had changed. It was the first time that many people in the country realised that black readers were as important to the *Mail* as white ones.

Following the *Mail's* campaign the incoming Labour government initiated the McPherson Inquiry which resulted in sweeping changes in the way the police handled racial crimes. Dacre said later, 'Newspapers come in for enormous criticism. Here was a case where they could be an enormous power for good. I'd like to think that we made a 'little bit of history that day'.

TWENTY-THREE

THE SIXTH FLOOR

David English was a man of strong emotions. At times they could be overpowering and when this happened his personality tipped over into the histrionic. John Winnington-Ingram's way of putting it was that David too often went 'over the top'. 'Every crisis was deemed capable of bringing down the house,' he said. By that he meant that David consistently overstated the problem, exaggerating the danger in order to prevail.

Another of English's colleagues, this time a subordinate on the *Mail*, said David frequently indulged in 'psychodramas'. If one were to flourish, so went the logic, one had to take a prominent role in these little productions. But even if this was an overstatement, English did harbour a 'them-against-me' mentality in which he, David, represented all that was right and good, and his enemies all that was unfair and unjust. In David's eyes his enemies were trying constantly to thwart him and the moral imperative he alone represented. It was necessary to overcome them in his quest for justice. This was the underlying subtext of David's psychodramas.

Then again, English entertained 'enthusiasms'. It was surprising how effusive he could become if he discovered you had one of these in common with him.

Were these faults? Hardly. They were the very qualities that had propelled him to the top of his field. While recognising that David wasn't perfect, Winnington-Ingram simultaneously spoke of his incredible talent, his undeniable contributions to the firm. 'Without David, the *Mail* would not exist today,' he said.

As far as his abilities as a newspaperman are concerned, David English was arguably the greatest Fleet Street editor of his time. He understood his power in much the same way that Northcliffe had, and used it politically and personally to effect changes he believed in.

But the characteristics that made him a great editor were at odds with his ability to function effectively as a high-level executive. Was David as good a chairman as he was an editor?

The truth was that David's emotionalism was a handicap to him in the executive environment he entered when he became chairman of

Associated Newspapers. And the tight control he had habitually exercised over his staff, that gave coherence to the editorial policies of the *Daily Mail*, was inappropriate in dealing with the independent-minded executives who inhabited the sixth floor of Northcliffe House. Entrepreneurial talent is by its very nature nonconformist and tight controls inhibit rather than support creativity in this quarter. Yet, when English began as chairman it seemed as though he was on the same wavelength as his new colleagues.

He told Roger Gilbert, managing director of Harmsworth Media, that his first priority was to get the firm back into television. By making that his primary goal, English was pointing to the company's most glaring failure in the field of media. In September of 1955 the then chairman of Daily Mail and General Trust, Vere's father Esmond, sold the group's 50 per cent share in Associated Rediffusion, the company that won the London Weekday Television franchise for ITV, just one month before its profits began to roll in. It was an inexplicable failure of nerve, the biggest mistake in Esmond's career, and it set the tone for the company's fortunes in television for the next four decades.

In fact, the one success Associated enjoyed in the field, a 37.5 per cent holding in a joint venture that won the franchise in Southern TV, was eventually lost, although Southern Television did enjoy creative and financial success for twenty years before the licence was awarded to a rival consortium. But another venture into commercial television, the company's 15 per cent investment in Northern Star Holdings, turned out to be nothing less than disastrous.

Northern Star controlled the ten metropolitan networks in Australia and in September 1990 the company was placed into receivership. DMGT's losses were in the region of £39.6 million, a huge loss in 1990 pounds. All in all, the company's record in commercial television had been dismal.

English intended to change all that and in 1994 it seemed his chance had come. The opportunity for Associated to begin building a national television network was glimpsed through the newly emerging technology of cable television. In the beginning it had been Bert Hardy who saw the opening, and his original model was based on programming that would consist of national news and low-cost entertainment. The well-known television producer Allan McKeown, associated with the popular series 'Birds of a Feather' and 'Lovejoy' came aboard. He brought with him a vast back catalogue of light entertainment with which to put Hardy's brainchild into operation.

The idea was to keep the trial channel ticking over until distribution was established by the cable companies. Coverage could then expand parallel to revenue so that the whole operation remained more or less solvent.

But on one of his many visits to New York, English became enamoured of New York One, a locally originated twenty-four-hour news channel owned by Time-Warner. At the heart of New York One was the concept of the video-journalist; that is, a reporter operating a camcorder and generating his own local news pieces. It quickly became one of David's 'enthusiasms' and when he returned, said Roger Gilbert, who had taken overall charge of the project, 'David had "the light of battle in his eyes"'.

If Roger Gilbert had reservations about David's New York model, Rod Gilchrist was adamant that it was unworkable. In addition to his duties as deputy editor of the *Mail on Sunday*, and before that as associate editor on the *Mail*, Gilchrist had accumulated a high level of expertise regarding television. He had been director of programmes at BSB for Associated Newspapers and was executive producer at Kensington Film and Television, and had made feature films for ITV and a comedy series for BBC Television. This experience and his belief that London was fundamentally different from New York, where he had previously lived, told him that David's concept was flawed.

So when David English offered Gilchrist the job of running Channel One, as it was called, Gilchrist gave David his opinion in no uncertain terms. He believed that Associated's new cable channel had a chance if it stayed within the original perimeters outlined by Hardy. 'But David had reached the point where he didn't want to hear about anything that wasn't a London news-based channel,' said Gilchrist. 'He wanted nothing to do with reruns of hit shows.'

What David wanted Gilchrist to do was implement his New York One model and he offered Gilchrist twice his current salary to do so. 'For ten times my salary, it will still fail,' Gilchrist told English. Gilchrist predicted the station would close within three years, with losses in the tens of millions of pounds. 'I begged him not to do it. And he begged me to do it. He said that if I did it he would give me a seat on the board of Associated and he was gobsmacked when I said it would make no difference.

'And he did actually say to me that if I didn't take this, there would be nothing for me at Associated Newspapers.' Gilchrist took this to mean he would not be appointed editor of a national title, as David had promised him in the past.* But Gilchrist believed the model David envisaged could never succeed in London and he stuck to his guns.

---

* After leaving the Teletext project, Gilchrist went back to his position on the *Daily Mail*, later assuming the position of deputy editor of the *Mail on Sunday*. He never did receive the editorship of a national title.

Soon after this Allan McKeown departed with a very substantial severance package and Bert Hardy's shoestring model was dropped in favour of the New York One concept. Forty local reporters were hired to operate a fleet of hand-held cameras, each generating his own news. But even at the relatively low salary of £25,000 per year, costs escalated quickly. And obviously, with this emphasis on local news, Channel One didn't have the same national appeal as the original model. Indeed, New York One, the original source of David's enthusiasm, had a viewing base of 11 million, many of them sophisticated New Yorkers with a high income base, ideal viewers from the point of view of revenue raising. But even at that, Time-Warner had run the free New York channel as a loss-leader and didn't actually intend to make money on it.

At English's Channel One, even as the possibility of gaining a national audience receded, revenue raising on a local basis was being severely curtailed by poor distribution. Essentially, the cable companies failed to reach a significant section of the public and there were virtually no viewers. As Roger Gilbert said later, 'Distribution was so patchy that the targets for Bert Hardy's original model were not being met. So even that model would have generated losses.'

But the losses now being absorbed by Associated were in the region of £10 million a year. In his career as an editor, David English had been able to rely on a distribution system set up and run by a management with an astonishing level of expertise. He could literally take their distribution skills for granted while he concentrated on creating a high-quality newspaper. By assuming cable distribution would catch up with him, David was being overly optimistic, so that the very optimism that had buoyed him up in the saving of the *Daily Mail* would count against him at Channel One.

In the case of Channel One, it was English's commitment to quality that brought about the losses, by some estimates £40 million, by others even higher. He understood how to make a quality product; he was impatient with fiscal restraints. And in the world of television, where costs can escalate at an astronomical rate, this impatience can be fatal.

But certain innovations did emerge from the failure of Channel One. Ironically, despite the costs incurred, the quality of the news coverage was tremendously good for the money spent, to the extent that techniques pioneered there became widespread in the industry. ITV learned to cut costs by watching Channel One, and the cable channel also had a strong influence on the way in which news was gathered and produced.

But though David was always highly innovative in his work, he could not grasp the harsh fiscal realities that came to bear in the field of television. In retrospect, Rod Gilchrist's earlier estimates of the losses that Channel One would accrue were very near the mark and his predictions of failure now seemed prophetic.

In another area, that of programming, David English's early attempts in television showed a basic lack of understanding of the high regulation to be found in the television field. He was to discover that the same controversy that worked very much in his favour on the *Daily Mail* could work against him in television.

English had been attracted to a real-life story of murder and deceit that took place in Northern Ireland in 1991. The mistress of Captain Duncan McAllister stabbed his wife to death in a crime of passion against her rival and English had given full play to the story in the *Daily Mail*. But a television drama he initiated, *Beyond Reason*, that was based on the same event resulted in criticism and censure. Carlton Television, the channel that had purchased and televised the drama, was ordered to carry an on-air apology to the victim's parents and husband in a ruling by the Broadcasting Complaints Commission. Ironically, the film had attracted a viewing audience of 12 million and was almost universally acknowledged to be a high-quality production.

Rod Gilchrist, who had made the film *Beyond Reason* after David suggested the topic, publicly disavowed the finding of the BCC. But whether or not the Commission's findings were balanced – and some believed the BCC had been overly sensitised by an earlier documentary, *Death on the Rock*, about the IRA shootings in Gibraltar – Associated was still stung by the censure. English had believed that high quality was the key to television, just as it had been for the *Daily Mail*, but in this he showed his naïveté, at least in the field of television.

Roger Gilbert explained it this way,

David never came to grips with the fact that rivals didn't want to compete with the *Daily Mail* in the winning of contracts. Developing programming is very hard work. It took time to make television programmes – time to win the contracts, time to make the programmes and time for the programme to air. Although the programmes might be good, the profits all too often were not. But it was irreconcilable with David's style to produce low-quality programming.

David had an almost naïve belief in good programming. He was eager to show that his team could transfer its creativity to the screen and he got lost in that.

The long and short of it was that David wasn't sufficiently cynical to compete successfully in television. Despite his reputation as being very tough, at the heart of him was an ethos committed to quality, creativity and controversy. In the world of television, that ethos would prove to be his undoing.

By contrast, David's contribution to the bid Associated made for the Public Teletext Licence was important. Before the Channel One disaster, in 1991, a committee composed of six high-level executives began reviewing all the television opportunities available to the company at that time. English was a member of the committee although he had not yet taken over as chairman of Associated Newspapers. Also on the committee were Bert Hardy, Roger Gilbert, Charles Sinclair, Michael Jones, who has since left the company, and Rothermere himself.

They decided that they would pursue Television Southwest and Wales TV. Ironically, the committee initially rejected the idea of bidding for Public Teletext. Teletext is an electronic text service operated in conjunction with Channels 3 and 4, and available on all new television sets. It utilises the spare lines on a television screen to provide a hidden text brought into view by using the 'text' button on a remote control. Teletext offers a range of news, sports, racing results, entertainment and other services. Its revenue base comes from two primary sources: banner advertisements and holiday sales.

Until then, Associated had been prevented from owning a national ITV franchise outright because of cross-media ownership prohibitions. Teletext was different. Regarded by the independent television companies as something of a 'Cinderella service', they didn't see Teletext's full commercial significance.

Again, it was Rod Gilchrist who originally brought Teletext, then known as 'Oracle', to the attention of the company. A professional contact named Richard Brooks came to see Gilchrist, who then set up a meeting with Brooks and Julian Aston in which Brooks asked if Associated would be interested in getting involved in a franchise bid for the service. Rod and Julian studied the service closely and immediately saw an opportunity.

But when Gilchrist initially approached English he wasn't at all enthusiastic. Gilchrist persisted and eventually English said to him, 'All right, go ahead, if you want to do it. But don't let it interfere with your duties on the *Daily Mail*.' So Gilchrist came in with his assistant Geraldine McKeown on their weekends off and started to work on the Compliance Document with Julian.

Aston, who later took over Channel One when Gilchrist rejected it, and Gilchrist quickly skimmed the most recent broadcasting act, finding what they thought was a loophole that the company could exploit. There was no restriction on the amount of the public Teletext licence that Associated could own, unlike an ITV licence in which it could own only 20 per cent. To Aston and Gilchrist it seemed too good to be true.

As managing director of Harmsworth Media, ultimate responsibility for developing the idea went to Roger Gilbert, and it was only after he read the material that Rod Gilchrist and Julian Aston had prepared that Gilbert realised Teletext was essentially 'an electronic newspaper'. Associated Newspapers was in a unique position to develop the concept. By 12 November Gilbert had written urgently to Charles Sinclair, advising him of the fact. If the company was going to bid, he told Sinclair, the documentation had to be submitted by 10 January 1992.

Everybody jumped in feet first. David had been away, but by the time he returned in mid-December, Charles Sinclair had begun negotiations with Philips with whom he had a strong relationship, having earlier brought them into the Whittle Communications partnership. Sinclair believed they would be the ideal partner for the venture.

In fact, with Teletext, distribution was assured because every new television set manufactured in Great Britain would have the capacity for the text. As a major manufacturer of televisions, Philips had been a pioneer in the development of Teletext technology so they were quick to come into the bid. Now, with little time remaining, the race was on.

Under this kind of pressure English became an invaluable member of the team. They were trying to assemble and write a high-quality document in order to win the franchise against strong competition, particularly from the ITV companies. Roger Gilbert said later,

David brought to the project absolute focus. His ability to get things done without distraction was like a tank rolling through.

One of the questions we were facing was how to provide information to the service by using news input from the *Daily Mail*. But one of the requirements for running Teletext was that the news put on the screen had to be unbiased and David saw instantly that this wouldn't work. He went to the Press Association to provide the information. It was the crucial breakthrough.

He also relied on Rod Gilchrist and Julian Aston to write the document, who along with Mark Alcock, the financial director of Harmsworth Media, put the application document together. Media Ventures, the 10 per cent minority participant, also brought in their representative, Christopher Turner, to work on the project.

In the meantime, Associated's consortium had won Television SouthWest with a bid of £8 million against TSW's renewal bid of £16 million. Ironically, TSW were ruled out for overbidding. Now began one of those comedies of error that sometimes can cause a reversal of fortune. The chief executive of TSW, Harry Turner, initiated a court action against the Independent Television Commission that challenged the ruling against his bid. That court action was due to be decided in January 1992. But because they needed to give their undivided attention to defending the suit, the ITC postponed the Teletext Application submission date a crucial three weeks. This gave Associated the extra time they needed to prepare their documentation.

Because of the delay, they were able to assemble a quality document that resulted in Associated's winning the franchise. Ironically, Harry Turner lost his challenge in court and Associated retained that bid as well. 'In a way,' said Gilbert later, 'Harry Turner helped us win Teletext.' Associated and its partner renamed the outlet West Country Television, and they were up and running.

By his own estimation, the securing of the Public Teletext licence became David English's greatest triumph as chairman of Associated.

By counterpointing the way David English handled Teletext Holdings Ltd and Channel One, one can see the strengths and weaknesses of his tenure as chairman of Associated Newspapers. In some ways he was suited to the job because intelligence and creativity always play an important part in carrying out any high-level job. He had as well a spark, or drive if you will, that gave him an edge. Then, too, as a figurehead for Associated, David was in his element. He became chairman of the Press Complaints Commission and also of ITN, and he excelled in these high-profile positions. He was adept at networking and his innate charm made him a natural at public relations.

But David did not possess that calm deliberate logic, the nerves of steel or the extreme patience of the strategic thinker, the very qualities that Vere had in abundance. And although he used his emotions as a driving force that often carried him through, he lacked the quiet cunning that an executive position entails.

David was handicapped by a kind of naiveté that caused him to believe his success in newspapers could easily be replicated in other related fields, if only he had the will. But television wasn't David's medium and he didn't have a feel for it.

Nor was the Internet. David English never truly believed the Internet would become a commercial force to be reckoned with. Speculating as to whether interactive digital television, Teletext or the Internet would become the prevailing technology, David believed that the Internet was a relatively minor development. If it did succeed, it would eventually be merged on to the television screen. In this, he may still be proven right. But he didn't understand that the company would need expertise and experience in the early technology in order to compete as a force in its evolved form. He took the cautious route, holding to a wait-and-see strategy.

As usual, it was Vere who saw the possibilities of technological innovation, insisting the company become involved in the Internet. In this, as in so many other areas, his long-term strategy eventually paid off for Associated Newspapers.

Vere Rothermere could also show a certain tenacity in acquiring new investments. After the fall of Communism in Eastern Europe in 1989 it suddenly became possible to acquire media holdings in former Eastern bloc countries. Vere's historical interest in Hungary had always been high, a result of his grandfather's colourful and fantastic history in that country.

Harold had become interested in Hungary as the result of a chance meeting with the adventuress, Princess Stephanie Hohenlohe. Convinced by her of the unjustness of the partitioning of Hungary dictated by the Treaty of Trianon at Versailles, Harold Rothermere published two editorials, protesting against the ceding of land containing 3 million Hungarians to Czechoslovakia, Romania and Yugoslavia. Overnight the first Viscount Rothermere became an icon in the country and, citing a precedent in Hungary of electing their kings, was actually invited to become the reigning monarch of Hungary. This he declined, agreeing instead to accept an honorary Doctor of Law degree from Szeged University.

Somehow the incredible event stuck in Vere's mind for many years and when the opportunity came about to invest in Eastern European countries he zeroed in on Hungary. In this effort he was opposed by several of the group directors who attempted to put a strict limit on the amount he could bid.

Under this handicap Vere asked David Kirkby to go to Hungary to bid for *Kisalfold*, the largest of the regional newspapers in that country. Because of earlier irregularities in which the selling agent, the Communist Party, had been accused of accepting bribes, Kirkby found himself being broadcast on public television as he made his bid. He said later,

The amount of money I was allowed was very small and I knew we wouldn't get it but I was nevertheless told to do my best. But it was quite clear after a relatively short period of time in these final negotiations that at the level I was pitching in we had no chance at all.

Slightly stung by the prompt rejection of his bid before the Hungarian public, Kirkby commandeered the only telephone available, where other bidders were gathered.

In clipped and indirect sentences I informed 'Lord R' of what was happening and recommended a much higher maximum bid. The answer was curt – 'Well, I think we should get it. Call me later.' The negotiations resumed and a price agreed within the recommended ceiling, and the title was bought to give Associated Newspapers its first trading presence in Hungary almost seventy years after the long association with Hungary began.

Though some had been against the investment, upon actually acquiring *Kisalfold* the company jumped in enthusiastically. Press specialists began immediately to apply their newspaper expertise to the project, bringing in colour and doubling the weekly pagination of the six-day-a-week newspaper. They introduced a women's page, and although it was necessary to increase the price, they lost only 1 per cent of their circulation while rival newspapers have suffered serious attrition. In fact, *Kisalfold* proved very popular and began making money right away. Today it is still making money.

In 1994, Associated began building a new print works in Györ , where *Kisalfold* is published. Vere's son Jonathan said later,

Kisalfold is our only business in a foreign-speaking environment and we have confidence in the investment. The only mistake we made was not to go further. In 1997 we led a consortium that acquired Danubius, the largest single radio station we run, and we're now looking into building a proper media company in Hungary.

In a way, *Kisalfold* was a cornerstone of Vere's policy of building on the company's history. If the company went forward by building on its past and in areas of expertise it had earlier developed, *Kisalfold* and Danubius were examples of that policy and, as such, it has proven to be a profitable investment as well.

The sixth floor of Northcliffe House is its own place, a maze of offices and dead-end passages than can lead a visitor astray. The only orientation is a measure of gold, red and grey carpet, a replica of the mosaic tile from Carmelite House that lines the hallway outside the chairman's suite and leads to historic Room One.

The diversification of Associated Newspapers likewise began as a haphazard affair that originated with Mick Shields in the 1960s. Investments in such far-flung interests as furniture, oil, taxis and pizza contributed to an eclectic pool of investments that appeared to the outsider to have little rhyme or reason. There was nevertheless a compelling reason for diversification at that time – to divert valuable capital resources away from the virtually uncontrollable Fleet Street operations. Indeed, these investments, along with Northcliffe Newspapers, the prosperous chain of provincial newspapers, were key to the company's survival during the years leading up to 1971.

Then on the verge of bankruptcy, the company passed from Esmond to his son Vere. Vere's innovations in the newspaper field – the resuscitation of the *Daily Mail*, the successful launch of the *Mail on Sunday*, the acquisition of the *Evening Standard* – all these investments in the national press put the company on a firmer fiscal foundation. That, plus Northcliffe Newspapers, made Associated uniquely asset-rich within the newspaper industry.

Because of the glamour of the field and the flamboyance of its practitioners, this has always been the sector of the Daily Mail and General Trust that drew the attention of the public. But the sixth floor is a beehive of industry involving little-known projects. 'The accountants', as they are called, are actually well-informed risk takers who move their chips around the investment table with a high level of expertise. They certainly do not crave public notice, preferring instead to operate quietly in the rarefied atmosphere of the sixth floor, investing and divesting large sums in a constant quest for solvency and profit. The spearhead for this policy had always been Mick Shields. It was Mick's genius that had led to the company's keeping its North Sea oil investments when Vere's father Esmond lost his nerve. Mick had also earlier masterminded the precursor to the Mori Poll, the National Opinion Poll.

In 1986, however, the company signalled a shift in its investment focus as it began a sell-off of non-media assets. Ticketmaster, Argus Shield security services, Purfleet wharf facility and the company's six West End theatres all went, as well as its 10 per cent holding in the London Cab Company with its fleet of 250 black cabs. A one-off investment in G. T. Rackstraw, suppliers of reproduction furniture to Harrods, was also dropped.

Instead, the company would now concentrate on expanding its media holdings, especially those areas in which it had established a level of expertise. One of its earliest attempts at this, in 1993, to launch a national press service, UK News, was defeated in-house, killed off by David English, who refused to let the *Daily Mail* and its sister publications subscribe to it on the grounds that it wasn't as good as the PA. David could be quite ruthless in eliminating the competition, whether it arose from his national competitors or fellow executives.

One managing director confessed that as a result of David's continuing worries about his own 'vulnerability', as he put it, he routinely submitted his plans to David's office first, even though this wasn't the customary chain of corporate command. 'It helped to eliminate any misunderstandings that might arise from those quarters,' he explained.

Others referred to David's continuing problems in dealing with ideas he didn't think of himself. Roger Gilbert later said,

> David believed in a creative élite and you were either in it or you weren't. He and his creative team were part of it, but it wasn't extended to others in the company. He didn't recognise creativity he had not fostered. It was also his way of keeping power, by keeping control of this 'élite force'.

But the investment wing of Daily Mail and General Trust was an irresistible creative force of its own. Vere had become interested in new media-based industries, and as a result the company zeroed in on certain selected sectors, most particularly the exhibition business and information publishing. The company eventually expanded to become one of the top ten exhibition organisations in the world, both for trade and consumer shows. The newly formed company, 'dmg world media', runs exhibitions around the globe, in such far-flung locations as Dubai, South America, China and North America.

Other sectors of interest included radio, information television, information publishing and financial publication. Patrick Sergeant had earlier pioneered the company's entry into the field of financial publishing with his far-sighted magazine *Euromoney*. In the 1960s he had persuaded Vere's father Esmond to invest £6200 in the launch of the periodical that specialised in business, later expanding it to include European and global market interests.

'It was almost a one-off,' said Peter Williams, who is group finance director of DMGT. '*Euromoney* is a business that expanded to a worth of £500 million in the last decade.' It was this success that led the company to acquire in 1997 the American periodical *Institutional Investor*.

'Whereas our early investments in 13–30 [later Whittle Communications] and *Esquire*, the *SoHo News* and *American Lawyer* had shown varying degrees of success, we were actually just getting our feet wet,' said Williams. 'Now we are targeting our acquisitions to match areas we know about.'

Whittle Communications was an example of the wet-foot philosophy. Through the years, as first half and then another quarter of DMGT's original investment in 13–30, was sold off, DMGT achieved a profit comfortably in excess of $150 million. Later, in 1994, when the company folded, DMGT generated a loss. Inside the company the logic was that if they had sold *all* of Whittle earlier, the investment would have yielded an even *higher* return with *no* loss. It was a circular argument that pitted optimists in the company against pessimists. And at DMGT, on 'the dark side',* as the financial sector was often designated by the editorial sector, pessimism was usually deemed the safer route.

But there was no doubt the company was growing in sophistication, learning from its past investments and tending towards areas where it had established a high level of expertise and profitability. Following that logic, it sold its share of West Country TV to Carlton Communications in November 1986 for £85 million. 'It was a good investment; we did well financially,' said Williams. 'But we weren't learning much about consumer television and we decided to let that sector go.'

Instead, the company concentrated on radio, acquiring fifty-five radio stations in Australia, largely through the efforts of a dynamic Australian named Charlie Cox who joined the firm in 1993, charged with developing its interest in the field. 'Vere was absolutely pushing for radio,' Cox said. 'He called it "good real estate", and it was my job to go out and get it.'

There were two reasons for going into Australia. The first was that cross-media prohibitions operating in the UK were preventing the company from going forward in certain selected areas. The other was the idea of spreading the risk. By going into a completely different geographical market, the firm was not limited to expansion in the UK economy alone.

By 1997 the company gained the national network in Hungary, paralleling the logic of DMGT's investments in newspapers there. Cox remembered the excitement on the day they won the international tender in Hungary against all comers:

I received a telegram from Vere who was delighted about it all. I was just

---

* It was called 'the dark side', ostensibly because the offices on that side of the atrium fell more in the shadow than the other side.

about to participate in a car race, and the telegram said, 'Congratulations to you and my cousin [Vyvyan Harmsworth] on this signal triumph. I hope you do as well in Australia with the V8s.'

Vere was incredibly entrepreneurial and sometimes when there was a bit of collateral damage around the table at finance committee meetings, Vere would wink at me as I left, and I knew we would get the money.

Meanwhile, the company went on to the Internet, launching 'Peoplebank', a recruitment business. This had a slow start, largely because it was too early. But another Internet initiative, 'thisislondon.com', won the Consumer Website Award of the Year for 1998. It is worth noting that the website had received the support of David English since its inception.

But how did the investment strategy at DMGT measure up overall? What was the general trend of the company? Were they succeeding? Well, if in March 1982 an individual had invested £1 in the Footsie One Hundred Index, he would by the year 2000 have made £9. But if, in the same time-frame, he had invested £1 in DMGT, he would have £129. By this standard the achievement of the company was nothing less than miraculous.

By 1995 Jonathan Harmsworth had joined the Board of Directors of the Daily Mail and General Trust, contributing a new voice to the invest-ment policies of the company and, as one director put it, 'bringing down the average age of the board considerably'.

The board was changing and the firm was changing. Nothing illus-trated that more than the sale of Carmelite House in 1998 for £60 million. Also sold were Northcliffe House in London and the building by the same name in Manchester that had withstood bombing raids during World War Two. These sales signalled the end of an era for Associated Newspapers. It became clear now that the very nature of the business was changing. And as it moved into the twenty-first century, the company was actively creating a new profit base to support its expanding investment in the provincial and national newspaper industry.

But one thing would not change, and that was the fundamental outlook for Associated Newspapers and its holding company Daily Mail and General Trust. Because of the family ownership, the company had been able to afford a commitment to long-term development. It was this sometimes difficult but always profitable policy that had been pursued under Vere Rothermere. It is the policy that will continue under his son Jonathan.

TWENTY-FOUR

A CLOCK OF GUILT

From the time he was seven years old Vere had been dreaming of having a son. He would name him Jonathan and the boy would be groomed to take over the publishing dynasty that had been founded by Northcliffe.

By the time that son was born, Vere was forty-two years old and the idea of a successor had grown even more important with each passing year. He took the boy into his confidence from an early age and it would not be an exaggeration to say that Vere's son Jonathan began receiving his training to take over the Daily Mail and General Trust virtually from birth.

But when Vere was a boy he had suffered enormously under the British educational system. He never knew why he did poorly at school. It was something to do with the highly regimented, examination-orientated methods of the public school system. Vere had enjoyed his studies at Eton, but his marks were mediocre to poor, and at the end of the day he felt he was a total failure, with no aptitude for learning. This caused an erosion of his confidence that very nearly brought him down.

Then something happened that changed everything. Vere was among the schoolchildren evacuated from England during the war and went to stay in America. There he was enrolled in Kent School in Connecticut, where he did well. He was impressed by the school and grateful to the teachers for 'bringing me up to snuff'.

Vere was not a slow learner. He was simply different. Most people learn by isolating skills one at a time and mastering each of them in turn. But Vere learnt in a manner sometimes called 'gestalt' by American educators, in which the learner must understand the entire gestalt of a set before he can begin to master individual skills within it. A pattern shared by only a small percentage of the population, the 'gestalt' learner can seem slow during the learning process. But once he has mastered the set he is usually more proficient than others in manipulating it. This might have been one of the characteristics shared by others in the Harmsworth family and it could account, at least in part, for the unique way of thinking certain of the family's members displayed.

Whether or not his son also shared this learning quirk, Vere decided against sending Jonathan to Eton. Jonathan went instead to Gordonstoun, where team spirit and peer pressure yielded tremendous benefit. 'It was Spartan, but I grew to love it,' Jonathan said later. 'I loved Scotland and I still end my showers with a blast of cold water.' He was referring to the fact that cold showers were mandatory for the younger students.

But even before Gordonstoun Vere had included Jonathan in many of his most difficult decisions, explaining in simple terms what was at stake in each of the challenges he met. So Jonathan had a memory of the launch of the *Mail on Sunday* and the newspaper war between the London *Daily News* and the *Evening Standard*, as recounted by his father. And seeing his father under pressure taught him a lot about what the future would hold for him. One of his earliest memories was of his father taking him to see the hot-metal presses running off thousands of copies of newspapers: 'How can this be, Dad?' he asked his father in amazement.

He also had flashes of himself as a youth downstairs in the family's Eaton Square apartment, with 'a wonderful nanny, a proper English nanny', who had lost a leg in an accident. 'I didn't know my mother then. I loved this old woman,' Jonathan said later. But the nanny turnover was high and Jonathan remembered making the life of at least one of them so difficult that she left in despair.

To a large degree Jonathan's childhood memories were happy ones. But what was difficult for him was the separation. Even though Vere didn't believe in divorce, thinking it could do his children harm, the formal separation turned out to be almost as painful. Jonathan said later,

> I dealt with it. My parents loved me. They showed me love. They showed emotion. That was strengthening.
>
> Even afterwards, my parents went on holidays together.
>
> My father gave me love and consideration. We would have dinner alone and it would be great. We talked about history. I loved listening to Dad.
>
> We went to Colorado together, riding in the mountains. I was under tremendous pressure to succeed, so out in the wild I felt great.
>
> Then, too, on the riding holidays I got to know him intimately. It was there he became a strong father figure to me.

The separation also had a direct impact on Jonathan's education. For two terms he attended the American School in St John's Wood in London. He loved it and wanted to stay. But his mother took him out, hiring a tutor and bringing him down to the South of France to stay with her in her villa at Cap d'Ail. Later he went to Kent School in Connecticut, where his father had gone when he was the same age. All in all, Jonathan would remember being pulled back and forth between British and American schools, as his parents alternated their views of what would give him the broadest background.

But when it was time for Jonathan to go to college, both parents did their best to find the right university for him. In fact, the selection of a university was one of his most pleasant memories. The time Jonathan had spent at Kent School had been highly successful and he seemed to both parents to enjoy American education. This had an influence on their decision to send him to the United States for his higher education. He said later,

> My parents were separated and somewhat eccentric, but they also wanted to give me as normal an upbringing as they could. So we all went on a trip to the East in the United States when I was sixteen.
>
> Dad rented a Ford LTD and we went round to Harvard, Amherst, Yale, the University of Connecticut, to visit all the universities I had applied to. We stayed in motels. It was normal for most kids, but for me it was an abnormal but terrific experience. My two parents were in one car, that was unusual, and we were having a great time.
>
> My mother left before I got to Duke. But once I got there I fell in love with it. It was warm, the cherry trees were in bloom. The teachers were obviously excellent. So that's how I chose Duke.

Duke University is located in Durham, North Carolina. Not a particularly well-known college in Britain, Duke is nevertheless one of the top ten academic institutions in the United States and it has the reputation for attracting well-adjusted, talented, upper-middle-class students. Its former affiliation with the Methodist Church, a mainstream religion in America, means it still attracts a high number of serious-minded young people with high ideals. After giving thought to the matter, Jonathan decided to major in history and philosophy.

But while Jonathan determined to take a hand in choosing what kind of education he would have, the education of his sisters was put on the back burner. To an extent this attitude was the result of the backward thinking of the upper classes in England. Daughters didn't need an education, so went the logic, since they would only grow up to get married and have a family. Then again, the thinking was a function of the archaic concept of primogeniture, which still had terrific influence on the family's attitude, probably because the title passed from eldest son to eldest son.

Camilla did become a homemaker, but she always felt the sting of not having had a better education. Geraldine also had children, two girls. But Geraldine felt the lack sorely, especially since she had literary talent. Both girls later came to believe they would have enjoyed and benefited from higher education.

Jonathan's upbringing was clouded by the family's belief in primogeniture. It was an old-fashioned notion, but in fact it performed the function of keeping the family assets together and Jonathan took that responsibility seriously. It did however, tend to keep the pressure on him, from the beginning and throughout his entire education, to succeed, because everything depended upon him.

He was nevertheless not an easy young man to tame. While he was at Duke, he took to 'travelling the North Carolina countryside', in the words of his father, 'obsessed by the local types'. What Vere was referring to was a dust-up Jonathan became embroiled in during his junior year at Duke, when he was twenty-one years old. He went to a bar with a couple of his friends to play basketball hoop, a popular game in America. When they came out, six or seven local youths were emerging at the same time. They began to make fun of Jonathan's curly hair and Jonathan picked a fight with one of them. Just as it became clear that Jonathan would win, the other youth's friends came in. One of them took Jonathan down, beating him on the head with a tyre iron, while another of them jumped in his car and tried to run him over, but accidentally smashed up the car instead.

Jonathan ended up in hospital in intensive care, as his father flew over, torn between fear and rage. 'I was *furious*,' said Vere. 'I vowed if he lived through it I would kill him.' What he did instead was to tell him there was no shame in running from an unfair fight and another important lesson that Jonathan eventually would take to heart: you should only fight 'when you *have* to fight'.

Although he was given a great deal of freedom, still Jonathan always felt he was on a short leash, with his mother keeping track of his movements almost obsessively. It was, in fact, his mother who introduced him to the woman he would marry.

Patricia had met Claudia Clemence at a social gathering in 1989 and, discovering that Claudia and she shared the same birthday, 5 May, she began urging the young woman that she should meet her son Jonathan. Eventually she persuaded Jonathan to invite Claudia to the Evening Standard Drama Awards in November 1991.

The relationship began as a friendship and Jonathan didn't want to lose it. 'It was Claudia's company I enjoyed,' he said later. It was new to him to have an attractive woman as a friend.

Eventually Claudia accompanied Jonathan and Vere to the Yukon, where Vere was relocating his Canadian assets. Vere's long-time business associate and best friend, Bob Morrow, arranged for the couple to go on a two-week riding holiday in the Yukon. They thought it was going to be a kind of 'five-star trek', but typical of Morrow and his very Canadian sense of humour, it turned out to be a real survival course in the northern wilderness. They had an Indian tracker, horses, a tent and very basic food, which actually ran out before the trip was over. 'We got on really well,' Jonathan said, 'and after that, I was sure. It was so fortunate to make a real bond with a woman. And Claudia returned the feeling. It was, well, *finding another soul.*'

For Claudia it was walking into unfamiliar territory. Her father was a property developer and her mother stayed at home to take care of their three daughters. They lived in the country in Essex while her father went into London to work during the week.

Claudia eventually went to Oxford, where she read Philosophy, Political Science and Economics. She loved the tutorials and studying with world authorities. Eventually she took her Master's in Comparative Government at the London School of Economics which, after Oxford, seemed easy. Then she went to work for an art dealer and later met Patricia, who urged her to go out with her son.

On the night Patricia died, Claudia and Jonathan were visiting her in her villa in France. The couple had come back from swimming at five o'clock in the evening because they usually had tea with Patricia then. But that day the door to her bedroom was closed. They knocked on it, trying to rouse her. At last they broke into her bedroom and found she had died.

They called an ambulance, and in due course the medics arrived and tried to revive her. But it was no use. After the medics left, Jonathan called the family members who made arrangements to come. Then Claudia and Jonathan sat in the living room, while outside a mistral began. The lights went out and the weather, blistering hot all day, changed. The evening had been overcast, with dark and threatening skies, and now the storm broke and rain started to fall. It must have seemed to the young couple that the very weather was in some way reinforcing the unhappiness of the day.

Patricia died on 12 August 1992 in her villa in the South of France, the villa that had earlier belonged to Greta Garbo. She was sixty-three years old. She had had wine earlier and apparently took some sleeping pills to get to sleep, as she had been doing for many years. But she had also been suffering from a summer cold and had been prescribed antihistamines to relieve general stuffiness. Later the coroner speculated that it might have been the addition of the antihistamines that put her over the threshold of safe drug consumption. But it was impossible to determine precisely if that was the cause of death. Certainly, the mixing of alcohol and sleeping pills can become lethal at any time.

Vere took her death hard. For many months afterwards he was in a depression; on 2 September 1992 he had a car accident in northern France that came close to costing him his life. But after all, he was lucky to have only a dislocated arm and several stitches in his ear. He said in the aftermath of the accident,

> I'm not enjoying life very much at the moment. I miss Patricia. I knew that Porsches aquaplaned in the rain and I didn't slow down. I wasn't caring if I died. But it would have been wrong to take someone with me.

He was referring to his mistress, Maiko Lee, who was in the car with him at the time of the accident and whom he later married. Yes, Vere felt very guilty about Patricia's death, desperately guilty – guilty that they had separated and couldn't work things out. But those who knew him well said he always tended to feel guilty about his relationships with women. Where women were concerned, he was like a clock of guilt, ticking. Certainly, none of those close to him took seriously the idea that he was trying to take his own life. They believed he simply felt terrible that Patricia had died.

As to Patricia, it was not unusual to hear people say that she had lived life as she wanted. They were referring to the constant round of parties and self-indulgent behaviour that many had seen her display. But nothing could have been further from the truth. Patricia wanted to be a helpmeet to Vere and she wanted to be taken seriously for her intellect. She wanted to be respected by her family and for them to know that she loved them. All that somehow slipped away, quite possibly because of an illness she never even knew she had.

At a service of thanksgiving and celebration for Patricia's life held on 2 October 1992 Vere spoke of his wife in loving terms, saying,

> Pat was an unusual person, as all who knew her would testify. She was a free and generous soul and also a very lonely one.
>
> She believed fervently in the importance of the *Daily Mail* and the other newspapers and their places in our national life … What I and my family owe to Pat is incalculable and can now never be repaid.

He then read a poem he had composed himself, about the nature of their singular love for one another.

I Love You, a Poem from a Husband to His Dear Wife

I was never old nor
Wise enough for you.
My pen has not the
Depth nor scan
My mind the reach
Nor season
To compose the
Strange music of your heart.

Oh, Lady with the
Mahler soul
Why have you me in
Thrall?

I have wept deep tears
Tinged with the
Blood of my life
At love's sweet and secret sea
Far below the
Burning sands of
Living.

TWENTY-FIVE

THE UNKNOWN VERE

Vere knew David, but David didn't know Vere.

'How is Vere?' David would ask Vyvyan Harmsworth if he had a meeting scheduled with his proprietor. 'How is the family?' Does he have any worries?' Even after all the years David and Vere had worked together, Vyvyan mused, his knowledge of his employer was still very tentative. But then, David was never in Vere's confidence.

Few were. But because of the family connection and his frequent contact with him, Vyvyan knew Vere as well as anybody. He saw and understood several different sides to the man. He knew his moods.

But nobody knew Vere completely. The popular public persona, fed by a media that didn't have a clue as to what Rothermere really was like, was that of a dimwit bumbler, and Rothermere delighted in that perception. He fed it by behaving whimsically in interviews and in public. He made baffling statements; he took up arcane issues. Yet as success piled upon success, it became increasingly clear that the press had got him wrong. Somebody came up with the word 'enigmatic', and for a time that was the buzz word used to describe the elusive Vere Rothermere.

The fact was that outsiders saw only what Vere wanted them to. In most of his personal interactions he purposely fragmented his personality, revealing only a small part of himself. Nor could he resist hamming it up on occasion. He was a terrific showman and anyone who understood they were seeing a performance was in for a treat. He was also changeable. One minute he might be the jester, the next King Lear.

Why did he do it? Was it camouflage – or self-protection? Probably both, maybe neither. He did get enormous pleasure out of bamboozling people. He set little traps and when a victim fell into one of them he was endlessly pleased. But at least part of his motivation had to stem from an unconscious desire to insulate the individual he was dealing with from the full force of his personality. He seemed intuitively to understand that most people would not be able to tolerate all the sides of his character. He was protean, multifaceted, changeable, complicated.

So David, the powerful David who could topple governments, often walked on eggshells when he saw Vere. He had a healthy regard for his own well-being and therefore a healthy fear of his proprietor. David stuck to the script – as did everyone – the script written by Vere. And in the essentials Vere always got what he wanted.

In terms of setting the policy for his newspapers he was somewhat tricky. He set only the policies he cared about deeply, and these were few. The others he left to David. This freedom itself created a minefield for the editor, because English only heard from his proprietor when he called it wrong. So part of setting policy was correctly guessing what Rothermere believed – without the benefit of actually being told.

Vere could be blissfully ignorant about what would be published next. On one occasion the *Daily Mail* serialised a biography of Malcolm Muggeridge written by former *Private Eye* editor Richard Ingrams. It revealed information about the private life of Pamela Berry, the well-known London social hostess and the mother of a good friend of Vere's, Nick Berry. When Berry and his French wife, Evelyne Prouvost, who owns the women's magazine *Marie Claire*, mentioned the matter to Vere, he replied honestly, 'I knew nothing about this.' If Vere *had* known he would have prevented publication. 'But', he said later, 'I was awfully glad I *didn't* know anything about it.'

This was his modus operandi.

Vere was a restless man, a nomad, constantly on the move from one location to another. 'If he were away from the office for more than two days he would call, asking, "What have I missed?" "What's in the headlines?"' said Kathy Campbell, his personal assistant for fourteen years. She said later,

> Three weeks was a long time for him. Occasionally he would be in Paris that long. He would spend two weeks in New York, one week in California. A lot of it was necessary. There were board meetings to attend in Canada and New York. And in Australia.

Campbell knew what few others knew: Rothermere was a workaholic. Only on the rarest of occasions did he miss checking in with the office every single day. 'If you faxed him correspondence, he would fax it back immediately,' said Campbell. 'He was the most "hands-on chairman" I ever knew.'

When Campbell went to work for Rothermere he was very difficult, a short-tempered man who didn't suffer fools gladly. It was so hard at the beginning that she wondered whether she would be able to stay. 'But he changed when he got his dog Ryu-ma, his Japanese Akita,' she said later. That was when Vere softened, making him easier to work for. The only throwback to his bad temper occurred on the third day of jet lag. Then he was easily angered, groggy and he could be cruel. 'Don't let me sign anything important on the third day!' he used to warn Campbell.

As well as being difficult, he was often very funny. He had a devastating and highly sophisticated sense of humour. After hearing a funeral oration promising rewards in the hereafter, Vere said, 'Heaven. It's not really for rich men, is it?' Another wicked bon mot was made in regard to his newspapers' great appeal for the middle market. 'My newspapers do well in the suburbs,' he said blandly, 'because all my editors are so suburban.'

Yet his pride in his newspapers was inestimable. He credited David with saving the *Daily Mail*, always referring to him as a 'newspaper genius'. And on 2 May 1992 he held a celebration of the twenty-first anniversary of the relaunch of the *Daily Mail*. It took place at Grosvenor House and his wife Patricia was the hostess. After the dinner, both he and David spoke warmly to the gathering about those early days. Vere talked about the dire predictions of failure reported in the popular press. 'As usual, the thousands were wrong!' he roared to tumultuous applause. He went on, 'This is very much David's day. David was and still is the greatest and most creative editor seen in Fleet Street since Northcliffe.'

Vere also singled out Jackie Shields for particular thanks because her husband Mick had contributed so much to the success of the company. And, poignantly, he thanked his wife Patricia who had helped so much to ensure the success of the newspaper.

Vere had every reason to be proud of his achievements. In the past twenty-one years he and David had built on the success of the relaunched *Daily Mail* by launching the now very valuable *Mail on Sunday*. Later Vere acquired the *Evening Standard*. His national titles dominated the middle market and his record was unassailable.

It was after this twenty-first anniversary celebration that he determined to leave behind a legacy in honour of his family. Very much aware of the Harmsworth family's rich history, Vere made it his business, especially in his later years, to promote several projects generously. After considerable thought he decided to continue with the philanthropy begun by his father and grandfather.

His grandfather Harold had founded two chairs for study, the Vere Harmsworth Professorship of Imperial and Naval History attached to St Catherine's College, Cambridge, and the Vyvyan Harmsworth Professorship of American History attached to Queen's College, Oxford.

Harold created these chairs in honour of his two sons Vere and Vyvyan who were killed in World War One.

In 1959 Vere's father Esmond had become the chancellor of Memorial University of Newfoundland, earlier founding the Rothermere Foundation for the benefit of Memorial University students who wanted to carry out postgraduate studies in Great Britain. The most important criterion for the award was that the studies pursued by the chosen students should benefit Newfoundland. It was natural for Vere to want to build on this work, as he had built on his grandfather's.

In this he was aided by Vyvyan Harmsworth, who had joined DMGT in 1982. Harmsworth had an impressive background, having worked first as an assistant equerry for Prince Philip from 1973 to 1975, then for the Prince of Wales as his first full-time equerry during 1975 and 1976. He had attained the rank of major in the army (Welsh Guards), putting in seventeen years of service, with two tours of duty in Northern Ireland in Belfast, the first in 1972 and then again in South Armagh in 1979. But besides bringing an illustrious background to the project, as a cousin of Vere, Harmsworth had his own sense of responsibility to family history as well.

Vyvyan had applied for the position with DMGT in 1981 and the story of how he got the job showed a lot about Vere's methods. First there was a waiting period of six months with no acknowledgement of Vyvyan's letter of application. Then, suddenly, Vyvyan got a call asking whether he could be at Northcliffe House by five o'clock that afternoon for an interview. He was not to be late since Rothermere had a social commitment at six o'clock. Harmsworth was caught without any cash and had to borrow £10 from the gardener for his train ticket to Waterloo. He made it by a hair.

At the end of the interview Rothermere said, 'I'll give you a job. How much do you want to be paid?' Not wanting to rock the boat, Vyvyan answered with what he considered a modest but fair sum. He found out only later that his secretary was paid £1000 more a year than he was. This was vintage Vere Rothermere. He had a reputation for giving people exactly what they asked for. But of course, Vyvyan wouldn't make this discovery for some time.

It was Harmsworth who first became aware of the idea of an American Institute through the work of David Fischer, who had been the Harmsworth professor of American History attached to Queen's College, Oxford in 1985–6. He was attempting to get all the American holdings at Oxford into one building. With that in mind, Fischer had organised a council responsible for raising the money. Vyvyan thought the idea a worthy one and approached Rothermere. Eventually, Harmsworth became a major fund-raiser on the project.

By 1995 the Rothermere Foundation was at the forefront of the fund-raising effort by donating an initial £1.6 million, with half a million also coming from Associated Newspapers.* Rothermere became co-chairman of the Founding Council, along with his sister, Esmé, Countess of Cromer.

The project grew and has expanded with the rise of the new technology. It is now envisaged as a living memorial to Rothermere that will use the Internet as a means of providing knowledge about American life. But the goal of the Institute is to be more than a simple academic repository of knowledge. It will also take on the broad brief to encompass art, literature and the cultural artefacts of the United States. The Institute intends to become the primary cultural and academic link of knowledge between the United States and Great Britain that uses the Internet. The Rothermere Foundation also set up a scholarship for students from Duke University, the alma mater of Vere's son Jonathan, to study at Oxford.

A second tier to Rothermere's philanthropy had been based on his grandfather Harold's initial involvement in Hungary in the late 1920s. Vere determined that commercial investment was the most intelligent way to support Hungary's emerging economy. Thus he continued to develop his original investment in the regional newspaper *Kisalfold* and the radio station Danubius.

But after opening the Hungarian Festival Magyarok (Britain Salutes Hungary), Vere was asked by the conductor of the Budapest Festival Orchestra to support them by becoming the Orchestra's international president. In a quite dramatic move he presented Rothermere with a programme from the celebration that had been signed by all the members of the orchestra, requesting him to take on this office. Vere accepted on the spot.

In December 1996 President Göncz invested Rothermere with the highest honour that can be given to a foreigner who is not a head of state – the Order of Merit of the Hungarian Republic, Middle Cross with Star.

Less well known than his work in Hungary, but also important, was Vere's philanthropic work with the City Ballet of London. He became honorary president of the company in 1997. He also sponsored the modern dance company, Ballet Rambert, for a tour of Hungary.

There were other acts of philanthropy, some involving employees who

---

* After Vere Rothermere's death DMGT, led by Vere's son Jonathan, provided another £1.5 million in order to name the Institute in memory of Lord Rothermere.

had fallen on hard times or who had become ill and needed expensive medical care. But Vere preferred never to let these acts of kindness be known, for the sake of the privacy of those he had helped and also to conceal his own sympathetic nature, which he considered to be a chink in the armour he customarily wore as a businessman and press proprietor.

Perhaps the most astonishing decision of Rothermere's later years was to join the Labour benches in the House of Lords. There was initial confusion as to his formal political allegiance in the Lords, since he had not been in attendance for some two years. Although he had traditionally been identified with the Conservatives, a spokesman for Rothermere said, 'If he had attended, he would probably have sat on the crossbenches.' But in May 1997 he went over, making a public statement that Labour 'are carrying out so many policies I believe in'.

The view appeared to be at odds with the editorial policy that had been established by the editor of the *Daily Mail*, Paul Dacre. After crossing over, however, Rothermere made a public statement supporting Dacre, saying that he was 'a great editor'. But, Vere stressed, 'we do not always share exactly the same views on politics.'

The day after he joined Labour, speaking on Radio 4's *The World at One*, Rothermere enlarged upon his statement:

> It is a free country and he [Dacre] is entitled to his views and to express them. But of course, if they start to affect the circulation that will be different.

About Tony Blair he had words of praise that were published in the *Evening Standard*:

> To me, Tony Blair is a young man and I became very aware of how much in touch he is with his own generation. That generation is now the age to take over. And, as I got to know him more and more, I realised that Tony Blair is the true representative of his generation, both mentally and physically. He understands absolutely the temper of the times and the spirit of the age.

Was this statement simply idle mischief on the part of the press baron? Was it aimed at showing Dacre the error of his ways? Or was Rothermere really enamoured of New Labour?

Insofar as New Labour carried out policies Vere approved of, that much he supported them, and at the time of his crossover he privately admitted to liking Tony Blair a great deal. He also wholeheartedly approved the policies that the Blair government were initiating, especially those that were, in mind, spirit and practice, closely associated with Conservative policies.

But so far as actually favouring New Labour was concerned, Vere indicated his decision had been, at least in part, a move inspired by pragmatism, aimed at neutralising the *Mail*'s continuing criticism of the Labour Government and perhaps motivated by a desire to keep those in the Labour Government guessing. It is interesting to note that at no time did Rothermere tell Paul Dacre to modify his editorial stance.

So the move was quintessential Vere Rothermere in that it was difficult to interpret and served a number of diverse purposes simultaneously. The crossover had provided a second point of view coming out of the *Daily Mail*, without compromising the editorial stance of its editor. It served to keep his editor on his toes. It encouraged New Labour to speculate that Vere Rothermere was perhaps at heart an ally ... and it made waves, something Vere loved to do.

In July 1993 Jonathan and Claudia Clemence were married at the Church of the Immaculate Conception in Farm Street, Mayfair. The couple soon moved to Glasgow, where Jonathan went to work at the *Scottish Daily Record* and *Sunday Mail*. There to learn all he could about the business, he worked first as a reporter, then as a sub-editor and later in the promotions and marketing departments. He also spent time as part of the management team. For Jonathan this was the beginning of the intensive period of training that would in the years to come prepare him to take over the Daily Mail and General Trust.

But after two years, the couple moved back to London, and Jonathan began commuting to work on the Essex *Chronicle Series*, a Northcliffe newspaper. Soon afterwards, he became managing director of Courier Newspapers in Tunbridge Wells, also part of the Northcliffe Group.

On 20 October 1994 the couple's first child was born, a son named Vere Richard Jonathan Harold Harmsworth. He would be called Vere, after Jonathan's father.

There was a saying at Associated Newspapers, a maxim that reflected the quick grasp the Harmsworths showed for the newspaper business: 'It's in the genes' referred to the brilliance of Northcliffe as the foremost editor and newspaper proprietor of the century. But the statement also implied the business acumen of Northcliffe's brother Harold, the first Viscount Rothermere. As regards Jonathan's quick grasp of managerial principles and newspapers in general, people were beginning to say, 'It's in the genes.'

For the young couple it was a time of stability, family life and happiness. They had settled into married life well; it suited both of them. Rothermere came to stay often, spending more and more time with his grandson. Vere had married his mistress Maiko in Paris on 15 December 1993 and the couple became involved in a hectic social life there and, in the summers, in Salzburg. Maiko, who had suffered a degree of ostracism while Patricia was alive, was now gaining new acceptance socially as Rothermere's wife.

In a sense the home made by his son became for Vere a port in the storm, where the pace of life was slow and leisurely, with long walks in the countryside and traditional Sunday lunches. By now Vere had seven grandchildren. Camilla had four children, the eldest a son, Sebastian, who was born in December 1990. His brother and sisters – Alexander, Imogen and India – followed in close succession. Camilla had married Andrew Yeates and lived near Jonathan and Claudia, so when Vere came to visit, he could frequently be found with Camilla and her children. A homemaker, Camilla devoted herself to her children, in her own words 'always trying to be there for them at school and social events'.

Later, after her father's death, Camilla and Andrew were divorced, but remained friends. Camilla went on to remarry the Reverend Hugh MacPherson Cameron on 16 September 2000.

Her sister Geraldine had two children, both of them girls. Her daughter Augusta was from her first marriage to Lord Ogilvy. Later that marriage was dissolved, she and David Ogilvy remaining in close touch. Several years afterwards Geraldine met the well-known and gifted poet Glyn Maxwell. Geraldine had been a model and, when she was younger, supported a number of environmental projects. But throughout the years she was also quietly writing poetry, giving unpublicised readings. She had gained a reputation of being a talented amateur when she met Glyn Maxwell.

The couple married and Maxwell took up a position as visiting professor and poet at Amherst College in Massachusetts, where the American poet Emily Dickinson had lived. Amherst was thought by many to be one of the finest private academic institutions in the world. The couple soon had a daughter, whom they named Alfreda, after Alfred Harmsworth, the great Northcliffe.

Sarah Holcroft, Patricia's daughter by her first husband Christopher Brooks, had long been considered a member of the Harmsworth family. She is married to the painter Harry Holcroft and the family lives in France. The couple have two sons: Harry, born in 1990 and Christopher, born in 1991.

Vere doted on his enlarging family, seeing them all regularly and speaking with his daughters by phone on a daily basis. If he wasn't staying with Camilla, he could be found with Jonathan and Claudia at their London flat. On the day when Jonathan and Claudia's second child, a daughter named Eleanor, was born, 17 October 1996, Vere was staying there.

Early in 1997 Jonathan went to work as deputy managing director of the *Evening Standard* and in December of the same year he became managing director. The point of his rapid succession in the company was to acquaint him, as quickly as was reasonable, with all the hands-on problems his employees encountered on a day-to-day basis. So when the day came that he had to take over from his father he would understand their point of view.

When Vere was seventy on 27 August 1995, a grand birthday party was held in Salzburg at the Schloss Leopoldskron that was attended by family, business associates and friends. The historical significance of the location of the party was that this was the mansion inhabited by Princess Stephanie Hohenlohe. She was the woman credited with acquainting Vere's grandfather Harold with Hungary's continuing problems with the partition mandated by the Treaty of Trianon that had been enacted in the aftermath of World War One. The mansion had belonged to the famous movie director Max Reinhardt who had to flee Austria as the Nazis rose to power.

A couple of years later Vere and Maiko bought a house in the Dordogne. Rothermere had been viewing property in the French countryside for years, so long that the French estate agents had given up on actually selling him anything. But when he did find what he wanted he bought it on the spot. The couple at first had no furniture and one Friday he went out and bought a prefabricated table. Vere sat happily the entire weekend, putting it together. He talked later about what a great time it was, because it was so far removed from the enormous responsibilities he had to carry in his work.

These were probably the happiest days of Vere's life. He had accomplished what he had set out to do in terms of the business and his family surrounded him. Unresolved problems still plagued him and he missed Patricia dreadfully, but for the first time in his life he was at peace.

Vere's doctor had been warning him for years of a growing health problem – high cholesterol – but he paid scant heed. He did a great deal of business over lunch or dinner and even after the warnings he continued to do so, eating rich foods and urging others to join him. He rarely drank alcohol at lunchtime, but in the evenings he drank red wine, because it was reckoned to be good for the circulation. He took up smoking cigars, against the advice of his friends, this after he was well into his seventies. In many ways Vere was an unapologetic bon viveur, indulging himself in the good life and taking very little exercise.

David English was the opposite. After suffering from a drastic bout of hepatitis, David had been forced to give up drinking and he had always eaten sensibly. In his later years, he tended to stick to white meat and vegetables, drinking plenty of water. He was a skiing buff and at every opportunity he went to Switzerland to ski, keeping himself in good physical shape for the sport.

It was highly ironic, then, that David the Spartan was destined to die before Vere the sybarite, and at a younger age. In many ways, David had lived a charmed life and he knew it. The first genuine suffering he had had to deal with was when his wife became ill with Alzheimer's disease.

To a close woman friend, Ann Leslie, David spoke of the heartbreak of his situation, that after years of hard work, when he and Irene had planned to take skiing holidays and enjoy themselves, she became so very ill. He was most grateful then to have work to do, because otherwise he didn't know how he would have coped.

Most people didn't know about Irene's illness, because David kept it purposely under wraps, in order to maintain her dignity. But she had been diagnosed with the disease as early as 1987. To his personal assistant Ina Miller, whose husband had died prematurely of cancer when he was only in his fifties, David always put on a brave front, saying that he believed life was made up of opposites. 'Life is a balance,' he would say to her.

> You shouldn't be bitter when you have had such good times. But I know that the good times have to be paid for, and I have to pay the price. It is unfair that Irene has to pay the highest price of all.
> But nature is about balance, night with day, summer with winter. And I know this is nature's way of balancing our lives.

David's life *had* been marvellous. He had been knighted in the Birthday Honours in 1982 and long before 1998, when he died, he was offered a peerage, which he turned down. In explanation he said he turned it down because he 'didn't think it proper' to have a peerage at the same time as his employer Vere. He told practically no one about this. But he knew he had succeeded at every level, had received every honour and accolade possible and, in his own words and from his own rather puritanical viewpoint: 'I know I have to pay now.'

But even in the face of his wife's illness, he managed to do what he could. Since Irene had become ill, he had worked with the Alzheimer's Disease Society. Less well known was his work on behalf of abused children for the 'Justice for Children Campaign' for the NSPCC. David was a highly religious man as well, attending church most Sundays. Ina Miller described him as being 'metaphysical by nature' and explained that David very much believed in an afterlife.

On the morning of 9 June 1998 David's chauffeur came to pick him up for work. But David didn't come down. When at last the chauffeur went up to check on him, he found David had collapsed on the floor. He had had a stroke. An ambulance rushed him to St Thomas's Hospital and almost at the same time as he was being taken out of his house by the ambulance staff, Paul Dacre was being informed of the fact by a News International man who was witnessing the event as it unfolded from his office.

Vere arrived from France at about nine o'clock that night, while Ina Miller was still there. As she watched Vere walk into the room, she saw him literally 'reel with shock'. 'Seeing David in bed with an oxygen mask over his face, deeply unconscious, Vere almost *imploded* from the shock of it,' she said afterwards. She speculated that it might have contributed to Vere's death later that year.

David died the next day, 10 June, at the age of sixty-seven, in a private room overlooking the House of Lords. 'It was the bitterest of ironies,' said Ina later. 'He was to be created a Peer of the Realm the following week, had he survived.'

All summer long, after David's death, Vere complained to Kathy Campbell of feeling worn-out. She urged him to see his doctor, but he wanted to put it off until the autumn, when he was scheduled to have his annual physical examination.

But Vere had been blessed with a strong constitution and good health was something he took absolutely for granted.

On 1 September 1998 he arrived at Northolt in the late afternoon, having travelled from his chateau in the Dordogne by private jet. An early meeting of the Board of Directors was scheduled for the next morning and there were papers that urgently needed his signature waiting for him at the airport. After he took care of that business, he checked in with Kathy Campbell, then went to his daughter Geraldine's house for a visit. From there, he went over to his son's apartment where he intended to stay the night.

During dinner Vere began to complain of chest pains and by 9.30 he had become restive. Shortly thereafter he suffered a massive heart attack.

The family called Vere's doctor and an ambulance. They both arrived shortly thereafter. When the medics arrived they attempted to revive him. But he died on the very bed he had shared with his wife Patricia.

The ambulance took Vere to the hospital where a young woman doctor laboured in vain to try to revive him by applying shocks to his heart.

Jonathan had rung his sisters and they arrived at the hospital, Geraldine with her teenaged daughter Augusta and Camilla alone. The family sat with the woman doctor who had tried to bring Vere back to life. She took a good deal of time explaining to them that they couldn't have saved him even if he had been in hospital. Once the attack began, it was inevitable that Vere would die. The family all sat there, stunned. A vicar came in and they prayed together.

Jonathan and Claudia returned home and the two of them went into the library, where they sat down, trying to make sense of what had happened. Then the telephone rang and within minutes it was ringing off the hook. All the calls were from people in the company.

The couple had only twenty minutes to compose themselves before Jonathan's responsibilities began.

TWENTY-SIX

ALL THE NEWS IN TWENTY MINUTES

The fourth Viscount Rothermere sat in his office, contemplating the first major challenge of his publishing career. It was early December 1998, only two months after his father's death, and Jonathan's plan for a free London daily newspaper, one of the best-kept secrets in Fleet Street, was speeding forward at a breakneck pace.

The free sheet was to be a tabloid and it would be distributed on the Underground. The final agreement with Underground officials had been signed, an editor had been engaged and everything appeared to be proceeding smoothly.

But rumours were rife and some of them were clearly based on fact. In the summer of 1998 Modern Times Group (MTG), a Swedish publishing company, had moved into London, having chosen the city as its global headquarters. They soon approached the London Underground with the idea of securing an exclusive distribution contract for a free sheet such as the one they were presently publishing, quite successfully, in Stockholm.

At the same time intelligence reports held that News Corporation had moved a group of journalists into a secret location, where they were preparing to relaunch the defunct title *Today* as a free newspaper. Rupert Murdoch was apparently planning to distribute the sheet on the streets of London and at large workplaces throughout the city, or so Murdoch MacLennan, managing director of Associated Newspapers, had been led to believe.

Another rumour had the Mirror Group out there somewhere, also plugging away at a free title – but this was never proven. What did turn out to be true was that News Corporation and MTG were joining forces to tender a bid in competition with Associated for distribution rights at the mainline stations and they planned to launch against Associated.

The irony of this was not lost on the new chairman of Daily Mail and General Trust. Earlier in the planning of *Metro*, News Corporation had indicated its desire to come in on Associated's venture. But Jonathan insisted on a majority shareholding in his company's favour. News Corporation refused. Now it was making plans of its own.

If News Corporation did go in with MTG, they would precipitate a newspaper war bigger than the one fought and won by Jonathan's father Vere against Robert Maxwell in 1987.* Then Maxwell's twenty-four-hour evening tabloid, the London *Daily News*, went head to head with Vere's newly acquired *Evening Standard*. It resulted in a total victory for Rothermere and one of the first body blows to Maxwell whose kingdom was destined to collapse like a house of cards. But could Associated hope to win this new war, waged by two able opponents?

'I was two months into the job,' Jonathan said later. 'We were haemorrhaging money on the project. But the most amazing part to me now, looking back, was that doubt never entered my mind. I believed in the project, and I knew it would go.'

London *Metro* was the brain child of Jonathan's father Vere. He had returned from one of his many trips abroad in the summer of 1997 and, over dinner at his son's flat, told him about reading an article on a small, obscure newspaper that was being given away free in underground stations in Stockholm. It was called *Metro* and since its inception in 1995 it had advanced to yearly net profits in the region of 40 per cent.

Other free newspapers quickly followed, most notably in Prague, Budapest and Gothenburg, and though none of these realised the same level of success as their Stockholm prototype, there were plans on the table for several more. Vere believed that London was the next logical place for such a newspaper and if that happened the free title would surely be an additional challenge to Associated's supremacy in the middle market. It seemed prudent to look into the idea and decide what to do, and Vere asked Jonathan to see to this.

At the time Jonathan was deputy managing director of the *Evening Standard*, he was twenty-nine years old and it did appear to him that his plate was full. He and a staff member nevertheless researched the matter and found out that *Metro* was owned by Modern Times Group, a division of a Swedish company called Kinnevik Group. It was headed by Jan Stenbeck, who had purchased the idea from two young Swedish journalists. They had noticed that commuters on the Stockholm tube did little more than stare out of the windows as they travelled to work and they saw 'a twenty-minute window of opportunity' for a free newspaper.

Stenbeck's career had thus far been a colourful one and he was known for his 'take-no-prisoners' style of operation. After earning an MBA from Harvard Business School, he worked his way up to becoming a vice-

---

* See chapter 18 for a full account of the war.

president at Morgan Stanley in New York before taking over the family business, Kinnevik Group, in 1977, the year both his father and his older brother died. At that time the company was an old-fashioned conglomerate of diverse holdings in farming, sugar factories, lumber and steel. Stenbeck quickly converted the group into an international holding that included telecommunications, media, finance, IT and the Internet, and within a short time it was listed on the Stockholm Exchange and on Nasdaq.

Jonathan believed what his father was telling him was interesting, but after the initial research he allowed the matter to drift. He was brought abruptly to order by a telephone call. 'It was more of an *eruption* than a phone call,' Jonathan recalled ruefully. 'He wanted me to get on with it.'

Murdoch MacLennan was also on the receiving end of a call from Vere, but he remembered the tone as being 'more exasperated than ferocious'. It was August. MacLennan was mid-budget. It was 'a terrible time' to consider a new project. He nevertheless found himself on a plane to Stockholm a short time later, alongside Jonathan, the two of them charged with finding out more about the Swedish *Metro* and how it worked.

MacLennan had managed to locate a former editor of the newspaper, Thomas Grahl, who had also been managing director of the newspaper. Unusually able and deeply intelligent, he was an independent thinker even by Swedish standards. Significantly, he had been sacked for his confrontational style in dealing with upper management, a fact he was hardly ashamed of and communicated freely to anyone who seemed interested.

On 12 August he, Jonathan and Murdoch all went to dinner together at La Famiglia, a small Italian restaurant chosen by Grahl, one that was popular in Stockholm with journalists and media types. There Grahl outlined in his deliberate Swedish way how such a newspaper could be organised and the pitfalls of the operation, most notably the protracted negotiations with the Underground that would be required in order to gain distribution rights. Said Grahl,

> I hadn't been able to understand MacLennan when he called me earlier because of his Scottish accent. And now Jonathan was gregariously laying out his plans openly in the restaurant. Stockholm is a small city where everybody knows one another and I was acutely aware of people I knew around me. Anthropologically, these two were from a different world. But I said, 'Well, if you want to see how it works, go down early the next morning.'

The two men did as Grahl suggested. What they saw was an entire underground populace, reading one newspaper intently for the duration of their journey to work. That newspaper was *Metro*.

When Jonathan told his father about the experience a few nights later he could barely restrain his enthusiasm. He told him he was convinced a London *Metro* would be a viable business opportunity and he wanted to go for it. 'I half think I should go it alone on this and just do it myself,' he told his father.

Vere, with the consummate logic that had characterised his entire career, made what for him was the obvious answer: 'But by doing it with Associated and DMGT, you *will* be doing it yourself, because ...*you own the company.*'

The London *Metro* may have been Vere's idea, but it was Jonathan's baby and to his way of thinking founding it was not a defensive move. It was a hot business opportunity for which he could scarcely contain his enthusiasm. For the next few months, from wherever he happened to be in the company at the time, Jonathan began the relentless pushing that was to become the salient characteristic of his leadership style.

Thomas Grahl was hired to spearhead the operation. For a time he *was* the project. He came over from Stockholm in mid-September 1997, holing up in a small office – 'it was more of a wedge that an office' – on the sixth floor of Northcliffe House. Here he worked in total isolation.

'I was this small secret fry, doing a feasibility brief and a business plan explaining the concept of *Metro* for the Finance Committee and later for the Board of Directors,' said Grahl.

The idea behind *Metro* was deceptively simple. The free sheet was to cover the news of the day, it went without saying. But it also had to be a quality production – not 'throwaway trash' like many free sheets, but something that looked good and that people wanted to read. It was to be produced by a small group of capable sub-editors, perhaps twenty to fifty in all, who would use wire services and photographs to bring out an interesting short read of news, features and sports. The paper's most salient characteristic would be a complete absence of political bias. And, most important, it would offer all this in the length of time it took to make a short trip on the Underground.

It was this last feature that had so attracted Jonathan to the project, because he immediately recognised the concept. It had been the organising principle behind the first issue of the *New York World* on the first day of the twentieth century. And it had been created by Alfred Harmsworth, later Viscount Northcliffe, Jonathan's great-great-uncle, when Joseph

Pulitzer invited the young newspaper publisher to produce the 'Newspaper of the Twentieth Century'. Then Alfred's slogan had been 'All the news in sixty seconds'.

Now Jonathan's slogan would be, 'All the news in twenty minutes', the length of the average tube ride to work, and it would become the newspaper of the twenty-first century.

During the first two months he worked on *Metro* the only people at Associated who knew of Thomas Grahl's existence were Jonathan, Murdoch, David English, Kevin Beatty, then managing director of the *Mail on Sunday* – and of course Vere. But even though these individuals knew about Grahl's existence, they knew little about the man.

For one thing Thomas Grahl was Swedish, speaking practically perfect but formal English, which he had taught himself after he became a journalist. Another little-known fact about Grahl was that he was a Fulbright Scholar who had spent two years in the United States, where he took a Master's degree in journalism. Still another – he was an exceedingly religious man, a member of the Pentecostal Church whose devotion to the evangelical cause was unflagging. His bright, casual manner in some ways camouflaged a highly ethical way of thinking that dominated his every action.

In this most secret of projects, Grahl was eventually joined by Ian Pay, who had been managing director of both the *Mail on Sunday* and the *Evening Standard*. Ian went to work alongside Thomas on a day-to-day basis, the two men moving to a secret office at 1000 Great West Road in Brentford. The pair were charged with the onerous task of convincing the London Underground that it would be safe, desirable and financially rewarding to give Associated Newspapers rights for the distribution of the London *Metro*.

It was decided that David English and Murdoch MacLennan would make first contact, thus placing negotiations on the appropriate corporate level. But they were surprised by the indifference they encountered. Safety issues alone precluded the possibility of such a venture, they were told. And in any case the money they were offering was insufficient.

It was now up to Thomas Grahl and Ian Pay to convince the Underground they had been too hasty in their first reaction. Kevin Beatty explained:

> These two guys were heroes. Thomas Grahl had real experience doing this with the Stockholm tube, and he was able to talk knowledgeably about the Underground's concerns and biases. And Ian Pay, as a commercial

manager, was able to impress them with his credentials in producing a good quality newspaper, something they were clearly worried about. The two men plodded away. They were methodical and practical. But it was an uphill grind.

A seemingly insurmountable concern of the Underground was the fire hazard presented by having tens of thousands of newspapers piled in bundles in each station. Nobody was forgetting the fire at King's Cross on 18 November 1987 that had taken the lives of thirty-one people. It was up to Associated to prove their newspaper was safe. So Ian Pay contacted Phil Dimes, the Quality Assurance manager at Associated, with a tall order – he hoped Dimes would be able to prove that newsprint wouldn't burn.

Before he came to Associated, Dimes had worked for the Printing Industry Research Association and through them, he became familiar with the Fire Research Association (FRS). Along with several similar research facilities, that organisation was created at the end of World War Two to get industry back on its feet. As an independent authority, the FRS carried more credibility than Associated, which was an interested party, Dimes said. And besides, Dimes was haunted by an image of him and his staff appearing in a home-made video, running around setting fires in their laboratory coats and 'looking like the Keystone Cops'.

He therefore recommended they pay the £3000-plus fee charged by the FRS to make the tests and to provide a professional film crew to video the results. In March 1998 Phil Dimes and Ian Pay drove up the M1 to Garston near Watford, where the FRS Burn Hall was located. Ian Pay said,

> It was here we would try to set fire to bundles of newspapers, hoping the newsprint would not explode, or create any pungent odours, or in fact burn. It seemed at the time a forlorn hope.

The first of the two tests involved the Calorimetric Measures of Heat Usage Rate, in other words, how much oxygen, carbon dioxide, monoxide, formaldehyde and nitrogen oxide a fire generated from bundles of burning newsprint would produce. But after three top sheets of the test bundle burned, the ashes blocked the flame and it went out. Since the bundles wouldn't catch fire, no toxic gases were emitted.

The second test, the Propane Burner Test, was more drastic. Four bundles of two stacks of newspapers one metre high were placed three inches apart, and a 4-radiant panel propane burner connected to a gigantic bottle of propane gas was directed towards them. Dimes said,

I thought, here's where it's all going to go horribly wrong. If you had walked between the two stacks, you would have been burned alive ...But in the event, only the top sheets burst into flames before a black pile of ash put out the fire. There was scorching on the front and sides of the stacks, and after a while they began listing, but they didn't burn. Forty-five minutes passed, then sixty, and we all realised that the improbable was true. Newsprint in bundles wasn't easy to set alight.

The men drove back down the M1 in a state of disbelief. Even though the tests had far surpassed their greatest hopes, it was hard to get their brains around it. Bundles of newsprint were essentially not flammable, and presented no clear and present danger in tube stations – hard though that was to grasp.

The professional videos of the fire test went a long way towards convincing Underground officials that newspapers could be safely distributed at tube stations. But they were equally concerned about loose sheets flying about. The idea of stapling had been around for a long time, but it was Thomas Grahl who put it into operation on *Metro*. Besides satisfying the concerns of the tube negotiators, it also would give the free sheet an ultra-upmarket look, one that would only enhance the product.

Another feature that contributed much towards convincing officials to come on board was Associated's offer of a one-page free advertisement with content to be decided by the Underground. It was a unique marketing opportunity, Ian Pay explained, with an entirely new product, one not to be missed. So this possibility of daily contact with travellers became increasingly attractive to the Underground officials, perhaps as attractive as any revenue the free newspaper might generate. Altogether, the package was becoming too alluring to reject. When the agreement was concluded near the end of 1998, Pay and Grahl had a lot to congratulate themselves over.

'Now we steam ahead,' Ian Pay remembered thinking. *Wrong*, it turned out. *Now* the two men had to assemble bins for 350,000 newspapers in 267-odd stations, and they had to be specially constructed, conforming to fire authority requirements.

But the biggest blow was that each tube station manager had to be won over to *Metro* individually. It was all well and good for the system to come to a favourable decision, one manager explained to Ian Pay, but he was the man who was accountable if something went wrong. Exasperated but undeterred, Thomas Grahl began mapping out individual stations, determining alongside the station managers the most sensible placement of bins and eventually getting them into position.

It would turn out that on the day of the launch the process was far from complete. But Associated rushed in individual distributors at tube stations where bins had not yet been installed.

'How did we do it?' Ian asked at the end of the day. 'Persistence and heartbreak. A lot of heartbreak. We promised the advertising industry a circulation of 350,000 and at the beginning they only got 180,000. Regardless of that they hung on. They could sense this was going to be a winner.'

On 10 June 1998 David English died unexpectedly of a stroke. The shock was devastating to the staff at Associated, but much more so to Vere Rothermere, who had worked with David for twenty-seven years. There was no question as to who would replace David English as editor-in-chief. It would be his protégé Paul Dacre, whom David had been grooming for a leadership post for over twenty years. But Vere was for a time paralysed and it wasn't until 16 July that Dacre was actually named to the position.

What this meant in terms of *Metro* was not immediately clear. But if a launch date early in 1999 was to be realised, there could be no slowdown. Recruitment of staff became the next urgent item on the agenda and management went forward.

Because of the strict secrecy of the project recruitment was being conducted by Charles Paterson of the London agency Search and Selection. The management at Associated assembled a panel to choose a launch editor from the candidates put forward by Paterson. Thomas Grahl, who believed the prototype for the London *Metro* would be similar to the Swedish *Metro* he had installed in Stockholm, was strongly in favour of hiring a woman candidate who was editor and director of the Guardian Media Group's provincial daily, the *Reading Evening Post*.

Kim Chapman had a background as a troubleshooter. She had made a career of taking over ailing newspapers, turning them around, reinvigorating them and returning them to profit. She had redesigned, restaffed and relaunched a number of such papers and, most important, 'made money'. The forty-three-year-old was also forthright and articulate, likeable and charismatic.

She seemed to Thomas Grahl the ideal candidate to launch the London *Metro*. Murdoch MacLennan also saw Chapman as 'a bright prospect'. Having passed the scrutiny of the panel, Chapman was pencilled in to meet David English, but because of David's death that interview never took place.

Meanwhile, Paul Dacre was working his way to the surface of his new position and became aware for the first time of the secret project. In those early days the fact that it was continuing apace and to a large extent independent of his input didn't bother him. He didn't feel passed over. He though of the project as 'a managerial thing, a free paper, OK. At sixteen hours a day, I had enough on my plate.' He accepted that it was a wonderful idea and put it at the back of his mind.

But even though the panel agreed Kim Chapman would be good as launch editor, she wasn't offered a job. The search was continuing when Associated Newspapers was dealt a second blow.

Vere Rothermere died of a heart attack on 1 September. That Vere died so soon after David English seemed highly significant at Associated Newspapers. In a way, every employee felt directly affected and all were set reeling. To Thomas Grahl, the outsider, it seemed as if Jonathan simply disappeared from the *Metro* project for a couple of months and even his colleague Ian Pay couldn't seem to shake his grief.

Pay had been working with Vere since the launch of the *Mail on Sunday* in 1982 and Grahl, who had never met the proprietor, became acutely aware that a giant had passed. But even despite this loss, the project went forward.

By November 1998 no candidate had been found whose credentials satisfied the panel as much as those of Kim Chapman and she was again approached. This time she was officially offered the job of launch editor for the project. She accepted and in a whirlwind of activity resigned her job at Reading, moved to London and began work setting up computer systems and links to output the material. She had never started from scratch before and the challenge was exhilarating.

By now Grahl and Pay had moved to a 'displacement' office in Surrey Quays that had been set up for the use of the staff of the *Daily Mail* or the *Mail on Sunday* in case of emergency. Chapman moved in with them, along with Nic Morrison, deputy night editor of the *Daily Mail* and launch editor of the *Daily Mail* in Scotland. The plan was to hire twenty-two journalists and that task was urgent. But Chapman knew what she was looking for. In an article in the *UK Press Gazette*, published after the announcement of the project, Chapman was quoted as saying,

> Everybody who works for us has to have the capability of doing each other's jobs. They have to be able to slot in if someone's off.

The tabloid, she continued, would be 'a distillation of news down to its essence for people who use the tube'. And in a reference to the Stockholm style of *Metro* that Thomas Grahl was planning, she added that there would be 'lots and lots of stories'.

It must have been at about this point that, as Paul Dacre remembered it, 'the alarm bells went'. He said,

> I kept asking to see a dummy. We didn't have a dummy. I got a few isolated pages with no overall pace, no target market, no shape. I was acutely aware that I was the new editor-in-chief and Jonathan the new proprietor. It could be very damaging if it flopped. The clock started ticking.

While Paul Dacre was shifting into gear on the basis of the dummy he had seen, the question was, 'Which dummy had he seen?'

In all, three dummies were floating, each intended for a different purpose. The first had been drawn up by Ian Pay with the help of the Slough-based advertising agency Clarke Hooper that Pay had worked with on previous occasions. Pay used the dummy with potential advertisers at a series of breakfasts to promote the London *Metro*. A second dummy had been prepared by Thomas Grahl with the help of the same agency. Grahl was using his dummy in the continuing negotiations with Underground officials to reassure them the paper was a proper one, devoid of lewd photographs of 'Page Three Girls' and the like.

A third dummy was in the process of being prepared by Kim Chapman and Nic Morrison, with the assistance of a brilliant editorial designer John Hill, a consultant who had worked successfully with the *Evening Standard*. It was in all likelihood the third dummy that Dacre saw. But the existence of the other two was probably clouding the overall plan for the free newspaper.

Paul Dacre didn't know Kim Chapman well. He had interviewed her twice, referring to her privately as 'a feisty girl' whose spirit he clearly admired. But he must have sensed she came out of an editorial and business ethos very different from his own.

To Dacre, with over twenty-five years of experience on Fleet Street, running a newspaper was like running a military campaign. His language was peppered with terms like 'my war council' and 'my trusted lieutenants'. He had a siege mentality and not without reason. 'Cut-throat' was a euphemism for the practices commonly employed on the Street. When one added in the Left–Right political biases of each of the London dailies, the atmosphere was most often poisonous. Vere had always referred to the newspaper business as 'open warfare'. Others in the field believed that the editor of a London daily was the last bastion of the dictator in a democratic society.

But Chapman had always worked on an egalitarian model. She set a brief for her team and people contributed to it creatively. Using this model, she had enjoyed a large measure of success. But would her method work in Fleet Street?

At the same time Thomas Grahl was having a hard time understanding why his Swedish model wasn't directly applicable in Britain. It was a high-quality, upmarket, spot-news approach, with a layout more diverse that the public in London was accustomed to seeing. But Grahl could see no reason why something different shouldn't work, and work well, in a new environment.

'Would that dummy have worked in Fleet Street?' Alistair Sinclair asked rhetorically.

'My professional instinct told me no.' As deputy editor on the *Mail*, Sinclair was part of the triumvirate Dacre always consulted before making final decisions.

As the second member of Dacre's ruling élite, Sinclair's great gift was his uncanny ability to strip an issue down to its essentials. He was deliberate and clear in his statements, but the overwhelming impression he gave was of a man having trouble bottling up his energy. He was a Type A personality in the guise of a Type B.

'*Metro* was a new concept in the market,' he said. 'It was a newspaper for the most discerning city in the world. On top of that, it had to appeal to people who didn't buy newspapers. It was a tall order – actually more difficult to achieve than launching a paid newspaper. And we were only going to get one chance at it.'

The third member of Dacre's 'war council' was Peter Wright. At the time he was consulted, Wright had been editor of the *Mail on Sunday* for just under three months. He was working from 9 in the morning until 9.30 at night and in his words, 'everything was a blur'. He was deeply involved in the process of killing off the Sunday newspaper's existing television listings and relaunching *Night & Day* in its stead.

The *Mail on Sunday* itself was being expanded from 104 to 128 pages and Wright was involved in making the strategic decision to move the review section back into the centre of the paper in order 'to make sense of 128 pages'. On the day he was first consulted on *Metro,* he was trying to solve the costing problems involved in a new, revamped *Night & Day.*

He was nevertheless intrigued by the novelty of *Metro* and by necessity came on to the council more as a sounding board for the ideas of the others than as an active participant in the process. Unlike Dacre, whose swift forward movement can be overwhelming, or Sinclair, whose stark honesty can be daunting, Wright's strength lies in his ability to give a reflective assessment on urgent matters. In looking over the dummy Paul and Alistair had already been poring over, Wright took his time, as was his way. Eventually he gave his opinion. Peter Wright thought the dummy 'extremely *worthy*'.

In the jargon of Fleet Street the word 'worthy' connotes a thoughtful, measured approach; intelligent, balanced and deserving of merit. It says, above all, that the project is worthwhile and even inspirational.

In other words it is the kiss of death.

TWENTY-SEVEN

A NATIONAL CONCEPT

Paul Dacre now unleashed the full fury of his talent on the *Metro* project. Using his office as the unofficial *Metro* headquarters, he began working one-on-one with the designer John Hill and the two of them laid out the altered dummies on Paul's coffee table. They were joined by Alistair Sinclair and Peter Wright. Given the punishing schedules of the élite triumvirate, who still had newspapers to publish, the work was fast and furious, done in a rush 'and all the better for it', Dacre would say later.

The new *Metro* would appeal to upwardly mobile Londoners, young people who sought an active social life. This audience tended to live in flats, they were gainfully employed and they were technologically astute. Turned off by politics, they wanted news without spin. Dacre said,

> I knew the young hated heavy politics and so *Metro* could have no ideology. It would be a politically free zone, a class-free read. We would use extensive graphics and lots of colour. This paper had to be totally different from our different products, but have the indisputable signature of Associated Newspapers.
>
> But two weeks before launch I knew something was missing. It came to me over the weekend. *Listings*! We had to have a middle section totally designed for youth and their leisure activities, with listings for clubs, theatres and sports events. We called it 'Metro Life' and it eventually included TV listings as well so readers would carry the newspaper home.

Alistair Sinclair, along with a number of specialists from the *Daily Mail* staff, was seconded to Surrey Quays and charged with putting the new plans into operation. Sinclair began a work schedule that started at 7.30 in the morning and ended with his falling into bed at 1 a.m. in a nearby hotel where he stayed for the duration.

By now, Jonathan was very much back on the scene as the project's main mover and shaker. But everything had changed. Now he carried the burden of power and responsibility that attached to being the new proprietor of the Daily Mail and General Trust.

'Paul hadn't been interested in *Metro* at first,' Jonathan said, 'but then he decided to come in.' Jonathan was well aware that Dacre's invasion of *Metro* was creating conflicts, but from years of watching his father run DMGT and Associated Newspapers, he was less dismayed than he might have been. He said later,

> Having 'yes men' around doesn't really give you the focus and commitment you need. So the firm has always had strong characters in it. You get big explosions from these characters, but we have always allowed diverse points of view …
>
> The level of competition in Fleet Street is robust, even more so inside the firm. Conflict is part of the process. Results are what matter and the successful outcome of these open conflicts can be seen in the brilliant products we produce.

The conflicts would culminate in what Alistair Sinclair later termed 'a fairly bloody few weeks'. At their end Kim Chapman was out. She was offered a different position, that of publisher of *Metro*, but she declined the job, choosing instead to leave the company. Soon thereafter she joined a small media group where she designed a new free newspaper, simultaneously becoming managing director of the group's local radio station in Basingstoke. In these twin positions she and her launch team worked together to create a 'Sight and Sound', a concept new to the British media while significantly boosting the audience of the station.

As to Grahl, he was appalled by what he called 'the inelegant ousting' of Chapman as editor. He also felt sorely the modification of his original prototype, and he resigned from his position as editorial and development director of London Metro Ltd. He was offered a different position at Associated, which he declined, and accepted another, which, in the end, failed to materialise.

It was sometimes thought in London that Grahl was bitter about his experience on the project. But that was not true. From the distance of time, he viewed it as fascinating, with characters he had never seen the likes of before. 'In the end,' he said, 'we all played our part in producing a completely new newspaper, and a very successful one at that.'

In autumn 1998, independent of the dramatic events now unfolding on *Metro*, Ian MacGregor, news editor at the *Daily Mail* for the past three years, wrote a letter to Paul Dacre. In it he said he felt ready for a new challenge. He heard nothing in return. Then, one morning the following February, Dacre called MacGregor into his office.

By afternoon, he found himself riding in a taxi to Surrey Quays with Alistair Sinclair to meet his new staff. He had been named launch editor of the new give-away newspaper *Metro*. MacGregor said,

> I was completely surprised. I knew about *Metro's* existence because I had read about it in the *UK Press Gazette*. Beyond that I had heard nothing. I was to put into practice, starting then, the ideas of Paul and Alistair.

Although he was only thirty-seven years old at the time, MacGregor had an impressive journalistic background. For sixteen months he had been New York correspondent for the *Daily Express* and was just finishing a stint back in London as that newspaper's deputy news editor when he was talent-spotted by the *Daily Mail*. He came in as deputy news editor but soon advanced to the post of news editor where his solid work attracted the attention of the *Mail* editorial staff.

Now MacGregor was joined by others from the *Daily Mail* – Jackie Annesley from 'Femail', Rory Clements from 'Good Health' and the then backbencher David Monk, as well as several other staff members. Those staff members who had been hired by Kim Chapman were already in place and, according to her brief, they were young and flexible. 'But they did well,' MacGregor said later. 'More than three-fifths stayed the course. And it was difficult, because their game plan had changed.'

MacGregor was astonished by their dedication. He put two people on the sports desk to edit four and six pages, and when it became eight pages he put on one more. What they and the other staff were doing was 'selecting what were the main stories of the day and deciding how to develop them'. Said MacGregor,

> We used the wire services, television, radio and the Internet.
>
> At the beginning we were doing the listings ourselves. And we could have no mistakes. Every day we were reading and rereading the copy. It was hard graft but it was great. It was exciting, the most exciting times of our careers.
>
> Our target audience were the Internet generation and when we ran promotions we would get as many as 60,000 entries per day, all by e-mail.

Metro was launched on 16 March 1999, more or less 'by stealth', as the catchphrase became. The new free daily was bucking a 6 per cent decline in overall newspaper circulation and the pundits were frankly sceptical it could succeed. It was generally considered that the newspaper would be a cheap production, little more than a spoiler. But when the finished product appeared the critics were dumbfounded. It was a polished, highly professional newspaper, commensurate in its own way with the *Mail* itself.

But almost from the beginning *Metro* was losing money. According to Jonathan: 'This was to be expected...But we were losing at a rate of about £1 million a week.'

In August 1999, at a time when Fleet Street pundits were still betting one way or the other on the free sheet's survival, Ian Pay, who had launched *Metro*, retired from Associated Newspapers. In his place was a young man Pay had hired in 1989 as a client sales executive on the *Mail on Sunday*. Since then Mike Anderson had steadily climbed the ladder in the advertising field, carving out an outstanding record for himself. But Mike believed the most useful experience he had in the field was as the marketing director at New PHD, where he helped win the UK's largest strategic planning account, British Telecom.

Anderson was an adherent of a basic tenet that had been developed at New PHD. In a nutshell, it held that the media had become more fragmented and as a result the simple concept of advertising during 'prime time' was no longer relevant. Instead, it was necessary to implement strategic planning. It was this principle, Mike believed, that helped him to recognise that *Metro* was the most exciting product of the fourteen newspapers published each day in London.

One morning at 5 a.m., Mike made the rounds with the distribution van, stopping at last at Waterloo Underground station, where 22,000 copies of *Metro* were distributed every day. As he watched the feeding frenzy at the bins, Mike realised that 'We were twenty minutes in people's lives!' he said. 'We weren't a newspaper, we were a moment.'

Thus was born the concept of the '*Metro* Moment'. It was a young reading audience, Mike realised. They were employed, affluent and were giving twenty minutes of undivided attention to *Metro*. They were reading their newspapers in the morning, leaving plenty of reaction time during the rest of the day. This was a very attractive proposition for advertisers.

Later, Mike came up with the concept of 'Young Urban Britain', and they became *Metro*'s reading audience.

Anderson pointed out that he had promised Ian MacGregor he wouldn't sell too many ads, 'and make his newspaper into a free ad sheet. Well, I kept that promise.' In so doing *Metro* had weathered the storm and in the first year the newspaper broke even.

Quietly, and indeed, very much 'by stealth', the newspaper began to take off. And grudgingly the very critics who had predicted its demise were forced to admit that it looked as if it were going to survive. Everyone at Associated breathed a little easier.

By November 1999 Ian MacGregor, who had been spending every minute on the project, felt able to celebrate Guy Fawkes Day with his family. On Bonfire Night, he and his wife Fiona Knight were just setting off with their baby son to a celebration when Ian heard the phone go. 'It was Paul Dacre,' Ian said,

> and he told me they wanted to launch in Manchester.
>
> 'When?' I asked.
>
> 'Next week,' he answered.
>
> So I spent the rest of Bonfire Night on the telephone calling staff to get them ready to go up in the morning.
>
> We took the train, a chap from Systems, a group of news reporters, a couple of staff members from the *Daily Mail*, and we planned the new newspaper out on the train.
>
> The *Daily Mail* has a centrally located office in Manchester. It has no windows and there were twelve of us with eight computers. We just piled into it and we all worked at one big table under unbelievable conditions. And the whole thing was done right there in secret.

The new provincial crew stayed at the Victoria Hotel, and Paul Dacre and Alistair Sinclair made a flying visit to the city to see how they were getting on.

Six days later they launched in Manchester.

For the first time since *Metro* began, the staff was meeting competition head on. The local newspaper, the *Manchester Evening News*, was fighting back with everything they had, launching their own *Metro* on the same day as MacGregor's team. Newspapers flooded the streets of Manchester, bombarding readers with vying headlines.

The opposing distribution teams each took up the cudgels of their own side and Associated's staff soon had the euphoric feeling they were at the centre of the universe. It was the stuff of newspaper legends and, as such, immensely exciting to the young staff.

They were soon dealt a blow, however; the title *Metro* in fact belonged to Greater Manchester Newspapers Ltd, a Guardian Media subsidiary who owned their competitor, the *Manchester Evening News*. A quick emergency meeting was called, where new names for *Metro* were considered. Mike Anderson said,

I wanted to call our newspaper '*Blue*', the colour of our masthead. Others suggested names like '*Orange*' or '*More Than*'. Everybody had an idea for a funky name. But what we came to was *News Northwest*. And everybody got used to it.

But even though they lost the title, in the minds of the editorial staff there was still a sense of exhilaration and triumph. Alistair Sinclair said,

Although we were the invaders, the reality was that the readers were keener to get their hands on our paper. We spoke to them and treated them as sophisticated young people. The *Evening News*'s paper wasn't that different from their own newspaper. It was local and almost didactic in its approach that local was good.

The *News Northwest* kept to the original London brief, to appeal to Young Urban Britain, and an almost cult-like reverence for the Associated product resulted. They were the trendy invaders, the wave of the future, and the staff knew and savoured the fact.

At the same time MacGregor was launching in Manchester, his deputy Kenny Campbell, who later was to become editor of *Metro*, was launching a Scottish edition for Edinburgh and Glasgow.

Associated's Manchester launch had taken place on 12 November 1999. By the end of the month, Edinburgh and Glasgow were also under siege. Birmingham was only a few days behind, with a 29 November start-up date. Six months later, in June of 2000, Newcastle was added, and Leeds in January of 2001. But even though the newspaper was popular with readers, to the local newspapers it was an act of war.

What had impelled Associated to launch so quickly in virtually every city in the North large enough to support a free newspaper? What had started this war?

It was rumoured that the Swedes, that is, Modern Times Group, intended to launch in Newcastle.

But when MTG's dreaded Newcastle launch did finally come about, the first issue showed that they were out of their depth in the British market. Said Mike Anderson, 'They led with the riots in Korea and that's hardly tops on Newcastle's list of high-interest topics.' Not only that, but they used the original approach of the Swedish *Metro*, packing 188 stories into twenty-four pages. To the practised eyes of the professionals at Associated it was clear that it was only a matter of time before the Swedes would fail in Newcastle.

Complicating the matter was a mighty legal battle. When MTG

launched in Newcastle, Associated Newspapers 'rushed into court and got an interim injunction against MTG, to stop them using the title *Metro*. And we won,' said Harvey Kass, legal director of the firm. But in another similar action a different outcome had resulted. 'In Manchester, where the local newspaper already held a weekly *Metro* title we lost,' Kass continued. This resulted in the earlier renaming of *Metro* as *News Northwest* and Manchester became the only city in which *Metro* was owned by someone other than Associated.

Like everyone else involved in the provinces, Neil Jagger, then circulation director of the *Evening Standard*, was drafted into the project at short notice. He had two and a half weeks to set up the distribution for the newspaper in Birmingham. For Jagger, who found himself working seventy hours straight, it was 'the most exciting time of my career. I didn't sleep because of a great adrenalin rush. It was too exciting to sleep.'

In record time he negotiated the distribution points. Lord Rothermere was attending a Northcliffe conference near Birmingham and he rang Jagger saying, 'Take me out to see the distribution in the city.'

The next morning, some time before 5 a.m., Jagger picked up Jonathan at his hotel, hoping that 'everything would be perfect for a visit from the chairman'. As Jagger remembered it,

> The copies were out and gone to all the bus and rail stations. There were 150 merchandisers giving the newspaper away at the main traffic junctions. And it was *great* on the streets. There were tactical battles, they were all jumping ahead of the bus queue in car parks, hotels … There were papers everywhere.

After seeing all this, Jonathan asked Jagger to take him to breakfast at a greasy spoon and Jagger headed towards Mr Egg, a place frequented by fruit and vegetable market workers, truckers, people who've been to all-night raves, the whole range.

It was all the same, in the words of Murdoch MacLennan, 'a tough time'. Associated was at war every place in the North where *Metro* had launched except in Glasgow and Edinburgh.

It was at this point that Associated's main competitor, Philip Graf, Chief Executive of Trinity Mirror, came up with the simple but brilliant idea of working together through a 'franchise', as the agreements eventually became known. Simply put, each party played to its strengths.

Trinity Mirror would take care of local advertising, distribution and printing in return for a share of the national advertising, and Associated would provide the editorial expertise, marketing and national sales.

It was ground-breaking stuff and one that allowed both parties to benefit. Very quickly all the regionals owned by Trinity Mirror soon signed up for the deal, leaving only the Guardian-owned Greater Manchester Newspapers group outstanding. And before long even they came in for the ride.

As the franchise idea took hold, entirely new possibilities came over the horizon and the company has been investigating them ever since. *Metro* had succeeded beyond the wildest dreams of anybody – except perhaps Jonathan himself.

In reflecting on this success, the new chairman of DMGT eventually believed that the entire *Metro* experience came down to the quality of the people who had worked on it. 'It's our staff. Our people are brilliant and highly professional. And one way and another, they made it work.' Of the new partnerships, he said,

With the new franchise arrangement, we broke even much more quickly than anyone thought possible. I fundamentally believe that if you produce a good newspaper which people like reading, that is *relevant* and entertaining, you will succeed.

Today *Metro* is the largest free newspaper in the world, the sixth largest newspaper in the country. *Metro* has won a host of awards, including 'the Media Brand of the Year 2000' from *MediaWeek*; 'Medium of the Year 2000' from *Campaign*; 'Best Morning Newspaper' of 2001 by the Plain English Campaign – to name only a few.

Metro has a circulation approaching a million. Just as important, it has the highest profile of readers in work in the country, with 72 per cent of its audience employed. Some 64 per cent have a desirable ABC1 profile and 74 per cent are under the age of forty-four. 'It is the profile every newspaper in the country wants,' said Mike Anderson, 'nothing short of breathtaking.'

This was the last great vision of the late Vere Rothermere, who 'once again turned out to be prophetic', as Murdoch MacLennan put it.

A result of the unwavering and energetic support of Vere's son Jonathan, the newspaper continues a tradition begun over a hundred years ago when Alfred Harmsworth, later Viscount Northcliffe, and his brother Harold, later first Viscount Rothermere, published their first newspaper. Then as now, the critics predicted that the Harmsworths would come to grief. Then as now they were wrong.

The Harmsworth newspaper publishing dynasty is the longest-lasting in the history of the British press – a triumph of the past, a harbinger of the future.

EPILOGUE

For over a quarter of a century David English and Vere Rothermere shared a common goal – to seize the middle market of the national press and make it their own.

Theirs was a different world from that of 1896, when Alfred Harmsworth and his brother Harold confounded the sages of Fleet Street by founding the *Daily Mail*. By 1971, when David and Vere sealed their alliance, the news business had changed drastically.

Broadcasting had overtaken print, the unions had a stranglehold on newspaper production and many believed the national press was finished. It was in this difficult climate that the two men relaunched the dying *Daily Mail* as a tabloid, in a win-or-lose-all gamble that might have ended the dynasty then and there. But they won and, in so doing, they defined a new middle-market audience for the *Daily Mail*. It was aimed at women readers, but somehow caught the imagination of men as well.

Time and again, during the years he led the company, Vere's courage held. From the relaunch of the *Daily Mail*, to the launching of the *Mail on Sunday*, to the war between the London *Daily News* and *Evening Standard*, Vere stood pat in the face of potentially ruinous losses. Again, during the takeover of Associated Newspapers by the Daily Mail and General Trust and the modernisation programme for the national and provincial titles, Vere did not falter. His last legacy to the company was the idea for the London *Metro*, which his son Jonathan carried out after his father's death.

Vere did what he set out to do: restore the failing prospects of the company. When he died in 1998, his titles were secure and the business on a firm footing. Even his worst critics admitted his record was unassailable. At his memorial service at Westminster Abbey, attended by his family, friends, business associates and the leaders of the land, Vere Rothermere emerged as a worthy successor to the press dynasty founded by his great-uncle Northcliffe and his grandfather Rothermere.

But the world was changing at a rate difficult to imagine. It was a time for young men, with rapid-fire reactions to technological change. When

David English died, Vere Rothermere knew his day was done. He had done everything he could. It was a new age.

Just before his death and speaking on behalf of Vere and himself, David English told how the two friends wanted to be remembered.

He said then, 'We are the men who saved the *Daily Mail*.'

CHAPTER SOURCES

Note about Titles

Both David English and Vere Rothermere requested that their formal titles be dropped for this volume. For consistency's sake then, I have omitted the titles of the following individuals: Sir Neill and Lady Cooper-Key, Sir Larry Lamb, Sir Max Aitken, Sir Patrick Sergeant, Sir James Goldsmith, Sir Jocelyn Stevens, Sir Denis Hamilton, Lord Beaverbrook, Lord Goodman, Lord Matthews, Lord McAlpine, Lord Bell, Sir Bernard Ingham and Lord Rawlinson.

1: The Night of the Long White Envelopes

Books include *Tales of the Redundance Kid or the Bedside Barry Norman*, Van Nostrand Reinhold, Berkshire, England, 1975; Peter Black's unpublished MS, *The Saving of the Mail*, 1976; S. J. Taylor, *The Great Outsiders*, Weidenfeld & Nicolson, London, 1996, *The Reluctant Press Lord*, Weidenfeld & Nicolson, London, 1998.

Articles include Press Association, wire copy, 12 March 1971; John Womersley, 'The Born-Again *Daily Mail*', unpublished MS, 2 October 1998; leader, *Spectator*, 1 May 1971; Bernard Levin, 'Profit and Dishonour in Fleet Street', *The Times*, 16 May 1971.

Correspondence includes Mick Shields, managing director, Letter of Redundancy (prototype), 15 March 1971; Vere Harmsworth to the editor of the *Spectator*, n.d.

Interviews include Howard French, 21 May 1992; John Winnington-Ingram, 28 October 1998, 26 October 1999; Julian Holland, 19 May 1992; David English, 14 May 1992, 29 November 1992; John Womersley, 22, 28 November 1992, 19 October 1998; Alwyn Robinson, 29 April 1992; Iain Smith, 23 November 1992. Also included are Barry Norman, 21 April 1992; Peter Black, 7 September 1992; Peter Burden, 23 March, 30 July 1992; Rhona Churchill, 14 August 1992; Norman Garrod, 16 July 1992; Brian James, 16 April 1992; Bernard Levin, 14 April 1992. Several sources remain anonymous at their request.

The name of the publishing company changed several times during this period. I use Associated Newspapers throughout this volume for the sake of consistency and clarity.

2: Poison

Books include Esmé, Countess of Cromer, *From this Day Forward*, Thomas Harmsworth Publishing Co., Stoke Abbott, 1991, Unpublished Memoirs; S. J. Taylor, *The Great Outsiders,* Weidenfeld & Nicolson, London, 1996; Florence Oakley, Unpublished MS; S. J. Taylor, *The Reluctant Press Lord,* Weidenfeld & Nicolson, London, 1998.

Correspondence includes Harold Harmsworth to Esmond Harmsworth (letter), 23 May 1918; Esmond Harmsworth to Margaret Hunam (letter), Saturday, n.d.; Florence Oakley to Vere Rothermere, 19 January 1987.

Interviews include Vere Rothermere, 26 February 1997, Esmé, Countess of Cromer, 14 March 1992, 28 January 1998, 24 July 1998; Lady Cooper-Key, 2 February 1997; Florence Oakley, 6 November 1998; the late Aiden Crawley, 22 June 1992. Anonymous sources.

3: Terms of Endearment

Books include S. J. Taylor, *The Great Outsiders,* Weidenfeld & Nicolson, London, 1996; *The Reluctant Press Lord*, Weidenfeld & Nicolson, London, 1998; *The Diaries of Evelyn Waugh*, ed. Michael Davies, Weidenfeld & Nicolson, London, 1976.

Correspondence includes Frank Humphrey to Esmond Rothermere (letter), n.d. December 1940.

Interviews include Vere Rothermere; Lady Jeanne Campbell, 10 November 1998; Kathy Campbell, 10 January 1997; Jenny Willis, 10 October 1998. Anonymous source.

4: Every Woman Needs Her Daily Mail

Books and magazines include Peter Black, Unpublished MS; *Campaign*, 7 May 1971.

Business documents include David English, Advertising Briefing Guide; Minutes, Board of Directors, Associated Newspapers Group Ltd; Foot, Cone and Belding, Account Documents for *Daily Mail.*

Correspondence includes Esmond Rothermere to Vere Harmsworth (telegram), 30 March 1971; David English to Vere Harmsworth (letter), 23 September 1971.

Interviews include Vere Rothermere; Alwyn Robinson; John Winnington-Ingram; Dennis Ridley, 25 April 1992; Bill Muirhead, 8 July 1992; John Standen, 11 August 1992.

5: Shell Games

Books include S. J. Taylor, *The Great Outsiders,* Weidenfeld & Nicolson, London, 1996; *The Reluctant Press Lord*, Weidenfeld & Nicolson, London, 1998; Peter Mathias, *Takeover*, Maclean-Hunter Ltd, Toronto, 1976.

Interviews include Frank Ryan, 22 September 1992; Vere Rothermere; Bill Turner, 30 September 1992; Bob Morrow, 22 May 1992.

6: The Gloves Come Off

Books include Peter Black, Unpublished MS.

Articles include Brian Freemantle, 'Touchdown at Midnight', *Daily Mail*, 7 April 1975; 'The *Mail* Wins Damages over Airlift Libel', *Daily Mail*, 1 August 1979; 'The Lives of the Children Matter Most', (leader), *Evening News*, 7 April 1975.

Interviews include Stewart Steven, 23 November 2001; John Womersley; Anthea Disney, 28 September 1992; Ian Wooldridge, 1 May, 3 June, 1992; Paul Callan, 28 November 1992; Nigel Dempster, 20 March 1990; Brian Freemantle, 14 July 1992.

7: On the Road

Books include Zola Budd with Hugh Eley, *The Autobiography of Zola Budd*, Partridge Press, Transworld, London, 1989.

Articles include John Edwards, 'I Watch the Tanks Roll In', *Daily Mail*, 1 May 1975; Ann Leslie, 'What a Momentous Night to Remember', *Daily Mail*, 11 November 1989; Ian Wooldridge, 'We just wanted to weep alone', *Daily Mail*, 7 September 1972.

Interviews include John Edwards, 7 May 1992; Ann Leslie, 3 July 1992; Ian Wooldridge, 1 May, 3 June 1992; Brian Vine, 1 June 1992, 11 February 1992.

8: In Love with the Pig

Interviews include Phillip Moffitt, 17 December 1992; Charles Sinclair, 8 September, 23 November 1992; Clay Felker, 29 September 1992; Tom Shields, 26 June, 3 September 1992; Wilma Jordan, 29 September 1992.

9: The Montagues and the Capulets

Books include Lewis Chester and Jonathan Fenby, *The Fall of the House of Beaverbrook*, André Deutsch, London, 1979 and the Associated Newspaper Group Ltd, Annual Meeting Minutes Books for 4 March 1977.

Interviews include John Winnington-Ingram; Jocelyn Stevens, 16 September 1992; Vere Rothermere.

10: The Old David Was No More

Books include Lewis Chester and Jonathan Fenby, *The Fall of the House of Beaverbrook*, André Deutsch, London, 1979; Robert Harris, *Selling Hitler*, Faber and Faber, London, 1986, p. 368, quoting Rupert Murdoch.

Articles include Stewart Steven, 'World Exclusive Disclosure: MARTIN BORMANN ALIVE', *Daily Express*, 25 November 1972; Stewart Steven, 'HIDEOUT OF THE NAZI MAFIA!', *Daily Express*, 29 November 1972; Stewart Steven, 'Exclusive: Exposed – The Amazing Truth about Britain's State-owned Car Makers, WORLD-WIDE BRIBERY WEB BY LEYLAND', *Daily Mail*, 19 May 1977; *UK Press Gazette*, 30 May 1977, quoting MP Ian Wrigglesworth; David English, 'A Message from the Editor to *YOU* the Reader', *Daily Mail*, 25 May 1977.

Correspondence includes John Womersley to S. J. Taylor (letter), 3 September 1998; Peter Grover to S. J. Taylor (letter), 10 February 1993; Harry Longmuir to S. J. Taylor (letter), 11 May 1992.

Broadcasting sources include David English speaking on the BBC, *The Editor's TV Programme*, 26 June 1977.

Interviews include Charles Wintour, 2 July 1992; Jocelyn Stevens; Arnold Goodman, 1 July 1992; Ted Jeffery, 12 March 1991. Other interviews include Jonathan Holborow, 2 September 1992; Stewart Steven, 28 July 1992; John Womersley; Ina Miller, 9 December 1998; Dickie Herd, 8 May 1992; David English; Vere Rothermere. Anonymous sources.

11: Better than the Lot of Them

Books include Lewis Chester and Jonathan Fenby *The Fall of the House of Beaverbrook*, André Deutsch, London, 1979; Associated Newspaper Group Ltd, Annual Meeting Minutes Books, 1978; Bernard Ingham, *Kill the Messenger*, HarperCollins, London, 1991; Alistair McAlpine, *Once a Jolly Bag Man*, Weidenfeld & Nicolson, London, 1997.

Interviews include Gordon Greig, 27 February 1992; Charles Wintour; David English, 22 April 1998; Stewart Steven, 23 November 2001; Peter Wright, 21 November 2001; Peter Grover, 17 October 2001; Chris Nicholson, 1998; Alistair McAlpine, 18 January 2002; Tim Bell, 14 December 2001; Bernard Ingham, 27 November 2001.

In an interview with Sally Taylor on 22 April 1998, David English confirmed his intentions, saying he intended to write a book about his relationship with Thatcher after his retirement. SJT said, 'A book like that would fetch a lot of money.' 'Indeed,' he replied.

12: Trial by Menu

Books include Esmé, Countess of Cromer, Unpublished Memoirs; Jane Wolfe, *The Murchisons*, St Martin's Press, New York, 1989; Charles Wintour, *The Rise and Fall of Fleet Street*, Hutchinson, London, 1989.

One article is included: Vere Rothermere, 'My Father, a Man in a Million', *Evening News*, 13 July 1978.

Correspondence includes David English to Vere Harmsworth (letter), 19 March 1975; John Hemingway to Sally Taylor (letter), 21 December 2001.

Interviews include Nigel Dempster; Vere Rothermere; Tom Shields; David English; Sarah Holcroft, 22 December 1993. Also included are Bob Morrow, 1 October 1992; Esmé, Countess of Cromer; John Hemingway, 23 November 1999. Anonymous source.

13: Two Patricias

Articles include Frances Wheen, 'She Got a Kick from Champagne', *Vanity Fair*, November 1992; Paul Harris, 'Tributes to Lady Rothermere's Courage, Kindness and Loyalty: In Memory of a Woman Who Reached for the Sky', *Daily Mail*, 2 October 1992; Diary, *Daily Express*, 16 January 1978.

Interviews include Vere Rothermere; Jenny Willis, 10 October 1998; Richard Compton Miller, 3 September 1998, John Hemingway; Jonathan Rothermere, 20 February 1994, 24 January 2000; Camilla Yeates, 20 January 1994. Also included are Alwyn Robinson; Kathy Campbell, 10 January 2000; Vyvyan Harmsworth, 7 February 2000; Dr Sheila Rossan, psychologist, Brunel University, 26 January 2000; Dr Geoffrey Lloyd MD, FRCP, FRCPsych, Harley Street, London. Anonymous source.

14: David at His Best

One book is included: Peter Rawlinson, *A Price Too High*, Weidenfeld & Nicolson, London, 1989.

Articles include David English, 'We Fought Them, We Beat Them and We Shall Go On Fighting Them', *Daily Mail*, pp. 6–7, 1 April 1981. Also included were Warren Adler, 'They Took Away My Son and Then Raped His Mind', *Daily Mail*, 29 May 1978; 'Legend in His Own Lunchtime, Special Edition', *Daily Mail*; 22 September 1983.

Interviews include Alwyn Robinson; John Royle, 18 June 1992; Howard Sabin, 18 June 1992, Peter Rawlinson, 15 August 1992; Tom Plate, 7 October 1992. Also included were Jim Hoge, 7 October 1992, Gil Spenser, 7 October 1992; Anthea

Disney; Peter Grover, 3 April 1992; Brian Vine, 1 June 1992; Norman Heath, 31 March 1992; Colin Reid, 30 August 1992; Des Nichols, 25 November 1992.

15: Up the Down Escalator

Books include Harold Evans, *Good Times, Bad Times*, Weidenfeld & Nicolson, London, 1983; Associated Newspaper Group Ltd, Minutes, 23 January 1983.

Interviews include David English; Bernard Shrimsley, 10, 16 February 2000; John Winnington-Ingram; Bill Pressey, 23 May 1992; Stewart Steven; Vere Rothermere; David Kirkby, 29 July 1992; Gordon Greig, 27 February 1992; Norman Heath; Peter Grover; Graeme Thomson, 7 May 1992; Charles Sinclair.

16: Editor-in-Chief of What?

Interviews include David English; Jonathan Rothermere; Vere Rothermere; Peter Grover; Ian Pay, 19 June 1992; Genevieve Cooper, 11 June 1992; Julie Lowe, 5 June 1992; Michael Leese, 12 June 1992; Charles Sinclair.

17: The 'Lead-the-Horse-to-Water' Factor

Books include Donald Read, *The Power of News: The History of Reuters, 1849–1989*, Oxford University Press, Oxford, 1992; John Lawrenson and Lionel Barber, *The Price of Truth*, Mainstream Publishing, Edinburgh, 1985; Lewis Chester and Jonathan Fenby, *The Fall of the House of Beaverbrook*, André Deutsch, London, 1979. Also included are Richard Bourne, *The Lords of Fleet Street*, Unwin-Hyman Ltd, London, 1990; Sir Denis Hamilton, *Editor in Chief: Fleet Street Memoirs*, Hamish Hamilton, London, 1989.

Articles include Lionel Barber, 'Fleet Street's Billion Pound Scoop', *Sunday Times*, 12 July 1983; 'The Battle of the Barons', *Sunday Times*, 12 May 1985; Also included are G. V. W., 'Death of Baron de Reuter, Head of Great News Agency, Inconsolable Grief for his Wife', *Daily Mail*, 20 April 1915; Maggie Brown, 'Fleet Street's Pigeon Pie', *Guardian*, 10 June 1982; Michael Davie, 'Fleet Street gold rush', *Observer*, 18 September 1983; *Sunday Times*, 12 May 1985.

One document is included: 'Statement in Open Court', read in the High Court of Justice, Queen's Bench Division, 1989-R-No. 3375.

Interviews include Tom Shields; Bill Pressey; Bert Hardy, 30 July, 4 September 1992; David English; Peter Carter-Ruck, 28 July 1992.

18: War

Books include Charles Wintour, *The Rise and Fall of Fleet Street*, Hutchinson, London, 1989; Tom Bower, *Maxwell the Outsider*, Heinemann, London, 1991; Tom Bower, *Maxwell: The Final Verdict*, HarperCollins, London, 1995.

Newspapers include first issue of the London *Daily News* and the relaunched *Evening News*, 24 February 1987.

Articles include Tom Bower, *Observer*, 4 January 1987. Michael Leapman was the journalist who tried, on 30 March 1987, to read every edition of the London *Daily News*.

Interviews include Magnus Linklater, 8 January 1990, 14 February 2000; Charles Wintour; John Leese, 4 December 1989; Charles Sinclair; Bert Hardy; Bill Pressey; Vere Rothermere.

19: An Elegant Transaction

Books include S. J. Taylor, *The Reluctant Press Lord*, Weidenfeld & Nicolson, London, 1998.

Articles include Clive Schmitthoff, *Journal of Business Law*, 28 December 1988; Raymond Snoddy and Nikki Talt, 'DMGT Offers 765p a Share for Rest of Associated Newspapers', *Financial Times*, 18 October 1988; 'City Comment', *Daily Telegraph*, 26 June 1986. A promotions pamphlet, 'HQP, A Modern Production Plant', 1989 is also included.

Correspondence includes Peter Williams to SJT (letter), 21 May 2000.

Interviews include Charles Sinclair, 31 January 2000; Simon Borrows, 14 February 2000; Marius Gray, 15 February 2000; Esmond Harmsworth, 28 February 2000. Also included is Jonathan Rothermere, 24 February 2000; Peter Williams, 30 October 1998; Richard Kent, Peter Burt and Nicholas Gold, all on 27 June 2000; Padraic Fallon, 13 November 2001; Rowland Mitchell, 29 June 2000; Vere Rothermere. Anonymous source.

John Hemingway was of great help to the author in preparing this chapter.

20: Flexo-Fury

Books include Linda Melvern, *The End of the Street*, Metheun, London, 1986.

Correspondence includes Murdoch MacLennan to SJT (letter), 21 December 1999.

Documents include John Winnington-Ingram, 'Address on Flexographic Printing', FIEJ Marketing Seminar, Austria, 1989 and Winnington-Ingram, Tape Recording made in Athens on Flexographic Printing, May 2000.

Interviews include Bert Hardy, 30 July 1992, 2 September 1992; John Winnington-Ingram; Linda Melvern, 21 February 2000; Bill Pressey; Peter Williams, 18 November 1998; Stuart Martin, 17 August 1992; Murdoch MacLennan, 4 February 2000; Tony Gamble, 30 November 1992; Allan Marshall, 9 and 21 November 2000; Vere Rothermere. Anonymous source.

21: David's Version

Articles include Andrew Alderson, 'At the Court of KING DAVID: Musical chairs at the *Mail*', *Sunday Times*, 12 July 1992; 'New Chairman for Associated Newspapers: and a New Editor for the *Daily Mail* after 21 years', *Daily Mail*, 11 July 1992; Steve Boggan, 'All change for Fleet Street editors', *Independent*, 11 July 1992; Melinda Wittstock, 'Editor of *Mail* resigns after 21 years to be chairman', *The Times*, 11 July 1992; Jane Thynne, '*The Times* triggers Fleet Street shuffle', *Daily Telegraph*, 11 July 1992.

Correspondence includes Vyvyan Harmsworth to SJT (e-mail), 10 February 2000.

Interviews include Peter Williams; Kathy Campbell, 1 February 2000; Louis Kirby, 23 March 1992; David English; Paul Dacre, 11 September 1992, 23 March 2000; Bert Hardy; Vere Rothermere; Stewart Steven; Dee Nolan, 16 September 1992; Jonathan Holborow.

22: MURDERERS

Articles include David Hughes and Jenny Hope, 'Ministers bow to *Daily Mail*'s campaigns', *Daily Mail*, 19 January 2001; 'THE CANCER THAT NO ONE TALKS ABOUT', *Daily Mail*, 2 November 1999; 'MURDERERS' (headline), *Daily Mail*, 14 February 1997.

Correspondence includes Caroline Monks, Office of the Attorney-General, to the Editor, *Daily Mail* (letter), 5 March 1996 (*sic*).

Interviews include John Dale, 23 November 2001; Paul Dacre, 18 October 2001; Alistair Sinclair, 15 November 2001; Peter Wright, 21 November 2001; Eddie Young, 21 November 2001; Peter McKay, n.d.

23: The Sixth Floor

Books include S. J. Taylor, *The Great Outsiders*, Weidenfeld & Nicolson, London, 1996.

Articles include 'First Film: A cautionary tale', *UK Press Gazette*, 27 March 1995.

Correspondence includes David Kirkby to SJT (letter), 18 September 1992; Vyvyan Harmsworth to SJT (e-mail), 13, 14 March 2000.

Interviews include John Winnington-Ingram; Roger Gilbert, 16 February, 16 March 2000; Rod Gilchrist, 12 March 2002; Julian Aston, 16 March 2000; David English; Peter Williams, 14 March 2000; Charlie Cox, 7 March 2002; Murdoch MacLennan, David Kirkby, Michael Polosi, 7 September 1992; Jonathan Rothermere. Anonymous sources.

24: A Clock of Guilt

Articles include Paul Harris, 'Tributes to Lady Rothermere's Courage, Kindness and Loyalty: In Memory of a Woman Who Reached for the Sky', *Daily Mail*, 2 October 1992.

Interviews include Jonathan Rothermere; Camilla Yeates; Geraldine Maxwell, 26 January 1994; Claudia Rothermere, 20 February 1994, 18 February 2000; Vere Rothermere.

25: The Unknown Vere

Articles include Edward Whitley, 'A Very Private Person', *Spectator*, 26 October 1991, pp. 16–20. It may have been Whitley who first used the word 'enigmatic' to describe Rothermere's personality. Also included is Paul Landale and Carol Midgley, 'Mail Proprietor Switches to Labour', *The Times*, 23 May 1997; Carol Midgley, 'Rothermere Says Readers May Move *Mail* to the Left', *The Times*, 24 May 1997; Vere Rothermere, *Evening Standard*, 23 May 1997.

Correspondence includes Vyvyan Harmsworth to SJT (e-mail), 10 February 2000.

Interviews include Vere Rothermere; Kathy Campbell; Esmond Harmsworth, 28 February 2000; Vyvyan Harmsworth; Claudia Rothermere; Camilla Yeates; Ina Miller; David English; Paul Dacre, 23 March 2000.

26: All the News in Twenty Minutes

Articles include Jean Morgan, 'London *Metro* will have 22 "job-swap" journalists', *UK Press Gazette*, 18 December 1998.

Correspondence includes Thomas Grahl to Sally Taylor (letter), 11 December 2001; Thomas Grahl to Sally Taylor (letter), 6 December 2001, drawing on

Affarsvarlden (Swedish Business Weekly), No. 43, 2001; Per Andersson and Norstedts Forlag, *Stenbeck; Ett Reportage om det Virtuella Bruket*, 2000; and Grahl's own personal experiences as editor and managing director of *Metro* Stockholm.

Interviews include Jonathan Rothermere, 21 August 2001; Thomas Grahl, 4 December 2001; Kevin Beatty, 9 November 2001; Phil Dimes, 2 November 2001; Ian Pay, 12 September 2001; Murdoch MacLennan, 19 September 2001; Paul Dacre, 18 October 2001; Alistair Sinclair, 15 November 2001; Peter Wright, 21 November 2001.

27: A National Newspaper

Articles include 'Spotlight on *Metro*, London's Free Newspaper for Commuters Defies the Cynics', *Campaign*, 23 July 1999; Ian Herbert, 'Newspapers battle it out in court over use of *Metro* title', *Independent*, 20 January 2000.

Correspondence includes Thomas Grahl to Sally Taylor (letter), 5 December 2001.

Interviews include Alistair Sinclair; Ian MacGregor, 15 November 2001; Mike Anderson, 28 September 2001; Jonathan Rothermere, 11 December 2001; Neil Jagger, 19 October 2001.

SELECT BIBLIOGRAPHY

Annan, Noel. *Our Age*, London: Fontana, 1991.

Associated Newspapers Group Limited, Annual Minutes.

Associated Newspapers Group Ltd., Board of Directors, Minutes.

Benn, Tony. *Out of the Wilderness*, Diaries 1963–67, London: Hutchinson, 1987.

Bielenberg, Christabel. *The Past Is Myself*, Chatto & Windus, 1968.

Black, Peter. *The Mirror in the Corner: People's Television*, London: Hutchinson, 1972.

Black, Peter. Unpublished MS, 1976.

Blyton, Enid. *Daily Mail Annual*, Daily Mail, London: Northcliffe House, 1944.

Bourne, Richard. *The Lords of Fleet Street: The Harmsworth Dynasty*, London: Unwin Hyman, 1990.

Bower, Tom. *Maxwell: The Final Verdict*, HarperCollins, 1995.

Bower, Tom. *Maxwell the Outsider*, London, Heinemann, 1991.

Brendon, Piers. *The Life and Death of the Press Barons*, London: Secker & Warburg, 1982.

Budd, Zola, with Hugh Eley. *The Autobiography of Zola Budd*, Partridge Press: Transworld, London, 1989.

Chester, Lewis and Jonathon Fenby. *The Fall of the House of Beaverbrook*, London: André Deutsch, 1979.

Crawley, Aidan. *Leap Before You Look: A Memoir*, London: Collins, 1988.

Cromer, Esmé. *From This Day Forward*, Stoke Abbott: Thomas Harmsworth Publishing Company, 1991.

Cromer, Esmé. Unpublished Memoirs, n.d.

Daily Mail and General Trust Limited, Minutes.

Edelman, Maurice. *The Mirror: A Political History*, London: Hamish Hamilton, 1966.

English, David. *Advertising Briefing Guide*. Associated Newspapers.

English, David, and the Staff of the *Daily Express*. *Divided They Stand*, London: Michael Joseph, 1969.

Evans, Harold. *Good Times, Bad times*, Weidenfeld & Nicolson, 1983.

Ferris, Paul. *The House of Northcliffe: The Harmsworths of Fleet Street*, London: Weidenfeld & Nicolson, 1971.

Foot, Cone and Belding, Account Documents for *Daily Mail*.

Hamilton, Denis. *Editor in Chief: Fleet Street Memoirs*, Hamish Hamilton, 1989.

Harris, Robert. *Selling Hitler*, Faber and Faber, London, 1986.

Hirsch, Fred, and David Gordon. *Newspaper Money: Fleet Street and the Search for the Affluent Reader*, London: Hutchinson, 1975.

Ingham, Bernard. *Kill the Messenger*, HarperCollins, 1991.

Irvine, Bert. Unpublished MS, 1972.

Junor, John. *Listening for a Midnight Tram*, London: Chapmans, 1990.

King, Cecil. *The Cecil King Diary, 1970–1974*, London: Jonathon Cape, 1975.

King, Cecil. *The Future of the Press*, London: MacGibbon & Kee, 1967.

King, Cecil. *Strictly Personal*, London: Weidenfeld & Nicolson, 1969.

Koss, Stephen. *Fleet Street Radical: A.G. Gardiner and the Daily News*, London: Allen Lane, 1973.

Koss, Stephen. *The Rise and Fall of the Political Press in Britain, Vols. I and II: Hamish Hamilton*, 1981.

Lawrenson, John and Lionel Barber. *The Price of Truth*, Mainstream Publishing, 1985.

Levy, H. Phillip. *The Press Council: History, Procedure and Cases*, London: Macmillan, 1967.

McAlpine, Alistair. *Once A Jolly Bag Man*, Weidenfeld & Nicolson, 1997.

Mathias, Philip. *Takeover*, Canada: Maclean-Hunter Ltd., 1976.

Linda Melvern. *The End of the Street*, London: Methuen, 1986.

Norman, Barry. *Tales of the Redundance Kid or the Bedside Barry Norman*, Berkshire, England: Van Nostrand Reinhold, 1975.

Pocock, Tom. *Alan Moorehead*, London: The Bodley Head, 1990.

Price, G. Ward. Unpublished MS, 1949.

Rawlinson, Peter. *A Price Too High*, Weidenfeld & Nicolson, 1989.

Read, Donald. *The Power of News: The History of Reuters, 1849–1989*, Oxford University Press, 1992.

Taylor, S. J. *The Great Outsiders*, London: Weidenfeld & Nicolson, London, 1996.

Taylor, S. J. *The Reluctant Press Lord*, London: Weidenfeld & Nicolson, London, 1998.

Taylor, S. J. *Shock! Horror! The Tabloids in Action*, London: Bantam, Corgi Books, 1991.

Waugh, Evelyn. *The Diaries of Evelyn Waugh*, ed. Michael Davie, London, Weidenfeld & Nicolson, 1976.

Wintour, Charles. *The Rise and Fall of Fleet Street*, London: Hutchinson, 1989.

Wolfe, Jane. *The Murchisons*, New York: St. Martin's Press, 1989.

Documents

'HQP, A Modern Production Plant,' Promotions Pamphlet, 1989.

'Statement in Open Court,' read in the High Court of Justice, Queen's Bench Division, 1989-R-No. 3375.

Winnington-Ingram, John. Flexographic Printing, FIEJ Marketing Seminar, Austria, 1989.

Periodicals

Adler, Warren, 'They Took Away My Son and Then Raped His Mind,' *Daily Mail*, 29 May 1978.

Alderson, Andrew, 'At the Court of King David: Musical chairs at the *Mail*,' *Sunday Times*, 12 July 1992.

Barber, Lionel, 'Fleet Street's Billion Pound Scoop,' *Sunday Times*, 12 July 1983.

Boggan, Steve, 'All change for Fleet Street editors,' *Independent*, 11 July 1992.

Brown, Maggie, 'Fleet Street's Pigeon Pie,' *Guardian*, 10 June 1982.

Campaign, (Leader), 7 May 1971.

Daily Express, 'Dairy,' 16 January 1978.

Daily Mail, 'The Cancer that no one Talks About,' 2 November 1999.

Daily Mail, 'Death of Baron de Reuter,' 20 April 1915.

Daily Mail, 'Death of Baron de Reuter, Head of Great News Agency, Inconsolable Grief for his Wife,' *Daily Mail*, 20 April 1915.

Daily Mail, 'Legend in His Own Lunchtime, Special Edition,' 22 September 1983.

Daily Mail, 'The Mail Wins Damages over Airlift Libel,' 1 August 1979.

Daily Mail, '*Murderers*,' 14 February 1997.

Daily Mail, 'New Chairman for Associated Newspapers: And a New Editor for the *Daily Mail* after 21 Years,' *Daily Mail*, 11 July 1992.

Daily Telegraph, 'City Comment,' 26 June 1986.

Davie, Michael, 'Fleet Street gold rush,' *Observer*, 18 September 1983.

Edwards, John, 'I Watch the Tanks Roll In,' *Daily Mail*, 1 May 1975.

English, David, 'A Message from the Editor to YOU The Reader'; *Daily Mail*, 25 May 1977.

English, David, 'We Fought Them, We Beat Them and We Shall Go On Fighting Them,' *Daily Mail*, pp. 6–7, April 1, 1981.

Evening News, 'The Lives of the Children Matter Most,' (Leader), 7 April 1975.

Evening News, (Re-launch Issue) 24 February 1987.

Freemantle, Brian, 'Touchdown at Midnight,' *Daily Mail*, 7 April 1975.

Harris, Paul, 'In Memory of a Woman Who Reached for the Sky,' *Daily Mail*, 2 October 1992.

Harris, Paul, 'Tributes to Lady Rothermere's Courage, Kindness and Loyalty: In Memory of a Woman who Reached for the Sky,' *Daily Mail*, 2 October 1992.

Herbert, Ian, 'Newspapers battle it out in court over use of Metro title,' *The Independent*; 20 January 2000.

Hughes, David and Jenny Hope, 'Ministers bow to Daily Mail's campaigns,' *Daily Mail*, 19 January 2001.

Landale, Paul and Carol Midgley, 'Mail Proprietor Switches to Labour,' *The Times*, 23 May 1997.

Leslie, Ann, 'What a Momentous Night to Remember,' *Daily Mail*, 11 November 1989.

Levin, Bernard, 'Profit and Dishonour in Fleet Street,' *The Times*, 16 May 1971.

London *Daily News*, 1st Issue, 24 February 1987.

Midgley, Carol, 'Rothermere Says Readers May Move *Mail* to the Left, *The Times*, 24 May 1997.

Morgan, Jean, 'London *Metro* will have 22 "job-swap" journalists,' *U.K. Press Gazette*, 18 December 1998.

Rothermere, Vere, 'My Father, A Man in a Million,' *Evening News*, 13 July 1978.

Snoddy, Raymond and Nikki Talt, 'DMGT Offers 765p a Share for Rest of Associated Newspapers,' *Financial Times*, 18 October 1988. *Spectator* (Leader), 1 May 1971.

Steven, Stewart, 'Exclusive: Exposed—The Amazing Truth about Britain's State-owned Car Makers, World-Wide Bribery Web by Leyland,' *Daily Mail*, 19 May 1977.

Steven, Stewart, 'Hideout of the Nazi Mafia!' *Daily Express*, 29 November 1972.

Steven, Steward, 'World Exclusive Disclosure: Martin Bormann Alive,' *Daily Express*, 25 November 1972.

Sunday Times, 'The Battle of the Barons,' 12 May 1985.

Thynne, Jane, 'The *Times* triggers Fleet Street shuffle,' *Daily Telegraph*, 11 July 1992.

U.K. Press Gazette, 'First Film: A cautionary tale,' 27 March 1995.

U.K. Press Gazette, 'Spotlight on *Metro*, London's Free Newspaper for Commuters Defies the Cynics,' 23 July 1999.

Whitely, Edward, 'A Very Private Person,' *The Spectator*, 26 October 1991, pp. 16–20.

Wittstock, Melinda, 'Editor of *Mail* resigns after 21 years to be chairman,' *Times*, 11 July 1992.

Wheen, Frances, 'She Got a Kick from Champagne,' *Vanity Fair*, November 1992.

Womersley, John, 'The Born-Again *Daily Mail*,' Unpublished MS, 2 October 1998.

Wooldridge, Ian, 'We just wanted to weep alone,' *Daily Mail*, 7 September 1972.

Correspondence

English, David to Vere Harmsworth (letter), 23 September 1971.

English, David to Vere Harmsworth (letter), 19 March 1975.

Grahl, Thomas to SJT (letter) 5 December 2001.

Grahl, Thomas to Sally Taylor (letter), 6 December 2001, drawing on *Affarsvarlden* (Swedish Business Weekly), No. 43, 2001; Per Andersson and Norstedts Forlag, *Stenbeck; Ett Reportage om det Virtuella Bruket*, 2000; and Grahl's own personal experiences as editor and managing director of *Metro* Stockholm.

Grahl, Thomas to SJT (e-mail), 11 December 2001.

Grover, Peter to SJT (letter), 10 February 1993.

Harmsworth, Vere to the Editor of the *Spectator*, n.d.

Harmsworth, Vyvyan to SJT (e-mail), 10 February 2000.

Harmsworth, Vyvyan to SJT (e-mail), 13 March 2000.

Harmsworth, Vyvyan to SJT (e-mail), 14 March 2000.

Hemingway, John to SJT (letter), 21 December 2001.

Humphrey, Frank to Esmond Rothermere (letter), n.d. December 1940.

Kirkby, David to SJT (letter), 18 September 1992.

Longmuir, Harry to SJT (letter), 11 May 1992.

MacLennan, Murdoch to SJT (letter), 21 December 1999.

Monks, Caroline, Office of the Attorney General, to The Editor, *Daily Mail* (letter), 5 March 1996 (sic).

Rothermere, Esmond to Vere Harmsworth (telegram), 30 March 1971.

Shields, Mick, Managing Director, Letter of Redundancy (prototype), 15 March 1971.

Williams, Peter to SJT (letter), 21 May 2000.

Womersley, John to SJT (letter), 3 September 1998.

Broadcasts

'The Editor's TV Programme,' BBC, David English speaking, 26 June 1977.

INDEX

Abitibi Paper Co., 57–62, 64–6, 241

Aboodi, Ed, 243

Acourt, Neil and Jamie, 275

a Court, Robert Holmes, 180

Adler, Warren, 164

Adweek award, 106

Aitken, Sir Max: and *Daily Mail/ Daily Sketch* merger, 5, 14; and relaunch of *Daily Mail*, 47; Ann Leslie leaves, 88; decline, 110; and *Evening Standard/ Evening News* merger, 114, 117; and Wintour's criticism of *Daily Mail*, 130; eagerness to sell to Matthews, 205

Alcock, Mark, 285

Alexandria, 32

Aly Khan, Prince, 22, 26, 28

Alzheimer's Disease Society, 310

America (magazine), 97

American Corporation, 266

American Institute, 303–4

American Lawyer (legal newspaper), 242–3, 291

American School, St John's Wood, London, 294

Anderson, Mike, 327–9, 332

Anderson, Robert, 180

Anglo-Canadian Paper Mills, Quebec, 33

Anglo-Newfoundland Company, 57, 60

Annesley, Jackie, 326

Argentina, 134

Argus Shields security service, 289

Arnette, Peter, 88

Arnold, Sue, 111

Associated Newspapers: expansion, 3; controls *Daily Mail*, 4n; losses, 14; David English takes over chairman-

ship, 27–80, 171, 256–7, 263–4, 286; Vere first works on, 34; corporate structure, 42; Vere's chairmanship of, 42, 143; and Canadian paper companies' deal, 57–65, 68, 241; acquires *Esquire* magazine, 98–9, 101–2, 106, 137; and *Evening Standard/ Evening News* merger, 110–12, 113–14, 117, 130, 206; and bid for *Sunday Times*, 180–1; publishes *People*, 183; Vere's management of, 199, 208, 234; benefits from Reuters deal, 209, 212; inherits provincial newspapers from Northcliffe Newspapers, 210; Harmsworth family holdings in, 227; Sinclair takes over as managing director, 227; wealth, 230–1; DMGT investment in, 231; modernisation and new technology, 232, 244, 246–9, 252–3; conflicts and disagreements in, 234; internal buyout, 234–9, 242, 333; and sale of Consolidated Bathurst, 242; at Harmsworth Quays, 244–5; moves to Kensington, 254–5; and television interests, 280–5; and Public Teletext Licence, 284; interests in Hungary, 288; investment policy, 289–90, 292; contributes to Rothermere Foundation, 304; and launch of free newspaper (*Metro*), 312, 316, 319, 330, 331

Associated-Rediffusion (TV company), 44, 280

Aston, Julian, 284–5

Athelhampton Hall, Dorset, 26, 28–9

Australian Press Agency, 202–3